A Raven's Battle-Cry

Medieval Law and Its Practice

Edited by

John Hudson (*St Andrews*)

VOLUME 27

The titles published in this series are listed at *brill.com/mlip*

A Raven's Battle-Cry

The Limits of Judgment in the Medieval Irish Legal Tract Anfuigell

By

Charlene M. Eska

TUTA SUB AEGIDE PALLAS · 1683 ·

BRILL

LEIDEN | BOSTON

Cover illustration: Detail of Trinity College, Dublin MS 1387, *olim* H.5.15, p. 8a1, §1 *Anfuigell* (*CIH* 2146.16). The image is reproduced by permission of The Board of Trinity College Dublin.

Library of Congress Cataloging-in-Publication Data

Names: Eska, Charlene M., author.
Title: A raven's battle-cry : the limits of judgment in the medieval Irish legal tract Anfuigell / by Charlene M. Eska.
Description: Leiden ; Boston : Brill Nijhoff, 2019. | Includes bibliographical references and index.
Identifiers: LCCN 2018057537 (print) | LCCN 2018057804 (ebook) | ISBN 9789004391987 (ebook) | ISBN 9789004342644 (hardback : alk. paper)
Subjects: LCSH: Law–Ireland–History–To 1500–Manuscripts. | Irish language–To 1100–Texts.
Classification: LCC KDK145 (ebook) | LCC KDK145 .E83 2019 (print) | DDC 349.415–dc23
LC record available at https://lccn.loc.gov/2018057537

Typeface for the Latin, Greek, and Cyrillic scripts: "Brill". See and download: brill.com/brill-typeface.

ISSN 1873-8176
ISBN 978-90-04-34264-4 (hardback)
ISBN 978-90-04-39198-7 (e-book)

This book is printed on acid-free paper and produced in a sustainable manner.

Printed by Printforce, the Netherlands

For Nick

Contents

Acknowledgements

Although writing a book and editing a text are solitary tasks, they are tasks rarely done alone. I am grateful to acknowledge the assistance from several institutions and scholars at various stages of this project.

First and foremost, I should like to thank the anonymous readers at Brill for their helpful suggestions for improvements. This project has benefitted greatly from their expertise. Any errors are, of course, my own. Particular thanks are owed to Neil McLeod, Paul Russell, and Joseph F. Eska who all have offered assistance at various points in the process of editing and translating the tract.

I should like to thank Virginia Polytechnic Institute & State University, College of Liberal Arts and Human Sciences, for a Niles Research Grant during the summer of 2014, which enabled me to view many of the MSS for this project. I also gratefully acknowledge the assistance of an American Philosophical Society Franklin Research Grant during the summer of 2015, which enabled me to conduct research in the UK and view more of the relevant MSS. Particular thanks is owed to the Department of English for a Research Leave during the Fall 2017 semester to complete the final stages of the book. During my research leave, I was fortunate to be granted status as an Honorary Research Associate in the Department of Anglo-Saxon, Norse, and Celtic at the University of Cambridge during Easter and Michaelmas terms in 2017. I am also grateful to Magdalen College, University of Oxford, for a Visiting Fellowship, October 1–December 31, 2017. Both institutions provided me with time, space, resources, and the opportunity to be part of warm and welcoming intellectual communities.

Parts of this book are based on papers given at: the Department of Anglo-Saxon, Norse, and Celtic, University of Cambridge; the forty-first, fortieth, and thirty-ninth annual meetings of the Celtic Studies Association of North America; the thirty-seventh, thirty-fifth, and thirty-fourth annual Harvard Celtic Colloquiums; and the fifteenth International Congress of Celtic Studies. The feedback and comments received from members of those audiences have been very helpful.

During the course of writing this book, I have had the pleasure of working in many libraries, and I should like to acknowledge the assistance I have received from the librarians at: Trinity College, Dublin; The British Library; the Royal Irish Academy; University Library, University of Cambridge; English Faculty Library, University of Cambridge; Weston Library, University of Oxford; Oxford Law Library, University of Oxford; Longwall Library, Magdalen College, Oxford (with special thanks to Daryl Green); and the Celtic Library, Jesus College, Oxford. In particular, I should like to thank the College Librarian at Jesus College, Owen McKnight, for his assistance and for making the Celtic Library such a comfortable space to work.

Debts of gratitude are owed to Dorothy Africa, Thomas Charles-Edwards, Sharon Paice MacLeod, Jeff Mann, Sarah McKibben, Giovanni Varelli, Ralph Walker, Malcolm Wallis (for sharing his knowledge of maritime law, especially as it pertains to shipwrecks), and M. Joseph Wolf. I should also like to thank the Porters Lodges at both Jesus College and Magdalen College, Oxford, for their assistance and many acts of kindness.

I should also like to thank the editorial and production teams at Brill for their professional assistance throughout the course of this project. In particular, I am grateful to John Hudson, Marcella Mulder, and Cas Van den Hof.

My mother, her husband, and my brother have offered encouragement throughout and have kept my spirits up at low points. My son, Nicholas Shipman, has kept me laughing the entire time, and to him this book is dedicated.

C.M.E.
Blacksburg, 2018

Abbreviations

AL	*Ancient Laws of Ireland*, 6 vols., eds. W.N. Hancock et al. (Dublin, 1865–1901).
BL	British Library
CCIH	Liam Breatnach, *A Companion to the Corpus Iuris Hibernici* (Dublin, 2005).
CIH	*Corpus Iuris Hibernici*, 6 vols. paginated consecutively, ed. D.A. Binchy (Dublin, 1978).
CLH	*Clavis Litterarum Hibernensium*, 3 vols., ed. Donnchadh Ó Corráin (Turnhout, 2017).
DIL	*Dictionary of the Irish Language*, gen. ed. E.G. Quin (Dublin, 1983), compact edition.
eDIL	*Electronic Dictionary of the Irish Language* http://www.dil.ie/
EIF	Fergus Kelly, *Early Irish Farming* (Dublin, 2000).
EIWK	T.M. Charles-Edwards, *Early Irish and Welsh Kinship* (Oxford, 1993).
GEIL	Fergus Kelly, *A Guide to Early Irish Law* (Dublin, 1988).
GOI	Rudolf Thurneysen, *A Grammar of Old Irish*, revised edition and translation by D.A. Binchy and Osborn Bergin (Dublin, 1946).
LEIA	*Lexique étymologique de l'irlandais ancien*, eds. J. Vendryes, E. Bachellery, and P.-Y. Lambert (Paris, 1959–).
MI	Middle Irish (*c.* 900–1200)
NAJCS	*North American Journal of Celtic Studies*
O'Dav	*O'Davoren's Glossary*, ed. Whitley Stokes, *Archiv für celtische Lexikographie* 2 (London, 1904), 197–504.
OI	Old Irish (*c.* 600–900)
RIA	Royal Irish Academy
SM	*Senchas Már* 'Great Tradition'
TCD	Trinity College, Dublin
ZCP	*Zeitschrift für celtische Philologie*

Grammatical Abbreviations

acc.	accusative	dat.	dative
act.	active	du.	dual
adj.	adjective	f.	feminine
adv.	adverb	gen.	genitive
comp.	comparative	imp.	imperfect
cond.	conditional	imper.	impersonal
conj.	conjunction	impv.	imperative

ind.	indicative
indef.	indefinite
interrog.	interrogative
m.	masculine
n.	neuter
neg.	negative
nom.	nominative
num.	numeral
pass.	passive
part.	particle
perf.	perfect
pl.	plural
poss.	possessive
pres.	present
pret.	preterite
pron.	pronoun
rel.	relative
sg.	singular
subj.	subjunctive
subst.	substantive
superl.	superlative
vbl. of nec.	verbal of necessity
vn.	verbal noun

PLATE 1 Trinity College, Dublin MS 1387, *olim* H.5.15, p. 8a1, § 1 *Anfuigell* (CIH 2146.16). The image is reproduced by permission of The Board of Trinity College Dublin.

PLATE 2 Trinity College, Dublin MS 1387, *olim* H.5.15, p. 16b21, § 1 *Aidbred* (CIH 2163.33). The image is reproduced by permission of The Board of Trinity College Dublin.

Introduction

'A raven's battle-cry is a misuse of judgments'. Thus begins the medieval Irish legal text *Anfuigell* 'Wrong Judgment' or 'Non-judgment', a collection of legal judgments on a variety of topics ranging from the property rights of widows to selling stolen goods to shipwrecks and beyond.[1] The text and accompanying commentary is extant in five main fragments found in three different manuscripts now housed in the libraries of Trinity College, Dublin, and the Bodleian Library in Oxford, with smaller fragments extant in manuscripts in the British Library and Royal Irish Academy Library.[2] Although the text itself is not complete, when one takes into account the legal commentary and glosses on individual words and phrases accompanying the text, *Anfuigell* and its associated legal material amount to one of the larger bodies of legal matter in the corpus of attested medieval Irish law.[3] This legal tract has never been edited or accurately translated and, as such, it constitutes a legal mystery box for scholars.

The largest corpus of pre-twelfth-century European vernacular literary, historical, and institutional texts, other than Latin and Greek, is in medieval Irish.[4] Because Ireland was never absorbed into the Roman Empire, the Irish legal system contains a wealth of tradition and custom found nowhere else in Europe, although influence from canon law and patristic sources is evident in some of the legal texts. The majority of the early Irish legal texts were originally redacted within a fairly narrow period of time, *c.* 650–800 CE, but most of the surviving texts are found in manuscripts which date to the fourteenth through sixteenth centuries.[5] The working habits of the early Irish lawyers and legal families were

1 See below 5 where the title of the text is discussed in greater detail.

2 Although *CCIH*, 164–165 lists seven main fragments, the last two fragments listed actually belong to the legal text *Aidbred* 'Claiming'. I am currently preparing a critical edition and translation of the text. There is further discussion of *Aidbred* in Appendix 5.

3 All of the text and commentary can be found in the semi-diplomatic edition of the Irish legal texts; D.A. Binchy, ed., *Corpus Iuris Hibernici*, 6 vols. (Dublin: Dublin Institute for Advanced Studies, 1978).

4 Robin Chapman Stacey, "Law and Order in the *Very* Old West: England and Ireland in the Early Middles Ages," in *Crossed Paths: Methodological approaches to the Celtic aspect of the European Middles Ages*, eds. Benjamin T. Hudson and Vickie Zieglar (Lanham, MD: University Press of America, 1991), 45.

5 *GEIL*, 2. For a discussion of the linguistic registers found in the medieval Irish legal corpus see Paul Russell, "The Languages and Registers of Laws in Medieval Ireland and Wales," in *Law and Language in the Middle Ages*. Medieval Law and Its Practice 25. Eds. Jenny Benham, Matthew McHaffie, and Helen Vogt (Leiden: Brill, 2018), 83–103.

 | DOI:10.1163/9789004391987_002

such that texts were copied with little change to the actual legal text, but an ever-growing body of legal glossing and commentary was continuously added and subsequently recopied with each new redaction. The end result is frequently a linguistically and legally layered text; sometimes we can see up to 900 years of linguistic evolution on a single manuscript page. *Anfuigell* is one of these layered tracts where the OI text itself can be dated anywhere from *c.* 750–900 CE on linguistic grounds, but the accompanying commentaries span the Middle Irish (900–1200) and Early Modern Irish (1200–1600) linguistic periods.

References to *Anfuigell* in other medieval Irish legal texts[6] make it clear that the text was known to the medieval Irish lawyers. The lack of modern attention to *Anfuigell* is not due to the text being considered unimportant by modern scholars, but largely to the text's fragmentary nature; the surviving material consists of fragments of the OI text, but copious amounts of commentary.[7] In fact, the main continuous collection of fragments from *Anfuigell* was not recognized as being part of a distinct legal text at the time that the catalog of Irish manuscripts in Trinity College, Dublin was published in 1921,[8] even though the text was known by its correct title, as evidenced by its mention in a list of Irish legal texts in John Lynch's 1662 *Cambrensis Eversus* 'Cambrensis Overthrown'.[9]

In the 1850s, John O'Donovan, as part of the Brehon Laws Commission, included the main fragments of *Anfuigell* in his transcriptions of the legal manuscripts known at the time. In that same decade, he also translated the text. Aside from the original transcriptions housed in the Royal Irish Academy Library, only a handful of the anastatic facsimiles of the transcriptions exist, and the translation has never been published.[10]

6 Such as the examples cited at *CCIH*, 164; *CIH* 1499.14 (O'Dav no. 862(3)) *amail ader Anfuigell* 'as *Anfuigell* says' (see Appendix 6); and *CIH* 2003, n. p (written in *marg. dext.* in Digest D (32)) *Anfuigell sin* 'that is *Anfuigell*' (see §12 and *CCIH*, 81). It should be noted that the material accompanying both of these citations is not found in the other fragmentary material related to *Anfuigell*, aside from *CIH* 2003.40–2004.2.

7 There are approximately 242 words from the OI text preserved across all the MS sources. This number does not include sections where the OI text is repeated, such as in §§51 and 54, and it does not double-count words in MS sources where the text is the same across all witnesses.

8 T.K. Abbott and E.J. Gwynn, *Catalogue of the Irish Manuscripts in the Library of Trinity College, Dublin* (Dublin: Hodges, Figgis, & Co., 1921).

9 John Lynch, *Cambrensis Eversus* (Saint Malo, 1662), 158; Matthew Kelly, trans. *Cambrensis Eversus*, 3 vols. (Dublin: The Celtic Society, 1848–1854), 2: 368–369; and *CCIH*, 161. Lynch gives the title of the text as *Anfuighilbreath.*

10 John O'Donovan's original transcription and translation were consulted in the RIA. Anastatic facsimiles of his transcription were consulted in the University of Cambridge's Uni-

Much of the early Irish legal *corpus* has yet to be edited, and those texts which were included in the *Ancient Laws of Ireland* have been the focus of much of the field's secondary scholarship on the legal material.[11] *Anfuigell* was not included in the *AL*. The *AL* is a six-volume (the sixth volume is a glossary) edition and translation of many of the early Irish legal texts. The work was undertaken as part of the Brehon Laws Commission, the volumes being published between 1865 and 1901 by multiple editors. While the importance of such a monumental task and its achievements should be adequately acknowledged and appreciated, the quality (or lack thereof) of the editorial methods and translations has rendered the work as a whole rather a disappointment and quite often misleading in places.[12] That being said, the *AL* still contains the only editions and translations of many of the Irish legal texts.

It should also be noted that the *Dictionary of the Irish Language* is historically orientated to those texts included in the *AL*, unless they have been edited more recently elsewhere. Although the transcripts of John O'Donovan and Eugene O'Curry are frequently cited in *DIL*, they are rarely translated. While there are numerous citations from *Anfuigell* in *DIL*, they are not labeled as such. The citations simply cite the O'Donovan or O'Curry transcription and the relevant MS citation. The citations are rarely translated even when one has been provided by O'Donovan or O'Curry. For some of the more problematic citations, however, *DIL* refers to the unpublished dictionary slips (housed in the RIA) compiled by Charles Plummer.[13]

A comparison of O'Donovan's transcription of *Anfuigell* with that found in the semi-diplomatic edition of the Irish laws reveals that the transcriptions differ greatly from each other, with that of Binchy being far superior. Their transcriptions, particularly as a result of decisions each scholar made regarding the

---

versity Library and the University of Oxford's Bodleian Law Library. Copies of both the transcription and translation are available on microfilms.

11 Although much focus on the field has been (and still is) on legal texts which are more or less complete and/or old enough to be considered linguistically and legally interesting, recent work in the field has shifted focus towards some of these fragmentarily attested texts, for example: Fergus Kelly, *Marriage Disputes: A Fragmentary Old Irish Law-Text*. Early Irish Law Series 6 (Dublin: School of Celtic Studies, Dublin Institute for Advanced Studies, 2014); and "*Di Ércib Fola*," ed. and trans. Neil McLeod, *Ériu* 52 (2002): 123–216.

12 See T.M. Charles-Edwards, "Review Article: The *Corpus Iuris Hibernici*," *Studia Hibernica* 20 (1980): 141–143. For further discussion of the *AL*'s shortcomings and the intellectual and political climate in which the work was undertaken, see *idem*, "Whitley Stokes and Early Irish Law," in *The Tripartite Life of Whitley Stokes (1830–1909)*, eds. Elizabeth Boyle and Paul Russell (Dublin: Four Courts Press, 2011), 161–174.

13 These are cited as 'Plummer MS notes' in *DIL*. The earlier fascicles did not make use of Plummer's notes, but they were included in the later fascicles.

expansion of final syllables in abbreviated words, are different enough from each other so as to create highly variant versions of the text. It should be noted that Binchy based his own transcription to a certain extent on O'Donovan's. O'Donovan's unpublished translation has serious flaws, which are mainly the result of his own transcription choices and the fact the he was working at a time when there were few—and, no reliable—editions of the legal texts and almost no secondary scholarship on the subject. Furthermore, he was also working without the lexicographical resources available to scholars now, such as *DIL*, the lack of which would have made his task as a translator very difficult. Despite these shortcomings, it should be stressed that his translations were drafts, so they cannot be criticized.

The contents of *Anfuigell* are varied and give scholars, amongst other things, a rare glimpse of the sordid side of medieval Irish society.[14] Many of the topics discussed in the text are treated nowhere else in the corpus of early Irish law. The text itself is divided into 58 distinct sections, most of which deal with a different legal topic. This arrangement is rather unusual in the early Irish legal corpus as many texts, excluding *florilegia*, tend to focus on one topic, e.g. *Bechbretha* 'Bee-Judgments' is concerned with the laws of bee-keeping,[15] *Cáin Lánamna* 'The Law of Couples' is concerned with divorce, etc.[16] An analysis of *Anfuigell* reveals that these topics include: legal remedies concerning injuries sustained at funerals (§ 3), illnesses contracted at funerals (§ 3), unlawful and lawful regulations (§ 14), entering land after having sold it (§ 11), plundering in revenge for having been plundered (§ 17), taking back loans before they are due (§ 12), bringing in outsiders for conducting a raid (and the resulting penalties should the mercenaries inflict more harm than they were hired to do) (§ 45), deceiving widows (§ 51), failure to attend a mustering (§ 32), and taking the clothing of a dead man and giving it to a third party with intent to do harm (§ 54). The text also deals with regulations concerning who has the right to

14 When reading any of the medieval Irish legal texts, it should be borne in mind that reality as depicted in the texts may or may not represent historical fact. For a discussion of how this distinction can inform our readings of the legal texts, see Robin Chapman Stacey, "Ancient Irish Law Revisited: Rereading the Laws of Status and Franchise," in *Understanding Celtic Religion: Revisiting the Pagan Past*, eds. Katja Ritari and Alexandra Bergholm (Cardiff: University of Wales Press, 2015), 99–119.

15 *Bechbretha*, eds. and trans. Thomas Charles-Edwards and Fergus Kelly. Early Irish Law Series 1 (Dublin: Dublin Institute for Advanced Studies, 1983).

16 *Cáin Lánamna: An Old Irish Tract on Marriage and Divorce Law*, ed. and trans. Charlene M. Eska. Medieval Law and Its Practice 5 (Leiden: Brill, 2010). A notable exception to this would be *Ántéchtae* (*Breth*) 'Splendid Propriety (of Judgments)', which also covers a wide range of legal topics like *Anfuigell*; *CCIH*, 166–169.

objects which wash up on a beach (§22), the right to take plunder from those slain in battle (§1), and a range of unethical land deals with their resultant fines (e.g. §27). While there is little of the Old Irish text itself preserved in the fragments, the true value of the material lies in the copious legal commentaries which accompany each fragment of the text. The commentaries expand upon the topics only partially alluded to in the fragments of the OI text.

Anfuigell is so-called because *anfuigell* is the first word in the surviving OI text.[17] It has been known by this title since at least Lynch's 1662 *Cambrensis Eversus*; he refers to it as *Anfuighilbreath*.[18] Although the word *anfuigell* itself can be analyzed as a negative prefix *an-* plus *fuigell* 'judgment', literally 'non-judgment' or 'not-judgment', not every situation presented in the text is necessarily an example of a 'non-judgment', but sometimes it is a 'misuse of judgment', an 'inappropriate judgment', or a situation where no correct judgment can be given due to a circumstance, such as a lack of witnesses; in such cases any judgment given would be a 'wrong judgment'. For example, in §1 *anfuigell* has a more figurative meaning such as 'misuse' or 'inappropriate'; the sense of the text and commentaries is that it is inappropriate to submit some types of cases to a judge, such as those dealing with the slain in a lawful battle, because no judgment for homicide can be given in those cases. It would be inappropriate for a judge to award *wergeld* to the victim's kin, and it would be inappropriate for a judge to prosecute anyone slain in battle for any injuries committed during the course of the battle. These are also examples of when it would be inappropriate for a lawyer to bring such a case to a judge; there can be no damages awarded to anyone under these circumstances. Section 30 serves as a warning to all judges to have witnesses whenever hearing a case and pronouncing judgment. Without witnesses, the plaintiff and defendant can deny the validity of the judge's judgment. The lack of witnesses as an impediment to judgment comes up repeatedly throughout the tract. For example, in §49 the commentary in source A explicitly states that a judge would be giving a false judgment if he were to award the case to either party because it was a case of uncertainty due to a lack of witnesses.[19] One must be aware that the meaning of *anfuigell* may have changed between the time of the composition of the OI text and some of the later commentaries.

Within *Anfuigell* we find the legal details that a *brithem* 'judge' needed to know in order to carry out his duties properly. As such, a collection of legal 'exceptions' and 'what-if' scenarios, which is largely what the commentaries

17 *CCIH*, 164.

18 Lynch, *Cambrensis Eversus*, 158; Kelly, *Cambrensis Eversus*, 2: 368–369; and *CCIH*, 161.

19 In addition, cf. also §§19, 20, 31, and 46.

provide, would have been of interest and use to lawyers and judges alike. Many of the scenarios presented in the commentaries concern the limits of judgment, in other words, scenarios where there can be no correct judgment because there is no proof, no witnesses, etc., and, thus, no means of determining which party in a dispute should receive a favorable judgment. These are situations where no judgment can lawfully be given. The penalties for a judge giving an incorrect judgment varied. If he made a minor mistake, he would be fined; if he made a more serious mistake, e.g. only hearing one side of a case, he would lose his position as a judge and also his honor-price.[20] In terms of procedure, the text *Cóic Conara Fugill* 'The Five Paths of Judgment', lays out the eight stages in a typical legal case, but those stages rest on the assumption that there is the proper matter of a legal case to argue before a judge.[21] In *Anfuigell*, we are dealing mainly with legal situations which do not have enough evidence to even begin the process of initiating a legal case, or if the process is begun, the case will ultimately fail for both parties at the stage of judgment.

Sometimes, however, the connection between the topics alluded to in the OI text and the commentary which follows is not always clear. For example, § 42 of the OI text refers to the intoxication of a lord, but the commentary, after two brief etymological glosses on drunkenness, is concerned with the lord's obligations to his clients. It should be borne in mind that we do not have a complete OI text and that each extract of the OI text was intended to prompt the recall of the whole passage from which it was drawn. The context of these extracts is frequently lost when only fragments of the OI text survive. A similar situation is found in the text edited by Fergus Kelly in *Marriage Disputes*, where, for example, Kelly remarks regarding § 26 of his text that 'it is not easy to explain how this section relates to the law of marriage'.[22]

---

20 *GEIL*, 54–55. There are two main texts concerned with judges: *Urcuilte Bretheman* 'The Forbidden Things of a Judge', *CIH* 2102.31–2103.32; and a commentary from Digest D (17) *Día fis cía is breitheamh i ngach cúis síosanadh* 'To find out who is a judge for every case', *CIH* 1964.21–1973.40. These texts have been lightly edited, but neither has been translated; see *GEIL*, 268 and 267, respectively; *CCIH*, 85, 280–282, and 79, respectively; Rudolf Thurneysen, "Aus dem irischen Recht V," *ZCP* 18 (1930): 362–364; *idem*, "Allerlei Nachträge," *ZCP* 19 (1933): 129; and Roland M. Smith, "Urchuillti Bretheman," in *Irish Texts* 4, eds. J. Fraser, P. Grosjean, J.G. O'Keefe (London: Sheed and Ward, 1934), 24–27.

21 *GEIL*, 190–213; *CCIH*, 233–234; *Cóic Conara Fugill*, ed. and trans. Rudolf Thurneysen in *Cóic Conara Fugill: Die fünf Wege zum Urteil*, Abhandlungen der Preussischen Akademie der Wissenschaften. Phil.-hist. Klasse; Nr. 7 (Berlin: Verlag der Akademie der Wissenschaften, 1926), 15–61; and more recently ed. and trans. Christophe Archan in *Les Chemins du Jugement: Procédure et Science du Droit dans l'Irlande médiévale* (Paris: De Boccard, 2007), 287–383.

22 Kelly, *Marriage Disputes*, 104.

Many of the situations presented in the commentaries are, in essence, case studies. For example, in the section on failing to arrive at a mustering (§ 32), we are given the exact circumstances under which each class of person, for example, kings, nobles, and commoners, is held liable or not for either themselves or their subordinates failing to respond. Not only does this section inform us about who should be at the mustering, but we are also provided with a detailed breakdown of the specific circumstances under which each person is held liable. This level of detail is what a judge needs to know in order to render appropriate judgments.

It is also possible, although speculative, that the complete text was originally presented in the same kind of rhetorical structure as another early Irish legal text, *Gúbretha Caratniad* 'The False Judgments of Caratnia'.[23] This legal text is structured as a conversation between a mythical judge, Caratnia, and a king, Conn Cétchathach, in which the king states that each judgment made by Caratnia is false. It turns out that in each instance the judgment given by Caratnia was correct because each case involved an exception to a basic legal principle. While we will never know whether *Anfuigell* followed a similar rhetorical structure, it is clear from the text and commentaries that *Anfuigell* likewise deals with exceptions to general legal principles, situations where either a case should not be taken to a judge or situations where no judgment can be given due to lack of evidence. Without such detailed legal knowledge, a judge would be in danger of making an incorrect judgment.

Given the tract's preoccupation with exceptions and/or additional details to general legal principles and the limits of judgment, it is likely that judges were the intended audience of the text. As mentioned above, *Gúbretha Caratniad* is also concerned with seeming exceptions to legal principles. In terms of texts for judges, it is likely that *Recholl Breth* 'Shroud of Judgments'[24] also fits within this category. *Recholl Breth* is divided into ten sections. Each section presents a scenario which appears to be legal at first glance, but actually involves some type of legal fault, such as contracts which do not recover anything or activities which can reduce a person's honor-price. These are legal activities which are of no legal benefit.[25] These three texts all illustrate the breadth and depth of knowledge required by a judge.

---

23 *Gúbretha Caratniad*, ed. and trans. Rudolf Thurneysen, in "Aus dem irischen Recht III," *ZCP* 15 (1925): 302–370; and *CCIH*, 262.

24 The text is numbered 13 within the *Senchas Már* legal tradition; see *CCIH*, 293; *CIH* 218.31–223.21, and *AL* 4: 50–65. A critical edition and translation of this text is currently in preparation by Charlene M. Eska.

25 For a discussion of this aspect of the text, see Charlene M. Eska, "*Recholl Breth*: Why It Is a

Many of the legal commentaries are structured within a logical framework that sets out a variety of 'if X and Y, then Z', 'if X and not Y, then W', circumstances whereby the fines determined will vary depending on which legal conditions have been met. This type of legal system-building is common not only in the Irish legal commentaries, but also in contemporary legal commentaries on the Continent.[26] One such example from the text to illustrate this type of conditional structure can be found in § 3 on injuries at wakes and funerals. Here the degree of liability (or not) for the mourning heir depends on the status of the person injured, whether the injury happened at the wake or removal, the type of injury received, and whether a guardian's permission was obtained. The conditions are set out in tabular form below for injuries to guests not considered legally competent.[27]

Harm to incompetent guests

	With guardian's permission		**Without guardian's permission**	
	Wake	**Removal**	**Wake**	**Removal**
Death	exempt	exempt	full fine	restitution
Injury	full fine	restitution	full fine	restitution

It is useful to bear this general type of structure in mind when reading the commentaries. For any section of the tract, the full range of variables for a given set of circumstance might be found not in one commentary, but spread across the commentaries found in several sources. An example where the full range of variables is found only when reading all the commentaries together is § 22

'Shroud of Judgments'," in *Ollam: Studies in Gaelic and Related Traditions in Honor of Tomás Ó Cathasaigh*, ed. Matthieu Boyd (Madison, NJ: Fairleigh Dickinson University Press, 2016), 182.

26 Katharine Simms, "The Brehons of Later Medieval Ireland," in *Brehons, Serjeants and Attorneys: Studies in the History of the Irish Legal Profession*, eds. Daire Hogan and W.N. Osborough (Blackrock, Co. Dublin: Irish Academic Press, 1990), 51–76; and *eadem*, "The Contents of Later Commentaries on the Brehon Laws," *Ériu* 49 (1998): 23–40.

27 The table has also been published in Charlene M. Eska, "A Medieval Irish Commentary on Wakes and Funerals from *Anfuigell* 'Wrong Judgment'," *North American Journal of Celtic Studies* 1 (2017): 36.

on shipwrecks. It is only by taking into account the commentaries that all the details regarding exactly how to divide up the value of the shipwreck can be established.

The significance of the material found in *Anfuigell* cannot be overly-emphasized, not only for historians of medieval Ireland, but also for scholars interested in medieval law and literature, and linguists (many forms in the text, especially verbal forms, are not attested elsewhere). For example, in the section on injuries sustained and diseases contracted at wakes and funerals, among the list of fines for death and injury, we are provided with a list of those who would have been present at the wake and removal. The list includes the family, various members of the community (including minors), and the keeners—those hired to recite poems of lament for the dead. While the tradition of keening is well-attested in early Irish literature and other sources such as penitentials, *Anfuigell* provides us with very early non-fictional evidence for the activity. This section also reveals what the medieval Irish understood about disease transmission, as there are fines payable by the mourning heir should he hide the fact that the deceased died from a disease known to be contagious. Finally, this same section of the text also provides the earliest non-fictional reference to what are the medieval precursors to the modern funeral games and other Irish wake activities documented by Seán Ó Súilleabháin.[28]

In the section described by the Trinity College, Dublin manuscript catalog as 'defrauding widows'[29] and by O'Donovan as 'to seduce a woman', the text (§ 51), instead, presents a much more sinister range of scenarios involving seduction, theft, and double-crossing. Within the Irish legal corpus, there is very little information about widows and their property rights. This section in *Anfuigell* provides the most comprehensive body of information that we have. The text lays out various scenarios under which a widow takes a lover and either gives her property to him or he steals it from her. Should she give her property to her lover but not have a full legal claim to it, fines are assessed against her for theft from her family, as they would have rights to any property that they should inherit from her. Should her property be stolen by her lover, fines are assessed against him based on the percentage of the property to which the widow had a legal claim and the percentage to which the family had a claim. This commentary highlights the vulnerable nature of widows and the variety of property they could possess in their own right, and provides valuable information regarding the ties that she had to her natal kindred.

28 Seán Ó Súilleabháin, *Irish Wake Amusements* (Dublin: The Mercer Press, 1967).

29 Abbott and Gwynn, *Catalogue of the Irish Manuscripts*, 252.

One of the many challenges to the editor when faced with such a large range of material is to make the tract accessible to a wide audience. The introduction includes summaries of each section of the tract in an attempt to guide the reader through what at times can feel like an overwhelming and bewildering series of fines and what-if scenarios laid out in the commentaries. Paleographical, linguistic, and legal notes are to be found in the footnotes to the sections of the edited tract itself. While I have tried to find a balance between technical and more general notes, scholars and students alike may feel that there are instances where they need more (or less!) information. Although *Anfuigell* covers many disparate legal topics, it does not deal with all aspects of the law. For a detailed overview of the Irish legal system, Fergus Kelly's *A Guide to Early Irish Law* and *Early Irish Farming* are indispensable.

Summary of the Text

Heading: Sources A and B[1] begin with a literary formula of stating the place, person, time, and cause of writing, which is not uncommon both in Irish legal and literary texts, although, as noted by Breatnach, not all four of these conditions need necessarily be present.[2] Robin Flower has argued that the Irish adopted this literary convention under the influence of Boethius' *De consolatione philosophiae*.[3] Regardless of whether this is the origin of this literary convention in Irish, the convention is clearly a result of Latin influence. None of the information regarding the time and place of composition need necessarily be accurate, even if historical figures are mentioned. For example, Finguine son of Cú-cen-máthair, who is mentioned in source B, was king of Munster 678–695,[4] but this information cannot be used to date the heading of *Anfuigell* because many of these formulaic beginnings were copied from text to text; the heading in source B derives from the later introductory material to *Cáin Ḟuithirbe*.[5] Source B also specifically identifies the title of the tract as *Anfuigell*.

§1 Title of the text and the property of those slain in battle: The first section of the text begins with a series of Isidorean-style quasi-etymological glosses on the title of the text. While these types of glosses can be found anywhere throughout the Irish legal texts, they tend to cluster around the beginning sections of the texts.[6] Here we can see the glossator hesitating between two

1 See the section on Manuscript Sources for the MS sigla used here and throughout. Source A is the main source for the tract.

2 *CCIH*, 355, n. 4. For a list of representative legal texts which contain versions of this formula, see *CCIH*, 354–362; the introductory formula from source B of *Anfuigell* is discussed on 360. See also Liam Breatnach's edition of *Cáin Fhuithirbe* in, "The Ecclesiastical Element in the Old-Irish Legal Tract *Cáin Fhuithirbe*," *Peritia* 5 (1986): 36–37; and Fangzhe Qiu, "*In senchas bith-nua:* The Traditionalisation of Early Irish Law," Medieval Law Conference, Dublin Institute for Advanced Studies, June 28, 2014. Available at https://www.youtube.com/watch?v=gIJutcPSjU8. Accessed November 7, 2017.

3 Robin Flower, "*Quidam Scotigena .i. Discipulus Boëthii* or Boëthius and the Four Conditions of the Tale," *Ériu* 8 (1916): 150–154.

4 *Cáin Fhuithirbe*, 45.

5 *CCIH*, 360–361.

6 For examples of the range of techniques and vocabulary employed in this style of glossing, see D.A. Binchy, "The Linguistic and Historical Value of the Irish Law Tracts," *Proceedings of the British Academy* 29 (1943): 211–212. The dismissive attitude of Binchy towards medieval glosses and commentary is no longer an accurate reflection of the field. For more recent discussions of etymological glossing and glossing in the legal texts, see Paul Russell, "Laws, Glossaries

 | DOI:10.1163/9789004391987_003

interpretations of *anfuigell*. The first involves interpreting the *an-* of *anfuigell* as *án* 'splendid'; the second interpretation understands *an-* as a negative prefix.[7] Both interpretations deal with submitting or not submitting to the decision of a judge who may or may not award *wergeld* for a person slain in battle.[8] Although Gwynn suggests that the glossator did not know the meaning of *anfuigell*,[9] both interpretations offered by the glossator make sense in their own way.

The sense of the law as given in the commentary is that while *wergeld* normally is awarded to the family of the slain victim, this is not the case when the victim has died in lawful battle. Thus, a judge should not award *wergeld* for anyone killed in battle. In fact, it is not even appropriate to submit such a matter for judgment as it cannot be prosecuted as homicide. The remainder of the material deals with taking the belongings from the slain. If someone takes any belongings from one of his slain fellow combatants, he is allowed to keep everything he takes if it is certain that the property would have fallen into enemy hands. If there is uncertainty on this point, he is allowed to keep half of what he takes; presumably the other half goes to the slain combatant's kindred. If it is certain that the enemy would not have gotten any of the belongings, he is not allowed to keep anything. If a man deposits belongings with a third party before battle, the third party keeps a portion of the value of the belongings according to the same set of circumstances laid out for taking the belongings of the slain from the battle-field.

---

and Legal Glossaries," *ZCP* 51 (1998): 85–115; *idem*, "*Quasi*: Bridging the etymological gap in early Irish glossaries," in *A Companion in Linguistics: A Festschrift for Anders Ahlqvist on the occasion of his sixtieth birthday*, eds. Bernadette Smelik et al. (Nijmegen: Stichtig Uitgeverij de Keltische Draak, 2005), 49–62; and Liam Breatnach, "The Glossing of the Early Irish Law Tracts," in *Grammatica, Gramadach and Gramadeg: Vernacular grammar and grammarians in medieval Ireland and Wales*, eds. Deborah Hayden and Paul Russell (Amsterdam: John Benjamins Publishing Company, 2016), 113–132.

7 *CCIH*, 164.

8 The Irish term *éraic* 'wergeld' refers to the fixed fine for homicide. The fine is set at seven *cumals* for every free person regardless of rank, and is payable to the victim's kindred; see *GEIL*, 125–126. Although the relative value of the currencies differs across texts, Kelly gives the following general guideline for the equivalencies: '1 milch cow = 1 ounce of silver = 2 *séts* = 1/3 *cumal*'; *GEIL*, 116. Although *cumal* means 'female slave', in the legal texts it is usually found as a unit of value rather than in its literal meaning; see *GEIL*, 112–113; *EIF*, 591–593; and Charlene M. Eska, "Women and Slavery in the Early Irish Laws," *Studia Celtica Fennica* 8 (2011): 29–39. *Sét* is the general term for any object of value; see *eDIL s.v.* 2 *sét*. It is also used as a unit of currency where it is usually equivalent to twelve scruples (there are twenty-four scruples in an ounce) or half a milch-cow; see *GEIL*, 114–116; and *EIF*, 589–591 for a full discussion of the meaning and various values assigned to this word.

9 E.J. Gwynn, "Miscellanea," *Ériu* 9 (1921–1923): 29.

§ 2 Various ways of breaking a contract: Like the first section, the second section begins with a quasi-etymological gloss on the first word of the OI text, i.e. *combach* 'breaking'. The section then discusses the various ways of breaking a contract. The first part deals with (1) the plaintiff suing the surety before the specified time of payment, and thus accruing fines as a result, and (2) the defendant evading the surety and accruing fines as a result. The second part deals with the conditions under which either or both of the contracting parties may withdraw from the contract.

According to early Irish law, all contracts should be made in front of witnesses and bound by sureties. The role of the surety is to ensure that each party fulfills his or her side of the terms of the contract. No one is allowed to act as surety for an amount greater than one's honor-price.[10] Honor-price is determined by social status and gender.[11] While the ability to contract is granted to most members of society, there are limitations on the types of contracts one can make depending on social status and gender. Those who are not considered legally competent, such as minors and those of unsound mind, cannot make valid contracts.[12] Contracts can be rescinded by either party within a period of twenty-four hours according to the commentary.[13] After that, the contract stands, even if the terms are disadvantageous to one of the parties, except if both parties wish to withdraw from the terms of the contract.

§ 3 The liability of the mourning heir for any injuries which take place at a wake or during the removal of the body to the graveside: The commentary in source A presents two different versions. The first version states that the mourning heir is exempt from any legal liability regardless of whether any of the mourners (be they considered legally competent or not) become ill or die from any contagion in the house, regardless of whether the heir was aware of the contagion. The second version is consistent with the material found in sources C and E where a complicated fine structure details the degree of liability for fatal and non-fatal injuries to both legally competent and legally incom-

---

10 For a discussion of the role of sureties in early Irish law and society, see *GEIL*, 158–163; Neil McLeod, *Early Irish Contract Law*. Sydney Series in Celtic Studies 1. (Sydney: University of Sydney, 1992), 14–28; and Robin Chapman Stacey, *The Road to Judgment: From custom to court in medieval Ireland and Wales* (Philadelphia: University of Pennsylvania Press, 1994), 27–54.

11 *GEIL*, 8–9.

12 *GEIL*, 160.

13 In earlier texts, contracts are said to be binding from nightfall on the day they are made. In later commentaries, the time is extended to twenty-four hours; McLeod, *Early Irish Contract Law*, 24–25.

petent persons. There are no fines associated with injury done to those considered legally competent, regardless of whether the injury takes place at the wake or removal. For those not considered legally competent according to early Irish law,[14] the fines are based on whether the injury is fatal or non-fatal, whether it takes place at the wake or removal, and whether those legally responsible for the injured party had given permission for their attendance at either event. Fines are higher for injuries sustained at the wake than at the funeral, and fines are higher when the legal guardian's permission was not obtained.

§ 4 The conditions under which a paying-surety (*ráth*) can withdraw from his obligations as a surety: Irish law recognized three types of sureties, the *ráth* 'paying-surety', the *naidm* 'binding-surety', and the *aitire* 'hostage-surety'. The *ráth*-surety guarantees with his own property that the contracting party for whom he is surety will fulfill his contractual obligations. If the contracting party defaults, the *ráth*-surety's property can be distrained. The defaulting party must then pay the surety a series of increasingly heavy fines until the *ráth*-surety is compensated for his property up to double the amount of the original debt along with honor-price and any other additional expenses.[15] The *naidm*-surety is able to use any means, including violence, to enforce a contract. While his own property is not at stake, his own honor-price is; thus it provides a great deal of motivation for him to ensure that the principal fulfills his legal obligations.[16] The *aitire* guaranteed the terms of the contract with his own person. If the principal defaults, the *aitire* is kept as a hostage by the other contracting party for up to ten days. If the principal does not pay his debts within that time, the *aitire* becomes a *cimbid* 'captive' and would have to ransom himself for the amount of seven *cumal*s. If either of these situations should come to pass, the defaulter owes the original amount of the debt and a series of heavy fines for defaulting.[17]

The commentaries state two main versions of the law. The first states that the *ráth*-surety, when he is surety for a non-kinsman, can withdraw from his obligations as a surety within twenty-four hours of entering into suretyship as

---

14 This category of people includes minors, women (not in all circumstances, however), those of unsound mind, dependent sons of living fathers, slaves, and unransomed captives; *GEIL*, 68.

15 *GEIL*, 168–171; McLeod, *Early Irish Contract Law*, 17; and Stacey, *The Road to Judgment*, 37–43.

16 *GEIL*, 171–172; McLeod, *Early Irish Contract Law*, 16; and Stacey, *The Road to Judgment*, 34–45 and *passim*.

17 *GEIL*, 172–173; McLeod, *Early Irish Contract Law*, 17; and Stacey, *The Road to Judgement*, 82–111.

long as he provides a replacement *ráth*-surety. If more than twenty-four hours have passed, he cannot withdraw without paying penalties. If he is surety for a kinsman, he cannot withdraw at all without paying penalties.

The second version states that the *ráth*-surety must obtain restitution of the other contracting party's chattels (i.e. whatever was given to the party for whom he acted as a surety must be returned to the other contracting party) within twenty-four hours to be able to withdraw from his obligations. He is not able to withdraw at all after that time unless someone else impugns the contract. If that is the case, the entire amount of the contract is impugned for a non-kinsman, and he receives restitution of his honor-price without interest. If it is for a kinsman, he is paid nothing except honor-price, or honor-price with restitution of any amount beyond his honor-price, if any of his own property has been diminished. In part, this section is parallel to what we see in § 2 where the parties of a contract have twenty-four hours to withdraw from the contract without penalty.

§ 5 Items which wash up on shore, including a boat full of goods and a *deorad Dé* 'exile of God':[18] Normally any items that are found on the shore or floating near the shore belong to the owner of the adjoining land (aside from seaweed and whales); however, anything brought in from the sea belongs to the finder, or at least a portion of it does, according to some texts.[19] If the *deorad Dé* can perform three miracles, he himself, his goods, and his ship are not confiscated. If he performs none or fewer than three, a portion of his goods and ship (i.e. the value of) are confiscated unless he can otherwise prove his identity. The point of the exercise is to prove that he is who he claims to be and is not a criminal who has been set adrift and subsequently washed up on shore.[20] The procedure described here is similar to that found in § 50 where a poet has to prove his identity by performing three acts of divination.

---

18 For voluntary exile as a form of penance and the legal status of the *deorad Dé*, see Thomas Charles-Edwards, "The Social Background of Irish *Peregrinatio*," *Celtica* 11 (1976): 43–59 and 53–54, respectively.

19 GEIL, 107–108; and Gearóid Mac Niocaill, "Jetsam, Treasure Trove, and the Lord's Share in Medieval Ireland," *The Irish Jurist* 6 (1971): 106–107. See also Fergus Kelly, "Drifting on the Ocean: Are Old Irish *cnoe gnáe* 'beautiful nuts' to be identified as sea beans?," in *Bile ós Chrannaibh: A Festschrift for William Gillies*, eds. Wilson McLeod et al. (Ceann Drochaid, Perthshire: Clann Tuirc, 2010), 211–218.

20 For setting adrift as a punishment, see Mary E. Byrne, "On the Punishment of Setting Adrift," *Ériu* 11 (1932): 97–102; GEIL, 219–221; and Pamela O'Neill, "Old Irish *Muirchrech* 'Sea-Boundary'," *Ériu* 67 (2017): 1–9. See also GEIL, 5–6 for the *murchoirthe* 'castaway', who has no honor-price unless he has been taken into service within the *túath*.

§ 6 Lawful and unlawful ordinances established by a *túath* 'community': If a lawful ordinance has been established by agreement in an assembly, all are obligated to follow it. If any repudiate it, they are liable for a fine. The ordinance stays in effect until all who agreed upon it repudiate it. If the established ordinance is unlawful, repudiating it does not incur any fines. Both of the commentaries state that the ordinances are to be established by a group of nine people deemed qualified to make an ordinance. The commentaries depend on the reader being familiar with both the etymological glossing tradition regarding the word *nós* 'ordinance, custom'[21] and the tradition in the *Pseudo-historical Prologue to the Senchas Már* of nine people, comprising nobles, scholars, and ecclesiastics, who composed the *Senchas Már* 'Great Tradition' legal compilation. Source B lists the nine people who are entitled to establish lawful ordinances, which differs in some ways from that found in *Sanas Cormaic* 'Cormac's Glossary' and the *Pseudo-historical Prologue to the Senchas Már*. Further discussion can be found in the edition below.

§ 7 Kinship: Section seven is devoid of any concrete context and is obscure to me, but, according to a note made by John O'Donovan in his translation of the commentary from source A, this section is about 'succession to ecclesiastical and lay lands'.[22] In early Irish society, kin groups had the following divisions: *gelḟine* 'white kindred', which encompassed one's immediate family to three generations;[23] *derbḟine* 'true kindred', which encompassed four generations, *íarfine* 'after kindred', which encompassed five generations, and *indḟine* 'end kindred', which encompassed six generations.[24] If an entire *gelḟine* should become extinct, the wider kin groups are entitled to a share in the deceased's property.[25]

§ 8 Violating protection: Every freeman in early Irish society had the ability to offer protection to another freeman of equal or lower rank (although some exceptions apply; for example, no one should offer protection to a slave).[26] The protection extends not only to the protector's house, but also to the precinct

21 *Sanas Cormaic*, no. 970; and § 8 of the *Pseudo-historical Prologue to the Senchas Már* in John Carey, "An Edition of the Pseudo-historical Prologue to the *Senchas Már*," *Ériu* 45 (1994): 1–32.

22 John O'Donovan, 159. For inheritance within kin groups, see *EIWK*, 61–73.

23 The definitions given here are post-700; *EIWK*, 55–56.

24 *EIWK*, 23–61.

25 The texts are not always consistent in their descriptions of how this system works; see *GEIL*, 102–104; and *EIWK*, 61–73.

26 *GEIL*, 141.

around the house, the extent of which varied by rank. Any injury inflicted on the person under protection was also considered to be an offense against the protector, and the offender was liable to pay the protector's honor-price along with any fines to the injured party or his kindred.[27] The commentaries outline the procedure for acquiring protection, which consists of seeking protection, formally acquiring the protection, and then agreeing to bring the matter to law. The commentaries then give a series of fines associated with violating someone's protection, which vary depending on knowledge or not of the protection, whether the violation takes place within or outside the precinct, and whether the injured person is an otherwise lawful party or a culprit. The topic of sanctuary/protection also appears in §§52 and 57.

§9 Inciting fear in others: The text begins with a comment about a pledge made in terror; any such pledge made under fear or duress would not be considered valid.[28] The commentaries deal with injuries which result from inciting fear in others; any pledge made in such a state would not be considered valid. The commentaries consist of two topics. The first topic is accidentally inciting fear in others, which results in injury to people and property. The second part deals with falsely saying that enemies are approaching, thus inciting fear. In both instances, the motive of the instigator determines the fines that he is responsible for. That being said, the commentaries suggest that in the second situation, the instigator most likely had ulterior motives such a homicide, injury, or theft and was not making a genuine mistake.

§10 The liabilities of the *aitire* 'hostage-surety':[29] Both commentaries state that the hostage-surety is only liable for that which was agreed upon at the time the contract was made. If the person for whom he went surety accrues other debts while the hostage-surety is being held by the other party of the contract due to the debtor defaulting, the hostage-surety is not liable for those additional debts.

§11 Entering land after it has been sold: The section presents a scenario where someone has sold land to another person, received payment for the land, but then the original owner proceeds to graze his animals on the land or tries to

27 *GEIL*, 140–142 and *CG*, Legal Glossary, *s.v. díguin*.

28 McLeod, *Early Irish Contract Law*, 56.

29 See the introduction to §4 for a discussion of the different types of sureties.

regain possession of it. If the purpose of entering the land is to graze his animals, he is liable for a fine for trespassing; if the purpose is to take back the land, he owes a fine for taking possession. One of the ways a person could take possession of land was through a process called *tellach* 'legal entry'. One of the stages in the process involved entering the land with livestock, which are then allowed to graze on the land.[30] In the scenario presented in this section, the original owner has no right to graze his animals on his former land if he has already received payment for the land. Grazing animals on land to which a person has no legal right occasions fines for trespass, and if the original owner is trying to reclaim his land, he owes fines for illegal entry.[31] The commentary then says that this scenario is different from the scenario where the price promised for the land has not yet been handed over. In that case, the land still belongs to the original owner, and he can do what he likes with the land without incurring any penalties.

§ 12 Loans:[32] The legal principles discussed are as follows. Anything given as a loan or rented without a fixed end-time for the loan or rent is able to be taken back by the owner at whatever time the owner wishes without the owner incurring any penalties for doing so. If a time had been fixed for their loan or rent, and the owner takes the item (i.e. livestock, land, tool, etc.) back before the determined time, the owner owes fines, which are determined by the nature of the item loaned or rented. If, however, the item was given for interest, hire, or as a commercial loan, the fines the owner is liable for are much higher. If necessity compels the owner to ask for the item back, it is given back with whatever interest the item earned. If it is not from necessity, the item does not need to be returned before the specified time. Source A adds to the above principle that the person who has the lent item can make full use of its labor or produce while the item is in his possession, as long as it was not part of the original terms that he could not make use of the produce or labor. If the items are given as a commercial loan or for interest and are taken back by the owner early to use their produce or labor or simply take the item back permanently, the owner is fined for doing so.

The commentaries from source J may or may not belong with the rest of the *Anfuigell*-related commentaries. The first four paragraphs of the commentary

30 *GEIL*, 186–188.

31 *GEIL*, 189.

32 See Neil McLeod, "*Ón* and *airliciud*: Loans in medieval Irish law," in *Celts and their Cultures at Home and Abroad: A Festschrift for Malcolm Broun*. Sydney Series in Celtic Studies 15. Eds. Anders Ahlqvist and Pamela O'Neill (Sydney: University of Sydney, 2013), 169–196.

concern pledges, the fifth paragraph concerns judgments on thefts, plunderings, and violations, and the sixth commentary concerns pledged items. Only the sixth paragraph is duplicated in another commentary in source A.

§ 13 The liabilities that a dog owner has for any injuries the dog inflicts on others:[33] Aside from paying any fines associated with the injury, the owner is also liable to pay for sick-maintenance for the injured person. Sick-maintenance is the early Irish social institution whereby the offender must pay for the medical expenses for anyone he injures and also provide food, accommodation, and substitute labor if the injured party is out of work as a result of the injury.[34]

§ 14 The king's ability to make laws: If a king is asked by his subjects to make a regulation, and the regulation he makes is lawful, his subjects are obligated to follow the regulation. Failure to do so results in fines for violating the regulation. If, however, the regulation made by the king is unlawful, the subjects are not obligated to follow it and the king owes a fine for making an unlawful regulation.[35]

§ 15 The obligations of the deceased's heirs:[36] The deceased's heirs are normally not liable for the deceased's personal offenses, provided the deceased did not die while committing an offense. If, however, the deceased left debts of his property, the heirs are liable for those debts. If the deceased was acting as a hostage-surety, that obligation is not passed on to his heirs. If he was acting as a paying-surety, the heirs are responsible for those liabilities. The commentaries in this section state that, if the deceased knew of his illness (and presumably impending death) and neglected any of his financial obligations, then his heirs are only liable for exact restitution. If, however, there was no neglect and any illness (and, thus, impending death) was unknown, the heirs must pay the debts and any interest owed.

§ 16 Unlawful raids: This section deals with unlawful raids in a territory and the liabilities of both the raiders for any injury and damage they inflict and the locals (i.e. those against whom the raid is conducted) for any injuries they might inflict on the raiders during the course of the raid. If the locals only had

---

33 *EIF*, 114–121.

34 *GEIL*, 130–134.

35 Creating legislation at the behest of his subjects was one of the duties of a king; *GEIL*, 21–22.

36 For liabilities associated with the dead and their heirs, see *GEIL*, 157.

the intent to apprehend the raiders or just to take back their own property from the raiders, but it is not possible to apprehend them or take back their property without killing the raiders, then there is no liability for killing the raiders. Two conditions are present: (1) the intent was not to kill the raiders, and (2) the locals did not have the ability to apprehend them or regain their property without killing the raiders in the process. If the locals did not intend on killing the raiders, but they could have apprehended them or taken back their property without killing the raiders, and the locals kill them anyway, the liabilities for killing the raiders are balanced against the damage done by the raiders and the text states that under these conditions counter-claims are allowed. The legal term *frithaigid* 'counter-claim, counterplea, disallowal' is used to refer to circumstances where additional liabilities may or may not be allowable.[37] Unfortunately, the commentary does not provide examples of what types of situations or injuries would be considered to be valid counter-claims, but the situation presented under these sets of conditions in the commentary is that additional liabilities could be taken into consideration in addition to balancing out the damage done by both the locals and the raiders. The use of unnecessary force is the legal trigger for the counter-claims. If the locals planned from the start that they were going to kill the raiders, regardless of whether or not they had the ability to apprehend them, then along with balancing the liabilities between the damage the raiders inflicted and the injuries inflicted by the locals, counter-claims are also allowed if they are sued for at the time the attack was made. If the counter-claims are not sued for at the time of the attack, they are not allowable, but both parties must balance their liabilities against each other. Here again we see intent as a conditioning factor to the fine structure.

The third paragraph of the commentary in source A is difficult as the end is missing. That being said, it is clear that the paragraph deals with who is liable for paying the resulting fines from the raid. Obviously, those who carried out the attack are liable. Their kinsmen who stand within close enough relation to them to be a kinsman-surety are also liable when the raider is not apprehended. The kinsman-surety, however, can still be liable for fines even if the raider is apprehended. This arises when the raider does not have the financial ability to pay for all of the damage that he has inflicted.

In terms of how raids and blood-feuds work legally, it is important to bear in mind that "an entire kin-group" has the right "to avenge attacks against any of its members. And the legitimate object of that vengeance is the entire kin-group of the attacker."[38] Not only are the kinsmen-sureties financially liable for

---

37 *eDIL s.v. frithaigid.*

38 Neil McLeod, "The Blood-Feud in Medieval Ireland," in *Between Intrusions: Britain and Ire-*

the crimes of their fellow kinsmen, their own lives are at risk if the raid, feud, etc. is not settled quickly. It is in the best financial interests of the kin-group to bring the perpetrator to justice because the perpetrator has the first level of responsibility for paying any fines that he owes. If he cannot pay what he owes, the kinsmen-surety can step in or the kin-group can decide not to pay any of the liabilities and hand the perpetrator over as compensation.[39] Not everyone has the financial responsibilities of being a kinsman-surety, even if related to the perpetrator. For example, poets, smiths, and churchmen are considered exempt from this obligation.[40]

The last part of the commentary shifts to what happens if a person accidentally kills someone else in mistake for one of the raiders. If he cannot apprehend him, and mistakenly kills an innocent man, there is no liability. If he could have apprehended him without killing him, then he owes the penalty for killing an innocent man. The usual legal ruling is that, if someone kills a thief in their own home (provided he does not recognize the person and does not have the ability to apprehend him), then there is no liability. If it turns out that an innocent man was killed by mistake, the fine is half that of murder. It is a similar situation to when someone thinks that they are trying to apprehend an outlaw, which one is legally entitled to do, but accidentally kills an innocent person by mistake.[41]

Source II equates the fines for killing raiders in one's own territory to those of diminished mental capacity where their crimes are usually the liability of their close kinsmen. The legal connection between these two situations is rather unclear, but perhaps rests on the theme of the kin-group's financial responsibilities for its members.[42]

§17 Raiding in retaliation for a raid: Section seventeen continues the topic of raiding from the previous section, but its focus is on raiding in retaliation for having been raided. Before conducting a raid in retaliation for a raid, the proper procedure is to give notice and fasting,[43] and if these things are ignored

land between the Romans and the Normans. Syney Series in Celtic Studies 7. Ed. Pamela O'Neill (Sydney: University of Sydney, 2004), 116.

39 *GEIL*, 125–127.

40 *eDIL s.v. inbleoga(i)n, inableogain*. Cf. §50.

41 For killing someone in mistake for a thief or outlaw, see *CIH* 1161.15–17 and 1067.30–31, respectively. Both of these passages are cited and discussed in Neil McLeod, *Bloodshed and Compensation in Ancient Ireland* (Perth: Murdoch University, 1999), 17–18.

42 *GEIL*, 92–93.

43 In early Irish law, *troscad* 'fasting' refers to the legal process by which someone seeks legal redress from someone else (usually) of a higher rank, such as a king or other noble, or, for

or evaded by the original perpetrator(s), then fines for evasion are added onto the damage done in the first raid, and there is the right to raid in retaliation resulting in no liability for up to a third of the damage done in the retaliatory raid.

The procedure detailed in source A is as follows. The first person conducts a raid but did not submit to law, in other words, he did not seek protection with a neutral third party (see § 8). Protection does not mean that one is absconding from the law, but seeking protection from a third party whereby a cooling off period is created and the neutral third party can help negotiate the terms for the amount of compensation owed for the raid.[44] If the second person conducts a raid to retaliate, he is not liable for up to a third of the damage and/or injury done during the retaliatory raid, and the remaining two-thirds of the penalties owed as a result of both raids is balanced out. Whichever one of them owes a balance, as it were, he pays the amount to the other.

If the first man submits to law, however, then there is simply a balancing of liabilities without counter-claims (this scenario assumes that a retaliatory raid was made before terms were reached or payment was made for the first raid). If both parties owe fines to each other, they can go to a judge for advice about how to pay, which is: they can balance their liabilities or cancel out everything. Whichever of them sues first is paid first. The last paragraph of the commentaries in sources A and C is difficult. It is unclear whether it forms a separate section of the commentary or follows on from the material immediately above. If it follows from the above, then whichever of them sues first, regardless of how much he owes, is paid first. If it does not follow on, then it assumes a situation where they did not seek the advice of the judge, and the one who is owed less is paid first, probably with the intent that the little compensation that he is owed will contribute towards the larger amount that he in turn needs to pay to the other party.

§ 18 Fines owed the king for cohabiting with a type of concubine: Section eighteen is problematic. According to the commentary, a king is owed a fine for another man cohabitating with a married woman. The *bé n-indles* 'non-owned

example, a poet or churchman. The plaintiff first must give *apad* 'notice' to the defendant. The fasting itself seems to take place at the defendant's residence from sunset to sunrise. During this time, the plaintiff sits outside the defendant's residence. If the defendant eats during this period of time while the plaintiff is fasting, he owes double the amount of what he is being sued. The point of the fast is to force the defendant to appoint a surety or give a pledge that the case will be submitted to justice. If the defendant agrees to submit the case, but the plaintiff continues to fast, the plaintiff loses his case; *GEIL*, 182–183.

44 McLeod, "The Blood-Feud in Medieval Ireland," 118–120.

woman' is a type of concubine. She is depicted in the texts as a married woman who has her husband's permission to cohabitate with another man. If the fine owed to the king is evaded, the original amount doubles, honor-price is owed, and the amount of five *séts*[45] is added on. This would have been a considerable amount to pay. How the king's own honor comes into all this (as per the text) is unclear, but, aside from moral implications, this situation would create additional revenue for the king. If the issue deals with the honor of the woman's husband and the amount the king is owed due to dishonoring his tenant, the situation makes more sense (although it should be borne in mind that the *bé n-indles* has her husband's consent to cohabitate with another man). The husband of the *bé n-indles* does not stand to inherit anything from her, nor is he responsible for any crimes committed by her.[46] The man cohabitating with her would receive a twenty-first of his own honor-price for any injury done to her.[47]

§ 19 When a promulgated law (*cáin*) has impugned a previous law (*cairde*):[48] The people governed by the new promulgated law have the option to have the amount of compensation for a crime owed in the previous law increased so that it will be equal to the amount owed under the promulgated law. This makes sense as many promulgated laws were temporary. Under this scenario, when the promulgated law expires the people will revert back to the previous law, but with the new higher amount of the compensation. All of this must be done with witnesses or mutual agreement, otherwise a criminal could deny that he owes the higher amount.

§ 20 Disputes regarding suretyship:[49] This section presents situations where 1) a surety says he is acting on behalf of the defendant, but the defendant denies that he is his surety, and 2) the surety and the defendant disagree over the amount that the surety agreed to guarantee. Unless there are witnesses, the defendant can deny the suretyship and the amount in question, but the surety is still responsible to pay any fines because he himself states that he agreed to

---

45 The term *sét* refers to any item of value. It is also used as a unit of currency where it is usually equivalent to twelve scruples (there are twenty-four scruples in an ounce) or half a milch-cow; see *GEIL*, 114–116; and *EIF*, 589–591 for a full discussion of the meaning and various values assigned to this word. See above 12n8.

46 Nancy Power, "Classes of Women Described in the *Senchas Már*," in *Studies in Early Irish Law*, ed. R. Thurneysen et al. (Dublin: Royal Irish Academy, 1936), 98–99.

47 *Uraicecht Becc* 'Small Primer', *CIH* 1607.11–12; and *AL*, 3: 72.6–7.

48 For promulgated law, see *GEIL*, 21–22.

49 Cf. §§ 4, 31, 46.

act as surety. The commentaries state that the only way to avoid such disputes is to have witnesses at the time of entering into the suretyship.

§ 21 Proving ownership between people of the same or unequal legal status: The terms *indraic* and *esindraic*[50] refer to those who are considered trustworthy or otherwise qualified to perform certain legal functions such as acting as a witness, and those who are not, respectively. The OI text deals with objects which are found on the shore and the right to claim ownership of the items.[51] The commentary deals with when the ownership of those items is in dispute. Regardless of the social status of the finder, it appears as if the item remains in the possession of the finder (and later purchaser) if the original item was in the finder's possession for longer than the prescribed period during which the original owner can claim their lost or stolen property. Usually any items that are found on the shore or floating near the shore belong to the owner of the adjoining land (aside from seaweed and whales); however, anything brought in from the sea belongs to the finder, or at least a portion of it does, according to some texts.[52]

§ 22 Shipwreck: Section twenty-two (see also §§ 5 and 21) is concerned with 1) dividing a shipwreck and 2) the share of the goods which the owner of a ship pays to the locals for permission to trade. According to the commentary, the goods from a shipwreck (including the ship itself) are divided into thirds: one-third for the owner of the land where the ship came ashore, one-third for the king of the *túath*, and the remaining third is divided amongst the people of the *túath*. The share of the king of the *túath* also includes the best *sét* 'item of value' from the ship. He in turn gives a share to the king of the province, who in turn give a share to the king of Ireland. The Church's clients and a lord's base clients are also obligated to give a third of their own share to their church or lord, respectively.[53]

50 See *eDIL s.vv. indraic* and *eisinnraic*, respectively.

51 Cf. §§ 5 and 22.

52 *GEIL*, 107–108; and Mac Niocaill, "Jetsam, Treasure Trove, and the Lord's Share," 106–107. See also Kelly, "Drifting on the Ocean," 211–218.

53 Clientship is the social institution where a lord advances a fief to a client in exchange for food rent and service. Base clients, although freemen, are not entirely independent of their lord because he purchases their honor-price; free clients pay a higher rent than base clients, but they do not give up their independence; *GEIL*, 29–33. Monasteries also had clients in a system that mirrored that of secular lords, although the rent and service requirements were different; *EIF*, 452–455; *Córus Bésgnai* § 9, in *Córus Bésgnai: An Old Irish Tract on the Church and Society*, ed. and trans. Liam Breatnach. Early Irish Law

The commentary from source A then presents a situation in which a ship came with the purpose of seeking out a specific lord. In this case, the owner of the land receives a *sét* worth an ounce of silver, the lord the ship was seeking receives half the ship's goods, and the captain and sailors keep the other half for commerce. If the ship was not seeking a specific lord, but came for commerce, half the goods are given to the *túath*, and the captain and sailors keep the other half for commerce. If the people of the *túath* do not wish to conduct trade, the division is the same as that given for the owner of the land and the lord.

Source O states that the owner of the shore owns whatever washes up on the shore up to the value of five *sét*s. The commentary then gives the same divisions as source A. The end of source O is noteworthy in that it mentions some of the ship's cargo which would have been given in exchange for firewood and fresh water from the owner of the land, e.g. hides, iron, salt, exotic nuts,[54] drinking horns, wine, and honey.

§ 23 Claims of prior right: If someone purchases a *sét* and the original owner wants to sell the *sét* to someone else afterwards, the original owner is not able to do so because the *sét* now belongs to the new owner. The second commentary in source A states that the *sét*s belong to the purchaser, even if the original owner wants to dissolve the contract or someone else wishes to purchase the *sét*s; cf. § 11. Source F defines a claim of purchase with prior right as a situation where someone bought the *sét* before it was taken from the original owner. A claim of purchase without prior right is defined as a situation where the *sét* is taken from the one who claims it before the *sét* has been bought. In the second scenario, the sale had been agreed upon and the goods taken, but the amount owed has not yet been paid. The claim of growth deals with anything born while it was in someone's possession, such as the case with the young of livestock.

§ 24 Clientship:[55] Clientship is the medieval Irish social institution where a lord advanced a fief of stock or land to someone else in exchange for food renders, military service, and a certain amount of labor. Clientship relationships were categorized as free or base. In a base clientship relationship, the

Series 7 (Dublin: School of Celtic Studies, Dublin Institute for Advanced Studies, 2017); and Colman Etchingham, *Church Organisation in Ireland AD 650 to 1000* (Maynooth: Laigin Publications, 1999), 363–393. See also § 24 for more on clientship.

54 See the references in the text and for § 5 for further discussion of some of these items.

55 *GEIL*, 29–33; and *EIWK*, 337–363.

lord advances the client *séts* of subjection, which are equal to the amount of the client's honor-price. A person may be in a base clientship relationship with more than one lord at a time, provided that the fief received from subsequent lords was not more than two-thirds of that which he received from the first lord. A lord and his base client may terminate the agreement at any time by mutual agreement. If only one party wishes to terminate the agreement, penalties apply. In a free clientship relationship, the lord does not advance *séts* of subjection, so the client is thus more independent and may even be of the same status as the lord. Free clientship relationships can be terminated by either party without penalties.

The commentary makes it clear that a lord cannot force someone to enter into a clientship arrangement with him; that would be unlawful. Once someone has entered into a lawful clientship agreement, the lord is able to enforce the obligations due from his client. Although it is possible to be in more than one clientship relationship simultaneously, the commentary suggests that this is improper when the second clientship arrangement involves an external lord. That being said, the interpretation of this part of the commentary is uncertain. The hostages referred to in the commentary are not hostage-sureties, but rather political hostages used as a means of enforcing authority.[56]

§25 Divorce and fosterage: This section of the text concerns how a wife's *coibche* 'bride-price, dowry' is to be divided in the event that a couple should divorce. If the separation is justified for both parties or unjustified for both[57] and they do not have an heir, the *coibche*, aside from the bed covering, is divided in two. If there is an heir, the *coibche* is used to pay the fosterage-fee.[58] If the amount of the *coibche* does not equal the fosterage-fee, it is added to until the full fosterage-fee is paid. If the *coibche* is more than the fosterage-fee, the surplus is returned. If the separation is justified as a result of wrong-doing by one spouse, the *coibche* is given to the lawful spouse and the spouse who committed the wrong-doing is responsible for paying the fosterage-fee.[59] Fosterage was a common practice in medieval Ireland where children from a young age were fostered with another family until fourteen or seventeen years of age; the legal texts are not consistent on this point. Not only did the fosterage arrangement teach children valuable skills, but it strengthened political bonds between households and created emotional bonds between the fosterling and

56 *GEIL*, 173–176.

57 Medieval Ireland allowed for the equivalent of the modern 'no fault' divorce.

58 For discussions of fosterage, see *GEIL*, 86–90; and *EIWK*, 78–81.

59 For legal justifications of divorce, see Kelly, *Marriage Disputes*, 4–6.

the foster-parents and siblings. The fosterage-fee was based on rank and gender; the fee for girls was higher. Children could also be fostered for affection, in which case there was no fosterage-fee.

§ 26 Disputed land: The glosses and commentary state that when land is in dispute, whomever has possession of the land is free to make use of it without liability (unless there is a prior stipulation on the land use) until the true ownership of the land has been proved.

§ 27 Selling land: This section states that once a person has sold land and received payment for it (cf. § 11), the original owner cannot take possession of the land again. If he were to do so, he would be liable for the fine for illegal entry. If the seller were to distrain the new owner's property in an attempt to get the land back, the seller would be liable for the fine of illegal distraint.[60]

§ 28 The evading kinsman: Section twenty-eight concerns an evading kinsman. If a kinsman paid the debts of an absconding kinsman, he had two ways to get compensated for paying the evading kinsman's debts. If the kinsman did not enter the absconding kinsman's land, the entirety of what is owed is paid to him along with the fine for evasion. If the kinsman decides instead to enter the absconding kinsman's land, he can make use of it for mast, grass, corn, etc. to offset what he is owed. This is one of the situations when it is not illegal to enter and make use of someone else's land.[61] The absconding kinsman is able to get his land back, but he has to pay what he owes his kinsman first.[62]

§ 29 The watchman:[63] If the watchman spots a ship before anyone else, he receives the equivalent of a *sét* worth six scruples, if the ship contains items such as feathers, hides, and iron; he receives a *sét* worth an ounce, if the ship contains gold, silver, exotic nuts, or drinking horns. If he spots a ship and does not say anything, he is liable for fines which depend on the certainty or not of the ship being seized. The watchman is fined for not mentioning that he

60 For illegal entry and distraint, see *GEIL*, 189 and 177–186, respectively.

61 *GEIL*, 189.

62 *CCIH*, 237.

63 Cf. §§ 5, 21, and 22. Acting as a watchman was one of the services clients owed their lord. The terms *fuba* 'attack' and *ruba* 'defense' refer to the compulsory military service base clients owed their lord. *Fuba* consisted of duties such as hunting wolves, horse-thieves, and pirates; *ruba* consisted of duties such as "patrolling the borders of the territory and strategic points such as promontories and mountain-passes;" *GEIL*, 31.

sees the ship because the value of the shipwreck's cargo would have been distributed amongst the community. His silence would deprive others of potentially valuable goods. It should be noted that this section does not deal with piracy or wrecking; it concerns salvaging the goods from a shipwreck.

§ 30 Disputes about judgments: As with § 20, in which a defendant can deny that the person claiming to be his surety actually is his surety and §§ 31 and 46, in which a surety can deny that he entered into a suretyship agreement, § 30 cautions any judge against giving a judgment unless it is in front of witnesses. If he does so, both parties to a case can deny the accuracy of the judge's judgment.

The commentaries present a scenario in which two parties consent to give their account of a situation to a judge and then abide by the given judgment, but they then deny the reported accuracy of their accounts or the judgment given. The judge must prove that the reported accounts were what were told to him, and he needs to prove the original judgment he gave them. If the judge proves he was correct, he gets a twelfth as payment. Judges were paid a fee equivalent to a twelfth of the amount involved in a case.[64] If the claimants consent to give their accounts to him, but not to his judgment, they can deny that the judge ever gave them a judgment, in which case the judge gets nothing. The judge gets a twelfth for the judgment for which he was asked, regardless of whether the claimants follow the terms of the judgment.

§ 31 Suretyship: Section thirty-one (see also § 4) concerns the paying-surety who denies that he entered into a suretyship agreement. Unless there were witnesses who can prove he entered into the suretyship, he can deny it.[65]

§ 32 Failing to attend a mustering and leaving your lord in hostile territory: This sections deals with fines associated with failing to attend a mustering or leaving one's lord in hostile territory. Clients were obligated to attend their lord at assemblies and participate in military service.[66] Fines are higher for leaving one's lord in a hostile territory than for not attending the mustering in the first place, and fines are also calculated based on status; nobles are fined at a higher rate than non-nobles. Anyone who has clients is also liable for fines, if he should tell his clients to abandon their lord in a hostile territory. If the clients

64 *GEIL*, 53.

65 Cf. §§ 20 and 30 where difficulties arise when there are no witnesses to suretyship agreements and judgments, respectively.

66 *GEIL*, 31.

abandon their lord without being told to do so, they are responsible for the fine. The commentary further states that fines are calculated according to the status of the one who pays, but honor-price payments are based on the status of the one to whom the honor-price would be paid.

§ 33 Mutilating the dead: This section details the fines associated with beheading or otherwise mutilating a dead body.[67] The fines are calculated based on whether the victim was a member of the clergy or not (the fines were double for mutilating the body of a cleric than a layman),[68] and whether the decapitated head or otherwise mutilated body was then exhibited. Fines for offenses committed against the dead body of a cleric were paid to the Church. The commentary states that two fines are due when the killer and mutilator are different people. If they are the same person and it was done at the same time, only the fine for killing or wounding is paid. If the same person mutilated the dead body at different times after the killing in outbursts of rage, the killer is responsible for both sets of fines.

§ 34 Warding off an attacker: The translation of the OI text is tentative, but the commentaries concern the fines for wounding or killing an attacker. If an innocent man is attacked, he is not liable for fines for any injury he inflicts while trying to ward off his attacker; § 35 also concerns killing or injuring another in self-defense. If he was able to ward off the attacker without killing him, he is exempt from liability for up to a third of any injuries he inflicts, while his attacker is liable for the full penalties of any injuries he inflicts on the innocent man. If they each wound the other, their liabilities are balanced out and whichever owes more after that, he pays the excess to the other. If the man attacked is wanted for a crime or debt, the attacker is exempt from any fines for injury. If the attacker was able to collect any fines that were due from the other party, he is exempt from liability for up to a third of the fines he might owe for injury, and the other party owes full fines. If both parties inflict injuries on the other, there is a balancing of liabilities and paying of the excess amount to whomever it is owed.

---

67 Presumably the scenarios presented in the commentary do not apply to killing someone in a lawful battle. As seen in § 1, no *wergeld* is awarded for killing someone in lawful battle. What is unclear is whether the fines apply to mutilating the bodies of those slain in a lawful battle or only more generally to mutilating the body of someone murdered or killed in a raid.

68 In this text, fines committed against the Church, the clergy, or any member of a monastic community are double what would normally be due to the laity.

§ 35 Self-defense: The topic of this section follows on from § 34 and concerns killing in self-defense. The first part of the commentary states that a person is exempt from any legal liability for killing an attacker provided that he did not have the ability to escape from the attacker. If this is the case, then he has to prove that he could not escape his attacker without killing him and that the attacker was, indeed, pursuing him. He is to do penance as stated in a penitential for the killing.[69] If the pursuer inflicted any injuries on the party he was pursuing (and the pursuer dies as a result of wounds received in the fight), the kindred of the pursuer pays the fines. If the pursuer made a confession to his heirs, they can deny that their kinsman was the pursuer, but the victim can deny this. If either inflicted any injury, whichever one is the pursuer owes the full fine for any injury done to the one pursued.

§ 36 Killing raiders: This section deals with liability for killing raiders (see also §§ 16 and 17). There is no liability for killing those who enter another territory to raid it or commit arson, as long as the raiders are not recognized, cannot be apprehended by the locals, and the original intention was not to kill them, but to apprehend them. The legal principles here are similar to those in § 16. The last part of the commentary states that the liability for a justified counter-raid is one-third, as in § 17.

§ 37 Loans and fosterage-fee: Section thirty-seven concerns *séts* which one has on loan. The OI text states that they should not be used to pay a fosterage-fee (see § 25). One presumes that the OI text in its complete form would have listed other things which should not be paid for with loaned *séts*. The commentary adds that lords should not give loaned *séts* as fiefs for clients. The latter part of the commentary is obscure to me. It appears to deal with liability for animate *séts* given as part of the fosterage-fee, which in part depends on whether there is knowledge of the location or not of the *séts*, and whether they were removed for safeguarding.

§ 38 Buying imported goods: The commentaries state that, if two *séts* are equally good on the day of a contract, even if one were to increase or decrease in value afterwards, then there is no compensation for increase or loss in the

69 According to the *Old-Irish Penitential*, anyone who kills another in a brawl must do penance for a year and a half or for forty nights, as long as 'he does not pursue the slaughter after the fight is won'; "The Old-Irish Penitential," trans. D.A. Binchy in *The Irish Penitentials*. Scriptores Latini Hiberniae 5. Ed. Ludwig Bieler (Dublin: Dublin Institute for Advanced Studies, 1975), v § 4; *CLH* no. 583.

value of the *séts* because they were equally good on the day that the contract was made. The commentary in source A then goes on to illustrate this with the example of buying a horse.

§ 39 Unlawful requests made by poets:[70] Although poets can make a request for clothes, arms, etc. as payment for a poem, the commentary states that, if the poet makes an unlawful request, especially if the intent is to cause shame, then the poet is liable to pay the full honor-price of the person in question and of the king. The commentary begins with unlawful requests, which are requests made of a king (or someone else) during a hosting or in his residence after he has already said that the item demanded by the poet was not going to be given in payment. It is also unlawful for the poet to make an unlawful request of others or to demand the forbidden items from a third party as payment for a poem. If the king (or other patron) has not yet given notice that certain items will not be given as payment for a poem, the fine is reduced to one-fourth of the person's honor-price. The poet should not ask for any item as payment which is worth more than one-seventh of the honor-price of the person from whom he is asking payment. The commentary also states that a poet who is on circuit, i.e. traveling outside his own territory and performing for others, can ask for payment in clothes or arms, but the overall payment should still not be greater than one-seventh of the patron's honor-price.

§ 40 Overly hasty sureties: Section forty deals with problems resulting from a binding-surety suing the other party to the contract before the agreed upon time for payment. It states that a surety who sues a defendant before the agreed time of payment is himself liable for fines as a result. The commentary then gives two different opinions regarding the payment of the original terms of the contract. The first opinion states that neither the defendant nor someone else pays the original debts. The second opinion says that the defendant should pay what was originally agreed upon at the originally agreed upon time.

§ 41 Contracts made in drunkenness: The commentary states that as long as the person remembers the contract in the morning, and it is as advantageous a contract as he would make while sober, the contract is considered legally binding. Any disadvantageous contract, however, is not binding unless he acknowledges it after twenty-four hours of regaining his senses. A variety

---

70 *GEIL*, 43–49. For the laws concerning poets, see *Uraicecht na Ríar: The Poetic Grades in Early Irish Law*, ed. and trans. Liam Breatnach. Early Irish Law Series 2 (Dublin: Dublin Institute for Advanced Studies, 1987).

of contracts are considered valid, even if made while drunk; these contracts include clientship, neighborhood, and joint-plowing agreements.[71]

§42 Intoxicating a lord: This short section continues the theme of intoxication from §41. The commentary begins with a quasi-etymological gloss on *mescbuide* 'intoxication'. The relationship between the OI text and quasi-etymological gloss, on the one hand, and the remainder of the commentary, on the other, is unclear. The remainder of the commentary states that the lord is responsible for giving judgment, proof, and testimony for his base clients and judgment only for his free clients. The responsibilities listed in the commentary are part of the standard responsibilities that a lord owes his clients.[72]

§43 The authority of the Church in legal matters: The commentary states that the Church's evidence is accepted as final proof regarding fines that are owed to it. If the people who owe the fines have a different church testify on their behalf, the proof of the first church can be contested.

§44 Flouting the authority of a nobleman: The commentary states that, if one evades legal responsibilities owed to a nobleman, then additional fines for evasion are incurred. The commentary then makes a distinction between the nobleman being evaded by someone who is not obligated to act as a paying-surety for him [i.e. the other party to a contract] and someone who is obligated to do so. If the other party to the contract evades the nobleman, he owes additional fines for evasion. If the nobleman's own paying-surety evades him, the surety is responsible for paying the nobleman's debts, or the lord choses the surety's fine for doing so.

§45 Mercenaries: The material here continues the topic of raiding discussed in §§16, 17, and 36, except here we find mercenaries who have been hired to carry out a specific raid in another territory. This is not the same situation where the *aire échta* 'lord of slaughter' and his group of men are hired to carry out vengeance in a different territory.[73] The *aire échta* and his men were professional avengers; there is no indication that we are dealing with that level of sophistication here, as the *aire échta* would be a member of one's own territory

71 *GEIL*, 154.

72 *GEIL*, 26–28.

73 See Neil McLeod, "The Lord of Slaughter," in *The Land beneath the Sea: Essays in honour of Anders Ahlqvist's contribution to Celtic Studies in Australia*. Sydney Series in Celtic Studies 14. Ed. Pamela O'Neill (Sydney: University of Sydney, 2013), 101–114.

and would not have been referred to as a *deorad* 'foreigner, outsider, mercenary' as the hired raiders are referred to in the commentary.

According to the commentaries, the first step necessary when hiring mercenaries is to make certain that their surety takes an oath that the mercenaries will not carry out any other attack than the one for which they have been hired. If this is the case and the mercenaries do more damage than they were hired to do, their employer is only liable for the attack he hired them to commit. If the employer does not get an oath from their surety, he is considered legally liable as an instigator for all the damage the mercenaries commit; he is also liable for all of the property that was not seized from the mercenaries.

If it is the case that the employer does not have an oath from the mercenaries and the mercenaries planned all along to commit many attacks, he is liable as an inciter, and everyone involved, regardless of whether they were directly involved in any given attack or not, are considered legally liable as accomplices. If the mercenaries intended only to make the attack for which they were hired, but some of them did more, it is only those directly involved in the additional attacks who are legally considered to be accomplices. Accomplices, culpable onlookers, and instigators are all considered legally liable to pay fines, which vary depending on the circumstances and degree of involvement with the crime.[74]

If, however, the mercenaries were hired to carry out a lawful attack, and they gave their oath not to do more than they were hired to do, but they did not have a surety acting on their behalf, the one who hired the mercenaries is only liable for the attack for which he hired them, provided that he himself was not capable of carrying out the attack. Any other damage that the mercenaries do, they pay for it if apprehended, or the employer pays for it if they are not. If the attack was unlawful (and with an oath but no surety), the employer is liable as an inciter. The additional damage should be paid by the mercenaries if they are seized, and by the employer if not, but they should in turn reimburse the employer for paying their fines. If there had been a surety on behalf of the mercenaries, he pays for the additional damage (provided he is not apprehended himself), and the mercenaries in turn repay the surety for his expenditures.

§46 Sureties denying their responsibilities: This section concerns sureties who enter into paying-suretyship, but deny afterwards that they did so (cf. also

74 *GEIL*, 154–157; and Jade Harman, "Causation in Medieval Irish Law," in *Language and Power in the Celtic World*. Sydney Series in Celtic Studies 10. Eds. Anders Ahlqvist and Pamela O'Neill (Sydney: University of Sydney, 2011), 97–122.

§§ 4, 20, and 31). According to the first commentary, when there are no witnesses to the fact, the surety can deny, with a compurgator, that he entered into the suretyship. The second commentary advises the plaintiff not to accept a surety unless he has a witness, otherwise the surety could deny having entered into the suretyship. As seen in §§ 4, 20, 30, and 31, it is unwise to enter into any legal action, such as contracts and judgments, without having witnesses. Without witnesses to the agreements, any person, whether in the role of surety, party of the contract, or judge, can deny their role or the extent of their role. In these situations, it is difficult for a proper judgment to be made because they are all examples of legal situations where nothing can be proved due to the lack of witnesses.

§ 47 Usucaption of land:[75] Although it was an offense to settle on someone else's land, if the settler's presence is uncontested for a period of time (the length of time varies depending on the circumstances), the settler is able to make a claim to ownership of the land due to uncontested use of it. The original owner is not able to claim land after it has gone into usucaption, if the owner is aware that someone had settled on the land in the first place. If the owner was unaware that the land was being occupied, the owner can make a claim on the land no matter how much time has passed. The same applies if someone not considered legally responsible, such as a minor, was aware that the land was being occupied; their acknowledgement has no legal authority.

§ 48 Revoking a legacy made to the Church: The commentary begins by stating that any offering made to the Church is binding from the time the offering is made. If someone unintentionally makes an offering to the Church which consists of stolen goods, the original owner is able to reclaim his property as long as he impugns the offer within the legally prescribed time. If someone intentionally gave stolen goods to the Church, he is liable for a fine of misrepresentation. As seen in other sections (§§ 33, 52, and 56), whatever fine is normally due to the laity, it is doubled when due to the Church.

The next part of the commentary states that, if the stolen goods were given to the Church to pay a fine or other obligation owed to the Church, then the person who gives them is liable to pay restitution to the Church.

The last part of the commentary continues the same subject matter. If the owner made a bequest and then took the goods away, he is liable for a heavy fine. If he later returned the goods to the Church, the fine is halved. The com-

75 *GEIL*, 109–110.

mentaries in sources A and E also state that the same fine structure applies to bequests made to laymen, but the original fine starts out as half, i.e. four doubles, what would be due to the Church, i.e. eight doubles. The amounts being doubled for the Church are given as penance and a fine for taking back the goods.

§ 49 Lawful and unlawful payments for poets: This section concerns lawful and unlawful rewards for poets (see also § 39). The commentary states that, if a poet makes a praise poem, then requests an unlawful (i.e. too high) payment for it and threatens to satirize his patron (or whomever he composed the praise poem for) if he does not receive the excessive payment, then the poet then is liable for the fine of theft for the amount above what was proper for the poet to request. An unjustified satire would require the poet to pay the patron's honor-price.[76] According to § 39, the amount of the payment for a praise poem should not exceed one-seventh of the honor-price of the patron.

In medieval Ireland there was a great deal of importance placed on the power of the spoken word.[77] Not only could a satire ruin someone's reputation within the wider community, thus causing shame and loss of honor, but there was also the sense that whatever the poet said had power beyond the actual words spoken. A praise poem gave the patron the qualities being praised; a satire could raise disfiguring red blisters of shame on the victim's cheeks. The threat of satire was very serious. Unjust satires were fined, but to ignore a just satire was a great shame; just satires could be used as behavioral correctives. In this commentary we see the poet abusing his power so that he may receive an unlawfully high payment for his poem by threatening satire if he does not receive the higher payment.[78]

---

76 *GEIL*, 137–139; and Roisin McLaughlin, *Early Irish Satire* (Dublin: School of Celtic Studies, Dublin Institute for Advanced Studies, 2008), 4.

77 For general discussions of poets in medieval Ireland, see J.E. Caerwyn Williams and Patrick K. Ford, *The Irish Literary Tradition* (Belmont, MA: Ford & Bailie, 1992), 30–63 and 153–177; and Patrick K. Ford, *The Celtic Poets: Songs and Tales from Early Ireland and Wales* (Belmont, MA: Ford & Bailie, 1999), xv–xxxi.

78 McLaughlin, *Early Irish Satire*, 3–7; *GEIL*, 43–49. Even in literary texts we see the lengths kings and nobles will go to in order to keep their honor intact. For example, in *Talland Étair* 'The Siege of Howth', the poet, Aithirne Áilgesach, 'Aithirne the Importunate', demands, and receives, King Echu's only eye and sleeps with the wife of the king of Munster, all of which was granted to the poet in order to avoid the poet destroying their honor; *Talland Étair: A Critical Edition with Introduction, Translation, Textual Notes, Bibliography and Vocabulary*, ed. and trans. Caoimhín Ó Dónaill. Maynooth Medieval Irish Texts 4 (Maynooth: Department of Old and Middle Irish, 2005), ll. 8–10, and 26–29, respectively.

The commentaries then compare this scenario to a situation where the *aire échta* 'lord of slaughter' is given an excess of food, which he then consumes before carrying out his duties. In this scenario, the *aire échta* is charged a fine of theft for the totality of the food he ate because he had not yet carried out his duties.[79] The commentators explain that the poet is fined only for the excess of the payment because he had already delivered his praise poem, and, thus, should only be fined for the amount above and beyond what his praise poem was worth.

The penultimate paragraph of source A concerns a situation where the poet and the patron disagree over whether the poet threatened to satirize the patron unless he got an excessive payment for his praise poem. Although it is not explicitly stated that there are no witnesses, this must surely be the case; if there were witnesses to the poet threatening satire, there would be proof and it would not be another situation of 'he said vs. he said'. The burden of proof in this situation lies with the plaintiff.

The final paragraph of source A deals with situations where 1) the plaintiff's excess of payment was given to the poet to balance mutual liabilities between the two or 2) the poet had forgiven payment for the poem. Both of these situations are to be treated as cases of uncertainty and presumably also do not have witnesses, as otherwise there would be certainty. As such, no judgment can be given in favor of the poet (or the plaintiff); any judge who decides in favor of either of them would be giving a false judgment. In very serious cases, a judge could lose his position for making a false judgment; at the very least, he owes a fine.[80] This is one of the few places in the tract (aside from § 1) where there is explicit mention of a judge making a false judgment.

§ 50 Taking a poet captive: If the poet can perform the three acts of divination, i.e. *teinm láeda*, *imbas forosna*, and *díchetal di chennaib*, he is thus able to prove himself as a poet and is entitled to the privileges thereof, e.g. having an honor-price and being released from the obligation of being a kinsman-surety. This is similar to the procedure described in § 5 where the *deorad Dé* has to prove his identity by performing miracles. The fullest explanation of these three acts of divination is found in *Sanas Cormac*:

> Imbass forosnae .i. dofūarascaib sec[h]ip rēt bas maith lasin filid ⁊ bes adlaic dó d'foillsiugad. Is amlaid di*diu* dognīther ōn .i. *con*cnā in file mīr

79 See McLeod, "The Lord of Slaughter," 101–114.

80 *GEIL*, 54–55.

do c[h]arna dirg muice nō c[h]on nō c[h]ait *ocus* dobir īarom for lic īar cūl na comlad ⁊ dichain dīchetal fair ⁊ adodpair do dēib īdal ⁊ cotagair dó ⁊ nī fagaib īarnabāroch, ⁊ dochain īarom for a dī bois ⁊ congair dēo īdal cuige arnā tarmascthar a c[h]odlud ⁊ dobeir a dī bois ima dī lecain ⁊ contuli ⁊ bīth*ir* og a foraire ar nachn-imparræ ⁊ nach toirmescae neach, agas doadbanar dō īarom annī aradmbí co cend nómaide nō a dōu nō a trī, fut ngair *con*messad ocind andbairt.

Et ideo imbas dicitur .i. bas disīu ⁊ bass anall im a agaid nō im a c[h]end. Atrorbe Pātraic anīsin, ⁊ an teinm laoda ⁊ fotroirgell a brīathar nā bad nimhe nā talman nach aon dogēnai, ar is dīultad bathis. Dīc[h]etal doc[h]ennaib im*morro* fodrācbad sōn i cōrus c[h]erdæ, ar is soas fodera sōn: nī ēcen audbairt do demnaib oca, acht aisnēis do c[h]ennaib a chnāmae fochēdōir.[81]

Imbas forosnai ['knowledge which illuminates'], i.e. it reveals whatever thing the *fili* ['poet'] pleases and what he needs to have revealed. This is how it is done: the *fili* chews a piece of the raw flesh of a pig or a dog or a cat. Then he puts it upon a stone behind the door, chants over it and he offers it to false gods and he summons them to him. He remains at that the next day, and chants over the palms of his two hands. He summons idol gods to him in order that his sleep may not be disturbed. He puts the palms of his two hands about his cheeks and sleeps, and people are watching over him so that no one might interfere with him or disturb him. And then the thing that he is after is revealed to him, for as long as three days, or twice that, or three times, or whatever time, long or short, that he may be involved in the offering.

And that is why it is called *imbas*: to wit, a palm [*bas*] on this side and a palm on the other around [*imm-*] his face or around his head. Patrick forbade that thing and the *teinm laída* ['chewing of pith'], and he pledged his word that there would not be heaven nor earth for anyone who practiced it, for it is a denial of baptism. *Díchetal de chennaib* ['incantation from ends'],[82] however, was left as an integral part of poetic art, for it is learn-

81 "*Sanas Cormaic: An Old Irish Glossary*," ed. Kuno Meyer, in *Anecdota from Irish Manuscripts* IV, eds. O.J. Bergin, et al. (Halle: M. Niemeyer, 1912), 64, no. 756. See also John Carey, "The Three Things Required of a Poet," *Ériu* 48 (1997): 41–58.

82 The meaning of *cenn* is ambiguous here; it has a range of meanings which would fit the context, including 'ends', 'tips', or 'heads'; *eDIL* s.v. 1 *cenn*.

ing that causes that: offering to demons is not necessary to accomplish it, rather narrating from the ends of bones straight off.[83]

§51 Abduction of women, theft of their property, responsibility for raising their children, and the role of the kindred: The OI text concerns defrauding widows. The commentary opens with a situation where a woman who has been abducted, whether by her consent or not, has given some of her property to her abductor. Whenever a woman has been abducted, the general operating principle is that her abductor assumes all liability for her and her actions while she is in his custody, but her natal kindred still has rights to all of her assets. For example, if she were to die while in a relationship of any type without her family's consent, her family would still retain rights to her inheritance and property. Even if the woman gives away her own property, her family is due compensation since she is away from them without their consent.

When a woman marries, early Irish law is clear that, while the woman's husband has legal rights over her, she still retains her own property. If he should die, the woman's son is her legal guardian. Assuming that the marriage produced any children, they are usually regarded as part of their father's kindred. If there are no children, her own kindred assume legal responsibility for her. She is not entitled to inherit from her deceased husband, but her children are. One can easily imagine a widow with young children living on the property that her sons inherited, thus creating a situation where the woman could be both emotionally and physically vulnerable. One could also envision a scenario where a widow without sons has moved back into her father's house (or her brother's house, if her father is deceased), also moving her own property from her marriage. In such a situation, one can easily see how both the woman's property and that of her family could be stolen during the abduction. Furthermore, we can see how a widow might be a prime target for abduction given the fact that she could well have a great deal of wealth as a result of her previous marriage.

The commentary then presents scenarios where a woman has been carried off and her property forcibly taken from her. Regardless of whether she had a hand in orchestrating her own abduction, if her abductor steals her property, she is owed compensation and honor-price, although only half the honor-price if she consented to her abduction. The commentary then goes on to discuss what type of property the woman had stolen from her. This is legally important because if she has consented to her abduction, she has therefore severed ties to her kindred and, accordingly, her honor-price is no longer calculated

83 Ford, *The Celtic Poets*, 47.

at half of her father's (or brother's, if her father is no longer alive) and has to be calculated in terms of the legal standing that her own property gives her. As Neil McLeod has discussed, *etarscarthach* 'separable' property is property sufficient for someone to be independent from the person on whose status their honor-price would normally depend. *Nemetarscarthach* 'non-separable' property is property one possesses, but it is not sufficient to maintain an independent honor-price. The catch to all of this is that it is not simply enough to have *etarscarthach* property, one must make good use of it. If the woman does not make good use of her *etarscarthach* property or only has *nemetarscarthach* property, she is entitled to restitution of her stolen goods, but no honor-price payment.[84] There are situations where a woman can maintain an independent honor-price, e.g. if she is an heiress with sufficient property, and some women had a greater amount of legal independence, such as a female physician. Depending on how successful her former household was, she could well have grown her own property considerably.[85]

Regardless of whether she consented to her abduction, if her abductor forcibly takes property belonging to her kindred, her kindred will be owed compensation, restitution, and full honor-price because it is a case of theft. If she gives her kindred's property away willingly, regardless of whether she was abducted willingly, she is owed nothing and her kindred is owed compensation and full honor-price. The next part of the commentary is difficult because part of it is missing. There is a similar and equally difficult commentary in *Cáin Lánamna*.[86] Mac Cathán, whom we cannot identify, and who may or may not be the actual son of a Cathán mentioned in two other commentaries in *Cáin Lánamna*, offers a different legal opinion. He suggests (in the commentary found in *Anfuigell*) that the woman should not have to pay her kindred restitution and compensation for goods she gave away willingly to her spouse, but that restitution of the goods is enough. That is what the 'fault' is, having to pay for the goods twice. The commentary ends with an alternative where the woman has stolen the goods, in which case there is no 'fault' because she owes restitution and compensation.

The commentary from source E begins much the same way as source A. If a woman is abducted against her will, she and her kindred are owed honor-price; if she consented to her abduction, she is owed nothing and her kindred is still owed honor-price because it was without her kindred's consent. If she dies

84 Neil McLeod, "Property and Honour-Price in the Brehon Law Glosses and Commentaries," *The Irish Jurist* 31 (1996): 280–295.

85 *GEIL*, 77.

86 *Cáin Lánamna*, § 36.

within a month of being abducted, her kindred is owed body-fine and honor-price. Because the kindred did not consent to the abduction, the kindred has legal rights over any child begotten on her within a month of her abduction. If, however, the father wishes to pay the kindred to acquire legal rights to his child, the child then acquires the legal status of a child of a betrothed *cétmuinter* 'spouse' or *adaltrach* 'concubine'. In a situation where the woman was abducted by force, the kindred can decide to retain legal rights to the child or not. If the kindred decides to give up legal rights to the child, the father is obligated to pay the kindred to acquire the legal rights to his child. If, however, the woman was willingly abducted, the father is not obligated to acquire legal rights to the child. If he wishes to acquire such rights, the woman's kindred is obligated to let those rights be purchased from them. If the kindred decides to freely hand over the legal rights to the child, the father has no choice but to accept it.

As is frequently the case in the commentaries, we are given a different legal opinion, this time coming from the text *Bretha for Macṡlechtaib* 'Judgments on Categories of Sons'. This legal text is part of the *Senchas Már* legal collection, but it is only fragmentarily attested.[87] According to this text, regardless of how the woman was taken, the father is obligated to take the child if given an opportunity to do so, although it could be the case that the kindred wants to keep the child; law does not require the kindred to give the child up, but it requires the father to assume responsibility if given the chance. We are told that a harlot, perhaps a condemnation on the woman who consents to her abduction, should return any child to its father if she does not have the means to support it, regardless of whether the child is from a recognized or secret union.

The commentary becomes more complicated in the next set of scenarios. Whereas up to now the commentary was treating children begotten within a month of the abduction, now it deals with children begotten after a month up to the point where the couple should be lawfully betrothed. These children are considered as being the child of an abducted *cétmuinter* or *adaltrach*, and have a lower status than those conceived within a month of the abduction. This implies that, if the woman remains long enough, i.e. more than a month with her abductor, then either she does not want to go back or the kindred cannot get her back. Because all of this is happening without the kindred's consent, the children will continue to have a lower status until the couple is legally betrothed. Whatever the case, the situation has changed and is beginning to look more like a legally recognized, albeit illegal, potentially long-term union.

---

87 Fragments of the text can be found in *CIH* 107.9–110.13 and 1546.26–1550.14; see *GEIL*, 270; and *CCIH*, 300–301.

Furthermore, it appears as if the woman's kindred can compel the father to acquire legal rights to his child if the child is conceived within the first month of her being away, but that power no longer applies if the woman remains with the abductor more than a month.

The commentary then moves on to discuss what happens if the woman is offered a bride-price by the abductor, which would then in turn change the status of their children and make their relationship legal. If she was carried off without her consent, but for the sake of her kindred accepts a bride-price, if her kindred does not oppose the union, she is paid the fine of a *cétmuinter* for her abduction (presumably by the abductor or his kindred). She in turn seems to pay to her kindred a lower fine, that of an *adaltrach*, presumably to compensate them for loss of her labor while she has been away. She comes out ahead financially in this case, but in effect she has more or less been forced into a marriage. If her kindred opposes the union, she pays them nothing. If she was complicit in her abduction and accepted a bride-price for the good of her kindred, or she was forcibly abducted but accepted a bride-price against the best interests of her kindred, she is paid the lower fine of an *adaltrach*, which she in turn pays to her kindred. She does not make any financial gain because of acting against the best interests of her kindred. If her kindred opposes the union, she pays them nothing. If the kindred opposes whatever union into which she has entered, they still retain rights to her assets and are not responsible for her liabilities. Furthermore, while she is away from the kindred with the status of one who has been abducted, the kindred has the choice of having, by way of compensation for the woman's labor that they are losing, another woman work for them, presumably paid for by the abductor, or they can choose to have their kinswoman contribute to the abductor's household without him contributing to hers. A second opinion is given that the woman's kindred has the right to both.

When the abducted woman is living with her abductor in this situation, the law reckons fines between them as between a husband and wife, up to the point where honor-price comes into play. The abducted woman can certainly injure her abductor, whom the commentary now refers to as her husband. (Marriage by abduction was recognized as a form of union in the laws.[88]) She can injure him without having to pay him honor-price, and if she should injure someone else, the abductor is responsible for paying any fines to the third party. Legally, the woman is still considered as stolen property, which means that, like stolen cattle, as long as she remains technically stolen, he is responsible for all of her liabilities while she is in his possession.

---

88 *Cáin Lánamna*, § 36.

§ 52 Seeking sanctuary of a church or monastic community: If the sanctuary is sought in a violent manner, the fines are double that due to a layman. This doubling of fines is seen in other sections concerning fines owed to the Church, i.e. §§ 33, 48, and 56. The commentary from source D adds that a king is not entitled to seek sanctuary in a church or monastic community without providing tithes, first fruits, and alms. The topic of sanctuary/protection also occurs in §§ 8 and 57.

§ 53 Repudiating a wife: The commentaries state that it is wrong to repudiate a wife without just cause. In such a case, the wife is entitled to her bride-price and honor-price. If there should be just cause to repudiate her, their separation is conducted according to the nature of the injury. *Cáin Lánamna* 'The Law of Couples' § 10 states that, if a couple should divorce by mutual consent or if they have each given the other cause for a divorce, then they each retain the property that they had when they entered the marriage, and the profits of their joint household are divided into thirds. According to § 13, if either spouse has reason to divorce the other, the share of the household profits derived from labor are forfeited to whichever spouse was well-behaved, as it were.

§ 54 Washing the clothing of the dead: The commentaries begin by stating that the clothing is *nesam* 'necessary' only after it has been washed. In legal texts, for example *Di Chetharṡlicht Athgabála* 'On the Four Sections of Distraint', four different types of 'necessary' or 'urgent' things are distinguished. These are 1) whatever is needed for 'life and sustenance', such as food and clothing, 2) what is 'needed to support a joint economy or household', 3) what is 'needed to discharge one's liabilities', and 4) what is 'needed to conserve one's normal resources', in other words, anything that one would need to borrow if it remained out of one's possession.[89] The clothing is not considered within the first classification of 'necessary' items until it has been washed. A period of delay is given for washing it. The commentaries both discuss a period of delay in the process of distraint so that the clothing can be washed.

Distraint refers to a series of procedures for enforcing a claim against another person by seizing their property without recourse to a legal court.[90] The first step in the process requires that the plaintiff give the defendant formal notice that the plaintiff intends on impounding the defendant's property.

89 D.A. Binchy, "Distraint in Irish Law," *Celtica* 10 (1973): 38.

90 Binchy, "Distraint in Irish Law," 22–71; and *GEIL*, 177–182.

After formal notice has been given, there is a period of delay of one, two, three, or five days depending on what the issue is, so, for example, failure to raise the funeral mound of one's lord has a delay of five days, taking the plaintiff's pigs has a delay of three days. During the period of delay, the defendant has the opportunity to stop the whole process by settling the matter at hand, i.e. paying fines due or otherwise fulfilling necessary obligations. If the defendant does nothing at all (not even giving a pledge that he is willing to come to terms), the plaintiff can then enter the defendant's land and remove cattle up to the value of the amount owed. This part of the process needs to be carried out in front of a legal advocate. The cattle are then taken to a private holding area, and this is followed by another period of delay. If the defendant continues to do nothing by the end of this delay period, the plaintiff can day by day take cattle from the holding area and they become his own. This process continues until all of the cattle owed to the plaintiff are formally his, assuming that the defendant continues to do nothing. Any cattle moved from the holding area to the plaintiff's property cannot be recovered by the defendant.

The commentaries in sources A and E next move to the topic of whether the clothing was intentionally not washed and then given to a third party with the intent to do harm. If harm results, then the full fines for the specific type of injury are to be paid to the plaintiff. If no harm results, source A gives two options, 1) either that the defendant is exempt from any fines, or 2) the defendant needs to pay the fine for the type of injury he intended to give the plaintiff by giving him or her the unwashed clothing. Source E states that in this instance double the value of the clothing is to be paid by the defendant on account of deception. The underlying assumption in both sources is that the clothing of the dead should always be washed before being given to someone else. The harm to which the commentaries allude probably deals with issues of disease. In other words, if someone died of a contagious disease, there would be the likelihood of passing the disease along to a third party if the clothing was not washed first. If, however, the clothing was given to discharge a fine from the defendant, it is treated either as a careless act of social utility, where restitution is the fine ('restitution' here is the legal term for a component of the compensation for injury), or it is treated like an injury due to negligence where full penalty fines are owed.

The second half of the commentary in source A starts much like the first half in that it gives the periods of delay in the distraint process, which depend on whether the clothing was originally washed or not. The second half is about what is owed to the Church for burying the dead. The deceased person's clothing being the minimum charge for this service. This charge was due even from the very poorest members of the ecclesiastical community.[91] More affluent members of the ecclesiastical community were also required to provide a heriot cow, which may or may not be an actual cow but perhaps a form of commuted payment rendered to the Church as part of the burial payment. It is hard to tell whether the payments listed here are only due from members of the ecclesiastical community, such as the monastic tenants, or whether they were also due from members of the secular community as well. The seven loaves are due after seven days, and a funeral feast after a month.[92]

If items belonging to the deceased were being taken to the Church as a donation, and they were stolen along the way, the owners of the property are owed a series of fines and the Church is owed nothing unless the theft took place on land owned by the Church, in which case the Church is owed fines for the theft taking place on the Church's land. If the property was due to the Church or if it was stolen to disgrace the Church, the Church is owed a series of fines instead, with honor-price being owed to the person who was conveying the property to the Church.

Although not part of the legal commentary under discussion, in § 67 of the ecclesiastical text *The Monastery of Tallaght*, clothing given to the Church is discussed.[93] *The Monastery of Tallaght* is an OI text that deals with some of the traditions associated with the monastery, which was founded in the eighth century by Máel Ruain. In this section of the text, we are told a tale of an anchorite, Laisren, who, while spending the night with one of the clerical students, sleeps on a cloak which had formally belonged to a married couple. Alas for Laisren, the cloak had not been washed beforehand, and the anchorite was troubled by dreams such that he had never experienced ever in his life. Laisren, much disturbed, then performs a vigil in which an angel appears and informs him that a demon had accompanied the cloak because it had belonged to lustful people. Once the cloak was washed, the demon left it.[94] While the legal commentary is concerned about actual physical contagion associated with unwashed clothing, this text is clearly concerned with the spiritual dangers that can result from being in contact with clothing from the laity. This is not to say that physical contagion was not also a concern, but the text highlights the spiritual dangers instead.[95]

91 Etchingham, *Church Organisation in Ireland*, 439–440.

92 Etchingham, *Church Organisation in Ireland*, 440–441; and Kelly, *Marriage Disputes*, 118–121.

93 I owe this reference to Morgan Davies.

94 "The Monastery of Tallaght," eds. and trans. Gwynn, E.J. and W.J. Purton, *Proceedings of the Royal Irish Academy* 29 C (1911): 115–179.

95 Westley Follett has suggested to me that the writer of the text probably had Leviticus 15 in

§ 55 Fishing rights: If someone owns the bank on both sides of a river, he can choose to have a weir on both sides of the river and keep a sixth of the profits from each side, or he can keep a third of the profits from one side. If he owns one side, he is entitled to a sixth of the profits. Anything more than that is owed to those who have a weir either above or below him, depending on which way the fish come to them, i.e. if the fish come from above his location, two-thirds of the surplus goes to those who have the weir below him.[96]

§ 56 Crimes committed against the Church: The OI text refers specifically to theft, but the commentaries do not list specific crimes. As seen in §§ 33, 48, and 52, the fines for crimes committed against the Church are double what would be due to a layman for the same crime. § 52 also lists penance as part what is due to the Church for crimes committed against it.

§ 57 Violating protection: The OI text in this section states that it is concerned with violating the protection of someone who is himself under protection. The OI text further states that an outsider in a territory cannot offer protection to another, and no one is entitled to a fine if their employees offer protection to a third party and their protection is violated (see also § 8). The commentary in source A states that, if someone who is an outsider (i.e. not originally from the territory) gives his own personal protection to another outsider who seeks him out, and if his protection is violated, then he is owed nothing because the protection was not ordered by a noble. If it were so, then the outsider (who offered the protection) would be entitled to the full range of penalties for violating his protection, and the noble who ordered the protection would be entitled to fines as well.

The commentary continues the theme of violating the protection of someone who is himself under protection; in this case, it deals with (free) dependent members of the household. Dependent members of the household are able to offer protection and the head of the household is entitled to a portion of his own honor-price if anyone violates their protection. If the head of the household ordered the protection, he is entitled to his full honor-price.

The first two paragraphs of the commentary from source D concern violating those whom the king has sent out (presumably on royal business) under his protection. The commentary states that whether outsiders or native freemen

mind when he wrote this section. Leviticus 15 discusses various forms of ritual impurity that can result from sexual activity.

96 *EIF*, 285–298, especially 287–289.

were violated, the king is owed his honor-price; what is unclear is whether his subjects offered protection, which was then violated, or whether they themselves were harmed. Based on the fact that the entire section focuses on offering protection while being under someone else's protection, the assumption is that the subjects offered protection to a third party, which was violated. Because the subjects were under the king's protection, so long as they plead the king's protection, both the subjects and king are owed honor-price. If the subjects do not plead the king's protection, neither they nor the king receive any portion of their honor-price.

If the subjects were not sent by the king, but they plead his protection, a third of the king's honor-price is due to him if they are dependent subjects. If they are independent, neither they nor the king receive anything. If the subjects plead their own honor-price instead, the king receives nothing.

§ 58 Defects in cattle: The final section of the text deals with defective items, particularly defects in cattle. The commentary concerns defects in *sét*s that are given in a contract or on condition and presents three scenarios. In the first, if the *sét* was perfect at the time it was transferred (or it does not survive at all), full restitution and full compensation are owed by the seller. In the second, if the *sét* was perfect when it left, but it was later found by the plaintiff to be damaged, he has to take it as it is, but he receives partial restitution and full compensation. The third scenario is when the *sét* is withered or lame when it left, i.e. was sold, or does not survive away at all. In this case, full restitution and incomplete compensation are owed to the purchaser.

Manuscript Sources

The manuscript sigla used for the first six sources are the same as those found in *CCIH*, 164–165.[1] They have been retained here for ease of reference. There is a concordance of manuscript sources and section numbers at the end of the list of sources along with a separate concordance of section numbers and manuscript sources with *CIH*. Due to the fragmentary nature of the source material, it is not possible to determine the textual relationship of the sources to each other. Furthermore, the fact that so many of the commentaries contain multiple variants of the same legal material attests to the compilatory nature of the scribes who assembled and arranged the material. This type of scribal activity is common not only in early Irish legal texts, but also in legal (both Roman and canon law) MSS on the Continent. The same tendency in both is to present only snippets of the text, as memory aids, each followed by a substantial commentary.[2] Because many of the commentaries come from multiple unnamed sources, it is not possible to reconstruct the origins of the source material unless the scribes provide that information. As can be seen from the attested sources, some of the legal material related to *Anfuigell* can be found embedded within other texts, such as *Bretha Éitgid* 'Judgments of Inadvertence',[3] but it is not possible to determine whether the compilers of the *Anfuigell* commentaries took the material from *Bretha Éitgid* or the compilers of *Bretha Éitgid* borrowed from *Anfuigell*.

1 Sources F and G as listed in *CCIH*, 165 actually belong to *Aidbred*; see the discussion of this text in Appendix 5, 304–306. Gaps in the lettering system of the MS sources below result from editing *Anfuigell* and *Aidbred* simultaneously; there is a great degree of overlap in the MS sources for both texts, and most of the first draft of the edited text for both was completed before I realized that I was dealing with two distinct texts rather than one. The purpose of retaining the sources as listed in *CCIH* is to make it clear where sources for *Anfuigell* and *Aidbred* overlap and where they diverge. The edition of *Anfuigell* does not use any of the same sigla used in *Aidbred* unless they refer to the same source.

2 *CCIH*, 50–51; Simms, "The Contents of Later Commentaries on the Brehon Law Tracts," 23–40; and Charlene M. Eska, "Varieties of Early Irish Legal Literature and the *Cáin Lánamna* Fragments," *Viator* 40 (2009): 1–16. For general discussion of the later Irish legal MSS, see Rowena Finnane, *Late Medieval Irish Law Manuscripts: A Reappraisal of Methodology and Context*. Sydney Series in Celtic Studies 13 (Sydney: The University of Sydney, 2013).

3 *Bretha Éitgid* is a medieval Irish legal text concerned with accidental injuries; *GEIL*, 272; *CCIH*, 176–182; and *AL* 3: 83–547.

 | DOI:10.1163/9789004391987_004

A TCD MS 1387, *olim* H.5.15,[4] pp. 8a1–16b19, *CIH* 2146.15–2163.32, *CLH* no. 685, *CCIH*, 88. The text as printed in *CIH* has been checked against the MS. While the MS in its current state is not complete, the contents of the MS are entirely legal. In this MS, *Anfuigell* is positioned between *Fothae Mór* 'Great Foundation' and *Aidbred* 'Claiming'.[5] This source contains the fullest version of the text and commentary. The scribe identifies himself in a note on p. 7a42 at the very end of *Findṡruth Fíthail* 'The Fair Stream of Fíthal' which reads 'Seaa*n* discribsit do m*ac* ædagai*n*' 'Seán wrote [this] for Mac Aedagáin'. The MS catalog prints the colophon as 'Seán doscrib do mac aedagáin',[6] but the text clearly has a later form of Latin *deṡcribo* and not the preterite/perfect of Irish *scríbaid*.[7] No date appears in the MS, but the catalog suggests the possibility of a fifteenth-century date.[8] There is nothing in the MS to suggest a date earlier or later than the fifteenth century.

The scribe generally distinguished the OI text from the commentary by using larger letter forms for the text, but sometimes, as seen in §48, the OI text is repeated within a block of commentary but not written in larger letters. Each new section of the OI text starts with a large, decorative initial letter. Many of the letters which begin new legal texts within the MS or new sections within a text are decorated with orange paint (see Plate 1 for the large initial marking the beginning of *Anfuigell*). The writing is in two columns in iron-gall ink. While the manuscript contains the occasional illegible marginal note, such as at the bottom of p. 7, no other scribes were involved with the copying of the text and commentaries. The scribe occasionally makes corrections to his work, some of which seem to have been made later than the main copying stage. These later corrections are often written in a lighter colored ink and with a wider cut pen, e.g. p. 11 between the columns of text. His usual method of cancellation is erasure. The scribe's hand varies at times between being neat and tidy, e.g. p. 8a3–6, and rather sprawling, e.g. the bottom of p. 24b. The scribe is also responsible for writing TCD MS 1337, *olim* H.3.18, pp. 871–874.[9] Both of these manuscripts were part of Edward Lhuyd's Irish manuscript collection.[10]

---

4 Abbott and Gwynn, *Catalogue of Irish Manuscripts*, 249–255. The material from *Anfuigell* is listed on 251–252. It is not listed as a distinct text.

5 See Appendix 5, 304–306.

6 Abbott and Gwynn, *Catalogue of Irish Manuscripts*, 249. The scribal colophon is not at the foot of p. 7a as the catalog states, but rather two thirds of the way down column a.

7 I should like to thank Paul Russell for discussion on this point.

8 Abbott and Gwynn, *Catalogue of Irish Manuscripts*, 249.

9 William O'Sullivan, "The Book of Domhnall Ó Duibhdábhoireann, Provenance and Codicology," *Celtica* 23 (1999): 277.

10 O'Sullivan, "The Book of Domhnall Ó Duibhdábhoireann," 277; and *idem*, "The Manuscript

B TCD MS 1337, *olim* H.3.18,[11] p. 436b, *CIH* 979.23–980.17, *CLH* no. 683. The text in *CIH* has been checked against the MS. This is a composite MS, sections of which date to the fifteenth and sixteenth centuries. The fragments of text and commentary follow a series of citations from various legal texts. The citations from *Anfuigell* break off due to a chasm in the MS. The scribe is unknown. See also *CCIH*, 43.

C Oxford, Bodleian Library MS Rawl. B 506, ff. 52c–53d, *CIH* 167.19–170.6, *CLH* no. 695. The text in *CIH* has been checked against the MS. This section of the MS dates to the fourteenth century and was written by an unidentified scribe who wrote for Brian Mac Aodhagáin (†1390). Ff. 16br–62v consists of legal material.[12] See *CCIH*, 21 for a description of the contents from *Anfuigell*. The material on stampeding cattle found at *CIH* 167.30–38 is edited and translated in Appendix 1 below because it is uncertain whether that material is actually part of *Anfuigell*.

D TCD MS 1337, *olim* H.3.18,[13] p. 439a–b, *CIH* 984.16–985.23, *CLH* no. 683, *CCIH*, 43. The fragment is acephalous and consists of a single folio written in two columns, half of which has been left blank. Unfortunately, the use of reagent now makes the reading of many words difficult; see also Binchy, *CIH* 984, n. f. The text in *CIH* has been checked against the MS. Source D begins with a fragment of commentary from § 51, corresponding to source A, *CIH* 2162.24. The scribe of this folio is unknown.

E TCD MS 1337, *olim* H.3.18,[14] pp. 456a–457b, *CIH* 1017.1–1018.25, *CLH* no. 683, *CCIH*, 44. The text in *CIH* has been checked against the MS. This section of the MS is acephalous and the scribe is unknown.

Collection of Dubhaltach Mac Fhirbhisigh," in *Seanchas: Studies in Early and Medieval Irish Archaeology, History and Literature in Honour of Francis J. Byrne*, ed. Alfred P. Smyth (Dublin: Four Courts Press, 2000), 439.

11 Abbott and Gwynn, *Catalogue of the Irish Manuscripts*, 149–150; images are available on the Irish Script on Screen website: https://www.isos.dias.ie/english/index.html. Accessed December 10, 2018.

12 Brian Ó Cuív, *Catalogue of Irish Language Manuscripts in the Bodleian Library at Oxford and Oxford College Libraries* (Dublin: Dublin Institute for Advanced Studies, 2001), 217; and Francis John Byrne, *A Thousand Years of Irish Script* (Oxford: The Bodleian Library, 1979), 23. Images of the MS are available on the Early Manuscripts of Oxford University website at http://image.ox.ac.uk/show?collection=bodleian&manuscript=msrawlb506. Accessed November 21, 2017.

13 Abbott and Gwynn, *Catalogue of the Irish Manuscripts*, 150.

14 Abbott and Gwynn, *Catalogue of the Irish Manuscripts*, 150.

F BL MS Egerton 88,[15] f. 4rb,[16] *CIH* 1271.29–33, *CLH* no. 689, *CCIH*, 52.[17] The text in *CIH* has been checked against the MS. The MS was written over a number of years in the 1560s and early 1570s by several scribes. The manuscript consists mainly of legal material and glossaries. This citation is from *Aidbred*.[18] The scribe of this material is Domhnall.[19]

H BL MS Egerton 88,[20] f. 54a in *CIH*, but f. 55ra in current library foliation, *CIH* 1432.20–26, *CLH* no. 689, *CCIH*, 65. The text in *CIH* has been checked against the MS. The citation is from a collection of citations on various topics with commentary. The text of this material is in Domhnall's hand.[21]

I TCD MS 1363, *olim* H.4.22,[22] pp. 55–57, *CIH* 1556.38–1558.9, *CLH* no. 684, *CCIH*, 68. The material in *CIH* has been checked against the MS. This is a composite legal manuscript. Pages 54–59 belong with TCD MS 1337, pp. 661–669.[23] The scribe of this section is unknown. The citation is part of a collection of citations concerned with *coirpdíre* 'body-fine'.

J TCD MS 1336, *olim* H.3.17,[24] *CLH* no. 682, *CCIH*, 79–82. This is a composite legal manuscript with sections dating to the fifteenth and sixteenth centuries. The material forms part of Digest D. For a discussion of the medieval Irish legal digests and their relationship to each other, see *CCIH*, 322–337. The text in *CIH* has been checked against the MS. For ease of reference, I give the citations from the digest listed by the section of *Anfuigell* followed by the section of Digest D: § 4 (39) *CIH* 2026.23–2027.6, cols. 545.33–546.26; § 7 (38) *CIH* 2026.3–13, col. 545.6–20; § 10 (39) *CIH* 2027.7–17, col. 546.27–42; § 12 (32) *CIH* *CIH* 2003.25–2004.2, col. 518.22–43; § 20 (39) *CIH* 2030.34–2031.18, col. 550.1–34; § 36 (33) *CIH* 2005.29–30, col. 521.6–8. Cols. 431–680 were written between 1574 and 1577 mainly by Aodhagán Mac Aodhagáin.[25]

15 Standish Hayes O'Grady, *Catalogue of Irish Manuscripts in the British Museum*, vol. 1 (London: The British Museum, 1926), 85–141, at 87.
16 *CIH* uses an older foliation system for this MS.
17 *CCIH*, 52 lists the source as *Anfuigell*.
18 See Appendix 5, 304–306.
19 O'Sullivan, "The Book of Domhnall," 291.
20 O'Grady, *Catalogue of Irish Manuscripts in the British Museum*, 101.
21 O'Sullivan, "The Book of Domhnall," 291.
22 Abbott and Gwynn, *Catalogue of Irish Manuscripts*, 202.
23 For the correct order of the fragments, see O'Sullivan, "The Manuscript Collection of Dubhaltach," 443.
24 Abbott and Gwynn, *Catalogue of Irish Manuscripts*, 128.
25 O'Sullivan, "The Manuscript Collection of Dubhaltach," 442. Images of TCD MS 1336 are

K Oxford, Bodleian Library MS Rawl. B 506, f. 62d, *CIH* 190.35–37, *CLH* no. 695, *CCIH*, 23. The text in *CIH* has been checked against the MS. The citation is part of a series of commentaries on various topics. The commentary concerns the dissolution of prescriptive rights. The scribe is the same unidentified scribe as source C.[26]

L BL MS Egerton 88, f. 54vb in current library foliation,[27] *CIH* 1431.15–31, *CLH* no. 689, *CCIH*, 65. The text in *CIH* has been checked against the MS. The material is from a collection of citations on various topics with commentary. *CIH* 1431.15–16 is in Domhnall's hand; the scribe of the remainder of the commentary is Cosnamhach Mac Fhlannchadha.[28]

M TCD MS 1387, *olim* H.5.15,[29] p. 6, *CLH* no. 685, *CCIH*, 88 and 253–257. The material in *CIH* has been checked against the MS; see also source A above. The citations are from *Findṡruth Fíthail* and correspond to *Anfuigell* as follows: § 15 *CIH* 2142.40–42; and § 49 *CIH* 2141.15–20.

N Oxford, Bodleian Library, MS Rawl. B 506, f. 30b, *CIH* 115.5–10, *CLH* no. 695, *CCIH*, 17 and 302–303. This material is from part of a section of commentary dealing with treaties and seems to be from *Bretha Cairdi* 'Treaty Judgments', text 31 in the *Senchas Már* 'Great Tradition' group of legal texts. The scribe is the same unidentified scribe as in sources C and K.

O TCD MS 1433, *olim* E.3.5,[30] *CLH* no. 687, *CCIH*, 176–182. The text in *CIH* has been checked against the MS. The citations from this source are from *Bretha Éitgid* 'Judgments of Inadvertence'. This is a composite manuscript containing a variety of legal texts and a copy of the *Lebor Gabála Érenn* 'The Book of Invasions of Ireland'. Parts of the MS date to the sixteenth century. The scribe of this section is unidentified. The section numbers of *Anfuigell* are given with the corresponding *CIH* and MS references: § 22 *CIH* 315.5–28, pp. 49b57–50a32;[31] § 32 *CIH* 330.9–42, p. 57a; § 34 *CIH* 278.5–10, p. 33a.

---

available online at the Irish Script On Screen website: https://www.isos.dias.ie/english/index.html. Accessed September 5, 2018.

26 Ó Cuív, *Catalogue of the Irish Language Manuscripts in the Bodleian*, 217.

27 O'Grady, *Catalogue of Irish Manuscripts in the British Museum*, 100–101.

28 O'Sullivan, "The Book of Domhnall," 291.

29 Abbott and Gwynn, *Catalogue of Irish Manuscripts*, 250.

30 Abbott and Gwynn, *Catalogue of Irish Manuscripts*, 308.

31 The commentary ultimately seems to derive from a fragmentary text on sea judgments, *SM*

P TCD MS 1337, *olim* H.3.18,[32] *CIH* 711.24–716.27, *CLH* no. 683, *CCIH*, 31. The material is from a series of citations from various texts. The text in *CIH* has been checked against the MS. Citations from *Anfuigell* are as follows: § 26 *CIH* 712.12–14, p. 185b, see also Digest D (12), *CIH* 1961.17–19; § 58 *CIH* 715.32–41, p. 191Ba–b. The scribe is unidentified.

Q RIA 1243 [23 Q 6], p. 6a, *CIH* 1148.37, *CLH* no. 677, *CCIH*, 49. This material is found in Digest A (13). The text in *CIH* has been checked against the MS.[33] This is a composite manuscript in which four of the five sections contain legal material; the citation here is from the first section. The first section is acephalous and dates to 1575. The material appears to be written in the hand of Saordhálach Óg.

R TCD 1337, *olim* H.3.18,[34] p. 628b, *CIH* 1063.20–26 and 1063.31–1064.3, *CLH* no. 683, *CCIH*, 45. The text in *CIH* has been checked against the MS. The citations are from a series of commentaries on a variety of topics. The scribe is unidentified.

S BL MS Cotton Nero A7,[35] f. 142b, *CIH* 2218.33, *CLH* no. 692, *CCIH*, 89. The citation is from part of *Bretha Nemed Toísech* 'The First *Bretha Nemed*'. The text in *CIH* has been checked against the MS. The MS dates to 1571 and is in the hand of Matha Ó Luinín.[36]

T RIA 1243 [23 Q 6], pp. 25b–26a, § 32 *CIH* 1169.19–1170.15, § 51 *CIH* 1178.34–1180.11, *CLH* no. 677, *CCIH*, 50. The text in *CIH* has been checked against the MS. The material is from *Bretha Éitgid*. The material from T is edited and translated in Appendices 2 and 3, respectively.

AA TCD MS 1336, *olim* H.3.17,[37] col. 434, *CIH* 1922.18–20, *CLH* no. 682, *CCIH*, 74. The text in *CIH* has been checked against the MS. The material is found in a sec-

38, *Muirbretha*; see *GEIL*, 276–277; and *CCIH*, 304–305 for a general discussion, although it should be noted that *CCIH* does not identify this citation as being from *Muirbretha*.

32 Abbott and Gwynn, *Catalogue of Irish Manuscripts*, 146.

33 Images of the MS and the catalog description are available on the Irish Script on Screen website at https://www.isos.dias.ie/english/index.html. Accessed November 21, 2017.

34 Abbott and Gwynn, *Catalogue of Irish Manuscripts*, 154.

35 O'Grady, *Catalogue of Irish Manuscripts in the British Museum*, 143.

36 O'Grady, *Catalogue of Irish Manuscripts in the British Museum*, 141.

37 Abbott and Gwynn, *Catalogue of Irish Manuscripts*, 126.

tion of Digest C (9) which deals with contracts bound under duress. Col. 434 is in the hand of Aodhagán Mac Aodhagáin.[38]

HH Oxford, Bodleian Library, MS Rawl. B 506,[39] f. 40rb41–vd27, *CIH* 138.34–139.31, *CLH* no. 695, *CCIH*, 18 and 308–309. The text in *CIH* has been checked against the MS. The material is from a series of commentaries on various topics, probably part of *SM* 46, *Díguin-tract*. The scribe is the same unidentified scribe as in sources C, K, and N.[40]

II RIA 1243 [23 Q 6], p. 37a, *CIH* 1202.32–39, *CLH* no. 677, *CCIH*, 50. The text in *CIH* has been checked against the MS. The citation is from a series of citations with commentaries on a wide range of topics. This part of the MS originally formed part of the Book of Domhnall Ó Duibhdábhoireann.[41] The scribe of this material is Domhnall himself.[42]

JJ BL MS Egerton 88,[43] *CLH* no. 689, *CCIH*, 57–58. The text in *CIH* has been checked against the MS. The citations are found in part of Digest B: § 9 (33), *CIH* 1318.22–23, f. 23vb in the current foliation system (f. 22d in *CIH*); § 30 (28), *CIH* 1314.36–1315.3, f. 22vb (f. 21d in *CIH*). All of this material is in Domhnall's hand.[44]

KK TCD MS 1337, *olim* H.3.18,[45] p. 873, *CIH* 1107.12, *CLH* no. 683, *CCIH*, 46–47. The text in *CIH* has been checked against the MS. The citation is from a collection of citations from various texts. Pages 871–874 are written in the same hand as source A.[46]

LL RIA 1243 [23 Q 6], p. 36a, § 35 *CIH* 1200.28–37, § 36 *CIH* 1201.22, *CLH* no. 677, *CCIH*, 50. The citations are from a collection of citations from various texts. The text in *CIH* has been checked against the MS. The text is in Domhnall's hand.[47]

---

38 O'Sullivan, "The Manuscript Collection of Dubhaltach," 442.
39 Ó Cuív, *Catalogue of Irish Language Manuscripts*, 222.
40 Ó Cuív, *Catalogue of Irish Language Manuscripts*, 217.
41 O'Sullivan, "The Book of Domhnall," 283.
42 O'Sullivan, "The Book of Domhnall," 292.
43 O'Grady, *Catalogue of Irish Manuscripts in the British Museum*, 96.
44 O'Sullivan, "The Book of Domhnall," 291.
45 Abbott and Gwynn, *Catalogue of Irish Manuscripts*, 157–158.
46 O'Sullivan, "The Manuscript Collection of Dubhaltach," 443; and *idem*, "The Book of Domhnall," 277.
47 O'Sullivan, "The Book of Domhnall," 292.

O'Dav O'Davoren's Glossary, BL Egerton 88,[48] *CLH* no. 689 for the manuscript and no. 889 for the text itself, §1 *CIH* 1477.14 (no. 292), f. 82rc; §54 *CIH* 1473.1–2 (no. 170), f. 81vb; §55 *CIH* 1468.8–9 (no. 60), f. 80rc. All material from BL Egerton 88 has been checked against the MS. There is a concordance of O'Davoren's Glossary entries to texts in *CCIH*, 109–156. Glossary entry no. 292 is written in the hand of Domhnall, no. 170 in the hand of Maghnus II, and no. 60 in the hand of Cormac mac an Chosnadhaigh.[49] O'Davoren's Glossary is extant in two independent versions: BL MS Egerton 88, fols. 79a–92c (*CIH* 1466.11–1531.24) and TCD MS 1317 *olim* H.2.15B, pp. 45–60 (120–135 in the old pagination). The TCD version of O'Davoren's Glossary was written in 1569 and lacks the letters *A* and *B*, most of *C*, and the section containing *S*, *T*, and *U* is badly damaged.[50] The TCD version is not printed in *CIH*. The two versions are referred to as E and F, respectively, by their editor, Whitley Stokes. Stoked edited the text twice: the BL version was edited in vol. 2 of the *Archiv für celtische Lexikographie* with emended readings from the TCD version.[51] Stokes edited the text first in *Three Irish Glossaries*, which does not take into account the TCD version.[52]

The first concordance which follows is a table of the MS sources for each section of the tract. The second concordance is a list of the MS sources and relevant *CIH* references for each section. The purpose of the concordances is to provide a means of being able to see the source distribution at a glance. The relevant *CIH* references are also given after each MS source within the edition itself.

---

48 O'Grady, *Catalogue of Irish Manuscripts in the British Museum*, 108–109.

49 O'Sullivan, "The Book of Domhnall," 291.

50 Abbott and Gwynn, *Catalogue of Irish Manuscripts*, 93; and *CCIH*, 100–108.

51 "O'Davoren's Glossary," ed. and trans. Whitley Stokes in *Archiv für celtische Lexikographie* 2, eds. Whitley Stokes and Kuno Meyer (Halle: M. Niemeyer, 1904), 197–504.

52 *Three Irish Glossaries*, ed. Whitley Stokes (London: Williams & Norgate, 1862), 47–124.

Concordances

Concordance of Sources and Sections of Text

	A	B	C	D	E	F	H	I	J	K	L	M	N	O	P	Q	R	S	T	AA	HH	II	JJ	KK	LL	O'Dav
Heading	×	×																								
§1	×																×									×
§2	×	×						×									×									
§3	×		×		×																					
§4	×	×							×								×									
§5	×	×																								
§6	×	×	×																							
§7	×								×	×																
§8	×	×						×			×										×					
§9	×																			×			×			
§10	×								×																	
§11	×		×																							
§12	×		×						×																	
§13	×																									
§14	×																									
§15	×											×														
§16	×																					×				
§17	×		×																			×				
§18	×																									
§19	×												×													
§20	×								×																	
§21	×																									
§22	×													×												
§23	×					×																				
§24	×																									
§25	×																									
§26	×														×											
§27	×																									
§28	×																									
§29	×																							×		
§30	×															×							×			
§31	×																×									
§32	×													×				×	×							
§33	×																									
§34	×													×												
§35	×																								×	
§36	×								×																×	
§37	×																									
§38	×							×																		

 | DOI:10.1163/9789004391987_005

(*cont.*)

	A	B	C	D	E	F	H	I	J	K	L	M	N	O	P	Q	R	S	T	AA	HH	II	JJ	KK	LL	O'Dav
§39	×																									
§40	×																									
§41	×																									
§42	×																									
§43	×																									
§44	×																									
§45	×		×																							
§46	×																									
§47	×																									
§48	×		×		×																					
§49	×											×														
§50	×																									
§51	×		×	×	×														×							
§52	×			×																						
§53	×			×	×																					
§54	×			×	×																					×
§55	×				×																					×
§56	×			×																						
§57	×		×	×	×		×																			
§58	×		×	×											×											

Concordance of Sections of Text and MS Sources with CIH

Heading: A 2146.15; B 979.23–26

§1: A 2146.16–38; R 1063.20–21; O'Dav 1477.14

§2: A 2146.40–2147.9; B 979.27–31; I 1557.21–30; R 1064.1–3

§3: A 2147.10–21; C 167.19–29; E 1018.18–25

§4: A 2147.22–37; B 979.32–37; J 2026.23–2027.6; R 1063.31–34

§5: A 2147.38–2148.2; B 979.38–41

§6: A 2148.3–14; B 979.42–980.11; C 167.39–168.8

§7: A 2148.15–25; J 2026.3–13; K 190.35–37

§8: A 2148.26–2149.26; B 980.12–17; I 1557.31–1558.9; L 1431.15–31; HH 138.34–139.31

§9: A 2149.27–2150.11; AA 1922.18–20; JJ 1318.22–23

§10: A 2150.12–24; J 2027.7–17

§11: A 2150.25–37; C 168.9–16

§12: A 2150.38–2151.30; C 168.27–169.3; J 2003.25–2004.2

§13: A 2151.31–36

§ 14:	A 2151.37–42
§ 15:	A 2152.1–4; M 2142.40–42
§ 16:	A 2152.5–17; II 1202.32–37
§ 17:	A 2152.18–32; C 168.17–27; II 1202.–38–39
§ 18:	A 2152.33–35
§ 19:	A 2152.36–2153.2; N 115.5–10
§ 20:	A 2153.3–11; J 2030.34–2031.18
§ 21:	A 2153.12–16
§ 22:	A 2153.17–40; O 315.5–28
§ 23:	A 2154.1–5; F 1271.29–33
§ 24:	A 2154.6–20
§ 25:	A 2154.21–26
§ 26:	A 2154.27–31; P 712.12–14
§ 27:	A 2154.32–34
§ 28:	A 2154.34–2155.15
§ 29:	A 2155.16–34; KK 1107.12
§ 30:	A 2155.35–2156.11; JJ 1314.36–1315.3
§ 31:	A 2156.12–17; R 1063.22–26
§ 32:	A 2156.18–2157.15; O 330.9–42; S 2218.33; T 1169.19–1170.15 (see Appendix 2)
§ 33:	A 2157.16–36
§ 34:	A 2157.37–2158.8; O 278.5–10
§ 35:	A 2158.9–18; LL 1200.28–37
§ 36:	A 2158.19–28; J 2005.29–30; LL 1201.22
§ 37:	A 2158.29–35
§ 38:	A 2158.36–2159.2; I 1556.38–1557.4
§ 39:	A 2159.3–21
§ 40:	A 2159.22–26
§ 41:	A 2159.27–39
§ 42:	A 2160.1–3
§ 43:	A 2160.4–6
§ 44:	A 2160.7–10
§ 45:	A 2160.11–27; C 169.4–16
§ 46:	A 2160.28–34
§ 47:	A 2160.35–2161.3
§ 48:	A 2161.4–21; C 169.17–21; E 1017.1–4
§ 49:	A 2161.22–37; M 2141.15–20
§ 50:	A 2161.38–39
§ 51:	A 2162.1–24; C 169.22–37; D 984.16; E 1017.5–39; T 1178.34–1180.11 (see Appendix 3)
§ 52:	A 2162.25–26; D 984.17–22

§ 53: A 2162.27–28; D 984.22–23; E 1017.40–43
§ 54: A 2162.29–2163.5; D 984.24–985.4; E 1018.1–5; **O'Dav** 1473.1–2
§ 55: A 2163.6–9; E 1018.6–10; **O'Dav** 1468.8–9
§ 56: A 2163.10–11; D 985.5–6
§ 57: A 2163.12–19; C 169.38–170.3; D 985.7–19; E 1018.10–17; H 1432.20–26
§ 58: A2163.20–32; C 170.4–6; D 985.20–23; P 715.32–41

Editorial Method

The edited text has been divided into a heading and 58 individual sections. These section divisions follow those laid out in MS source A, which contains the fullest version of the textual fragments and commentary. The scribe of source A regularly starts each new section of material with a larger initial letter, which is often decorated with orange paint.

Italics are used to indicate expansions of scribal abbreviations, e.g. § 1 am*ail*. [Square] brackets are used for editorial insertions, e.g. § 3 'rotair[c]ed', and (round) brackets for editorial deletions, e.g. § 8 i*n*dil(si)s*ech*. Italic *h* is used to indicate that the scribe used a *punctum* or *spiritus asper* instead of writing the actual letter form. However, I have retained the convention of leaving the *punctum* over lenited ⟨f⟩ and ⟨s⟩, e.g. § 8 ṡær, § 15 ḟe*r*t, and § 8 [ḟ]it*ir*, when it appears in the MSS and when restoring those letters. Punctuation and capitalization have been silently added. The punctuation of the text and translation are intended to match as far as possible. Paragraph breaks have also been silently added in some places where they do not occur in the MSS. Whenever a different version is signaled in a source by the phrase *gné aile* 'another version', a paragraph break has been inserted.

The OI text itself is printed in bold to distinguish it from the commentaries. Variant readings of the text, however minor, are given in the critical apparatus. The readings in source A are generally given preference, but other MSS are used when they provide a better reading or to supply material not present in source A. For example, in § 8, source A preserves only two words of the OI text, while source L preserves an additional fifteen words. In this case, A is given preference where available, but the remainder of the material is supplied by L. No attempt has been made to normalize the OI text as doing so would only create a cumbersome critical apparatus. The commentaries are printed in alphabetical order according to source sigla. Where two or more commentaries differ only in matters of orthography, one is printed with the text and the other is to be found in the appendices. While many of the commentaries repeat aspects of the same material, different sources treat some of the material differently in orthography, arrangement, emphasis, and general content. Thus, these commentaries are printed along with the commentaries from source A rather than printed in an appendix.

Notes of a paleographical or linguistic nature are generally confined to pages containing the Irish text. Notes relating to content or translation issues are to be found under the English translation. Where words have been left untranslated, e.g. *sét* 'item of value', an explanation is given in the textual notes or

 | DOI:10.1163/9789004391987_006

section summary the first time the word appears. These words are all listed in the Glossary.

When the material as printed cosmetically differs from *CIH*, no note is made, e.g. § 3 *CIH* 2147.11 'lucht' for 'lu*cht*'. *CIH* does not have a consistent editorial method across all six volumes. The approach adopted here has been to expand every MS suspension, abbreviation, etc. and print the expanded material in *italics*, even when the expansions are unambiguous. All of the material printed in *CIH* has been checked against the relevant MS source. When there is a different reading from *CIH* which is not simply a matter of editorial method, it has been noted in the concordance of variant readings to *CIH* in Appendix 4. Where the difference is significant for understanding the text or commentary, it has been indicated in the footnotes for that section as well.

The MS abbreviation *im̄* has been expanded throughout as MI *immurro* instead of OI *immurgu* because it appears only in the MI commentaries. MS *dō* has been expanded as 'd*ano*'. Lenited ⟨d⟩ and ⟨g⟩ are frequently used interchangeably orthographically. This is very common in the Irish legal commentaries. I have not emended these forms except in cases where there is the potential for confusion, e.g. § 36 *CIH* 2158.26 MS 'fog*ail*' for 'fod*ail*'.

Notes on Dating and Orthography

Dating a fragmentary legal text is fraught with difficulties, mainly as a result of a combination of how little of the OI text is extant and the lack of diagnostic criteria in the fragments of text. That being said, the text can be dated to the OI period from the following pieces of linguistic evidence. Compound verbal forms are generally preserved (compound verbs gradually become simple verbs during the course of the MI period), e.g. § 1 *-acairther* (pres. ind. pass. sg. prototonic form of *ad-gair*), but some of the prototonic forms, such as § 1 *-tucthar* (pres. subj. pass. sg. prototonic form of *do-beir*), survive through the MI period. Thus some of the prototonic forms found in the OI text cannot be used in and of themselves to conclusively establish an OI date for the text. Nasalization after neuter nouns is preserved in the phrases § 9 *gell n-uathbais* and § 36 *burach n-indraig*. None of the linguistic evidence suggests a date before *c.* 750 CE, and even a date of composition as late as 900 cannot be ruled out.

The commentaries themselves are on the whole very difficult to date precisely due to the fact that the same source can preserve two commentaries with different linguistic dates. It should be noted that § 9 source AA (Digest C (9)) contains two examples of object agreement markers which do not appear to be fossilized, e.gg. *nodberat* (3 pl. pres. subj. of *beirid* with a class C n. object agreement marker) and *atrenat* (3 pl. pres. ind. of *as-ren* with a class B n. object agreement marker), which suggests that this commentary dates to the OI period. Aside from the commentary to source AA, the others date to no earlier than the MI period. For example, in § 3 the commentaries of A and C both use forms of *indisid* 'say, tell, relate', which came to replace OI *ad-fét* during the MI period. Source A also has a form of *eplaid*, which came to replace OI *at-baill*. There is also the later form of the nasalizing conjunction *dia*, i.e. *dá*. In § 6 source C there is an example of the common MI confusion of the preverbs *no*, *ro*, and *do* found in *nabeith*. Independent pronouns, such as those found in the commentaries in source I § 2, are common. The most comprehensive discussion of the dating of MI legal commentaries can be found in the introduction to Fergus Kelly's *Marriage Disputes*.[1]

Orthographically, ⟨ch⟩ is sometimes found for ⟨th⟩, e.g. § 57 *CIH* 2163.29 'le*ch*olb' for expected 'lethcolb', but the interchange between internal ⟨ch⟩ and ⟨th⟩ is not uncommon in MI as it shows the reduction of /Θx/ > /x/.[2] During the MI period lenited outcomes of /d/ and /g/ merge as /ɣ/ > /∅/, resulting in ⟨d⟩,

1 Kelly, *Marriage Disputes*, 18–21.

2 Liam Breatnach, "An Mheán-Ghaeilge," in *Stair na Gaeilge*, ed. Kim McCone et al. (Maigh

 | DOI:10.1163/9789004391987_007

⟨g⟩, or ⟨∅⟩ being used interchangeably, e.g. § 9A *fogla* for OI *fodla*, and § 57E *sarugu*[d] for OI *sárugud*. Length marks on long vowels are usually omitted in the MS sources. There is frequent interchange between ⟨o⟩, ⟨a⟩, and ⟨u⟩ used to indicate a short vowel in non-palatal syllables, e.g. § 8 *isrenur* for *asrenar*, and § 12C *goiti* for OI *gaite*. This last example also illustrates the frequent interchange between ⟨e⟩ and ⟨i⟩ to indicate a short vowel in palatal syllables. These are but a handful of examples of MI features found in the sources.

Nuad: Roinn na Sean-Ghaeilge, Coláiste Phádraig, 1994), 234; and Kelly, *Marriage Disputes*, 15.

Anfuigell

Text, Variants, Commentary, and Translation

Heading

p. 8a Locc do*n* luib*ar*-sa Fuithribe Corm*aic* A.[1] [*CIH* 2146.15]

Incipit de Anfuigell, ⁊ locc do Fuit*hr*i*m*e Corm*aic*, ⁊ aimsear do aimsir Fi*nd*gui*n*e (m*ei*c cæ gan mat*h*air) m*ei*c Con Gen Mathair,[2] ⁊ tucaid a denma ainceas br*eith*emn*uis* do cuir f*or* Cu*m*ain i *n*-Ai*n*e Cliach iar leg*h*ud leig*hind*; ⁊ nir leg*h* fen[e]ch*us* roi*m*e riam, co ndechaid isin tuaisceart dia foglann[3] B.[4] [*CIH* 979.23–26]

---

1 The heading was written by the scribe in *marg. sup.* and enclosed by a rectangle of orange paint.

2 The scribe wrote the correct version of the name immediately following the mistake in the text. He indicates the correction with *no*. See also Binchy, *CIH* 979, n. g.

3 'foglann' against *CIH* 979.26 'foglaim'. The end of the word consists of four minims. Binchy, *CIH* 979, n. h, suggests *foglann* as a possible reading.

4 *CCIH*, 360–361, suggests that the material in source B is a later introduction. The following citation should be noted from Breatnach's edition of *Cáin Fhuithirbe* (his source E); see *Cáin Fhuithirbe*, 36–37: TCD MS 1337, [p. 151 (xvi)] Loc do[n] liub*ar*-sa Fuit*hr*i*m*e Cormaic; ai*m*s*er* do ai*m*s*er* Fi*n*dgai*n*e (meic cae ci*n* mat*h*air) meic *Con* Ce*n* Mat*hair* 'The place [of composition] of this book is Fuithrime Cormaic; and its time [of composition] is the time of Findguine son of Cú-cen-máthair', *CIH* 687.37–38.

Heading

The place [of composition] of this book is Fuithirbe Cormaic[5] A.[6] p. 8a

Here begins [the book] on *Anfuigell*, and the place [of composition] is Fuithrime Cormaic, and its time [of composition] is the time of Finguine mac Cú-cen-máthair, and [the] reason for composing it is that Cumain [was] perplexed regarding an adjudication in Áine Cliach after studying ecclesiastical learning; and he had never studied Irish law, so he went to the North to learn it B.[7]

5 Fuithrime Cormaic is also known as Mag Fuithrime. The location has been identified as being in Muckross Demesne. For a discussion of the evidence for this identification and of Cormac's association with the place, see Seán Ó Coileáin, "Mag Fuithirbe Revisited," *Éigse* 23 (1989): 24–26. For the Munster origin of *Cáin Fhuithirbe*, see *Cáin Fhuithirbe*, 45–46.

6 For a discussion of the Heading, see the Introduction, 11.

7 A slightly different translation of this passage can be found in *Cáin Fhuithirbe*, 37; and CCIH, 360. See also the Introduction for further discussion of the Heading.

p. 8a2[8] **§ 1 Anfuigell[9] breath[10] brangaire catha**

.i. is fir-fuigell, ł is fir liu*m con*id coir dul i fuigell i*n* br*eith*eman adera gan er*aic* isnahiib ara nde*n*ait na b*ra*[i]n gaire iarna toiti*m* isin cath coitcend comarleict*hi*. ł an aca diultad, *conach in*dula i fuigell in[11] br*eith*eman adera er*aic* isi*n* fer f*or*a ndenait na b*r*ain duba a ngaire iarna toiti*m* isi*n* cat*h* coit*chenn* comarlect*hi*.

---

1 Source R does not contain any of the OI text.

---

8 The scribe intentionally begins the text on the second ruled line of p. 8a even though he usually writes 'above top line' throughout the manuscript. The commentary following the first given line of the text starts on the first line and then continues on the third ruled line; Neil Ker, "From 'Above Top Line' to 'Below Top Line': A Change in Scribal Practice," *Celtica* 5 (1960): 13–16.

9 The scribe has written the material from the main text in larger letters than that used for the commentary. For § 1, the material from the OI text is embedded within the paragraph.

10 The opening line of the text is also found in *O'Davoren's Glossary*, where Stokes has chosen to expand the suspension mark following ⟨br⟩ as *-eith*. Gwynn, "Miscellanea," 29 suggests emending the reading given here and by Stokes (below) to *breitheman*, and suggests translating the first line of the text as 'The wrong decision of a judge is a raven's call to battle'. See also Abbott and Gwynn, *Catalogue of the Irish Manuscripts*, 251.

11 *CIH* 2146.19 reads 'mbr*eith*eman' as does O'Donovan, p. 1586, but cf. the ⟨m⟩s in 'comarleict*hi*' in the same line of the MS and the ⟨m⟩ in 'br*eith*eman'. The scribe tends to leave a little space between his ⟨i⟩s and ⟨n⟩s when they are in a sequence. He also tends to start his ⟨m⟩s with a larger serif on the first minim than he uses for the following two minims. In this instance, the first two minims have comparatively larger serifs than the third minim, which does not have a serif at all. The scribe frequently has a larger serif on the first minim of his ⟨n⟩s and no serif at all for the second minim.

§1 A raven's battle-cry is a misuse of judgments[12] p. 8a2

i.e. it is a *fír-fuigell*, a 'true-decision',[13] or I believe it is true that it is correct to submit to the decision of the judge who may award no *wergeld*[14] for the ones over whom the ravens cry when they die in a lawful battle.[15] Or *an*[16] negating it [i.e. *an fuigell*], so that it is not proper to submit to the decision of the judge who awards *wergeld* for the man over whom the black ravens make their cry when they die in a lawful battle.

---

12 For a discussion of this section, see the Introduction, 11–12. Gwynn, "Miscellanea," 29 translates the first line of the text as "The wrong decision of a judge is a raven's call to battle." A more literal translation of the first line of the text is 'A raven's battle-cry is an inappropriate [basis for] judgments'. I should like to thank Neil McLeod for valuable comments on this line of the text. The sense of the first two lines of the text is that it is inappropriate for a judge to award *wergeld* for deaths which occur in lawful battle because they are not prosecuted as homicide. Although *anfuigell* means 'non-judgment', 'wrong judgment', the text suggests that we understand the word not so much in its literal sense, but more figuratively, because a raven's battle-cry is not literally an incorrect judgment. If there were a 'wrong judgment' here, it would be if the judge awarded *wergeld* for someone slain in battle, which is alluded to in the second etymological gloss below. Ravens are often associated with battle fields in medieval Irish and Welsh literature; see, for example, Kim Heijda, "War-goddesses, Furies and Scald Crows: The Use of the Word *badb* in Early Irish Literature" (Final Thesis, University of Utrecht, 2007), especially 68–71 https://dspace.library.uu.nl/handle/1874/21638. Accessed June 1, 2018; Maria Tymoczko, "The Semantic Fields of Early Irish Terms for Black Birds and Their Implications for Species Taxonomy," in *Celtic Language, Celtic Culture: A Festschrift for Eric P. Hamp*, eds. A.T.E. Matonis and Daniel F. Melia (Van Nuys, CA: Ford and Bailie, 1990), 155 and 159–161; and *Breudwyt Ronabwy: Allan o'r Llyfr Coch o Hergest*, ed. G. Melville Richards (Caerdydd: Gwasg Prifysgol Cymru, 1948).

13 This quasi-etymological gloss implicitly depends on interpreting the *an-* in *anfuigell* as *án* 'splendid'; *CCIH*, 164. One wonders whether the etymological gloss originally contained *án* 'splendid', e.g. *án-fuigell*, but that the *án* later shifted to *fír* 'true' because it provided alliteration with *fuigell*.

14 The Irish term *éraic* 'wergeld' refers to the fixed fine for homicide. The fine is set at seven *cumals* for every free person regardless of rank, and is payable to the victim's kindred; see *GEIL*, 125–126; and the Legal Glossary in *Críth Gablach*, ed. D.A. Binchy. Medieval and Modern Irish Series 11 (Dublin: Stationery Office, 1941), *s.v. éraic*. It should be noted that *éraic* is also used to refer to a fixed penalty payment for injury. In other words, in cases other than those involving homicide, *éraic* is simply a fine for bodily injury.

15 I am interpreting the phrase *cath coitcend comarleicthi* 'common permitted battle' to refer to a general battle as opposed to an unlawful raid.

16 *an-* is a negative prefix. The commentator continues his analysis of the word *anfuigell* in the Isidorean etymological tradition.

Ni h-acairther nech dotuit a cath

.i. nochan [a]c*arth*i[17] i[n][18] nech toites isi*n* cath coit*chenn* co*mar*lect*h*i, .i. am*ail* ata bla fer cat*h*a.[19]

Is diles cia facabar and

.i. do sé*t*aib ona[20] ⁊ erraig é ait*h*ni ⁊ *air*licthi, u*air* is oi*n* in baile i n-upt*ha*[21]

Is diles cia tucth*ar* as

.i. seoit a loc*h*ta co*m*cat*h*a budei*n* t*u*cas, ⁊ ci*n*dti co mb*er*dais in lucht eli, ⁊ orra-su*m* romeb*aid* .i. *ar*i*n* luc*h*t isa seoit, ⁊ is diles do uile. Masa cu*n*dtab*ar*t*ach* i mberdais fo *n*a b*er*dais in lu*cht* eli, is dilsi a l*e*t*h*i. Dia*m*ad ci*n*dti

17 I follow the emendation suggested by Binchy, CIH 2146, n. k.

18 I follow the emendation suggested by Binchy, CIH 2146, n. l.

19 See CIH 272.28, from *Bretha Éitgid* 'Judgments of Inadvertence', for the second half of the gloss; see also AL 3: 214–215.

20 For the legal terms *ón* and *airliciud*, see Mcleod, "*Ón* and *airliciud*," 169–196. McLeod suggests that *ón* refers to a private loan and *airliciud* refers to a commercial loan, 189.

21 Binchy, CIH 2146, n. m, notes that the lenited ⟨t⟩ was inserted above the line of text.

Anyone who dies in battle is not prosecuted

i.e. the one who dies in a lawful battle should not be prosecuted, i.e. just as there is immunity for combatants.

Whatever is left there is forfeit

i.e. of *séts*[22] loaned and requisitioned, deposited and borrowed,[23] because it is a loan in a perilous place.[24]

Whatever is taken away is forfeit

i.e. the *séts* of his own fellow combatants that he may take, and [if it is] certain that the other people [i.e. the opponents] would carry [the *séts* away], and they were defeated, i.e. the people from whom [the] *séts* are [taken], and all [that he carries away] is forfeit to him.[25] If it is uncertain whether the other people would or would not carry [away the *séts*], half of it is forfeit [to him]. If it is certain that they would not carry [away the *séts*], he is to be

---

22 For a discussion of the word *sét*, see the Introduction, 12n8.

23 The vn. *airlicud* refers specificially to commercial loans, in contrast to *ón*, which refers to private loans; McLeod, "*Ón* and *airliciud*," 189.

24 On loans and lending in general, see *GEIL*, 117–118; Liam Breatnach, "*Cáin Ónae*: An Old Irish Law Text on Lending," in *Mír Cúrad: Studies in Honor of Calvert Watkins*, eds. Jay Jasanoff, H. Craig Melchert, and Lisi Oliver (Innsbruck: Institut für Sprachwissenschaft der Universität, 1998), 29–46; and McLeod, "*Ón* and *airliciud*," 169–196. Kelly notes that Heptad 48 discourages lending property for dangerous activities, such as lending a boat, lending a sword for a battle, and lending a dog for hunting, because of the likelihood that the lender will not be able to recover his property undamaged or at all. The heptad further states that it is not possible to recover property loaned to a man who dies unless the property was bound by sureties; see *CIH* 44.1 *oin fir atbaill*. § 4 of *Cáin Ónae* 'Regulation of Loan' contains the similar phrase (citing Breatnach's edited text and translation, 38–39 and 41) *ón mblá n-apthan* 'a loan in perilous places', literally 'a loan of the places of death', *CIH* 571.27. In his discussion of this section of the text, Breatnach (41) notes in a gloss at *CIH* 1993.24 that *baile* replaces *blá*, i.e. *is ōin a* [*m*]*baile n-apthan* 'it is a loan in a place of death'. From a legal standpoint, the material given in *Anfuigell* is consistent with what is found in the heptads on lending and in *Cáin Ónae*, i.e. items given in loan to a person who has died are not normally recoverable and a battlefield would, indeed, be a place of death.

25 The sense of the passage is that one is allowed to take the valuables of one's fellow combatants if the fellow combatants have been defeated in battle and it is certain that the enemy would take the valuables if they were left behind. In this case, any valuables taken from one's defeated fellow combatants become one's own property.

na b*er*dais, is b*eth* gi*n* ni. ł is s*ét* imluaid ⁊ *aile déc* mas ece*n* tadall tigi br*eitheman*, ⁊ mai*n*ib eci*n* adall t*ige* b*reitheman*, is s*ét* *im*luaid nama. T*r*ian isan ait*h*ne æ*nuair*e ar cul i*n* cat*h*a, ⁊ orra romeb*aid*, ⁊ ci*n*dti co *m*b*er*dais in fiall*ach* eli. Masa cu*n*dtab*air*t i mb*er*dais, is *seiss*id.[26] Masa ci*n*dti co*na*[27] b*er*dais, i*n*t ain*m*rai*n*de gab*us* an u*air* ud ł in blog do lo isi*n* bliad*nai*, cu*r*ab e i*n*t ain*m*rai*n*de-si*n* do *dech*m*ad* na h-ait*h*ne bes do-su*m*.

Cid fo*dera* t*r*ia*n* *ar*an at*h*ne-seo[28] ⁊ *cona* fuil *acht dech*m*ad* *ar*na h-ait*h*nedaib eli?[29] Is e i*n* fat*h*: *Ar*a gai[b]t*h*(b)igi[30] ⁊ *ar*a h-aicbeli do a gab*ail* do lai*m* a coi*m*et i*n* bail[e] a r*ucus*t*ar* hi. Cid fo*dera*, u*air* is gaibtec*h* ⁊ is aicbeil, nac*h* e a dilsi uile ata do? IS e fa*th*: *Ar*a *m*et rob i*n*det*h*b*ir* a gab*ail* do lai*m* alt na h-u*aire*-si*n*. Cid fo*dera* u*air* is i*n*d*eth*b*ir* ní do it*ir*? IS e fa*th*: U*air* *tuc* les na *séotu* o esi*n*ill co h-i*n*ill A. [*CIH* 2146.16–38]

---

26 The ⟨id⟩ are written above the line of text.

27 The ⟨a⟩ is written as a subscript; see also Binchy, *CIH* 2146, n. o.

28 *-seo* is omitted at *CIH* 2146.33.

29 Although the scribe includes this question with the preceding block of material, semantically it fits better with commentary that follows it in the MS.

30 I follow the emendation suggested by Binchy, *CIH* 2146, n. p.

without anything. Or he [gets] a *sét* [for] wielding weapons and a twelfth[31] if it is necessary to visit a judge's house [to decide the matter], and if it is not necessary to visit a judge's house, he [gets] only a *sét* [for] wielding weapons. A third for depositing [property with someone] for an hour away from [lit. behind] the battle, and they were defeated, and [it is] certain that the other warband would carry [away the *sét*s]. If it is uncertain whether they would carry [away the *sét*s], it is a sixth. If it is certain that they would not carry [them away], the proportion[32] that the aforementioned hour, or the fraction of the day, bears in respect to the year, is that proportion of a tenth of the deposit [which is awarded] to him.

What is the reason that there is a third for this [type of] deposit and there is not but a tenth for the other [types of] deposit? This is the reason: On account of the perils and dangers to him taking it in hand to guard it in the place where he took it. What is the reason, when there is peril and danger, that not everything which he has is forfeit? This is the reason: On account of the extent that it may be unjustified to take it in hand at that point of time. What is the reason when it is unjustified that there is anything for him at all? This is the reason: When he took the *sét*s with him from a dangerous place to a safe place A.

31 The fee judges charged both the defendant and the plaintiff was one-twelfth of the total amount involved in the legal case. It is worth noting that in the commentary the defendant is awarded both his *sét* and the fee he would have had to pay the judge, i.e. the twelfth. One assumes that the defendant is awarded his court costs because such a case never should have been brought to a judge in the first place, it being an example of an *anfuigell breth*, i.e. an inappropriate use of judgments; *GEIL*, 53 citing the evidence from gloss four of Heptad 25; *CIH* 24.26–27; and *AL* 5: 212.22. I should like to thank Neil McLeod for this reference.

32 The word *ainmrainde* is of uncertain meaning, but it seems to refer to a specific share or amount of the total; see *eDIL s.v. ainmm*. Regarding the percentage that he receives, it is calculated at a tenth of the percentage of one hour within a year. In other words, 24 is multiplied by 365, giving 8,760 hours in a year. One-tenth of 8,760 is 876, so the amount he receives is 1/876, which is effectively nothing. The percentage is so low presumably because the goods were never in any danger of being carried off in the first place. Although there is nothing of the burlesque in the commentary, the convoluted method of signifying that the compensation amounts to nothing worth claiming is similar to what is found in some medieval Welsh legal texts, where the shame of pursuing what amounts to worthless compensation factors in as a means of social control; see Nerys Patterson, "Honour and Shame in Medieval Welsh Society: A study of the role of burlesque in the Welsh laws," *Studia Celtica* 16/17 (1981): 73–103.

⁊ tai*n*ic leo o esi*n*ill co h-i*n*ill, ⁊ roscar f*r*iu i *n*-inill R. [CIH 1063.20–21]

Bran .i. fiach, [*ut est*][33] anfuig*ell*[34] br*eth*[35] b*r*angaire *catha*[36] O'Dav.[37] [CIH 1477.14]

33 I follow the emendation suggested by Gwynn, "Miscellanea," 29; see also Binchy, CIH 1477, n. c.

34 CIH 1477.14 reads 'an fuig*ell*'; Stokes' edition reads 'an fuig*ill*'. The reading given here follows Gwynn, "Miscellanea," 29. See also CCIH, 164.

35 CIH 1477.14 reads 'br*eth*'; Stokes' edition reads 'br*eith*'.

36 Binchy, CIH 1477, n. d notes that the MS abbreviates *catha* as 'k.a.'.

37 O'Dav no. 292.

And it came with them from a dangerous place to a safe place, and they left it in a safe place R.

Bran 'raven', i.e. raven, *ut est* a raven's battle-cry is a misuse of judgments O'Dav.[38]

38 Stokes offers the following translation of entry no. 292: "*bran* i.e. the raven ... raven-cry of battle;" the form *fuigill* is obscure to Stokes; see *O'Davoren's Glossary*, 243.

§2 Combach nadma

.i. bach [.i.] brised, co*m*briss*ed* nasc*airecht*[*a*][39] dona fec*h*emnaib, .i. do*n* fech*emain* t*oicheda*[40] ⁊ do bidbaid,[41] forsi*n* t*re*b*aire*. Ci*n*d*us* on? Is an*n* so o*n*: I*n* fech*em* toiche*d*a dori*n*de dei*n*e toicheda f*orin* t*re*b*aire* resi*n* re-si*n*, co n-icann *cóic séoit* ⁊ i*n*ecl*ainn*, ⁊ dilsi a fia*ch* do ne*m*ag*ra* f*or*in treb*aire*. ⁊ rolec i*n* bidb*a* el*od* na t*re*b*aire* i*ar*sna re, co n-icann *cóic séoit* ⁊ e*n*ecl*ainn*, ⁊ na feich risa raibe d'ic t*ara* cen*n*. ⁊ ass *ed*-si*n* as co*m*bac*h* nad*m*a an*n*.

Dias doroi*n*e cu*n*dr*ad* an*n* si*n*, ⁊ ata cac*h* fer dib [im]masech ac tia*cht*ai*n* t*air*is. ⁊ ma*n* rotoc*h*ait*h*sed*ar* na *ceth*ra h-u*aire* *fichit*, is cuimgec*h* cac*h* fer dib [im]masech tia*cht*ai*n* t*air*is. ⁊ ma rotocait*h*et*ar* na *ceth*ra h-u*aire* *fichit*, noc*h*a cui*m*gec*h* iat tia*cht*ai*n* t*air*is. ⁊ da*m*ad [i][42] n-æ*n*fe*cht* dotisdais t*air*is, roba cui*m*gec*h* iat tia*cht*ai*n* tairis A. [*CIH* 2146.40–2147.9]

1 Sources **A**, **B**, and **I** all agree, although Binchy, *CIH* 1557, n. j, notes that an ⟨m⟩ or ⟨ni⟩ following *combach* in **I** has been expunged. **R** reads 'I*n* Co*m*bac*h* nad*m*a' 'The breaking of a contract'. Above the line of the text in **A**, the scribe has written 't*r*iall tait*h*mig*h* cu*n*dartha so sis', translated by Breatnach, *CCIH*, 164 as 'this below [concerns] setting about dissolving a contract'. Breatnach suggests that this scribal note does not indicate the start of a new legal text, but it serves as a sub-heading within *Anfuigell* instead. The material following the extract of the text in **I** is just different enough from **A** to justify printing it in full. **B** does not have any of the material immediately following the two words of the text, but it does contain a version of the commentary closer to that found in **I** than **A**.

39 The text has been emended to the gen. sg. of *nascairecht* on the basis of the syntax of the clause and to reflect the linguistic parallelism between the phrases *combrissed nascairechta* and *combach nadma*.

40 The expansion of '.t.' follows Binchy, *CIH* 2146, n. r.

41 '.i. do*n* … bidbaid' were written interlinearly by the scribe and are meant to be an explanatory gloss on *fechemnaib*.

42 I follow the emendation suggested by Binchy, *CIH* 2147, n. a; see also the version of the commentary in **B** and **I**.

§2 Breaking a contract[43]

i.e. *bach* 'breaking' [i.e.] breaking,[44] contending against suretyship by the parties of the contract, i.e. by the plaintiff and by the defendant, against the surety. How does it come about? It comes about like this: The plaintiff sued prematurely [lit. committed 'swiftness of suing'] against the [defendant's] surety before that time,[45] so he pays five *séts* and honor-price, and forfeiture of his debts due [to him] as a result of unjust suing[46] against the [defendant's] surety. And the defendant evaded the surety after the time, so he pays five *séts* and honor-price, and the debts for which he was [secured] are to be paid on his behalf. And this is what is breaking a contract then.

Two people made a contract in that case, and each one of them separately withdraws from it; if the twenty-four hour period [prescribed by law] has not passed, each one of them is able separately to withdraw from it. And if the twenty-four hour period [prescribed by law] has passed, they are not able to withdraw from it. And if they would [both like to] withdraw from it at the same time, they are able to withdraw from it A.

43 For a discussion of this section, see the Introduction, 13.

44 The phrase *bach* [.*i.*] *brised* is an Isidorean-style etymological gloss on *combach* analogically based on *combrissed*. The phrase *bach .i. brised* is found in the H[4] version of the *Lecan Glossary*, CIH 951.35, but it is not in the version found in *The Book of Lecan* as edited by Stokes; see Paul Russell, "The Sounds of a Silence: The Growth of Cormac's Glossary," *Cambridge Medieval Celtic Studies* 15 (1988): 7; and "The Lecan Glossary," ed. and trans. Whitley Stokes in *Archiv für celtische Lexikographie* 1, eds. Whitley Stokes and Kuno Meyer (Halle: Niemeyer, 1898), 50–100. *Combach* 'breaking, destroying, cutting' is the vn. of *con-boing* 'breaks, defeats' followed by *nadma*, the gen. sg. of *naidm* 'contract, pledge, bond'. Similarly, *combrissed* is the vn. of *combrisid* 'breaks (mutually, completely)'. Since the verb *combrisid* (and also its vn.) is easily analyzable as a compound of *com-* 'together, mutually' and the verb *brisid* 'breaks, destroys, defeats', it is understandable how the synonym *combach* could also be analyzed as a compound consisting of *com-* and a verbal form *bach* with a meaning similar to that of *brisid*, thus creating a syntactic parallel between *combach nadma* and *combrissed nascairechta*.

45 The sense is that the plaintiff sued for debts owed to him before they were due.

46 Source A has *nemagra*, which is a compound of the negative prefix *nem-* and *acrae* 'suing, bringing action'; cf. *anacra* 'impossibility of suing, bad suing, unjust suing', *eDIL* s.v. 1 *anacra*.

.i. dias doro*in*e cu*n*drad*h* an*n* sin, ⁊ ita gach fer dib ag tia*cht*ai*n* t*air*is i*m*asech. ⁊ man*ar* t*h*ochaithed*ar* na ceith*re* h-u*aire* *fich*it, is cui*m*gech gach fer dib tia*cht*ain t*air*is. ⁊ ma rot*h*ochaithed*ar* na *ceithre* h-u*air*e *fich*it, noch*o* chui*m*gech nech dib tia*cht*ain [tairis].[47] ⁊ is cui*m*gech iad maraen i *n*-aen*acht* tiachtain t*air*is cach u*air* is ail leó B. [*CIH* 979.27–31]

.i. f*or*si*n* trebaire .i. do*n* feich*emain* t*oicheda* ⁊ do*n* biudbad. Cinnis si*n* on? Is
p. 56b an*n* so on: I*n* feich*em* t*oicheda* | dori*n*e deini t*oicheda* f*or*san trebaire reisi*n* re, co n-ici*nn* *cóic* *séoit* ⁊ enecl*ainn*, ⁊ dilsi a fiach do ne*m*ac*r*a do gres forsi*n* t*r*ebaire. ⁊ roleig in biudbad el*od* na trebaire i*ar*sna re, co n-ican*n* *cóic* *séoit* ⁊ enecl*ainn*, ⁊ na feich risa ndechaid d'ic t*ar*a cen*n*. ⁊ is *ed*-si*n* is co*m*bach nad*m*a an*n*.

Dias doroine cun*nrad* an*n* si*n*, ⁊ ata cac*h* fer dib ac tia*cht*ai*n* tairis. ⁊ mu*n*ar tocait*hiter* na ceit*h*re uaire *fichit*, is cui*m*gech cac*h* fer dib tia*cht*ai*n* t*air*is. ⁊ ma rotocait*hter* na *ceth*re uaire *fich*it,[48] *no*c[h]o cui*m*gech nech dib tia*cht*ai*n* t*air*is. ⁊ is cui*m*cech iat m*aræn* i n-æn*acht* t*air*is cac*h* uair is ail leo I. [*CIH* 1557.21–30]

.i. cor da sochon*n* cu f*is*[49] cu t*rebairi*[50] e-seic, ⁊ is fastait*h*i[51] ot*h*a na *ceithri* u*aire* *fich*it amac*h* it*er* diub*air*t ⁊ b*unad* *cunnartha*,[52] ce robai ne*cht*arde[53] do*n* dis dori*n*de i*n* [cor] (dis)[54] aca co*m*b*r*ised*h* R. [*CIH* 1064.1–3]

---

47 I follow the emendation suggested by Binchy, *CIH* 979, n. i.
48 The ⟨it⟩ were written above the line by the scribe.
49 I follow the expansion suggested by Binchy, *CIH* 1064, n. a.
50 I follow the expansion suggested by BInchy, *CIH* 1064, n. b.
51 For this vbl. of nec., see also *Di Astud Cor* §§ 1, 7, 15, and 23; and *GOI* § 717.
52 I follow the expansions suggested by Binchy, *CIH* 1064, n. d.
53 The scribe wrote *nechtarde* a second time, but expunged it by underlining; see also Binchy, *CIH* 1064, n. e.
54 I follow the emendation suggested by Binchy, *CIH* 1064, n. f.

i.e. two people made a contract in that case, and each one of them withdraws from it separately. And if the twenty-four hour period [prescribed by law] has not passed, each one of them is able to withdraw from it. And if the twenty-four hour period [prescribed by law] has passed, neither of them is able to withdraw from it. And they can jointly withdraw from it at the same time whenever they desire B.

i.e. against the surety, i.e. by the plaintiff and by the defendant. How does it come about? It comes about like this: The plaintiff | sued prematurely p. 56b
against the [defendant's] surety before that time, so he pays five *sét*s and honor-price, and forfeiture of his debts forever as a result of unjust suing against the surety. And the defendant evaded the surety after the time, so he pays five *sét*s and honor-price, and the debts for which he [i.e. the surety] went [into suretyship] are to be paid on his behalf. And that is what 'breaking a contract' means [lit. is] then.

Two people made a contract in that case, and each one of them withdraws from it. And if the twenty-four hour period [prescribed by law] has not passed, each one of them is able to withdraw from it. And if the twenty-four hour period [prescribed by law] has passed, neither of them is able to withdraw from it. And they can jointly withdraw from it at the same time whenever they desire I.

i.e. that is a contract [made by] two legally competent people with knowledge, with a surety, and it is to be secured from the twenty-four hour period [prescribed by law] onwards, both unwitting overpayment and [the] original contract,[55] though one of the two who made the contract [desires] to break it [i.e. the contract] R.

---

55 The sense of this last clause is obscure to me. Perhaps it means that both the original terms of the contract and any unwitting overpayment are bound once the twenty-four hours have passed.

§3 Nemed duine guba

.i. is am*al* ne*med*[56] ci*n* er*aic* do co*m*arba i*n* dui*n*e ara *n*de*n*t*ar* in guba.

Gne [aile]:[57] Is [s]l*an*[58] do*n* co*m*arba cia eblit lu*cht* i*n* cai*n*ti do*n* gal*ar* dobui tall, gidat codnaig cidat ecodn*aig*, cid targaud g*in*cob[59] ed, cia be fis gal*air* ginco be.

Masa codn*ach* rotairgest*ar* i*n* dui*n*e a h-aititi*n* a fi*n*e, cid do*n* cainiud cid don i*m*arc*h*ur, cid marb*ad* cid beocned, is [s]l*an*.

Masa ecodn*ach* rotairgest*ar* i*n* dui*n*e, cid do*n* c*h*ai*n*iud cid don i*mar*chu*r*, ⁊ cid a n-adaig cid i n-ecmais, is lanfia*ch* [nó aithgin].[60]

p. 8b Mas | beoc*h*ned, *acht* mas do*n* cainiud, is lanfia*ch*, u*air* uabar ca*ch* cai*n*ed. Mas don i*m*archu*r*, is a b*eth* am*al* i*n*det*h*bi*r* torba im aithg*in*.

1 neim*h*ed*h* C nemedh E. || gub*h*a C.

56 Binchy, *CIH* 2147.10 questions whether '*-med*' is the correct expansion of the final syllable.

57 I follow the editorial suggestion by Binchy, *CIH* 2147, n. c.

58 I follow the editorial suggestion of Binchy, *CIH* 2147, n. b.

59 One or two letters have been erased between the ⟨c⟩ and ⟨ob⟩.

60 The commentary in A sets up two broad scenarios between injury done to those who are legally competent on the one hand, and those who are not legally competent, on the other. The commentary first provides the general scenario for injury done to those legally competent, i.e. the mourning heir is exempt from legal liability. The commentary next provides a general scenario for injury to those who are not considered legally competent. After this, the commentary goes into greater detail regarding different combinations of scenarios for type of injury, location of injury, etc. regarding those who are not legally competent. The phrase *nó aithgin* has been added to the sentence here to bring not only the fine structure in line with that of the remainder of the commentary, but also to establish the parallelsism between this sentence and the previous one, i.e. both provide broad scenarios for injury. The broad scenario presented for injury to those who are legally incompetent needs to capture the full range of scenarios described below. Without the addition of *nó aithgin*, the broad scenario presented is incomplete and inconsistent with what is described in further detail later in the commentary. I should like to thank Neil McLeod for providing the solution to this textual problem.

§3 A mourner is [like] a *nemed*[61]

i.e. the heir of the person for whom the mourning is performed is like a *nemed*[62] without [liability for] *wergeld.*

Another version: The heir is exempt from legal liability though the keeners may die from the sickness which was there, whether they are legally competent or incompetent, whether invited[63] or not, whether there is knowledge of the sickness or not.

If it is a legally competent person whom the person [i.e. the mourning heir] invited with the acknowledgement of his kindred, whether to the wake or to the removal [lit. 'carrying' of the body],[64] whether fatal or non-fatal injury, he is exempt from legal liability.

If it is a legally incompetent person whom the person invited, whether to the wake or to the removal, [whether fatal or non-fatal injury is the result] and whether in the presence or absence [of his kindred], it is full fine [or restitution].

If it is | a non-fatal injury, but it [i.e. the invitation] is to the wake, it is full p. 8b
fine because every keening is an [unnecessary] vanity. If it [i.e. the invitation] is to the removal, it is treated as a careless act of social utility regarding [the payment of] restitution.

---

61 A full discussion of this material can be found in Eska, "A Medieval Irish Legal Commentary on Wakes and Funerals from *Anfuigell* 'Wrong Judgment'," 27–44 and in the Introduction, 13–14. The edition and translation presented here differs from that published in *NAJCS*.

62 While *nemed* generally means anything that is 'sacred' or 'priviliged', in the legal texts it refers to those who are considered to be of a privileged rank such as kings, lords, clerics, and poets, and thus have 'special legal privileges'; *GEIL*, 9; and *eDIL s.v. neimed.* Those who have *nemed* status cannot have their property distrained by the standard procedure and instead must be fasted against, contracts with *nemeds* are unenforceable should they default due to their high status, and *nemeds* are also 'immune from some legal obligations'; *GEIL*, 9. See also Riita Latvio. "*Neimed*—Exploring Social Distinctions and Sacredness in Early Irish Legal Sources," in *Approaches to Religion and Mythology in Celtic Studies*, eds. Katja Ritari and Alexandra Bergholm (Newcastle, UK: Cambridge Scholars Publishing, 2008), 220–242.

63 In legal contexts, forms of *do-áirci* have a range of meanings, including 'bring, conduct, lead'; see *eDIL s.v. do-áirci.*

64 For a general discussion of bearing a body for burial, see Susan Leigh Fry, *Burial in Medieval Ireland, 900–1500* (Dublin: Four Courts Press, 1999), 88–92.

Mas a n-ecmais a fi*n*ech*air*e, mas do*n* cai*n*ed, cid marb*ad* cid beocned, is lanfiach. Mas don i*m*arcu*r*, cid marb*ad* cid beocned, is a b*eth* am*al* inde*th*bi*r* torba i*m* ai*th*gi*n*.

⁊ da tecmad fis ceneile i*n* gal*air* aice ⁊ nir i*n*dis, ma rofas fog*ail* de, is a b*eth* am*al* inde*th*bi*r* torba im ai*th*gi*n*, no cu*m*[ad][65] lanfia*ch* A. [*CIH* 2147.10–21]

.i. mad cod*h*nac*h* rat*h*airgest*ar* in duini, cid du*n* c*h*ainiud*h* cid dun i*m*cur, cid*h* beoc*h*ned*h* cid m*ar*b*h*c*h*ned*h*, is [s]lan.

Mas ecod*h*nac*h* rat*h*airgest*ar* duni a aititi*n* a cod*h*nac*h*, masa m*ar*bud*h*
f. 52d cid*h* dun c*h*ainiud*h* cid*h* dun i*m*uc*h*ur, is [s]lan. Masa beo|c*h*ned*h*, mas dun c*h*ainiud*h*, is lanfia*ch*.

Mas dun imuc*h*ur, is am*al* indeit*h*beir torb*h*a, ⁊ aithg*h*ei*n* an*n*.

Mas i n-eccmais a cod*h*nac*h*, *acht* mas du*n* cai*n*iud*h*, cid beoc*h*ned*h* cid*h* marbud*h*, is la*n*fia*ch*.

Mas dun i*m*uc*h*ur, cid*h* beoc*h*ned*h* cid*h* m*ar*bud*h*, is ai*th*g*h*i*n*. Da teccmad*h* aiccbeili in gal*air* accu ⁊ nir i*n*nisetar, da teccmad*h* fog*h*al d'as de, cu *m*bet*h* aithg*h*ein and C. [*CIH* 167.19–29]

65 I follow the editorial suggestion made by Binchy, *CIH* 2147, n. d.

If it is in the absence of his family group, if it [i.e. the invitation] is to the wake, whether fatal or non-fatal injury, it is full fine. If it [i.e. the invitation] is to the removal, whether fatal or non-fatal injury, it is treated as a careless act of social utility regarding [the payment of] restitution.

And if it should happen that the family knew of the illness he[66] had and did not tell [anyone], if harm results from it, it is treated as a careless act of social utility regarding [the payment of restitution], until it would be full fine A.

i.e. if it is a legally competent person whom the person [i.e. the mourning heir] invited, whether to the wake or to the removal, whether non-fatal injury or fatal injury, he is exempt from legal liability.

If it is a legally incompetent person whom the person invited with the acknowledgement of his guardians, if fatal injury [is the result] whether [the invitation is] to the wake or to the removal, he is exempt from legal liability. If it is a non-fatal injury, | if it [i.e. the invitation] is to the wake, it is full fine. f. 52d

If it is to the removal, it is treated as a careless act of social utility, and restitution then.

If it is in the absence of his guardians, but if it is to the wake, whether non-fatal or fatal injury, it is full fine.

If it is to the removal, whether non-fatal or fatal injury, it is restitution.

If it should happen that they have [knowledge] of a dangerous sickness and they did not tell [anyone], if injury should result from it, it would be restitution then C.

66 The pronoun 'he' refers to the deceased.

.i. masa cod*h*naid*h* rotairced*h* and, cid do*n* gub*h*a cid*h* do*n*n imarchur, ce 'n-adaig[67] cid a n-ecmais a fi*n*e, cid beochned*h* cid marbchned, is [s]lan.

Masa h-eccodnaid[68] rotair[c]ed ann, ⁊ iss a fiadhnaise a fine, ⁊ is marb*h*[ud] cid dan gub*h*a cid*h* da*n*n i*m*archur, is [s]lan.

Masa beocned*h* roferad air, masa don guba, is am*al* anfoit inde*th*b*ir* im lanfiach a beocneid*h*e d'ic ris bodei*n*. Mas do*n* i*m*archur, is am*al* indethb*ir* torba im aithgi*n*.

Mas a n-ecmais a fi*n*e, cid beocned*h* cid*h* marb[chnedh],[69] *acht* mai go [*read* acht mas don] guba, is am*al* anfoit inde*th*b*ir* im lanfiach. Mas do*n* imarchur, is am*al* inde*th*b*ir* torba im aithgin. Finit ame*n* fi*nit* E. [CIH 1018.18–25]

67 The word *adaig* was inserted above the line of text; see also Binchy, CIH 1018, n. f. A few letters have been erased after the sequence ⟨cen⟩.

68 The letters ⟨ccodnaig⟩ were inserted above the line of text; see also Binchy, CIH 1018, n. g.

69 I follow the editorial suggestion made by Binchy, CIH 1018, n. h.

i.e. if they are legally competent people whom he invited there, whether to the wake or to the removal, whether in the presence or absence of their kindred, whether non-fatal or fatal injury, he is exempt from legal liability.

If they are legally incompetent people whom he invited there, and it is in the presence of his kindred, and it is a fatal injury whether [the invitation is] to the wake or to the removal, he is exempt from legal liability.

If it is a non-fatal injury that has been inflicted on him, if it [i.e. the invitation] is to the wake, it is treated as an injury due to negligence regarding the payment to himself of the full fine for his non-fatal injury. If it is to the removal, it is treated as a careless act of social utility regarding [the payment of] restitution.

If it is in the absence of his kindred, whether non-fatal or fatal injury, provided that it is to the wake, it is treated as a case of injury due to negligence regarding [paying the] full fine. If it is to the removal, it is treated as a careless act of social utility regarding [the payment of] restitution. It finishes, amen, it finishes. E.

§4 Guugud[70] rathachais .i. el*ud* a raith*e* do neoch t*et*[71] i rat*h*ig*hus*; ni coir ni dernait*er*[72,73]

Dui*ne* docuaid[74] a rathac*h*as an*n* si*n*, ⁊ rob ail leis tia*cht*ain as. Masa rait*h* ainfi*ne*,[75] ma*n* rotocaith na *ceth*ra h-u*ai*re [fichit],[76] is cui*m*gec*h*[77] cac*h* fer

---

1 Gud*h*ugud*h* **B** [G]uug **J** I*n* Gudug*ud* **R**. A large space has been left for the capital ⟨G⟩ to be added later in source **J**; see also Binchy, *CIH* 2026, n. f. ‖ rataigis ⁊rl- **B** rathaig*h*eas **J** rathaiges **R**. **R** also has a paragraph which contains the citation 'I*n* gudug*ud* rat*h*ac*h*ais' (*CIH* 1063.23), but the commentary which follows the citation, while similar in subject matter, does not directly relate to the commentaries here; see §31. ‖ Binchy, *CIH* 2026, n. g, notes that *do neoch tet i rathigus* is written above the second line of the text in the MS in the same size handwriting used to differentiate the main text from the commentary. The scribe clearly forgot the phrase initially as he includes reference marks to indicate its correct placement in the sentence. 2 .i. el*ud* … dernait*er* is only found in **J**; the scribe has written this material in the same large size script as the rest of the OI text.

---

70 All of the forms in the MS sources seem to derive from a form such as *gúugud*, which appears to be the vn. of *gúaigidir* 'falsifies', derived from *gáu* 'falsehood, misstatement, false judgment'. Although *eDIL* does not list a vn. for *gúaigidir*, see *GOI* §723 for verbal nouns formed from deponent denominative verbs. The spelling variants in the MSS are the result of the fact that in MI both internal and final lenited /d/ and /g/ are realized phonologically as /∅/ and, thus, ⟨d⟩ and ⟨g⟩ are orthographically interchangeable with each other in these positions.

71 The verbal form *tet* (only found in source J) is a later MI pres. 3 sg. rel. for OI *téite*; see *eDIL s.v. téit.*

72 Other than the first two words of the text, sources **A**, **B**, and **J** have only the commentary beginning *duine dochuiadh* in common, although parts of the second commentary in source **A** overlap with **J**. The verbal form *-dernaiter* is the MI 3 sg. perf. ind. pass. rel. of *do-gní.*

73 The majority of the material from the commentaries is printed and translated by Rudolf Thurneysen, *Die Bürgschaft im irischen Recht*, Abhandlungen der Preussischen Akademie der Wissenschaften. Phil.-hist. Klasse; Nr. 2 (Berlin: Verlag der Akademie der Wissenschaften, 1928), 42–43 and 50. Thurneysen seems to be following the text as printed in O'Donovan's transcript (757), in that he leaves out the portion of the text '*ni coir ni dernaiter*', which is also missing in O'Donovan. Curiously, Thurnesyen prints the opening words of the text as 'Gudhug rathaigheas' and notes that they should be read as 'Guugud rathaighis', 42, but the transcript prints the opening words as 'Duug rathaigheas'; cf. also *CIH* 803.33–34 'guudhud rathachais'. The copy of the transcript I examined at the University Library, University of Cambridge, is very faint, and there appears to be a faded question mark over 'Duug'. If O'Donovan has offered an alternative reading, it is too faint to be seen. The J commentary as printed in *CIH* differs in many ways from both that printed by Thurneysen and by O'Donovan.

74 The ⟨u⟩ was written above the ⟨a⟩; see Binchy, *CIH*, 2147, n. e, where he states that the ⟨a⟩ was written above the ⟨u⟩.

75 The ⟨a⟩ is written subscript; see also Binchy, *CIH* 2147, n. f.

76 The emendation is suggested by Binchy, *CIH* 2147, n. g.

77 The ⟨u⟩ is written above the ⟨i⟩.

§4 [Turning a promise] of paying-suretyship [into] a lie,[78] i.e. evasion of his paying-suretyship[79] by someone who enters into paying-suretyship; what was done is not proper[80]

A person who entered into paying-suretyship in that case, and he wants to withdraw from it. If he is a paying-surety for a non-kinsman, if the twenty-four hour period [prescribed by law] has not passed,[81] each one is able to

78 While *guugud* conveys a notion of an activity being 'fraudulent' or otherwise 'false' in some way, the commentary deals with removing oneself from the obligations of being a paying-surety. For the circumstances in which a contract can be impugned, see *Di Astud Cor* §1; and McLeod, *Early Irish Contract Law*, 58–83. In these circumstances, there is no legal remedy available for the contracting party.

79 For the obligations of the paying-surety, see *GEIL*, 168–171.

80 For a discussion of this section, see the Introduction, 14–15.

81 See McLeod, *Early Irish Contract Law*, 24–25 for a discussion of the later legal provision where contracts are binding after a period of twenty-four hours.

tia*cht*ai*n* as *acht* co faca[82] raith a comaice*n*ta dara esi; ⁊ ma rotocait*h* na *ceth*ra h-u*aire* *fichit*, nocha cui*m*gech hi tia*cht*ai*n* as ł co faca feich d*ar*' esi. Masa rait*h* fi*n*e hi,[83] o rac*hus* i*n*d do g*re*s, noc*h*a cui*m*gech i tia*cht*ain as ł co faca feic*h* dara[84] esi .i. u*air* is [si] i*n*[85] *cóic*id [ṡ]lecht[86] *fichit* in Cor*us*a Fi*n*e ⁊rl-.

Gne *aile*: Co*n*nic dligth*ech* fei*n*[87] a dichor de re re *ceithre* n-u*aire* *fichit* co tarr*acht*ain na[88] h-aithgi*n*a. Maine tarras im*murro*[89] in aithgi*n*, ni c*um*aic a dichu*r* de it*ir*. Ni c*um*ai*n*g im*murro* a dichu*r* de o cet*r*i u*aire* *fichit* a*m*a*ch*, gia tarr*us* genco tarr*us* i*n* aithgi*n*, mani ti nec*h* *aile* fo curu. Dia ti im*murro*, tic fo chu*r*u i*m*on uilidet*aid* in tan is t*ar* cenn anfine ⁊ ni rodigbait [a] *séoit* *ar* scath a t*r*eb*aire*. Ma rodigbait im*murro*, is c*er*taithgi*n* in loigi en*ech* nama[90] ci*n* los ci*n* as.

In tan[91] im*murro* is t*ar* cenn fi*n*e, teca*r* fon forc*r*aid fuil for log en*ech* an*n* *con*a icann[92] ni *acht* log en*ech*[93] nama co los ⁊ as; i*n* tan na rodigbait [a] *séoit* ar scath a t*r*eb*aire* si*n*. Ma rodigbait im*murro*, is log en*ech* co los ⁊ as,[94] ⁊ aithg*in* na fo*r*c*r*aide gi*n* los gi*n* as A. [*CIH* 2147.22–37]

---

82 The first ⟨a⟩ is written subscript; see also Binchy, *CIH*, 2147, n. h.

83 The ⟨hi⟩ were inserted above the line; see also Binchy, *CIH*, 2147, n. i.

84 The second ⟨a⟩ is written subscript.

85 The emendation is suggested by Binchy, *CIH* 2147, n. j.

86 The emendation is suggested by Binchy, *CIH* 2147, n. k; cf. source J.

87 A letter has been erased after *fein*.

88 The ⟨a⟩ is written subscript.

89 The ⟨im̄⟩ were inserted above the line.

90 The first ⟨a⟩ is written subscript.

91 Approximately three letters were erased after *tan*; see also Binchy, *CIH* 2147, n. l.

92 One letter was erased after this word.

93 The rest of the line was erased; Binchy, *CIH* 2147, n. m, estimates fifteen letters followed *enech*.

94 The sequence ⟨⁊ as⟩ was written above the line; see also Binchy, *CIH*, 2147, n. i.

withdraw from it provided that he [the paying-surety] gives a paying-surety of the same nature in his place; and if the twenty-four hour period [prescribed by law] has passed, he is not able to withdraw from it unless he gives penalties in its place. If he is a paying-surety for a kinsman, once he has entered into it [i.e. the suretyship], he is not able to withdraw from it unless he gives penalties in its place, i.e. because it is the twenty-fifth section of *Córus Fine*, etc.

Another version: He [i.e. the surety] is able lawfully to remove himself from it [i.e. the suretyship] within a period of twenty-four hours provided he affects[95] the restitution [of anything the secured party received from the other contracting party]. If he has not affected the restitution [of the other contracting party's chattels], however, he is not able to remove himself from it at all. He [i.e. the surety] is not able, however, to remove himself from it [i.e. the suretyship] from twenty-four hours onwards, whether or not he has affected the restitution, unless someone else impugns the contract. If he [i.e. someone else] impugns [the contract], however, he impugns the total amount of the contract when it is on behalf of a non-kinsman, and his [the surety's] *sét*s did not diminish on account of his suretyship [i.e. his property had not diminished as part of his obligations as a paying-surety]. If they diminished, however, it is exact restitution of honor-price[96] only without interest.[97]

When, however, it is on behalf of a kinsman, he impugns the amount exceeding the honor-price then so that he does not pay anything except honor-price only with interest, when his *sét*s did not diminish on account of his suretyship. If they diminished, however, it is honor-price with interest, and restitution of the amount exceeding [the honor-price] without interest A.

---

95 Although the usual meaning of *tárrachtain* is 'obtaining, finding, seizing', the sense in the commentary is that it is the surety's responsibility to make certain that anything which the secured party obtained from the other contracting party is returned to the other contracting party in the same condition. If exact restitution of the chattels is not possible, the equivalent must be provided in its place; for discussion of this legal principle, see McLeod, *Early Irish Contract Law*, 37.

96 If it was necessary for the paying-surety to use some of his own property to fulfill the financial obligations of the secured party, the paying-surety was entitled to receive both the amount of his own honor-price and the value of the propery he used to fulfill the contract; see McLeod, *Early Irish Contract Law*, 17.

97 The formula *los* ⁊ *ás* 'calves and milk' is generally used to refer to interest on livestock, i.e. the value of the progeny and milk the cows will produce while in someone else's possession; McLeod, "*Ón* and *airliciud*," 179–180.

.i. dui*ne* do*ch*uaid*h* a rathaig*h*es an*n* sin, ⁊ rob ail leis tia*cht*ain ass. ⁊ masa rait*h* anfi*ne* hé, manar t*h*o*ch*aith na ceit*h*ri *h*-uair *fich*it, is tualai*n*g he tia*cht*ain ass *acht* go ḟaga rait*h* a *ch*omaigi*n*ta t*ar*a eis. ⁊ ma[98] rot*h*o*ch*aith na *ceithri* h-u*air*e *fich*it, noc*h*o tualai*n*g he tia*cht*ai*n* ass *acht* go ḟaga feich t*ar*a eisi. ⁊ masa rait*h* ḟi*n*e hí, o rac*hus* i*n*d do g*r*es, *noch*o tualai*n*g hi tia*cht*ai*n* ass *no* go ḟaga feich t*ar*a h-eisi B. [*CIH* 979.32–37]

.i. na dernt*ar* si*n* o *ceithre* u*air*e *fich*it amac .i. u*air* nac*h* coir .i. conic fein a dichur de re re ceit*h*re n-uair *fich*it co tarr*achtain* na ait*hgen*a. Ma*n*a tarr*us* *imm*u*rr*o in ait*hgin*, ni cumaing a dic*h*ur de it*ir*; ⁊ ni *cumh*aing *imm*u*rr*o a dic*h*ur de o cet*h*re u*air*e *fich*it amac*h*, cia tarrus an aithg*in* ci*n*co t*ar*rast*ar*, col. 546 mana ti nech *aile* fo coraib*h*. Dia ti *imm*u*rr*o, tic fo cu*r*a iman uilet*aid* in ta*n* | is t*ar* cean*n* ainfine ⁊ ní rodi[g]bait[99] [a][100] seoit *ar* scat*h* a t*r*eb*air*i.

Mad rodigbait *imm*u*rr*o, is c*er*tait*hgin* in[101] loig*h* enec nama ci*n* los ci*n* as. In tan *imm*u*rr*o is t*ar* cen*n* fine, teca*r* fo*n* fo*r*c*raid* [ḟ]uil f*or* log*h* einec *con*a ican*n* ni *acht* log*h* einec nama ci*n* los ci*n* as, in tan na rodi[g]bait [a] *séoit* *ar* scat*h* a treb*air*i si*n*. Mad rodi[g]bait *imm*u*rr*o, is log*h* ein*e*c co los ⁊ as, ⁊ ait*hgin* na fo*r*c*raid*e ci*n* los ci*n* as.

98 Binchy, *CIH* 979, n. j, notes that an ⟨n⟩ was erased after ⟨ma⟩.

99 The emendation is suggested by Binchy, *CIH* 2026, n. h.

100 The emendation follows that of Thurneysen, *Bürgschaft*, 50.

101 Thurneysen, *Bürgschaft*, 50, suggests reading 'in' as '⁊'.

i.e. a person who entered into paying-suretyship in that case, and he would like to withdraw from it. And if he is a paying-surety for a non-kinsman, if the twenty-four hour period [prescribed by law] has not passed, he is able to withdraw from it provided that he gives a paying-surety of the same nature in his place. And if the twenty-four hours have passed, he is not able to withdraw from it unless he gives penalties in its place. And if he is a paying-surety for a kinsman, once he has entered into it, he is not able to withdraw from it unless he gives penalties in its place B.

i.e. let that not be done from twenty-four hours onwards, i.e. because it is not proper, i.e. he is able to remove himself from it within a period of twenty-four hours provided he affects the restitution [for the other contracting party].[102] If, however, the restitution was not affected [for the other contracting party], he is not able to remove himself from it at all; and he is not able, however, to remove himself from it from twenty-four hours onwards, whether or not the restitution was affected, unless someone else may impugn the contract. If he [i.e. someone else] may, however, [impugn the contract], he impugns the total amount of the contract when | it is on behalf of a non-kinsman,[103] col. 546
and his [i.e. the surety's] *séts* did not diminish on account of his suretyship.

If, however, they diminished, it is exact restitution of[104] the honor-price only without interest. When, however, it is on behalf of a kinsman, the amount exceeding the honor-price is impugned so that he pays nothing except honor-price only without interest, when [his] *séts* did not diminish on account of his suretyship. If they diminished, however, [he pays] honor-price with interest, and restitution of the amount exceeding [the honor-price] without interest.

---

102 Cf. Thurneysen, *Bürgschaft*, 42.

103 The word *ainfine* can be used for anyone who is not of one's own kindred.

104 Both sources A and J have the same grammatical construction with the gen. of *log*. It is known from other legal texts that no one can act as a surety for more than the value of his honor-price; *GEIL*, 169. The sense here seems to be, according to Thurneysen's interpretation of the passage, that, if the contract has been impugned and the surety has had pay out from his own property in the process, then the surety is owed what he originally paid out and also the amount of his honor-price if the case involved someone from outside his own kindred; see Thurneysen, *Bürgschaft*, 50. Cf. the slightly different fine structure in A. It is possible that one of these sources is corrupt.

G*ne* *aile*:[105] In treb*aire*, *acht* mas t*ar* cen*n* ainfi*ne* docuaid, tic fein fo coraib f*ri* re *ceithre* n-u*air* *fich*it cosi*n* mbidb*aid* do tab*air*t isi*n* co*m*urr*adus* *cét*na ɫ cosi*n* aithg*in* rodi[g]b*ad* *ar* scat*h* a laim*h*e d'aisic amuig*h*. Mas t*ar* cen*n* fine *immurro* docuaid*h*, tic fein [fo coraib][106] *co*n*a* biad *acht* re c*er*taith*gin* loig*h* einec *co* *n*-as ⁊ los ⁊ cosi*n* im*arcraid* ata f*or* log*h* ein*ech* anuas d'aisic amuig*h* ci*n* los ci*n* as. Mad i*ar*sna *ceithre* uai*re* *fich*it *immurro*, ni cu*m*aing nech dib*h* ti*acht*ain t*air*is *acht*,[107] mu*na* ti fi*ne* fo coraib*h*, ⁊ tic-side fo coraib riasna reib*h* i*n*a[d][108] dír.

Duine dochuaid*h* i rat*h*aig*hus* an*n* sin, ⁊ rob ail leis tia*cht*ain as. ⁊ masa rait*h* ainfi*ne* e, ma*nar* tocait*h* na *ceithre* uai*re* *fich*it, is tualaing e tia*cht*ain as *acht* co fag*h*ba rait*h* a co*m*aice*n*ta t*ar*a h-eisi. ⁊ ma rotocait*h* na ceit*h*re u*air*e *fich*it, noch*an* tualaing é tia*cht*ain as ɫ co fagba feich t*ar*a eisi. ⁊ masa rait*h* fi*ne* í, o rag*hus* in*n* do g*r*es, noch*an* tualaing i tia*cht*ain as ɫ co fagba feich t*ar*a eisi, u*air* is do *cóic*[id] sle*chta* *fich*it in Cor*us*a Fi*ne* J. [*CIH* 2026.23–2027.6]

105 Written in *marg. dext.*; see also Binchy, *CIH* 2026, n. i.

106 Binchy, *CIH* 2026, n. j, suggests emending the text to 'fo curu'; the other instances in source J of *fo* with *cor* have *cor* in the dat. pl. or in the acc. pl. In source A, *cor* is in the acc. pl. in this construction. I have emended the text here to be consistent with the usage in the rest of this particular commentary.

107 Binchy, *CIH* 2026, n. k, suggests reading MS 'tairis̄' as 'tairis s̄'.

108 Emendation suggested by Binchy, *CIH* 2026, n. l, for OI *indid*, 3 sg. pres. cop. combined with the prep. *i n-*.

Another version: The surety, except if it is on behalf of a non-kinsman that he undertook [the suretyship], he himself can impugn the contract within a period of twenty-four hours with the offending party [i.e. the party who now lacks the required surety] to bring forward a person of the same legal capacity [as the surety who withdrew] or with the restitution of what was diminished on account of his hand [i.e. on account of his obligation as a surety][109] to be given back. If it is on behalf of a kinsman, however, that he undertook [the suretyship], he himself can impugn the contract so that there is nothing [to pay] save for exact restitution of honor-price with interest and with the amount exceeding the honor-price to be given back without interest. If it is after the twenty-four hours, however, neither of them is able to withdraw from it, unless a kinsman impugns the contract, and he [i.e. a kinsman can] impugn a contract within the periods of time in which it is allowed.[110]

A person who entered into paying-suretyship in that case, and he would like to withdraw from it. And if he is the paying-surety for a non-kinsman, if the twenty-four hour period [prescribed by law] has not passed, he is able to withdraw from it provided that he gives a paying-surety of the same nature in his place. And if the twenty-four hours have passed, he is not able to withdraw from it unless he gives penalties in its place.[111] And if he is a paying-surety for a kinsman, once he has entered into it [i.e. the suretyship], he is not able to withdraw from it unless he gives penalties in its place, because it is from the twenty-fifth section of *Córus Fine*[112] J.

---

109 For idioms with *lám* 'hand' used to express the obligations of a surety, see McLeod, *Early Irish Contract Law*, 23–24; and the quotation from *Ántéchtae* 'Splendid Propriety (?)' edited and translated in *idem*, "*Ón* and *airliciud*," 181.

110 For the specific periods of time within which contracts can be impugned, see *Di Astud Cor* §1.

111 The sense of the passage is that the surety can withdraw from his obligations as a surety after twenty-four hours have passed as long as he provides the amount that he originally stood for as surety and perhaps other penalties for withdrawing. In other words, even if the surety himself withdraws, he leaves behind the amount of the debt in question so that the contract would remain valid.

112 *Córus Fine* 'The Ordering of the Kindred' is a fragmentary legal text pertaining to the kin-group, as the title suggests; see *GEIL*, 270; and *CCIH*, 237 for reference to the passage above.

I*n* gudug*ud* rathaiges,[113] fo cor*aib* na t*r*eb*air*i teac*ar*[114] an*n*-sideic, *con*a bia ré ní is mo na re log e*nech* t*ar* cen*n* f*ir* fi*n*e, ⁊ *con*a bia re ní it*ir* t*ar* cen*n* a*n*fine. ł is e fei*n* obr*us* a se*n*a na dechaid a t*r*eb*air*i re ni it*ir*, ⁊ *noch*u cu*m*aing u*air* atait fiad*ain* and R. [*CIH* 1063.31–34]

113 See the critical apparatus above.

114 The imper. pass. of *do-icc* 'comes', *teacar* here, is normally used with an indefinite agent. In this case, it is used to refer to an unspecified surety.

The [act of turning a promise] of paying-suretyship into a lie, [he is] under the bonds of the surety who comes then, and he will not be [a surety] for any [amount] which is greater than the amount [of his] honor-price on behalf of a kinsman, and he will not be [a surety] for anything at all on behalf of a non-kinman. Or it is he himself[115] who rejects his denial that he entered into surety for anything at all, and he is not able [to deny it] because there are witnesses there R.

115 I am uncertain of the referent here. Perhaps this refers to the secured party who is rejecting the surety's denial that he entered into suretyship on his behalf.

§5 **Reim nena ⁊rl- is dil*es* cia fagab*ar* and**

In deor*ad* de: Ma dorigne na t*r*i f*er*ta sai*n*emla i*ar* tia*cht*ain do*cum* tire, nosær*a* fe*n* co lu*cht* a b*air*ce. Mai*n*i derna *acht* æ*n*f*er*t ł da ḟ*er*t, no ci*nco*[116] derna f*er*t it*ir*, masa ci*nd*ti *con*id deor*ad* de cena, nosærand *con*a crud, ⁊ co*m*-rai*n*d b*air*ce f*or*a mbi 'na eth*ar* uile o si*n* a*mach*[117] A. [*CIH* 2147.38–2148.2]

In deor*ad* de: Ma dori*n*de t*r*i ferta faillsig*h*i ag tia*cht*ain do*cum* *th*ire i fiad-*nais*e rig*h* ⁊ tuait*h*i, i[s][118] saíre dó *con*a sé*t*aib ⁊ a b*air*c. ⁊ mana derna *acht* ł ded*he* dib, is s*air*e do *con*a sé*t*aib, ⁊ co*m*roi*n*d b*air*ce dligt*h*ig*h*i f*or*a b*airc*. ⁊ amail c*h*leirech he fei*n* a n-Eir*inn*[119] im besgna ris B. [*CIH* 979.38–41]

1 rem **A**, rei*m* **B**. ‖ is … and **A** Binchy, *CIH* 2147, n. n, queries whether this phrase is out of place because it is also found in part of the OI text from §1 **A**, *CIH* 2146.22–23.

116 The ⟨co⟩ were inserted above the line with a reference mark by the scribe.

117 The last three letters of *amach* were written below the first two in *marg. dext.* by the scribe.

118 See also Binchy, *CIH* 979, n. k.

119 Binchy questions his expansion of the final syllable of this word; *CIH* 979.41.

§5 Course [over the] wave,[120] etc. whatever is left there is forfeit[121]

The *deorad Dé*: If he performed three distinct miracles after coming ashore,[122] he exempts himself along with the cargo of his ship.[123] If he performed only one or two miracles, or he did not perform a miracle at all, if it is certain that he is a *deorad Dé* indeed, he exempts [himself] along with his possessions, and a share [of the goods] of the boat for whomever is wont to have [a share] in every boat in such cases[124] A.

The *deorad Dé*: If he performed three evident miracles [after] coming ashore in the presence of the king and the *túath*,[125] he is exempt along with his *séts* and his boat. And if he performed only one or two of them [i.e. miracles],[126] he is exempt along with his *séts*, and a share [of the goods] of a lawful boat for his boat. And he himself is treated as a cleric in Ireland concerning the custom with regard to it B.

---

120 According to *eDIL s.v.* 1 *nena*, the phrase *réim nena* refers to a procedure whereby a *deorad Dé* 'exile of God' who lands on the shore of a territory outside his own can keep himself, his goods, and his boat from being confiscated by proving his profession. Normally whatever goods are cast upon the shore belong to the owner of the land which borders the shore; *GEIL*, 107–108; Mac Niocaill, "Jetsam, Treasure Trove, and the Lord's Share in Medieval Ireland," 106–107. The *deorad Dé* is depicted as a pilgrim or hermit in the legal texts; see *eDIL s.v. deorad*. As mooted by *eDIL*, it is possible that *nena* here is actually from *en* 'water'. Regardless of how one interprets *nena*, the sense here refers to a journey by sea and subsequent arrival on land.

121 For a discussion of this section, see the Introduction, 15.

122 On the *deorad Dé* being considered a miracle-worker, see Fergus Kelly, "The Recovery of Stolen Property: Notes on legal procedure in Gaelic Ireland, Scotland, and the Isle of Man," in *Tome: Studies in medieval Celtic history and law in honour of Thomas Charles-Edwards*, eds. Fiona Edmonds and Paul Russell (Woodbridge: The Boydell Press, 2011), 167–168.

123 The ship's crew is conspicuously absent in this commentary and in the one from source B. It is possible that the commentary envisages a boat small enough to be controlled by one person. A more literal rendering of the phrase *lucht a bairce* as 'people of his boat', i.e. 'crew', would add the crew to the commentary, but such an interpretation is mitigated against by the mention of the *deorad Dé*'s *crod* 'property, wealth' listed later in the commentary.

124 For dividing up the goods of a shipwreck, see §22.

125 The word *túath* encompasses a range of meanings, including 'people, country, territory, laity'. Often translated as 'tribe' in early secondary sources, the words 'community' or 'territory' more accurately reflect the way the word is used in the legal texts; *eDIL s.v.* 1 *túath*.

126 It is possible that some material has been left out of B; cf. the material in source A.

§6 Nós tuaithe ⁊rl-

Masa nos dligth*ech* dorigned isi*n* tuait*h* a co*mæn*taid, noc*ha* dleg*ar* do neoch dib a t*h*urbrod, ⁊ da nd*er*na, icad er*aic* ina tu*r*brod. ⁊ cia rob*eth æn* ł deda ris amuig, urail*id* dlig*ed* orra tia*ch*ta*in* fai, ⁊ da nd*er*nat a tu*r*brod, ic*at* er*aic* ina tu*r*b*r*od. ⁊ cenco b*eth acht æ*nno*n*bu*r* aca de*n*am do mait*h*ib, roba [a](e)*cht*[127] dligth*ech* e u*air* no*n*bu*r* bis a ses ui*me*.[128] ⁊ noc*ha* cui*m*get-sec

1 nos **A**, nois **C**. ‖ tuathe **C**. ‖ ⁊rl- *om.* **C**.

127 Binchy, *CIH* 2148, n. a, queries whether this should be read as *acht*.

128 The commentaries in A and B rely on the reader being familiar with the etymological glossing tradition, especially with regard to the word *nós*. The entry for *nós* (no. 970, YBL version) in *Sanas Cormaic* is as follows: 'Nōs .i. nóe-fis .i. fios nonbuir .i. tri righ, tri suid, tri h-espaic, .i. sui litri ⁊ sui filidechta ⁊ sui bérlai Feine, ⁊ robadar uile ag denam ind tSenchusa Mair, unde dicitur Laogaire, Corc, Daire dur, Patraic, Binen, Cairnech choir, Ros, Dubtach, Fergas co feib, nai sailgi sin Senchuis Moir'. *'Nós*, i.e. 'nine-knowledge', i.e. knowledge of nine people, i.e. three kings, three scholars, three bishops, i.e. a scholar of letters and a scholar of poetry and a scholar of legal language, and they all composed the *Senchas Már*, *unde dicitur* Loegaire, Corc, Daire [the] Firm, Patrick, Benen, Cairnech [the] Just, Ros, Dubthach, Fergus with excellence, these are nine supports of [the] *Senchas Már*.'; see also *Cormac's Glossary*, trans. John O'Donovan and ed. Whitley Stokes (Calcutta: Irish Archaeolgoical and Celtic Society, 1868), 122; and the Early Irish Glossaries Database http://www.asnc.cam.ac.uk/irishglossaries/texts.php?versionID=9&readingID=17964#17964. Accessed July 2, 2018. A shorter version of this also appears in *Dúil Dromma Cetta*: 'Nós .i. fis nonbuir .i. tri ríg, tri h-espuig, tri filid'; *Dúil Dromma Cetta*, ed. Whitley Stokes in "Irish glosses, edited by a member of the Council from a manuscript in the library of Trinity College, Dublin [H. 3. 18, p. 61, col. 1]," *Transactions of the Philological Society* 6 (1859): 191; *CIH* 618.32 and 1076.9–10; and the Early Irish Glossaries Database http://www.asnc.cam.ac.uk/irishglossaries/texts.php?versionID=2&readingID=19073#19073. Accessed July 2, 2018. While the etymologies provided in these types of glossaries are not usually correct by modern standards, this one probably is. (Whether the etymology is 'correct' or not is beside the point as it makes no difference in the way the word is used here.) Its analysis of the etymology of *nós* as an original compound of *noí* 'nine' and *fis* 'knowledge' is most likely accurate, even though it is not transparent that *nós* is originally a compound; for another example of a non-transparent compound, cf. *cubus* 'conscience', formed from *com* 'with' and *fis* 'knowledge'; *GOI* § 201 (b). See also *eDIL s.vv.* 1 *noes* and *nós*; and *LEIA*, *s.v. nós*. Likewise, *séis* 'design, plan, arrangement' at the end of the sentence continues the underlying etymological gloss in the commentary and refers to the tradition of the nine people composing the *Senchas Már*. The entry on *séis* from *O'Clery's Glossary* is also relevant to understanding the commentary: 'Seis .i. soifios .i. fios mait*h*' *'Séis*, i.e. 'good-knowledge', i.e. good knowledge'; *Foclóir nó Sanasán nua: A new Vocabulary or Glossary*, ed. Mícheál Ó Cléirigh (Louvain: 1643), 115; cf. *O'Clery's Glossary*, ed. and trans. Arthur W.K. Miller in "O'Clery's Irish Glossary," *Revue celtique* 5 (1881–1883): 45. Many of the entries in O'Clery's Glossary were probably derived from earlier sources; Russell, "Sounds of a Silence," 9. Of note are the etymological glosses on *córus* in §§ 1 and 16, respectively,

§ 6 A *túath*'s ordinance,[129] etc.[130]

If a legal ordinance was established in the *túath* by agreement [in an assembly], none of them has the right to repudiate it, and if any should do so, let him pay a fine for repudiating it. And though there may be one or two people opposing it,[131] law requires them to submit to it, and if they should repudiate it, let them pay a fine for repudiating it. And though there is only a group of nine dignitaries[132] establishing it, it would be a lawful stipulation because nine people are in agreement about it.[133] And these [i.e. the nine dignitaries]

---

of *Córus Bésgnai*: '.i. cōirsēis, sēis choir, in bāfesa gnāe *nō* aībind', 'i.e. the 'arrangement properly', 'proper arrangement' of the 'delightful' or pleasant 'beneficial knowledge'', and '.i. comaircim caidi aithne in neich dleg*ar* dona fēinib a fīs choir', i.e. 'I enquire' what are the characteristics of that which is due from the commoners according to 'proper knowledge''; see 184 and 194 of the edition for discussion of these etymological glosses. What we have in § 6 of *Anfuigell* then are two alternative etymologies for the second element in *nós*: 1) *noí-fis* 'nine-knowledge' and 2) *noí-séis* 'nine-sense'. On the use of *séis* < Latin *sensus* in the OI glosses, see Pierre-Yves Lambert, "The Expression of 'sense, meaning, signification' in the Old Irish Glosses, and particularly in the Milan and Saint-Gall Glosses," in *Grammatica, Gramadach and Gramadeg: Vernacular Grammar and Grammarians in Medieval Ireland and Wales*, eds. Deborah Hayden and Paul Russell (Amsterdam: John Benjamins Publishing Company, 2016), 85–100. Alice R. Taylor-Griffiths, a doctoral candidate in the Department of Anglo-Saxon, Norse, and Celtic at the University of Cambridge, is currently conducting research on glossing and etymological glossing in the early Irish legal corpus.

129 Generally, *nós* refers to any custom or procedure that has been established by tradition or precedent; see *eDIL s.v.* 1 *nós* and cf. *eDIL s.v.* 1 *noes, naes, noís* 'law, custom, ordinance'. It it quite possible that the word intended in the OI text is *noes*, which is also spelled *nos*; both words were frequently confused for each other. It is also possible that *nós* and *noes* (and its variants) are all variant spellings of the same word.

130 For a discussion of this section, see the Introduction, 16.

131 The phrase *ris amuig* is more literally rendered '[holding] out aginst it'; I should like to thank Neil McLeod for discussion of this phrase.

132 Source B provides a list of the nobles who could establish a procedure or custom.

133 The sense of *séis* here refers to the nine people designing/planning the ordinance in much the same way that the glossing tradition refers to nine people composing the *Senchas Már*.

a tur*b*rod ł co rabat uile aca tur*b*rod. ⁊ iss *ed* fo*dera* a tur*b*rod can nech aca astad*h* u*air* da mb*eth* [nech][134] aca ast*ad* ni tur*b*ro[b]t*h*a[135] e.

Masa nos i*n*dligth*ech* doro*n*sat[136] in tuath, is [s]l*an*[137] dib a tur*b*rod iar tai*n*. ⁊ ce b*eth* æ*n* ł deda dib ris amuig do dligth*ech*aib, noc*h*an u*r*ail*enn* dliged orra taid*echt* fai, ⁊ da nda*m*tar dlig*ed*, *con*necat a tait*h*m*eth*.[138] ⁊ noc*h*a cui*m*get im*murro* na h-i*n*dligth*ig* na raibe f*or* a*ir*d tia*ch*ta*in* fai *con*da tait*h*m*eth*, *acht* nocha dleg*ar* doib ceana airisea*m* air A. [CIH 2148.3–14]

.i. nos dlig*thech* dorig*h*ned isin tuaith a*nd* sin: Noc*h*o dleg*ar* do neoch dib*h* a thur*b*rod, ⁊ da nderna, icaid er*aic* i*n*a tur*b*rod. ⁊ ge rob*eth* aen ł ded*h*e dib ris amuich, urailid*h* dlig*ed* orro tia*ch*t*ain fae, ⁊ da nderna a tur*b*rod, icad er*aic* i*n*a thur*b*rod. ⁊ gengo b*eth acht* ae*n*nonba*r* aga denam da mait*h*ib, robo besgna dlig*h*th*ech* hé u*air* nonba*r* bis a seis ui*m*e; *nocho* c*h*ui*m*gech a tur*b*rod *no* go robad uile aga thur*b*rod. ⁊ is *ed* fodera a thur*b*rod: Gan nech aga astad*h*, u*air* da *m*b*eth* nech aga ast*ad*, ni tur*b*roidthea he.

Masa nos i*n*dligth*ech* doronsad i*n* tuat*h*, is [s]lan doib a tur*b*rod. ⁊ ge rob*eth* aen ł deid*h*e ris amaig*h*, noc*h*on u*r*aile*n*d [dliged][139] orro tia*cht*a*in* fai, ⁊ da ndamth*ar* dlig*ed* doib, *conach* eagad [read *conecat*][140] a t*h*aithmech.

Nonba*r* dleg*ar* do dena*m* nosa dlig*h*t*h*igh .i. rí ⁊ fil*i* ⁊ briug*u* ⁊ eps*cop* ⁊ fer leig*h*i*n*d ⁊ oll*am* ⁊ aig*h*ne ⁊ *aire* forgill ⁊ *air*chindeach B. [CIH 979.42–980.11]

134 I follow the editorial suggestion made by Binchy, CIH 2148, n. b; cf. the commentary from source B.

135 See also Binchy, CIH 2148, n. c.

136 Although *doronsat* is the MI 3 pl. *s*-pret. of *do-gní*, it is used with the sg. subject *túath* because *túath* is being used here as a collective noun. Cf. the same construction in source B below. See Kim McCone, *The Early Irish Verb*, 2nd ed. (Maynooth: An Sagart, 1997), 234; and GOI § 539.

137 See also Binchy, CIH 2148, n. d.

138 Here and below for *taithmech*; see also Binchy, CIH 2148, n. e and cf. source B. *Taithmech* is the vn. of *do-aithbig*. The form *taithmeth* is a result of the sequence ⟨ech⟩ being misread at some point for ⟨eth⟩; within both sequences of letters, it can be very difficult to differentiate internal ⟨c⟩ from internal ⟨t⟩ in the Insualr script. In source A, the final syllable is written ⟨⁊̇⟩ for ⟨eth⟩, which is clearly a misreading of an earlier ⟨ech⟩ as ⟨eth⟩.

139 I follow the emendation suggested by Binchy, CIH 980, n. b; cf. the commentary from source A.

140 See Binchy, CIH 980, n. c and cf. source A.

cannot repudiate it until they all repudiate it. And the reason it is repudiated is that no one adhered to it, because if there were anyone adhering to it, it would not be repudiated.

If the *túath* established an unauthorized ordinance, they are free to repudiate it afterwards. And though there may be one or two of those [dignitaries] who are entitled [to propose a legal ordinance] opposing it, law does not require them to submit to it, and if the law is accepted, they are able to annul it. And the [dignitaries] who are unauthorized [to annul the ordinance] because [lit. who] they were not present [at the assembly] are not able, however, to repudiate it until it is annulled [by those dignitaries who were present], but it is not required for them, moreover, to abide by it A.

i.e. a lawful ordinance which was established in the *túath* in that case: None of them has the right to repudiate it, and if any should do so, he pays a fine for repudiating it. And though there may be one or two of them opposing it, law requires them to submit to it, and if any should repudiate it, let him pay a fine for repudiating it. And though there is only a group of nine dignitaries establishing it, it is a lawful custom because nine people are in agreement about it; [they] cannot repudiate it until all [of them] repudiate it. And the reason [for] its repudiation: No one adhered to it because if there were anyone adhering to it, it would not be repudiated.

If the *túath* established an unlawful ordinance, they are free to repudiate it. And though there might be one or two opposing it, [law] does not require them to submit to it, and if the law is accepted by them, they are able to annul it.

Nine people who are entitled to establish a lawful procedure, i.e. king and poet and hospitaller and bishop and head of a monastic school and chief poet and advocate and *aire forgill*[141] and monastic superior B.[142]

---

141 The 'lord of superior testimony' was the highest non-royal grade. For discussion of the position of the *aire forgill*; see CG, Legal Glossary, *s.v. aire forgill*.

142 A similar list is provided in § 8 of the *Pseudo-historical Prologue to the Senchas Már*. Although the list in source B is different, it still consists of three nobles, three men of learning, and three ecclesiastics like the list in the *Pseudo-historical Prologue*; see also Kim McCone, "Dubthach Maccu Lugair and a Matter of Life and Death in the Pseudo-historical Prologue to the *Senchas Már*," *Peritia* 5 (1986): 9; and D.A. Binchy, "The Pseudo-historical Prologue to the *Senchas Már*," *Studia Celtica* 10–11 (1975–1976): 22. The later Yellow Book of Lecan version of *Sanas Cormaic*, for the entry on *nós*, has the same list at the *Pseudo-historical Prologue*; see *Sanas Cormaic*, no. 970; the Early Irish Glossaries Database: http://www.asnc.cam.ac.uk/irishglossaries/texts.php?versionID=9&readingID=17964#17964. Accessed July 2, 2018.; and Carey, "An Edition of

.i. masa besgna ł nos[143] dlig*thech* darigned*h* acin tuaith, nucu dleg*ar* dib*h* a turbrod, ⁊ i*n*ti turbrabas he, icad*h* eraicc i*n*a turbrod. ⁊ cid*h* æn ł ded*h*a dib nabeith[144] i n-eccmais, uralid*h* dlig*ed* orro tuide*cht* fæ, ⁊ da turbrat he, icat eraicc ina turbrod*h*, ⁊ [...][145] na cu*mh*aing iat a turbrod*h* ł cu rabat uili 'ga turbrod*h*. ⁊ is *ed* fod*er*a a tu*r*brod*h* it*ir*, da nd*er*nta ca*n* nech aca[146] astud*h*, ⁊ da mbeith, nucu dige*n*ta. Masa nos inddlig*thech* he, nuccum [ḟ]uil eraic *air*i*n*ti[147] na raibi 'ca denu*m* i*n*a turb*r*od. ⁊ cid*h* æn ł ded*h*a dib*h* nabeith i*n*a ecmais, nucun uraileann*n* dlig*ed* orro tuid*hecht* fæ; cu*n*neccat dichur da n[d]amthar dliged*h* daib*h* C. [CIH 167.39–168.8]

---

the Pseudo-historical Prologue," 26. Neil McLeod notes that the tradition of nine people establishing a law code is also found in the Theodosian Code. While McLeod suggests that there is no evidence that the compilers of the *Senchas Már* borrowed from the Theodosian Code, the reign of Theodosius is mentioned in the *Pseudo-historical Prologue to the Senchas Már* at CIH 339.17; *idem*, "External Influences on Medieval Irish Law: AD 600–1600," *Australian Celtic Journal* 11 (2013): 34–35.

143 The scribe wrote ⟨gna⟩ after ⟨nos⟩ but indicated their proper position with reference marks; see also Binchy, CIH 167, n. j.

144 The form *nabeith* shows the MI confusion between *no-*, *ro-*, and *do-*; McCone, *The Early Irish Verb*, 196–197.

145 Based on the corresponding material in source B, the scribe of C has left out a few clauses; see also Binchy, CIH 168, n. a.

146 The second ⟨a⟩ is written subscript.

147 Between the ⟨t⟩ and the ⟨i⟩, the scribe wrote a ⟨h⟩, which he deleted by putting a *punctum delens* under it.

i.e. if a lawful custom or ordinance was established by the *túath*, [none] of them has the right to repudiate it, and the one who repudiates it, let him pay a fine for repudiating it. And though one or two of them may be absent [i.e. from the assembly], law requires them to submit to it, and if they should repudiate it, let them pay a fine for repudiating it, and …[148] they are not capable of repudiating it until they all repudiate it. And the reason for repudiating it at all, if they have established it, [is when there is] no one adhering to it, and if there may be, they are not able to do so [i.e. to repudiate it].

If it is an unauthorized ordinance, no fine for its repudiation is imposed on the one who was not there when it was established. And though one or two of them might be absent from it [i.e. the assembly], law does not require them to submit to it; they are able to renounce [it] if the law is accepted by them C.

148 A clause or two is missing here; cf. the two commentaries above.

§7 Condall[149] coecdac*h* is *cethorch*at do bl*iadna* .⁊rl-.

p. 9a Cuic coecait it*er* cach da gelfi*ne* g*r*aid ecl*as*a et*arru* fei*n*, *ceithri*[150] *coec*ait[151] it*er* gelfi*ne* ⁊ derbfi*ne*, t*ri* *coecait* it*er* *gelfini*[152] ⁊ iarf*ini*, da *coecait* it*er* *gelfini* ⁊ i*n*dfine, *coeca* it*er* *gelfini* ⁊ ai*n*fine, *coeca* it*er* cach da n-a*n*f*ini* g*r*aid ecl*as*a.[153] Cuic *cethorcha*it[154] it*er* da gelf*ini* g*r*aid tuait*he* et*arru* buden, *ceith*ri *cethorcha*it[155] it*er* gel*ḟini* ⁊ derbfi*ne*, t*ri* *cethorchait*[156] it*er* gel*ḟini* ⁊ i*ar*fi*ne*, da (.lx.) *cethorchait*[157] it*er* gel*ḟini* ⁊ i*n*dfi*ne*, (.lx.) *cethorchait*[158] it*er*[159] *gelḟini* ⁊ anfi*ne*, (.lx.) *cethorchait*[160] it*er* cac*h* da n-anfi*ne* g*r*aid tuait*he*.

---

1 Condull **A**. **K** does not contain any of the text. The commentary from **K** is part of a section headed *taithmeach rudhartha* 'dissolving of a prescriptive right'. ‖ .l.ach **J**. **A** contains no further words from the text. The fragment of the text from **A** is written at the bottom of p. 8b. ‖ .xxxx.at **J**.

---

149 *Condall* might be a form of *condail*, which is perhaps the vn. of *con-dáili*, 'division, share'; see *eDIL s.vv.* 1 *condail* and *con-dáili*. Alternatively, *eDIL s.v. condall* 'stalk, stubble aftermath' queries whether the form found in *Anfuigell* has a specific legal meaning; *eDIL* cites this passage, but offers no suggestions, and references *connlán* 'band, assembly, troop', which is derived from *condall*. If one accepts the meaning 'assembly', then the passage may be concerned with the proportional representation of each division of the kindred (metaphorically reckoned also for ecclesiastics), with the lowest representation for the more distant kindred. The specific interpretation of this section is obscure to me.

150 After the OI period, the forms *ceithri* and *cethra* are used for all genders and cases; see *eDIL s.v. cethair*.

151 The text abbreviates the form as '.l.ait'.

152 The text uses the abbreviation 'g.f.' for *gelḟine*.

153 Source A does not contain the sequence ⟨ł a⟩ as printed in *CIH* 2148.18. Binchy counted the last two syllables (the first of which is suspended) of *eclasa* twice.

154 The ⟨it⟩ are written above the line.

155 The scribe originally wrote '.xxx.', then added ⟨it⟩ above the Roman numerals. The correct number should be the gen. pl. of 40. The scribe later added one more ⟨x⟩ above the line in front of ⟨it⟩, thus providing the correct number. In this section we can see the not uncommon confusion of Roman numerals in the legal commentaries.

156 The scribe later corrected '.lx.' to '.xl.' by inserting the correction above the line with a reference mark; Binchy does not note this correction, although he does print the corrected text at *CIH* 2148.20.

157 The scribe later corrected '.lx.' to '.xl.' by inserting the correction above the line with a reference mark; Binchy, *CIH* 2148, n. h, comments on this correction and the other two below.

158 The scribe later corrected '.lx.' to '.xl.' for a third time employing the same method of correction.

159 The word *iter* is added in *marg. dext.*; see also Binchy, *CIH* 2148, n. i.

160 The scribe corrected '.lx.' to '.xl.' for the fourth time by putting the corrected text *marg. sin.*

§7 Assembly of fifties and forties for a year, etc.[161]

Five fifties between each two *gelḟine*s of the ecclesiastical grade among themselves, four fifties between *gelḟine* and *derbḟine*, three fifties between *gelḟine* and *íarfine*, two fifties between *gelḟine* and *indḟine*, fifty between *gelḟine* and *ainfine*,[162] fifty between each two *ainfine*s of the ecclesiastical grade. Five forties between [each] two *gelḟine*s of the lay grade among themselves, four forties between *gelḟine* and *derbḟine*, three forties between *gelḟine* and *íarfine*, two forties between *gelḟine* and *indḟine*, forty between *gelḟine* and *ainfine*, forty between each two *ainfine*s of the lay grade. p. 9a

161 For a discussion of this section, see the Introduction, 16.

162 The word *ainfine* refers to a 'stranger kindred'; see *eDIL* s.v. 1 *ainfine*.

In cutr*uma* bias it*er* gel*ḟini* ⁊ d*er*bfi*ne* gurab i*n* cutr*uma*-si*n* bias it*er* d*er*bfi*ne* ⁊ i*ar*fi*ne* ⁊ it*er* i*ar*fi*ne* ⁊ i*n*dfi*ne*; ⁊ i*n* cutr*uma* bias it*er* gelfi*ne* et*ar*ru bude*n* cu*r*ub i*n* cutr*uma*-si*n* bias it*er* d*er*bfi*ne* et*ar*ru fe*n* ⁊ i*n* cac*h* fi*ne* at*ar*ru fei*n* u*air* gelfi*ne* cac*h* fi*ne* i*n*dte fadesi*n* A. [*CIH* 2148.15–25]

.i. cuig *coec*at it*er* g*ac* da geilfi*ne*[163] g*r*aid*h* ecl*as*a et*ar*ru fein, ceit*h*re *coec*at it*er* geilfine ⁊ derb*h*fi*ne*, t*r*i *coecat* it*er* gelfine ⁊ i*ar*fine, da *coecat* it*er* *gelfini* ⁊ in*n*f*ini*, cæg*a* it*er* *gelfini* ⁊ ainf*ini*, cæg*a* it*er* g*ac* da ai*n*fine gr*aid* ecl*as*a. Cuig cet*hr*acit it*er* da ge*l*fine g*r*aid*h* tuait*h*e et*ar*ru budei*n*, ceit*h*re *cethracit* iter *gelfini* ⁊ derb*h*fine, t*r*i *cethracit* iter *gelfini* ⁊ iarfine, da *cethracit* iter *gelfini* ⁊ in*n*f*ini*, cet*h*racit it*er* *gelfini* ⁊ ainf*ini*, cethr*a*cit eit*er* da anf*ini* g*r*aid*h* *tuait*he et*ar*ru fei*n*.

In cutr*uma* bes it*er* *gelfini* ⁊ derb*h*fi*ne* gu*r*ab e in cutr*uma*-si*n* bes it*er* derbfi*ne* ⁊ i*arfini* ⁊ it*er* i*arfini* ⁊ in*nfini*; ⁊ in cutr*uma* bes it*er* *gelfini* et*ar*ru budei*n* gu*r*ab e in cutr*uma*-si*n* bes it*er* d*er*b*h*fine et*ar*ru fei*n* ⁊ i *ngach* fine et*ar*ru fei*n* u*air* *gelfine* g*ac* fi*ne* in*n*te fadeisi*n* J. [*CIH* 2026.3–13]

Cuig cæcait itir gac*h* da geilfini g*r*aid*h* ecailsi et*ar*ro budein, ceit*r*i cæccait it*er* geilfi*ne* ⁊ deirb*h*fine, t*r*i cæcait it*er* geilfine ⁊ i*ar*fine, da[164] cæca it*er* geilfine ⁊ indfi*ne*, caeca it*er* geil | K.[165] [*CIH* 190.35–37]

163 The first ⟨i⟩ is written subscript. In the sequence ⟨ei⟩, the scribe consistently writes the ⟨i⟩ subscript.

164 The word *da* was added above the line with reference marks; see also Binchy, *CIH* 190, n. d.

165 The text ends abruptly at the bottom of column 62d. This is the last vellum page of the manuscript; Ó Cuív, *Catalogue of Irish Manuscripts in the Bodleian*, 215.

The proportion that is between *gelḟine* and *derbḟine* is the [same] proportion that is between *derbḟine* and *íarfine* and between *íarfine* and *indḟine*; and the proportion that is between *gelḟine*s among themselves is the [same] proportion that is between *derbḟine*s among themselves and for each *fine*[166] among themselves because each *fine* [has] a *gelḟine* in itself A.[167]

i.e. five fifties between each two *gelḟine*s of the ecclesiastical grade among themselves, four fifties between *gelḟine* and *derbḟine*, three fifties between *gelḟine* and *íarfine*, two fifties between *gelḟine* and *indḟine*, fifty between *gelḟine* and *ainfine*, fifty between each two *ainfine*s of the ecclesiastical grade. Five forties between each two *gelḟine*s of the lay grade among themselves, four forties between *gelḟine* and *derbḟine*, three forties between *gelḟine* and *íarfine*, two forties between *gelḟine* and *indḟine*, forty between *gelḟine* and *ainfine*, forty between [each] two *ainfine*s of the lay grades among themselves.

The proportion that is between *gelḟine* and *derbḟine* is the [same] proportion that is between *derbḟine* and *íarfine* and between *íarfine* and *indḟine*; and the proportion that is between *gelḟine*s themselves is the [same] proportion that is between *derbḟine*s themselves and in each *fine* among themselves because each *fine* [has] a *gelḟine* in itself J.

Five fifties between each two *gelḟine*s of the ecclesiastical grade among themselves, four fifties between *gelḟine* and *derbḟine*, three fifties between *gelḟine* and *íarfine*, two fifties between *gelḟine* and *indḟine*, fifty between *gel*[*ḟine*] | K.[168]

166 *Fine* can refer to both a kinsman and the kindred in general; see *eDIL s.v.* 1 *fine*.

167 O'Donovan notes in his translation of this commentary (p. 159) that the material deals with the "succession to ecclesiastical and lay lands" and that a better version is found in TCD MS 1338, *olim* H.3.17, col. 545, which is source J (*CIH* 2026.3–13) translated below. That being said, the material in both commentaries is identical apart from the fact that the language in J is a little later than that in A.

168 The text breaks off incomplete.

§8 Collud sida, sid*h* i*ar* ng*air* snad*h*ad do diguin isren*ur*, cia dosli dilsi i*n* chai*ch* ima ndigonur and

Mas[169] aircsi ⁊ atac*h* ⁊ tairgsi dlig*id*, ce b*eth*[170] ce*n*go[171] b*eth* i*n* com*airce* i maigi*n*, is lan*e*necl*ann* an*n* do*n* com*airci*.

Masa aircsi ⁊ tairgsi[172] dlig*id*, ⁊ i*n* com*airce* i maigi*n*, is l*eth*e*n*ecl*ann* an*n* do*n* com*airci*. ⁊ mai*n*e fuil in co*mairce* a maigi*n*, is [s]l*an*, ⁊ is e-si*n* ni digui*n* nabi di *m*aigi*n* nabi di gu*air*e,[173] gaibes gi*n*. Gia b*eth* airgsi ⁊ atac*h*, mai*n*e fuil tairgsi dlig*id*, noc*h*an am*al* t*ar*ba. Dilsig si*n* uile ⁊ *cona m*b*eth* ar com*airci*, ⁊ dai*n*e bud sl*an* do tab*air*t on altoir maine betis f*or* com*airci*.

1 Collod*h* **B**. I and HH do not contain any of the OI text. ‖ sid*h*a ⁊rl- **B**, sid*h*a **L**. The text ends at this point in **A** and **B**, although **B** resumes after a gap of three words at *CIH* 980.15. The remainder of the OI text has been supplied from source **L**. ‖ Snad*h*ud*h* **B**. ‖ digu*in* **B**. The text ends at this point in **B**.

169 Material similar to that in the commentaries from sources A and B can be found in *CIH* 138.34–139.31; see *CCIH*, 18.

170 The words *ce beth* were added in *marg. dext.*; see also Binchy, *CIH* 2148, n. i.

171 The ⟨go⟩ were inserted above the line by the scribe; see also Binchy, *CIH* 2148, n. k.

172 The ⟨t⟩ was inserted above the line by the scribe; see also Binchy, *CIH* 2148, n. l.

173 Cf. *CIH* 1436.22–23 'Ni digui*n* nabi do maigi*n* nabi do guaire gaibhus gin'; see also *eDIL s.v. gúairiugud* and *CIH* 1347.6, 20, and 22 for the gen sg. form *guairethi*. The form *guaire* possibly is a shortened form of *gúairiugud* 'false imprisonment'; during the MI period, lenited /g/ and /d/ became /∅/ word internally and finally, which could result in the shortened form seen here.

§8 Violation of peace, a peace-offering[174] is paid after a cry that protection has been violated, although each who is violated there is entitled to a claim [of compensation][175]

If it is seeking[176] and refuge and offering of law;[177] whether or not the protector[178] may be in a precinct,[179] it is full honor-price then [that is paid] to the protector.

If it is seeking and offering of law, and the protector [is] in a precinct, it is half honor-price then [that is paid] to the protector. And if the protector is not in a precinct, he is exempt from legal liability [i.e. the one who violates the protection], and that is not violation of protection when he [i.e. the protector] is away from the precinct or when there is false imprisonment, [this is what the] book has. Although there may be seeking and refuge, if there is not an offering of law, it is not like a benefit. These are all [as] culprits[180] and are not under protection, and people whom it would be lawful to take from the altar[181] if they were not under protection.

---

174 The word *síd* is used here to refer to the compensation owed for violating someone's protection.

175 For a discussion of this section, see the Introduction, 16–17.

176 Although *aircsiu* is the usual legal term for the crime of looking on while an offense takes place (*eDIL s.v. aircsiu*), the commentary (below) explains the word as the act of looking for legal protection.

177 The phrase *taircsiu dligid* refers to the act of offering an appeal to law or being open to a legal settlement. In terms of the procedure for legal sanctuary, one must seek protection, acquire protection, and then agree to bring the matter to a judge or other qualified person to negotiate a legal settlement. Frequently the neutral third party with whom one has protection helps guide all parties through the process; see McLeod, "The Blood-Feud in Medieval Ireland," 118–120.

178 This passage is complicated by the fact that *commairge* can refer to both the person providing protection and the protection/refuge itself. In this section, the word switches between both meanings.

179 For a discussion of providing someone with legal protection, see GEIL, 140–141. Every freeman is able to offer protection to anyone of equal or lower rank; see GEIL, 141 for exceptions to this principle. The protection extends not just to the house, but also to the area (precinct) around the house. If a person is harmed within the precinct, the perpetrator owes compensation to the injured party for the injury and must also pay the householder compensation for violating his protection (*díguin*). See also CG, Legal Glossary, *s.v. díguin*; and McLeod, "The Blood-Feud in Medieval Ireland," 116–117.

180 The word *dílsech* can refer not just to an outlaw, but also to any person who is considered a culprit, guilty, or otherwise deprived of legal rights; see *eDIL s.v. dílsech*.

181 Cf. §52.

Inan*n* dilsec*h* f*or* co*mairci* co t*airg*si*n* dlig*id* ⁊ i*n*dil(si)*sech*[182] for co*mairci* (co) cin[183] tairgsi*n* dl*igid* im lanenecl*ainn* i ce*chtar* de. ⁊ ciama[d] dils*ech* e, iss *ed* dleg*ar* gell i*n* corp*diri* a lai*m* na[184] com*airce no* co tair dlig*ed* et*ar*ru ⁊rl- Lan*e*necl*ann* isi*n* dils*ech* a ci*n*d cilli ⁊ i *n*du*n* rig ⁊ a t*r*eb *air*ech, ⁊ lan i fiad*naise* ⁊ l*eth* a maigi*n* ⁊ in æ*n*mad ran*n fichit sechtar* maigi*n*. ⁊ les i*n* fer*ann* *secht*[ar] m*aigin*[185] an*n* si*n*, ⁊ manbud les, noc*h*a biad nac*h* ni do. A dualg*us* fiad*naise* ł ferai*n*d ata si*n* isi*n* dils*ech* ⁊ ni[186] a dualg*us* com*air*ce. Fis ⁊ anfis na com*airce* do riag*lad* a l*eth* risi*n* dilsech: *Acht* ma rofit*ir* a b*eth* ar com*airci*, is lanencl*ann* do*n* com*airci* an*n*. Mai*n*e fit*ir*, is [s]l*an*.

Int i*n*dils*ech* im*murro*, cia rofit*ir* gi*n*co fit*ir* a b*eth* ar com*airci*, is lanencl*ann* an*n* do*n* co*mair*ci. Sl*an* in dia*n*s*ar*ug*ud*, ⁊ sl*an* anfis na com*airce*, ⁊ sl*an* in com*airce* borblachais.

⁊ iss *ed* is diansar*ugud* an*n* a rad na de*m*ad dlig*ed*, ⁊ nocha leg*ar*[187] do re do ead*h* risa t*airsed* do dlig*ed* do tairgsi*n* uad fei*n* ł o*n*ti ara ta com*air*ge.

Is *ed* is a*n*fis com*airce* an*n*: Noc*h*an [ḟ]it*ir*[188] a b*eth* ar com*airci*.

Is *ed* is com*airce* borbl*achais* an*n* a rad na de*m*ad dlig*ed* ł 'da fagai*n*d slige t*r*et culfeit*h*, dob*er*ai*n*d i*n*de'.[189] & cid sl*an* na nechi-si*n* i l*eth* risi*n* co*mairci*, noc*h*a sl*an* gan er*aic* na fogla doronad an*n* d'ic.

Is *ed* is at*ach* and a rad 'atai*m* for co*mairci*'.

182 See also Binchy, *CIH* 2148, n. m.

183 A later hand added the correction above the line; Binchy, *CIH* 2148, n. h notes the correction but not the hand change.

184 The ⟨a⟩ is written subscript.

185 I follow the editorial suggestion of Binchy, *CIH* 2148, n. n.

186 The word *ni* was inserted above the line by the scribe; see also Binchy, *CIH* 2148, n. o.

187 Binchy, *CIH* 2149.6 questions his expansion of the final syllable. O'Donovan transcribes 'leg*ad*'.

188 I follow the emendation suggested by Binchy, *CIH* 2149, n. b.

189 Binchy, *CIH* 2149, n. c, is uncertain whether these letters should be divided as 'ind e' or 'i nde'; O'Donovan transcribes them as 'ind é'.

It is the same for the culprit[190] under protection with offering of law and the lawful person under protection without offering of law regarding full honor-price for each of them. And though he is a culprit, a pledge of the body-fine is required from the hand of the protector until law comes between them, etc. Full honor-price for the culprit within a church's boundary and in a king's fort and in a chief's household, and full [honor-price] in [front of a] witness and half in a precinct and a twenty-first outside a precinct. And [the protector is] with him in the land outside the precinct in that case, and if he [i.e. the protector] is not with him, there is nothing for him.[191] That is by right of witness or land regarding the culprit and not by right of protection.

Knowledge and ignorance of the protection regarding legislating with respect to the culprit: But if he [i.e. the one who violates the protection] knows that he is under protection, it is full honor-price for the protector then. If he does not know, he [i.e. the one who violates the protection] is exempt from legal liability.

The lawful person, whether or not he [i.e. the one who violates the protection] knows he [i.e. the lawful person] is under protection, it is full honor-price then for the protector. Exempt from legal liability [is] the forcible violation, and exempt from legal liability [is] ignorance of the protection, and exempt from legal liability [is] violent protection.

And this is what is forcible violation then, his saying that he would not yield to law, and he is not allowed time for which he should come to offer a legal settlement from him himself or from the one under whom there is protection.

This is what is ignorance of protection then: He does not know that he is under protection.

This is what is violent protection then, his saying that he would not yield to law or 'if he is slaughtered by a host behind your back, I would give compensation for it'. And though those things are exempt from legal liability in respect to protection, he [i.e. the one who violates the protection] is not exempt from paying the fine of the injury he would make there.

This is what is refuge, then, his saying 'I am under protection'.

---

190 Here, as above and below, the sense is not strictly 'outlaw' so much as 'culprit, guilty party, one outside the law'.

191 The sense here is that the culprit must be in the company of his protector while outside the inner precinct. If not, he can be killed without penalty.

Is *ed* is airgsi an*n*, a faicsi*n* re cois na com*airce* an*n* si*n* ł re*m*e.

Is *ed* is t*air*gsi an*n*, tairgsi dlig*id* aige fei*n* ł aca*n* com*airci*. Dilsig[192] si*n* mai*n*e be*th*is f*or* co*mairci*.

Is cutr*um*a gab*us* gre*im* i l*eth* risi*n* com*airci* dlig*ed* do tairgsi*n* di budei*n* ⁊ do*n*ti ata arin[193] com*airci*. ⁊ o bias[194] fis na com*airce* ⁊ tairgsi dlig*id*, ce b*eth* ci*n*co be i*n* com*airce* i maigin, is lane*n*ecl*ann* an*n* do*n* com*air*ce. Urias*acht*[195] na co*mairce* do co*mar*leg*ud*, cid a maigi*n* cid a *secht*ir *m*aigi*n*, is lane*n*ecl*ann* an*n* do*n* com*airci*. Airgsi ⁊ at*ach* ⁊ tairgsi dlig*id* ac dils*ech*; *airc*siu ⁊ at*ach* ac indil*sech*, ⁊ nochon fuil t*air*gsi dlig*id*, uair noc*h*an fuil aice ni 'ma t*air*g[s]en*n* dlig*ed*.

p. 9b Ma tait aræ*n* ac indilsech, .i. *air*gsi ⁊ at*ach*, is laneneclann an*n* do*n* com*airci*. Muna fuil [acht neachtar de],[196] is l*eth*e*n*ecl*ann*. ⁊ mu*n*a fuil ni dib, is [s]l*an*. No, ci*n*co b*eth* ni dib-si*n* an*n*, co mb*eth* lane*n*ecl*ann* do*n* co*mairci* a dualg*us* fog*l*a re h-i*n*dils*ech*. Masa tairgsi dlig*id* ce*n* at*ach* ce*n* airgsi, aisec na *sét* rug*ad* do *m*uin na co*mairce*, ⁊ toibget*ar* i*n* com*airce* corp*díre* i*n*ti rom*ar*ba, ⁊ co*mar*dug*ud* ci*n* frith*aigid* et*ar*ru A. [*CIH* 2148.26–2149.26]

.i. fl*aith* doc*h*uaid*h* do dena*m* c*h*ana t*ar* cen*n* a t*h*uait*h*i a*n*d sin, ⁊ ma rotur-b*r*od*ar* luc*ht* na tuaithe hi, is sma*cht* t*u*rb*r*od*h*t*h*i cana i*ar*na h-esg*air*e uai-t*h*ib*h*.

Masa[197] atach ⁊ *air*cse ⁊ t*air*cse dlig*id* ⁊ co*mair*ce a maigi*n*, is laneneclan*n* don co*mair*ce a *m*aigi*n*.

Et damdis i*n*d*í*lsi iad im*murro*, robo lan a t*r*eib ⁊ i fiadnaisi | B.[198] [*CIH* 980.12–17]

192 The ⟨g⟩ was inserted above the line in the same later hand that has made other corrections to the text; Binchy, *CIH* 2149, n. d, notes the correction but not the change in hand.

193 The ⟨in⟩ were inserted above the line by the scribe; see also Binchy, *CIH* 2149, n. e.

194 The ⟨a⟩ is written subscript.

195 Binchy, *CIH* 2149.16 questions his expansion of the final syllable; O'Donovan expands the final syllable the same way Binchy does. See source I below.

196 See source I, *CIH* 1558.7 and the editorial suggestion of Binchy, *CIH* 2149, n. g.

197 This commentary starts at *CIH* 980.15.

198 The text breaks off incomplete at this point in the MS at p. 436b.

This is what is seeking then, his looking for the protection immediately in that case or previously.

This is what is offering then, offering of law by him himself or by the protector. Those are [as] culprits if they were not under protection.

The obligation is the same with regard to the protector to [make an] offer of law himself and to the one who is under protection. And when there will be knowledge of the protection and offer of law, whether or nor the protector may be in the precinct, it is full honor-price then for the protector. [If he has] the protector's permission to leave, whether in a precinct or outside a precinct, it is full honor-price then for the protector. Seeking and refuge and offering of law by the culprit; seeking and refuge by the lawful man, and there is not offering of law because he does not have anything regarding which to offer to law.

If the lawful person has both, i.e. seeking and refuge, it is full honor-price then for the protector. If he has [only] one of them, it is half honor-price. And if he has none of them, he is exempt from legal liability. Or, although he would have none of those then, there would be full honor-price for the protector in compensation for injury to the lawful person. If there is offering of law without refuge, without seeking, restitution of the *sét*s which were guaranteed by the protector, and the protector exacts body-fine from the one who murdered, and a balancing of liabilities between them without counterclaims A. p. 9b

i.e. a lord who went to make a law on behalf of his *túath* in that case, and if it was violated by the people of the *túath*, there is a fine for violation of the law according to the proclamation [made] by them.

If it is refuge and seeking and offering of law and protection in a precinct, it is full honor-price for the protector in a precinct.

And if they were unlawful, however, it is full [honor-price] in a household and in presence of | B.[199]

199 The commentary breaks off here.

Slan[200] do ca*ch* gr*ad* tuaithe i*m* co*m*airci do denu*m* cein bes t*air*igsi[201] dligid, ⁊ mu*n*a be tairigsi dlig*id*, is fiach didi*n*. Cinco be tairigsi dlig*id* im*murro*, is [s]l*an* do*n*n ecl*ais* frisna reib am*ail* atbeir cain, ⁊ fiach didi*n* i*ar*sna reib
p. 57a am*al* in tuath.[202] | ⁊ *no*chan eicin atach ł aircsi ł taircsi dlig*id* ag indilsech.

Is *ed* is atach and a rad*h* 'ataim f*or* com*air*ce'.

Is *ed* is *air*csi a*n*d, .i. faicsin na com*air*ce re cois in uair-sin ł reime.

Is *ed* is taircsi[203] dlig*id* and, .i. t*air*csi dlig*id* aici fein ł acan com*air*ce.

Iss *ed* is diansa*r*u(du)g*ud*[204] and: Rofitir a b*eth* for com*airci* ⁊ *noch*a ranaic uada dligi[d] do taircsin.

Iss *ed* is anfis com*air*ce and: Ni fitir a b*eth* for comairci.

& is cutruma geibis gr*ei*m a leith risin comhairci dligi do taircsin di budein ⁊ do*n*tí ata forin comairci.

Iss *ed* is co*m*airci borblac*h*ais and: Neimdeiti*n* dlig*id* an co*m*air*ci.

Uriasacht na co*m*air*ci (*co*na) [do][205] co*m*arleca, cid a maigin cid a *sechtar*
p. 57b maigi*n*, is lanenecland an*n* don co*ma*[i]*r*(i)ci. Ai(*a*)*r*icsi[206] ⁊ atac*h* | ⁊ t*air*gsi dlig*id* ac dilsich.

Aircsi ⁊ atach ic indilsich,[207] ⁊ ni fuil taircsi u*air no*con [ḟ]uil aici ní ima tairc[s]i dligi.

Ma táit aroen oc indilsich[208] *air*csi ⁊ atach, is lan[en]ecland[209] and do*n* com*air*ci.

Mun fuil *acht* nea*chtar*de dib aici, is leath[en]ecland.[210]

Munu fuil ní dib-si*n* it*ir*, is [s]l*an*; ł d*an*o chena cinco beith ní díb-si*n* aici. Co *m*beith laneneacl*ann* and don com*airci* a dualgus fod*h*la indilsi I. [*CIH* I 1557.31–1558.9]

200 Cf. also Appendix 2, *CCIH*, 470.14–471.10, TCD MS 1337, *olim* H.3.18, p. 662a.
201 The ⟨g⟩ was added below the line by the scribe; see also Binchy, *CIH* 1557, n. k.
202 The ⟨u⟩ was added below the line by the scribe; see also Binchy, *CIH* 1557, n. l.
203 The first ⟨i⟩ is written superscript.
204 I follow the editorial suggestion made by Binchy, *CIH* 1557, n. m.
205 Cf. source A, *CIH* 2149.17 *do*.
206 See also Binchy, *CIH* 1558, n. a.
207 There is a black stain, possibly ink, after the ⟨d⟩ and the ⟨il⟩ are very hard to see.
208 'oc indilsich' against *CIH* 1558.6 'ocon dilsich'; cf. source A above.
209 See also Binchy, *CIH* 1558, n. b.
210 See previous note.

Exempt from legal liability for each grade of a *túath* regarding performing [the duties of] protector as long as there is offering of law, and if there is not offering of law, there is debt of protection. Though he may not offer law, however, the Church is exempt from legal liability for the times as the law says, and debt of protection according to the times as the *túath*. | And not by p. 57a
compulsion [should there be] refuge or seeking or offering of law by a lawful person.

This is what refuge is then, his saying 'I am under protection'.

This is what seeking is then, i.e. searching for the protector close to that time or previously.

This is what offering of law is then, i.e. offering of law by him himself or by the protector.

This is what forcible violation is then: He knows that he is under protection and he was unable to offer law.

This is what ignorance of protection is then: He [i.e. the one who violates protection] does not know that he is under protection.

And the obligation in regards to the protector to offer an appeal to law himself is the same as the one who is under the protection.

This is what violent protection is then: Not recognizing the right of the protector.

[If he has] the protector's permission to leave, whether in a precinct or outside a precinct, it is full honor-price then for the protector. Seeking and refuge | and offering of law by the culprit. p. 57b

Seeking and refuge by the lawful person, and there is not offering of law because he does not have anything regarding his offering of law.

If the lawful person has seeking and refuge at the same time, it is full honor-price then for the protector.

If he only has one of those two, it is half honor-price [for the protector].

If he does not have any of those at all, he [i.e. the violator] is exempt from legal liability; or moreover in the case that he does not have any of those. There is full honor-price then for the protector in compensation for injury to a lawful person I.

.i. is uais[211] ernith*er* na s*ét*, no in coirp*díre*, ł geall in coirp*diri* ⁊ na ene*clainne* a laim na com*airce*, cia tuillt*er* ł cia *ar*illnith*er* dilsi in caich ima nderna in s*arugud* co t*ar* dligh*i* it*er* in lu*cht* dorinde in m*arbad* ⁊ fine[212] in lo*cht*a rom*ar*b*ad* and. ł ernith*er* lanene*clann* don com*airci* cia tuillt*er* ł cia *arr*illnit*er* dilsi intí robui *ar*in com*airci*.

Inand dilsec *ar* com*airci*[213] gu t*ar*gsi*n* dlig*h*i ⁊ in*n*dilsec f*or* com*airci* gin t*ar*gsi*n* dlig*h*i im lanene*clainn* do*n* co*mairci* a ce*ch*t*ar* de uair nochan fuil aigi ní 'ma t*arg*[s]*inn* dlig*h*i.

Uair lan*e*necl*ann* isi*n* n-i*n*dilsec*h* a cin*n* cill*e* ⁊ a ndun rig*h* ⁊ a t*r*eib*h* aireac*h*,[214] ⁊ lan i fiad*naise* ⁊ l*eth* a maig*in* ⁊ an æ*n*m*ad* ran*n* *fich*it a *sechtar* m*aigin*. ⁊ a dualg*us* fiad*nai*si no ferai*nn* ata si*n* isi*n* n-i*n*dilsec*h*, ⁊ noc*h*a[n a][215] dualg*us* comairce. ⁊ fis ⁊ anfis na com*airce* do riagailt reisi*n* n-i*n*dilsec*h*. ⁊ lanene*clann* ontí dorin*n*e in s*a*rug*h*[ud] ma rofit*ir* a b*eth* *ar* com*airci*, ⁊ man fit*ir* is [s]l*an* do. ⁊ cia rofit*ir* gi*n*go fit*ir* i*n*t i*n*dilsec*h* do b*eth* f*or* com*airci*, go mb*eth* ene*clann* an*n*.[216] ł d*an*o gom*ad* sl*an* ai*n*fis ce*ch*t*ar* de L. [*CIH* 1431.15–31]

In m*h*aig*hen* dig*h*ona-so i*n*niseas leob*ur* dona grad*h*aib*h*: Mas *ar* cu*mair*ce
f. 40c atat na daine | resa *n*dernad*h* in fog*h*al, gid*h* m*ar*b*h*ad*h* gid cnedug[ud](al)[217] gid seoit ruccad*h* uaithi[b], is aircsiu ⁊ atac*h* ⁊ t*air*csiu dlig*h*id*h* du riagail i lleit*h* risi*n* com*airgh*e an*n*.

Ma tat a t*r*iur an*n* is lan n-ei*n*ecl*ainn*e dona co*mair*gib an*n* gid*h* a maig*h*in gid*h* *sechtar* maig*h*in. Masa atach ⁊ aircsiu dlig*id* is let*h*enecl*ann* do*n* comairge an*n* gid a maig*hin* gid*h* *sechtar* maig*h*in.

Masa aircsiu ⁊ taircsiu dlig*h*id, mas a maig*h*in, is let*h*enecclan*n* do*n* com*airgh*e and. Masa *sechtar* maig*h*in, is [s]lan gen ni do*n* comairg*h*e an*n*. Dilsig*h* se*n* mai*n*e beitis f*or* com*airgh*e.

---

211 The words *icus ł*, which followed *uais*, have been expunged by placing a *punctum delens* under each letter; see also Binchy, *CIH* 1431, n. g.

212 Binchy, *CIH* 1431, n. h suggests that the lenition mark over the suspension is an error.

213 The words *ar comairci* were written in *marg. sin.* with references marks; see also Binchy, *CIH* 1431, n. i.

214 The second ⟨a⟩ is written subscript.

215 I follow the emendation suggested by Binchy, *CIH* 1431, n. j.

216 The word *ann* was written in *marg. sin.* with reference marks; see also Binchy, *CIH* 1431, n. i.

217 I follow the emendation suggested by Binchy, *CIH* 138, n. d.

i.e. it is *úais* 'nobly' the *sét ernither* 'is paid',[218] or the body-fine, or a pledge of the body-fine and of the honor-price in the hand of the protector, whether each deserves or merits a claim regarding the violation made in contempt of law between the people who did the killing and the kin-group of the people killed there. Or full honor-price is paid to the protector whether the one who was under the protection deserves or merits a claim.

It is the same for the culprit under protection who offers law and the lawful person under protection who does not offer law regarding full honor-price for the protector for each of them because he does not have anything regarding his offering of law.

Because [it is] full honor-price for the lawful person within a church's boundary and in a king's fort and in a noble's household, and full [honor-price] in the presence of [a witness] and half in a precinct and a twenty-first outside a precinct. And that is for the lawful person by right of witness or land, and not by right of a protector. And knowledge or ignorance of the protection regarding legislating with respect to the lawful person. And full honor-price from the one who made the violation if he knew that he was under protection, and if he did not know, he is exempt from legal liability. And whether or not he knew the lawful person to be under protection, there is honor-price then, or there is no liability for each of them on account of ignorance L.

[Regarding] the area around a house under an owner's protection, the book about the grades[219] says: If the people | against whom the injury was made, f. 40c
whether killing or wounding or their chattels were taken from them, are under protection, it is seeking and refuge and offering of law according to the law because of the protector then.

If [those] three things are there, it is full honor-price for the protectors then whether in a precinct or outside a precinct. If there is refuge and offering of law, it is half honor-price for the protector then whether in a precinct or outside a precinct.

If there is seeking and offering of law, if it is in a precinct, it is half honor-price for the protector then. If it is outside a precinct, he [i.e. the one who violates the protection] is exempt from legal liability without anything [i.e. a fine] for the protector then. Those people are as culprits if they are not under protection.

218 *Uais ernid* is a frequent Isidorean-style etymological gloss on *as-ren* 'pays'.

219 I have not been able to identify this source.

Masa indilseac*h* [ḟ]uil arin com*air*ge an*n*, masa m*ar*bad ram*ar*bad*h* he *arin* com*airgh*e is tria*n* n-eneclain*ne* du*n* com*airgh*e an*n* i maig*h*in ł let*he*neclan*n* *sechtar* maig*hin*.

Masa c*h*ned*h* rafe*ar*ad an*n*, int ainmrai*n*ne da enecl*ainn* fei*n* [ḟ]uil aconti *arar* fe*ar*ad*h* i*n* c*h*ned*h* g*ur*ub e i*n*t ai*n*mrai*n*ne-sin da enecc*lainn* fei*n* bes do*n* com*airgh*e i maig*h*in ł let*h*enecl*ann sechtar* maigi*n*.

Masa ṡeoit[220] ruccad*h* uaid*h*, is lan n-eneclai*n*ne dan com*airgh*e an*n*, i maig*h*in, masa cleit*he* ł letheneclan*n* sec*h*tar maig*h*in. Masa lu, is let*h*ene-cl*ann* don comairg*h*e an*n* i maig*hin* ⁊ *secht*mad*h* i[221] sec*htar* maigi*n*. Gid*h* leis fei*n* in fe*ar*an*n* gingup leis, ata sei*n* do*n* com*airgh*e, .i. *ar*a beit*h* indil-sec*h*.

Mas a dualg*h*us fogla indilsigh, masa marbad*h* darig*h*ned*h* an*n*, is lan n-eneclain*ne* do*n* c*h*om*airgh*e an*n* i fiad*naise* ⁊ l*eth* i maig*h*in ⁊ i*n*n æ[n]-mad*h*[222] ran*n fichit sechtar* maig*h*in.

Masa c*h*ned rafe*ar*ad*h* air, int ai*n*mrai*n*ne da enecl*ainn* fein [ḟ]uil donti f*or*ar fe*ar*ad*h* i*n* cnead*h* gurub e i*n*t ai*n*mrain*ne*-sen da eneclan*n* fein bes donti i ndernad fiad*nais*e hi.

f. 40d Iss ed*h* is fiad*nais*e an*n* a denu*mh* i *n*-æ*n*tig*h* | ł i *n*n-æn*air*ec*h*t ris, ⁊ leth[223] i mbia do isna (mait*h*ib*h*)[inadaib][224]-se*n* ota sen i*m*mac*h*, gurup ed*h* bes do i maigi*n*, ⁊ i*n* æ*n*mad*h* ran*n fichit* sec*htar* maig*hin*. ⁊ leis fei*n* in fe*ar*and sec*htar* maig*hin*. ⁊ manbad*h* leis, nucu biad*h* ni do it*ir*. Gid*h* laiss gi*n*gup lais i*n* fe*ar*and, dobiad*h* do i*n*ni adrubram*ar* romaind, .i. leat*h* i *m*maigin ⁊ lan i fiad*h*naise.

Masa seoit ruccad and ⁊ ni ruac*h*tud*ar ar* com*air*ge, l*eth*eneclan*n* isi*n* clei-*th*e i *m*maig*hin* ł i*n*n æ*n*m*h*ad*h* ran*n fichit* sect*ar* m*h*aig*h*in.

220 Binchy, *CIH* 139, n. a, states that the lenition mark was added later. In my opinion, I do not believe that to be the case. The mark of lenition is no different from the range of lenition marks in this section of the MS. While some of them are lighter or darker than others, and some are more oblong than spherical, there is nothing that any of these 'later' lenition marks have in common with each other. Thus, I do not believe that any of the lenition marks Binchy states were added later in this section of the MS were added by anyone other than the scribe.

221 Binchy, *CIH* 139, n. b, queries whether this word should be omitted.

222 I follow the emendation suggested by Binchy, *CIH* 139, n. c.

223 The ⟨l⟩ was inserted above the line with a reference mark; see also Binchy, *CIH* 139, n. d.

224 I follow the emendation suggested by Binchy, *CIH* 139, n. e. It appears as if the scribe has misunderstood the first three minims in his exemplar; see further below in source HH.

If it is a lawful person who is under the protection then, if he was killed under the protection, it is one-third honor-price for the protector then in a precinct or half honor-price outside a precinct.

If a wound was inflicted then, the one on whom the wound was inflicted has the designated amount of his own honor-price so that the designated amount of his own honor-price is for the protector in a precinct or half honor-price outside a precinct.

If *sét*s were taken from him, it is full honor-price for the protector, then, in a precinct, if it is of great value, or half honor-price outside a precinct. If it is of small value, it is half honor-price for the protector, then, in a precinct and a seventh outside a precinct. Whether or not he himself was with him on the land, those [fines] are for the protector, i.e. with regard to he who is lawful.

If it is in compensation for an injury [done to] a lawful person, if he was killed then, it is full honor-price for the protector then [if it was done] in his presence, and half in the precinct, and a twenty-first outside the precinct.

If a wound was inflicted on him, the designated amount of his own honor-price is for the one on whom the wound was inflicted [and] the designated amount of his own honor-price may be for the one in whose presence it [i.e. the injury] was made.

This is doing it [i.e. the injury] then against him before[225] the same house | f. 40d
or the same assembly, and he will have half in those places henceforth, and he will have it in a precinct and a twenty-first outside the precinct. And he himself [i.e. the protector] is with him in the land outside the precinct; and if he was not, he would not have anything at all. Whether or not he was with him in the land, he would have that which we mentioned previously, i.e. half in the precinct and full [honor-price] in his presence.

If *sét*s were taken then and they had not come[226] under protection, half honor-price for an item of great value in the precinct or a twenty-first outside the precinct.

225 The sense is that the injury was done to him in front of witnesses at a house or at an assembly.

226 The form *ruachtudar* is a MI 3 pl. pret./perf. pass. of *ro-saig*.

Masa lu, *secht*mad*h* eneclain*n*e and i maig*hin*, ł t*r*ian na h-æ*n*mad*h* rain*n*e *fichit* ge*n*mot*h*a t*r*ian *secht*maidh na h-ae*n*mad*h* rain*n*e *fich*et an*n sechtar* maig*h*in.

Masa g*h*ait seoit nucun [ḟ]aici*m* ni do*n* tuait*h* an*n* maini gataith*er* iat asa taig*h*, ⁊ d(o)[a][227] gataite*r*, is enecc*lann* d'ḟir in tig*h*i an*n*.

Masa ṡær[228] ł slet*h* ł *for*cur darig*h*ned*h* isna h-inadaib-sei*n*, nucu*n*n [ḟ]aicmit ni do neoc*h* and, *acht* donti risa ndernad*h* in ḟog*h*al an*n*, *acht* mai*n*e rap*h* a dualg*hus* comairg*he*; *acht* manip a tig*h* darig*h*ned*h* in slet*h*ed*h*, ⁊ mas ed*h*, is eneclan*n* d'fir i*n* tig*h*i an*n* HH. [*CIH* 138.34–139.31]

227 I follow Binchy, *CIH* 139, n. f.

228 Binchy, *CIH* 139, n. g, queries whether MS *ṡær* represents *sár* 'outrage, humiliation, insult' or *aer* 'sport, amusement; air'. One wonders whether Binchy was also thinking of *áer* 'satirizing, defaming'. Given the context, *sár* seems to be the best semantic fit.

If it is an item of little value, one-seventh of [the] honor-price then in a precinct, or a third of a twenty-first besides a third or a seventh of the twenty-first then outside the precinct.

If *séts* are stolen I do not see[229] anything for the *túath* if they are not stolen from the house, and if they are stolen, it is honor-price for the man of the house then.

If an insult or rape by stealth or rape by violence[230] was done in those places, we do not see[231] anything for anyone then except for the one against whom the injury was done then, except a domesticated animal in compensation for the protector; except if the rape by stealth was done in his house, and if it is, it is honor-price for the man of the house then HH.

229 The sense here is obscure to me. Perhaps it is along the lines of: 'in the book I do not see ...'.

230 For the different categories of rape distinguished by Irish law, see *GEIL*, 134–137, and Lisi Oliver, "Forced and Unforced Rape in Early Irish Law," *Proceedings of the Harvard Celtic Colloquium* 13 (1993): 93–105.

231 The sense is obscure to me, but cf. the similar construction above.

§9 Gell n-uathbais ⁊rl-

In imraic*h*ne: Na h-uili cned rof*erustar* b*era* ⁊ alla ⁊ dre*m*en*na* ⁊ ruib ⁊ anurraid ⁊ i*n*dils*ig* ⁊ fiall*aig* ne*m*bescna fo*r*na dai*n*ib rote[c](t)*h*et*ar*[232] an*n*, is er*aic* fo*r*na dai*n*ib rias*ar* te[c](t)*h*ed[233] an*n* fo aicn*ed* na fog*l*a etg*id*[234] riasar i*m*getar. Mas ria i*ndethbirius* fog*l*a, is lanfiach na cned rofer*ustar* b*era* ⁊ alla ⁊ d*r*emen*na* fo*r*ru d'ic f*r*iu. ⁊ mas re h-espa, is l*eth*fia*ch* na cned rof*erustar* b*er*a ⁊ alla ⁊ fo*r*ru d'ic f*r*iu. ⁊ mas re torba, ⁊ conicfatis a fast*ad* gi*n* t*air*mesc ngni*mraid*, is ait*h*gi*n* uait*h*ib i*n*dib, ⁊ man*ar* etast*ar*, is [s]l*an* doib.

1 Source **JJ** begins with ⁊ but lacks the abbreviation ⁊rl- at the end. The text of source **A** agrees with **AA** and **JJ**, but note uat*h*bais **AA** and **JJ**.

232 I follow the emendation suggested by Binchy, *CIH* 2149, n. h.

233 See previous note.

234 For this legal term meaning 'category of culpable act', see *Bretha Éitgid*, *CCIH*, 385.3; and McLeod, *Bloodshed and Compensation*, 9.

§9 A pledge of terror, etc.[235]

The error: All wounds that stakes and rocks and cliffs and animals and outlaws and lawful people and unregulated *fían*-bands[236] have inflicted on the people who fled then, *wergeld* [or a fine for physical injury] [is paid] by the people from whom they fled then according to the category of culpable act from which they fled. If it is for an unnecessary injury, the full fine of the wounds that stakes and rocks and cliffs have inflicted on them [i.e. on those who fled] is to be paid to them. And if it is from folly, half the fine of the wounds that stakes and rocks have inflicted on them [i.e. on those who fled] is to be paid to them. And if it is from utility,[237] and they could have safeguarded them without hindering work, restitution [is paid] from them [who could have safeguarded them] to them [who were injured], and if they could not have [safeguarded them], they are exempt from legal liability.[238]

---

235 For a discussion of this section, see the Introduction, 17. For contracts bound under duress and their invalidity, see McLeod, *Early Irish Contract Law*, 55–56.; see also *AL* 4: 268.25. Although, on the surface, it appears as if the OI text does not directly relate to the subject matter of the commentary, they are, in fact, related. The commentary deals with injury which results from falsely inciting fear in others. Any pledge made in such a state would not be considered valid. Pledges (or any statements) made as a result of fear or intentional duress are not considered valid, even if the fear was caused by mistake. It should be noted that the OI text could be translated as 'of pledges of terrors' if one were to understand both words in the gen. pl. rather than n. nom. sg and gen. sg., respectively; the case forms are identical for both words. The commentary deals with two main topics. The first is when someone unintentionally incites fear in others which results in injury to others or their property. The second topic deals with intentionally stating that the enemy is at hand (when they are not). The commentary suggests that this scenario is when it is not a case of genuine error, but rather with an ulterior motive, such as causing someone else's death, injury, or stealing their property. The fines in this situation are based on the motive. I should like to thank Neil McLeod for help interpreting this section.

236 *Fían*-bands were groups of warriors who are associated both in the literary and legal texts as being not only outside the law, but also outside the structured framework of civilized society. That being said, they are also sometimes depicted as being in the service of kings; see Kim McCone, "Werewolves, Cyclopes, *Díberga*, and *Fíanna*: Juvenile delinquency in early Ireland," *Cambridge Medieval Celtic Studies* 12 (1986): 2–10; and *idem*, "Hund, Wolf und Krieger bei den Indogermanen," in *Studien zum indogermanischen Wortschatz*, ed. Wolfgang Meid (Innsbruck: Institut für Sprachwissenschaft der Universität, 1987), 101–154. The commentary envisions a *fían*-band that was not associated with a particular ruler (or at least not with their own territory), and, thus, unregulated.

237 On the meaning of *esba* and *torbae*, see McLeod, *Bloodshed and Compensation*, 9.

238 For the responsibilities and liabilities of performing (dangerous) acts of social utility, see McLeod, *Bloodshed and Compensation*, 11.

Ma robat*ar* *séoit* aca, ⁊ ma r*u*csat-s*om* te*cht*ug*ud* i*na* sét*aib*, is a n-aisec uai*th*ib co fia*ch*aib gaite. ⁊ mas a muda docuat*ar* at*ar*ru, is aithg*in* a *sét* d'ic friu. In tan is re torba doimthigest*ar* na dai*ne*,[239] ⁊ nir fetsat a taiscid ci*n* tair*m*isc gni*mraid*, is [s]lan.

Int i*m*or[ṡ]lon*n*[ed][240] na*m*at im*murro*, is fia*ch* a fa*th*a f*or*ru, f*or*na dai*n*ib dorat f*or*ru e. Mas *ar* daig*in* m*ar*b*th*a, is lanfia*ch* na cned rof*erustar* *bera* ⁊ alla ⁊ d*r*emen*na* ⁊ ruib ⁊ anurr*aid* ⁊ in*n*dilsi ⁊ f*iallaig* n*embescna*[241] f*or*sna dai*n*ib rote[c](t)*h*est*ar*[242] an*n* d'ic dona dai*n*ib dorat f*or*ru he. Mas *ar* daig*in* espa, is l*eth*fia*ch* na cned rof*erustar* *bera* ⁊ alla d'ic friu. ⁊ mas *ar* daig*in* na*m*at do b*eth* doib fei*n* isi*n* crich, ⁊ noch*an* lam*ustar* a sloi*n*ded f*or*ru, is [s]l*an*. Ma robat*ar* *séoit* aca ⁊rl-.

Gne *aile*:[243] Mas e i*n*ti risa nd*er*nad i*n*d fua*ch*tai*n* dorigni i*n*d i(n)*m*rai*ch*ni,[244] is cet*hraimth*e corp*diri* na cneidi[245] is airde ⁊ *cethraimth*i[246] dire na *sét*, ⁊ *cethraimthe* e*n*ecl*ain*ni [f]uil isna *sét*aib ł [f]uil isi*n* cneid, cidbe dib b*us*[247] mo. Co cæ*macht*ain tesairc*th*i sin, ⁊ mai*n*e cæ*m*nac*air* tes*argain*, i*n*ti dorigni i*n*d fua*chtain* is og[ṡ]lan[248] do. Mas e im*murro* i*n*ti dorigne i*n*d fua*ch*tai*n* dorigne i*n*t imar[ṡ]l*onned*, is lancorp*dír*e na cneidi is *air*de rof*er*ad ari*n* fer *aile* uad ⁊ landire na *sét*, ⁊ *in* enecl*ann* [f]uil laisna s*éu*tu ł laisi*n* cneid, gidbe de b*us* mo.

239 Immediately following the ⟨d⟩ there is a diagonal tear in the vellum which does not show any sign of repair. The tear seems to have been in the vellum before the scribe wrote the text as there are no visible erasure marks and the scribe left a space after the ⟨d⟩ to accommodate the tear.

240 Although this word is not listed with a gender in *eDIL s.v. immarsloinnded*, the nom. sg. form of the article, *int*, is usually only used for m. nom. sg. nouns which begin with a vowel; *GOI* §468.

241 Cf. 2149.28; and see Binchy, *CIH* 2149, n. i. As above, emended to 'fiall*aig*' instead of 'fiall*ach*'.

242 After the ⟨t⟩ the ⟨e⟩ has been erased; a tall ⟨e⟩ follows the erasure.

243 The MS reads *gne .ii.*

244 See Binchy, *CIH* 2149, n. j.

245 The ⟨c⟩ was inserted above the line; see also Binchy, *CIH* 2150, n. a.

246 The ⟨ti⟩ are written above the line.

247 The ⟨b⟩ was inserted above the line; see also Binchy, *CIH* 2150, n. b.

248 I follow the emendation suggested by Binchy, *CIH* 2150, n. c.

If they [i.e. those who fled] had *sét*s, and if they took their *sét*s [away from them], they [i.e. those who took the *sét*s] are to restore their *sét*s [to their owners] along with penalties for theft. And if they [i.e. the *sét*s] went [astray] in their possession, restitution for their *sét*s is to be paid to them [i.e. to the owners]. When it is from useful work that the people departed, and they were not able to [safe]guard them without hindering work, they are exempt from legal liability.

Falsely claiming an enemy attack,[249] however, a fine for them [on account of] their motive, for the people who did that to them [i.e. a penalty for those who intentionally falsely stated there was an enemy]. If it is for the sake of killing [that someone falsely said that there was an enemy or otherwise incited fear], the full fine of the wounds that stakes and rocks and cliffs and animals and outlaws and lawful people and unregulated *fían*-bands have inflicted on the people who fled then are to be paid by the people who did it [i.e. falsely stated there was an enemy] to them. If it is because of folly, half the fine of the wounds that have been inflicted by stakes and rocks are to be paid to them. And if it is because of enemies of their own in the territory, and they had not dared to mention them [i.e. the enemies] to them, they are exempt from legal liability. If they had *sét*s, etc.

Another version: If it is the one against whom the assault was made who made the error, it is one-fourth of the body-fine of the highest wound [i.e. one-fourth of the wound which has the greatest fine] and one-fourth of the compensation of the *sét*s, and one-fourth of the honor-price that is for the *sét*s or which is for the wound, whichever of them may be greater. That is with the ability to protect [them from injury], and if there was not the ability to protect [them from injury], the one who made the assault is completely exempt from legal liability. If it is, however, the one who made the assault who falsely claimed an enemy attack, it is the full body-fine of the highest wound that was inflicted on the other man by him [which is owed] and full compensation of the *sét*s, and the honor-price which is for the *sét*s or for the wound, whichever of them may be greater.[250]

249 Lit. 'the misnaming of enemies'.

250 This paragraph deals with the compensation owed to those who were injured. If the person who made the error is injured, he is owed one-fourth of the compensation for his most serious wound. If the person who did the misnaming is also the assailant, the assailant owes full compensation for the most serious wound inflicted on the other party and full compensation for any damage to his property, along with the honor-price payment for the injured party or his property.

Gne *aile*: Int i*m*ar[ṡ]lon*n*[ed] *nam*ad[251] .i. fiach a fatha f*or*ro an*n*. Ma ar daigi*n* fog*l*a ris fei*n* no fria s*éutu*, is lanfia*ch* i*n*dtib a ndis, ar is anfot inde*th*b*ir* friu cid ar daigi*n* ne*cht*ar de. Diam ar daigin espa, is l*eth*fia*ch* i ce*cht*ar de. Dia*m* ar daigi*n* a n-anacuil fei*n*, is ait*h*gi*n* i ce*cht*ar de. Diam iat fei*n* no*techt*aig*ed* na s*ét*, is fia*ch* gaide A. [*CIH* 2149.27–2150.11]

ni dil*es* ní dobe*rar* t*r*e uathbas. Ma t*r*e imraichne ł im*ar*sloin*ned* nam*h*at, ł cabet urr*aid no*dbe*r*at,[252] atrenat[253] a ndob*eir* nech doib*h* t*r*e uathbas AA. [*CIH* 1922.18–20]

ni dil*es* ni dob*er*ar ar uat*h*bás JJ. [*CIH* 1318.22–23]

251 Binchy, *CIH* 2150, n. d, comments that ⟨nam⟩ seem to have been erased along with the following word *fiach*. In the MS, ⟨ad⟩ are legible above the line, ⟨nam⟩ are not legible at all, and *fiach* is still visible despite the erasure. For this MS reading, see *CIH* 2149.37.

252 This verb is the 3 pl. pres. subj. of *beirid* with a class C n. object agreement affix. For object agreement affixes in early Irish, see Joseph F. Eska, "Where Have All the Object Pronouns Gone? The growth of object agreement in earlier Celtic," *ZCP* 57 (2009–2010): 25–47; and Aaron Griffith, "Old Irish Pronouns: Agreement affixes vs. clitic arguments," in *Formal Approaches to Celtic Linguistics*, ed. Andrew Carnie (Cambridge: Cambridge Scholars Publishing, 2011), 65–93.

253 This verb is the 3 pl. pres. ind. of *as-ren* with a class B n. object agreement marker.

Another version: Falsely claiming an enemy attack, i.e. a fine for them [who falsely claimed the enemy attack] then [on account of] their motive. If it is for the sake of inflicting injury against him himself or to his *séts* [i.e. if the intent is to cause injury to someone else or someone else's property], full fine for both of them [i.e. for the injured person and his property], because it is inexcusable negligence regarding them though for the sake of either of them [i.e. for injuring someone else or someone else's property].[254] If it is because of folly, it is half fine for each of them [i.e. injury to another or his property]. If it is because of protecting oneself, it is restitution for each of them [i.e. the injured party or his property]. If it is they themselves [i.e. those who falsely claimed an enemy attack] who took possession of the *séts*, it is the fine of theft A.

That which is given through terror is not lawful. If it is by error or falsely claiming an enemy attack, or though sureties may give it, they pay that which anyone gives to them through terror AA.

That which is given because of terror is not lawful JJ.

254 The interpretation of this sentence is tentative.

§10 Imdegail ait*ire* ⁊rl-

Na h-uile neic*h*i risa ndech*aid* int ait*ire* ⁊ i*m*a r*u*cad a*m*ac*h*, is *ed*[255] dlega*r* a n-ic tara ce*nd*. ⁊ cemad ail ni aile d'ac*r*a air-si*m acht* ani ris rug*ad* amach e ⁊ ro*acht*aig*ed* air, nocha dlega*r* a n-ac*r*a air. ⁊ a den*am* do*n*ti o r*ucad con*ar *acht*aig air *acht* sin, ⁊ is [s]l*an* do-*som* can[256] ni uad isa h-ait*h*le.

p. 10a Gne *aile*: Int ait*ire*, na h-huili neic*h*i | ima ndech*aid* a n-ait*irius* on *cét*la ⁊ rofas air o si*n* amach, is fola si*n* a ce*nd* in ait*ire*. Na h-uile neiche nar *acht*aig*ed* er o[n][257] *cét*lo ⁊ nar fas[258] er o si*n* amac*h*, nocho*n*[259] fola si*n* a ce*nd* i*nd* ait*iri*.[260]

Gne *aile*:[261] Int[262] ait*ire* tuc*ad* re fiac*h*aib airit*he*, ict*air* tara ce*nd*; ⁊ na h-uili fog*la* na ro*acht*aigit f*air in* cetla, ni h-ict*ar* ni[263] dib-si*n* tara ce*nd*.

1 Imdeag*ail* J.

255 The phrase *amach is ed* was written *inter. col.* by the scribe with reference marks; see also Binchy, *CIH* 2150, n. e.

256 *Can* is a variant form of *cen*; *eDIL s.v. cen.*

257 I follow the emendation suggested by Binchy, *CIH* 2150, n. g.

258 The ⟨s⟩ was added above the line by the scribe.

259 For the MI use of *nochan* combined with the copula (also in J below), see *eDIL s.v. nícon* (f).

260 The final ⟨i⟩ was added below the line by the scribe.

261 'Gne .ii.' is written *inter. col.* by the scribe; see also Binchy, *CIH* 2150, n. h.

262 The ⟨i⟩ was added below the line by the scribe.

263 It is possible that one letter has been erased after *ni*, but I cannot make out what it may have been.

§10 Protection of a hostage-surety, etc.[264]

All the things for which the hostage-surety[265] went surety and regarding which he was brought away, they should be paid on his behalf. And though there might be the desire to sue him for another thing besides the thing for which he was brought away and which he had agreed on, it is not right to sue him for them [i.e. for other things].[266] And it is proven by the one from whom he was brought [i.e. by the person who had physical custody of the hostage-surety] [that there was not] a term of agreement for him except that [i.e. what was originally agreed upon], and he [i.e. the hostage-surety] is not legally obligated [to pay] anything [additional] afterwards.[267]

Another version: The hostage-surety, all the things | regarding which he p. 10a
entered into hostage-suretyship from the first day and which arose[268] afterwards, that is a consideration for the hostage-surety. All the things that he had not agreed on from the first day and which did not arise afterwards, that is not a consideration for the hostage-surety.

Another version: The hostage-surety who was brought for particular debts, they are paid on his behalf [i.e. the party for whom he went surety is responsbible for paying what is owed]; and all the offenses that they did not agree on the first day, nothing is paid for them on his behalf.

264 For a discussion of this section, see the Introduction, 17. The 'protection' referred to is not physical protection, as seen in §§8, 52, and 57, but rather the hostage-surety's role in guaranteeing the secured party's debts.

265 For the role of the hostage-surety in Irish law, see Stacey, *The Road to Judgment*, 82–111; *GEIL*, 172–173; and McLeod, *Early Irish Contract Law*, 17–18. Unlike the paying-surety or the binding-surety, the hostage-surety guaranteed the terms of the contract with his own person. In the commentaries here, the secured party has defaulted and the hostage-surety has been taken hostage by the other party to the contract. The commentaries state that even if the defaulter continues to accumulate other fines and/or debts while the hostage-surety is held, the hostage-surety is not liable for any of those additional debts, only for the original terms of the contract.

266 The sense is that the hostage-surety can only be sued for that which he initially agreed to act as surety.

267 Thurneysen, *Bürgschaft*, 68 provides a translation (in German) of *CIH* 2150.12–24; see also *CCIH*, 88.

268 The sense of *rofas*, pret./perf. 3 sg. of *ásaid* 'grows, develops, arises', is that anything connected with (or a situation that developed regarding) what the hostage-surety originally guaranteed is his responsibility.

Mad e i*n*ti [i][269] fil lai*m*[270] dogni fogla ⁊ se 'na lai*m*, is co*mar*da[d] at*ar*ru ⁊ na feich *f*risi*n* fuil ait*ire*. Na fogla dorigne roi*me*: ⁊ ni t*ar*dat a fol*ad* do i lo tab*ar*ta ait*ire*, ni ditin do ait*ire* ce acraith*er* inois t*ara* ce*n*d, *acht* a *m*b*eth* ci*n* ti*n*cisi*n* co roslanaite*r*[271] ait*ire* A. [*CIH* 2150.12–24]

.i. eim[272]-diten in ait*ire* is *ed* dleg*ar* a de*n*am*h*.

Na h-uile neche risi ndech*aid* int eit*ire*[273] ⁊[274] ima ruc*ad* am*ac*, is *ed* dleg*ar* a n-ic t*ara* cen*n*. ⁊ ciam*ad* ail ni *aile* d'ag*r*a air-si*m* *acht* aní risi ruc*ad* amac*h* e ⁊ ro*acht*aig*ed* air, noch*an* dleg*ar* a n-ac*r*a air. ⁊ a denam do*n*ti o *r*uca *conar acht*aig*h* air *acht* sin, ⁊ is [s]l*an* do-som ca*n* ni uada asa h-ait*h*le.

Int ait*ire*: Na uile neche i*m*a ndech*aid* a n-ait*irus* o*n* cé*t*ló ⁊ rofas *air* o si*n* am*ac*, is fola si*n* a cen*n* an ait*ire*. Na h-uile neche n*ar acht*aig*h*[ed][275] air o*n* cé*t*lo ⁊ n*ar* as *air* o si*n* amac*h*, noch*a*n fol*ad* sin a cen*n* in ait*ire*. Int ait*ire* *t*uc*a*[d] re fiac*h*aib *air*ith*e*, ict*air* t*ara* cen*n*, ⁊ na h-uil*i* fog*la* na ro*acht*aig*h* f*air* in cé*t*la, ni h-ict*ar* ni dib*h*-si*n* t*ara* cen*n*.

Mad e inti i fil i laim*h* dogni na fog*h*la ⁊ se 'na laim*h*, is co*mar*dug*ud* et*ar*ru ⁊ na feic*h*[276] *f*risi fil ait*ire*. Na fog*h*la dorig*h*ne roi*me*: ⁊ ní .⁊rl- J.[277] [*CIH* 2027.7–17]

269 I follow the emendation suggested by Binchy, *CIH* 2150, n. i; cf. 2027.16.

270 The phrase *i láim* is used to indicate that someone is under the protection of a surety; McLeod, "*Ón* an *airliciud*," 181; and *idem*, *Early Irish Contract Law*, 23–24.

271 The ⟨ai⟩ were inserted below the line by the scribe; see also Binchy, *CIH* 2150, n. j.

272 The ⟨i⟩ is written subscript. It is usual in 'etymological' glosses for the prefix *im-*, when it is the first element in a compound, to be glossed by *éim-* 'swift'. For this style of glossing, see Binchy, "The Linguistic and Historical Value of the Irish Law Tracts," 210–212.

273 The first ⟨i⟩ is written subscript.

274 A feature of the scribe's writing is that he inserts a *punctum* on the base line before every Tironian note.

275 Cf. source A above.

276 The ⟨i⟩ is written subscript.

277 Binchy, *CIH* 2027, n. b, notes that the MS breaks off incomplete at this point owing to a chasm in the MS. He refers to *CIH* 2150.22 ff. for the continuation, i.e. the last part of source A above. *CCIH*, 82, notes the chasm as well, but further comments that the following material in the MS deals with the same subject matter.

If the one who is under his protection [i.e. under the protection of the hostage-surety] commits offenses and [i.e. while] he is under his protection, there is a balancing between them [i.e. the offenses] and the penalties for which he is hostage-surety. The offenses he made previously: And they do not come into his [i.e. the hostage-surety's] consideration on the day of taking the hostage-suretyship, [and] the hostage-surety is not a protection for him though it is now sued on his behalf, but it may be untendered until he compensates the hostage-surety[278] A.

i.e. 'swift-protection'[279] of the hostage-surety is what he is required to do.

All the things for which the hostage-surety went surety and regarding which he was brought away, they should be paid on his behalf. And though there might be a desire to sue him for another thing besides the thing for which he was bought away and which he had agreed on, it is not right to sue him for them [i.e. for other things]. And it is proven by the one from whom he is brought [that there was not] a term of agreement for him except that, and he is not legally obligated [to pay] anything afterwards.

The hostage-surety: All the things regarding which he entered into suretyship from the first day and which arose afterwards, that is a consideration for the hostage-surety. All the things that he did not agree on from the first day and which did not arise afterwards, that is not a consideration for the hostage-surety.

The hostage-surety who was brought for particular debts, they are paid on his behalf, and all the offenses that he did not agree on the first day, nothing is paid for them on his behalf.

If the one who is under his protection commits offenses and [i.e. while] he [i.e. the secured party] is under his protection, there is a balancing between them [i.e. the offenses] and the penalties for which he is hostage-surety. The offenses he made previously: And [they do] not, etc. J.

278 The last sentence of the paragraph is difficult. The sense seems to be that, if the secured party committed offenses before the hostage-surety took up his suretyship (and the liabilities for these offenses were not agreed on by the hostage-surety), then the hostage-surety is not responsible for whatever is owed by the secured party. If the secured party is sued for these previous offenses while owing compensation to the hostage-surety, the hostage-surety needs to be compensated first.

279 See the note on the Irish for this compound.

§11 Ecor tar folaid ⁊rl-[280]

.i. feran*n* rorec*ustar*[281] dui*ne*, ⁊ i*n*dni rogell*ad* tara ce*n*d dogab*ad* do he ɫ dosia*cht* i*n*a lai*m* ce*n*a.

Acht ma dochuaid ari*n* feran*n* asa h-aithle, (*acht*) mas ar daigin cait*h*me feoir ɫ arba, is la*n*fiach du*n*acait*h*e no l*eth*fia*ch* du*n*acait*h*e uad.

Mas ar daigi*n* in t*echt*ait*h*e, is lanfia*ch* no l*eth*fiach t*echt*ait*h*e tiri, cu cu*n*d, co coibne, ɫ ci*n* cu*n*d, ce*n* coibne, uad an*n*.

Caide deif*ir* et*ar*u[282]-si*n* ⁊ i*n* bail[e] ata: 'Tir ara n-i*n*gellt*ar*[283] log na ruirth*er*,' *con*a sl*an* do*n* dui*ne* dul arin feran*n* a*n*d-seic, ⁊ *con*ach sl*an* dul air a*n*d so? Is [s]i an d*eth*b*ir*: Andi rogell*ad* t*ar* ce*n*d and f*er*ai*n*d an*n*-side noc*h*an[284] fagba*r* do he, ⁊ is e anarra[285] is gaire les aca*n* fer amuig a f*eran*n fen aris do. (.i.)[286] [ɫ] i*n*di rogell*ad* t*ar* cen*n* in ferai*n*d an*n* so dogab*ar* do, no[287] rosia*cht* ina lai*m*, ⁊ coir cia rob*eth* er*aic* uad[288] a ndul arin fera*n*d.

---

1 | [f. 53a] Eccor dar folaid*h* C.

---

280 For similar material, see *Di Astud Chirt ⁊ Dligid* 'On the Confirmation of Right and Law', *CIH* 224.35–225.13; *AL* 5: 426–493; and *CCIH* 293–294.

281 The ⟨t⟩ and its accompanying suspension mark were added above the line by the scribe; see also Binchy, *CIH* 2150, n. k.

282 Binchy, *CIH* 2150, n. l, queries whether the final letter should be read as ⟨u⟩ or ⟨a⟩. The letter was added in below the line by the scribe and is very difficult to read with certainty.

283 The ⟨t⟩ and its accompanying suspension mark were added above the line by the scribe; see also Binchy, *CIH* 2150, n. m.

284 After the ⟨a⟩ the scribe left a gap to accommodate the tear in the vellum.

285 Binchy, *CIH* 2150, n. n, queries whether *anarra* should be read as *an arra*; but cf. *CIH* 168.15 *œnarra*.

286 Binchy, *CIH* 2150, n. o, queries whether *.i.* should be omitted.

287 This word was added above the line by the scribe.

288 The ⟨a⟩ is written subscript.

§11 Entering property, etc.[289]

i.e. property which a person has sold, and what was promised for it was taken by him or his surety had obtained it [i.e. the payment] already.[290]

But if he went onto the land afterwards, if it is for the purpose of consuming grass or corn, the full fine of human-trespass[291] or half fine of human-trespass [is paid] by him.

If it is for the purpose of taking possession, full fine or half fine of taking possession of land, with the head of his kindred, with a kinsman, or without the head of his kindred, without a kinsman, [is paid] by him then.[292]

What is the difference between those things and where [it says]: 'Land for which a price is promised that was not paid', and the person going on the land then is free [to go on the land], and he is not free to go on it here?[293] The difference is: That which was promised for the land then [in the first circumstance] is not taken by him, and the plaintiff considers that the closest substitute is to get his own land back again. [In the second circumstance] either that which was promised for the land here is taken by him, or his surety had obtained it [i.e. the payment], and though there might be a fine from him for going on the land, it is proper [to fine him for entering the land after accepting payment for it].

---

289 For a discussion of this section, see the Introduction, 17–18.

290 Literally 'it had come into his hand already'; cf. the idioms involving *lám* 'hand' and suretyship in §§4 and 10.

291 Early Irish law distinguishes between *duine-chaithig* 'human-trespass, trespass committed by a person' and *rop-chaithig* 'animal-trespass'. Even if there is a situation where the animals themselves are found on someone else's land, it can be considered a case of *duine-chaithig* if the animals were, for example, driven onto the land with the intent to do harm; *GEIL*, 142–144; and *EIF*, 134–142 and 431–432.

292 The sense of the first paragraph is that once someone has sold land and received payment for the land, the original owner has no right to enter the land either to graze his animals or to try to take possession of the land again. If he enters the land to try to repossess it, it does not matter whether the head of his kindred or another kinsman is with him; he is still charged fines for illegal entry; *GEIL*, 189; and *EIF*, 432–433.

293 The commentator is quoting from another legal text, which is not specified. The commentator then uses the common rhetorical device of question-and-answer to illustrate the point. For this rhetorical device in the medieval Irish legal texts, see Alice R. Taylor-Griffiths, "*Gúbretha Caratniad*: Agreement and disagreement in the classroom," *NAJCS* 2 (2018): 105–132.

Gne *aile*: Fer*ann* rorec (duine) nec*h*[294] su*n*d, ⁊ gidbed*h* fog*ail* dogne an*n* si*n*, is lanfiach uad i*n*d am*al* dui*ne* *aile*; ⁊ taibg*eth*-sui*m*[295] fiac*h* a t*h*ire, cid t*r*eb*air*e cid aiti*r*e fil f*r*is A. [*CIH* 2150.25–37]

.i. fe*ar*an*n* rarecast*ar* duni an*n*-si*n*, ⁊ i*n*ni ragellad*h* da cind (b)[d]agab*ar* do he ł rasiac*h*t ina laim*h* c*h*eana.

Ma dac*h*uaid*h* *ar*in fe*ar*an*n* asa at*h*li-sin, mas *ar* daig*hin* chait*h*m*h*i a [ḟ]eoir[296] ł arb*ha*, is lanfiac*h* ł leit*h*fiach dui*ne*c*h*aic*h*thi.

Mas ar daig*h*in a et*ar*sc*ar*t*h*a ris uili, is lanfiac*h* tec*h*taig*h*thi, co cun*n*, co coibni, ł can c*h*und, can coibne an*n*. I b*h*ail ata tir *ar* ingellt*ar* log*h* nad*h* rirt*er*, nucu [ḟ]rith[297] i*n*ni ragellad da c*h*ind*h* i*n* fe*ar*aind and-sid*h*e, ⁊ is e æn*ar*ra is gori leisin duni a fe*ar*and fein *ar* sein C. [*CIH* 168.9–16]

---

294 The scribe corrected *duine* to *nech* by adding 'no nec*h*' above the line; see also Binchy, *CIH* 2150, n. p.

295 The form *taibgeth* is obscure to me. It might be a 3 sg. pres. ind. form of a simplex verb to *do-boing*.

296 For the emendation see Binchy, *CIH* 168, n. c; and cf. *CIH* 2150.27.

297 See Binchy, *CIH* 168, n. c.

Another version: Someone sold land here, and although he might trespass in that case, the full fine [is paid] by him then as [would be the case with] another person; and he[298] recovers the fine of his land, whether there is a surety or hostage-surety for it A.

i.e. land which a person has sold then, and what was promised for it was taken by him or his surety had obtained it [i.e. the payment] already.

If he went on the land afterwards, if it is for the purpose of consuming grass or corn, [he owes the] full fine or half fine of human-trespass.

If it is for the purpose of taking [it] from him entirely,[299] [he owes the] full fine of taking possession, with the head of his kindred, with a kinsman, or without the head of his kindred, without a kinsman then. When land for which is promised a price was not paid, [and] that which is promised for the land is not demanded then, and the person considers the closest substitute is to get his own land [back] because of that[300] C.

---

298 Although the commentary is not explicit, the sense seems to be that the new owner of the land is the one to whom the penalties are paid if the previous owner trespasses on the land.

299 In other words, if he entered the land with the intention of taking possession of it from the new owner.

300 Cf. the second paragraph of source A above.

§12 Fortacht re ⁊rl-

Na(n)[301] h-uile ræta dob*e*rar[302] ar oi*n* no *ar* focraic ci*n* ci*n*d*eth* re, is [s]l*an* d'fir bu*n*aid a tab*air*t cuice cidbe u*air* b*us* maith les, ⁊ dilsi na focraice do. Ma roci*n*d*eth* re fo*r*ru, dianu*s*[303] *tu*ca cuice, is fiach foi*m*ri*m*e uad i*n* cach ni a ta gni*mrad*, ⁊ fia*ch* du*n*acait*h*i masa fera*nn*, ⁊ fia*ch* gaite i*n* lac*ht*a, masa ni 'ca ta lac*ht*; *cóic sét* masa tigi, ł fia*ch* foi*m*rimi.[304]

Mas ar fuill*em* im*murro* ł ar comai*n* no ar airleg*ud*,[305] is fia*ch* gaite f*air* a tab*air*t ne*ich* do*n* trede-so cuice ci*n* fi*ar*faig*ed*. Mas do rer dlig*id* nosacra*nn*,[306] ⁊ masa d*eth*b*irius* dob*eir* air a cui*n*dcid, a tab*air*t do *cu*si*n* cut*ruma* rotuills*et*. Masa[307] i*n*d*eth*b*irius* im*murro*, nocho ti*mair*gi*n*d dlig*ed* fori*n* fer aca tait a tab*air*t go fo*r*ba na reie,[308] ł noscui*r*e*n*d uad[309] gi*n* fuill*em* no ci*n* focraic ł ci*n* comai*n* cid i nder*ed* i*n*d re.

Cid e i*n* fer amuig d*ano* noscu*r*e*n*d uad i n-i*n*detb*irius*, is a naisic *con*a fuill*em* cid a tosa*ch* i*n*d re n-*us*at*h*cuir uad. Masa d*eth*b*irius* im*murro* dob*eir* air i*n* thath[ch]u*r*,[310] is a tab*air*t *cu*sani rot*h*uilset.

1 ⁊rl- *om.* C. None of the OI text is preserved in source J.

301 The ⟨a⟩ was written subscript. The scribe wrote two ⟨n⟩s and did not erase the second one.

302 The scribe wrote ⟨ar⟩ a second time at the end of the word, which were subsequently erased; see also Binchy, *CIH* 2150, n. q.

303 The form *dianus* is the conj. *día n-* followed by a 3 pl. object agreement marker.

304 The expected form is *foimrime*, but it appears as if the scribe forgot the final ⟨e⟩ and inserted an ⟨i⟩ below the line, which partially merges with the final minim of the ⟨m⟩.

305 The scribe originally wrote *airill-*, but he then turned the second ⟨i⟩ into an ⟨l⟩ and wrote the ⟨eg⟩ and suspension mark on top of the ⟨ll-⟩. The result is rather messy.

306 It appears as if the scribe erased the letters following ⟨no⟩ and then attempted to get the remainder of the word to fit into the available space. The final ⟨n⟩ with a suspension mark was added below the line; see also Binchy, *CIH* 2151, n. a.

307 The scribe inserted ⟨sa⟩ below the line; see also Binchy, *CIH* 2151, n. b.

308 I understand the *reie* to be a gen. sg. of *ré* 'time, period of time'. After this form, the scribe wrote two ⟨ł⟩s or two ⟨l⟩s, each with a suspension mark, and he then erased the first character. Binchy, *CIH* 2151, n. c, notes that what he sees as ⟨l⟩ with a suspension mark has been erased. He queries whether the sequence should be read as 'reie' or 'rei ele'. The form the scribe uses for both ⟨l⟩ with a suspension mark and ⟨ł⟩ is the same, so the reading is ambiguous.

309 The ⟨a⟩ is written subscript.

310 I follow the emendation suggested by Binchy, *CIH* 2151, n. d.

§12 Benefit of a period [of possession], etc.[311]

All the things given for loan or for rent without a fixed period of time,[312] the owner is free to take them back at whatever time he likes, and he has the rent.[313] If a time had been decided for them [i.e. if they determined the loan or rental was for a specific period of time], if he takes them back [before the determined time], a fine for unauthorized use is [owed] by him [i.e. the lessor] for each thing that has labor [i.e. for every item that is used for work], and a fine of human-trespass if it is land, and a fine for stealing milk, if it is a thing which has milk [i.e. cows]; five *sét*s if it is a house, or a fine for unauthorized use.

If it is for interest, however, or for hire [of inanimate chattels],[314] or for lending, there is a fine of theft for him [i.e. the lessor] taking back any of these three things without asking. If it is according to the law that he sues for them, and if necessity causes him to ask for them, they are given to him with the amount [i.e. interest] they earned. If it is non-necessity, however, law does not compel the man who has them to return them until the end of the [specified period of] time, or he returns them without interest or without rent or without [any profit from] hire though it might be at the end of the [specified] time.

Though the defendant,[315] however, returns them without necessity, they are restored with their interest, though it might be at the beginning of the time that he returned them. If necessity causes him, however, to return [them], they are given back with what they earned.

311 For a discussion of this section, see the Introduction, 18–19. The phrase *fortacht ré*, literally 'help of time', refers to the advantages either the lender or the borrower has in each of the scenarios presented in the commentaries; *eDIL s.v. fortacht*. For example, it is to the advantage of the lessor not to specify a period of time for the loan or rent because he can then take the item back whenever he wants without penalty. It is to the advantage of the lessee to specify the period of time for the loan or rent because the lessor would be fined for taking the item back before the specified period of time was over.

312 On loans and lending, see GEIL, 117–118; *Cáin Ónae*, 29–46; and McLeod, "*Ón* and *airliciud*," 169–196.

313 The literal meaning of *dilsi na focraice do* is 'possession of the rent for him'; in other words, the owner retains any rent paid by the borrower.

314 For *commaín* referring to inanimate items for hire, see McLeod, "*Ón* and *airliciud*," 183.

315 Although the phrase *fer amuig* usually refers to the plaintiff, here it seems to be used for the defendant, i.e. the borrower.

Gne el*e*: Na s*éoit* gill ⁊ ait*h*ne ⁊ urlamais, sl*an* do*n*ti a tait a lai*m* a la*cht* ⁊ a ngni*mrad* do cait*h*em *acht* man*ar acht*aiged a ne*m*cait*hem*; ⁊ ma ro*acht*aig*ed*, is fiach gaite isi*n* l*acht* ⁊ fia*ch* foi*m*ri*m*e isi*n* ngni*mrad*.

Gne *aile*: Na s*éoit* fuillmeda ⁊ na s*éoit* co*m*ai*n*e ⁊ na s*éoit* cun*nar*ta ⁊ na s*éoit* err*aig* ⁊ *air*lict*h*i, *acht* ma t*ucus*t*ar* dui*n*e cuice amuig iat, mas *ar* daigi*n* cait*h*me a l*ach*ta ⁊ a ngni*mraid*, masa s*éoit* aca ta l*acht*, is lanfia*ch* no l*eth*fiach gaite i*n* la*ch*ta a*nn* fo c*ét*oir.

p. 10b Masa s*éoit* aca ta gni*mrad*, is lanfia*ch* foi*m*ri*m*e, ł l*eth*fia*ch* | f*oimrime*[316] isi*n* ngni*mrad* co *dechm*a[i]d,[317] ⁊ la*n* enecl*ann* o *dechmaid*[318] amach.

Mas *ar* daigi*n* a n-et*ar*sc*art*h*a ris uile, is lanfia*ch* no l*eth*fia*ch* gaite a*n*d fo c*ét*oir.

Na s*éoit* focreca ⁊ o*n*a co ci*nn*iud re: *Acht* ma t*ucus*t*ar* dui*n*e cuice amuig iat riasiu tai*n*ic in re, cid *ar* daigi*n* a n-et*ar*scar*th*a ris do g*re*s cid ar daigi*n* cait*h*me a l*ach*ta ł [a][319] ng[n]i*m*raid,[320] masa s*éoit* aca ta l*acht*, is lanfia*ch* g*aite*[321] ł l*eth*fia*ch* g*aite* in l*ach*ta an*n* fo c*ét*oir. Masa s*éoit* aca ta gnimr*ad*, is lanfiach foi*m*ri*m*e no l*eth*f*iach* f*oimrime* isi*n* ngnimr*ad*[322] co *dechm*aid, ⁊ lan*e*n*e*cl*ann* no l*eth*e*n*ecl*ann* o *dechm*aid[323] amach. ⁊ noc*h*(a)on[324] [ḟ]uil fiach g*aite* na s*ét* uair is leis fei*n* iat.

In oi*n* ci*n* ci*n*de*th* re: Os ni f*or*sna fu*ir*m(ig)it*er*[325] aigi, as [s]i a aig*h*i a thimg*aire*. Mas ar foc*r*aic t*ucus*t*ar* in dui*n*e a f*er*a*n*d, ma t*ucus*t*ar* cuigi amuig he riasiu t*ucus*t*ar* re na foc*r*ecca, cid *ar* daigi*n* a et*ar*scar*th*a ris uili cid ar daigi*n* cait*h*me feoir ł arba, is lanfia*ch* no l*eth*fia*ch* dui*n*e*ch*ait*h*e an*n* A. [*CIH* 2150.38–2151.30]

316 See also Binchy, *CIH* 2151, n. e.

317 I follow the emendation suggested by Binchy, *CIH*, 2151, n. f; see also *CIH* 2151.25. The ⟨ad⟩ were inserted above the line.

318 See Binchy, *CIH* 2151, n. f.

319 See Binchy, *CIH* 2151, n. g, and cf. *CIH* 168.37.

320 See Binchy, *CIH* 2151, n. h.

321 See also Binchy, *CIH* 2151, n. i.

322 Binchy, *CIH* 2151, n. k, notes that the scribe made an erroneous suspension mark for ⟨m⟩ above the ⟨g⟩.

323 The ⟨aid⟩ were added above the line by the scribe.

324 See also Binchy, *CIH* 2151, n. h.

325 I follow the emendation suggested by Binchy, *CIH* 2151, n. l; cf. also *CIH* 168.40. The last ⟨i⟩ was inserted above the line by the scribe.

Another version: The *séts* of a pledge and deposit and custody, free for the one in whose hand they are to use their milk and their labor unless he stipulated not to use them; and if he [i.e. the lessor] stipulated [not to use them],[326] there is a fine for stealing the milk and a fine for unauthorized use for the labor.

Another version: The *séts* of interest and the *séts* of hire and the *séts* of sale and the *séts* of requisitioning and of a commercial loan,[327] if a person took them away with him, if it is for the purpose of using their milk or their labor, if the *séts* have milk, there is a full fine or half fine for stealing the milk then immediately.

If the *séts* have labor, there is a full fine for unauthorized use, or a half fine | for unauthorized use of the labor up to ten days, and full honor-price p. 10b
from ten days onwards.

If it is for the purpose of taking them [i.e. the *séts* themselves] from him entirely, there is a full fine or a half fine for theft then immediately.

The *séts* of rent and of loan with a fixed period of time: If a person took them away with him before the [determined] time came, whether for the purpose of taking them from him permanently, or for the purpose of using their milk or their labor, if the *séts* have milk, there is a full fine for stealing or a half fine for stealing the milk then immediately. If the *séts* have labor, there is a full fine for unauthorized use or a half fine for unauthorized use for the labor up to ten days, and full honor-price or half honor-price from ten days onwards. And there is not a fine for stealing the *séts* because they are his own.

The loan without a fixed period of time: When it is something for which a time is not fixed, its time is [when] it is demanded back [i.e. if no fixed time limit is set for the loan, the time limit is whenever the item is asked back]. If it is for rent that the person gave the land, if he took it back before the time of the rent which he gave,[328] whether for the purpose of taking it from him entirely, or for the purpose of consuming grass or corn, there is a full fine or a half fine of human-trespass then[329] A.

---

326 The beginning of this paragraph is translated and discussed in McLeod, "*Ón* and *airliciud*," 182.

327 The beginning of this paragraph is translated and discussed in McLeod, "*Ón* and *airliciud*," 183–184; cf. §1A.

328 This clause might be corrupt; cf. the material in C at *CIH* 169.1–3. The general sense seems to be that the owner has decided to take the land back from the renter before the end of the fixed rental period.

329 Cf. §11 for fines for trespassing on land.

.i. na seoit fuilliuma ⁊ na seoit errig*h* ⁊ na seoit *air*liccthi.

Ma t*h*uccast*ar* duini cuici amuich iat aris, *acht* mas *ar* daig*h*in a n-et*ars*-*car*t*h*a ris uile, is lanfiac*h* ł leithfiach goti and fo c*ét*oir.

Mas *ar* daig*h*in cait*h*m*h*i a lac*h*ta ł gni*m*raid*h*, masa seoit aca ta lac*h*t, lanfiac*h* ł leit*h*fiac*h* goiti in lac*h*ta an*n*. Masa seoit acca ta gni*mh*rad*h*, is lanfiac*h*
f. 53b ł leithfia*ch* foi*m*rime an*n* cu deachmaid*h*,[330] | ⁊ laneneccl*ann* ł let*h*eneclan*n* o dec*h*maid*h*.

Na seoit foc[h](c)ra[icce][331] ⁊ na seoit ona cu ci*n*niud*h* re (re):[332] Ma t*h*u*c*ust*ar* duini cuci iat riasiu tainic in re, cid*h* ar daig*h*in a n-et*ar*s*car*tha ris uili, cid*h* *ar* daig*hin* cait*h*m*h*i a lac*h*ta ł a gni*mh*raid*h*, is lanfiac*h* ł leit*h*fiac*h* goiti isi*n* lac*h*t, ⁊ lanfiac*h* ł leithfiac*h* foimri*m*e isi*n* gni*mh*rud*h* cu *dech*maid*h*, ⁊ lanenecl*ann* no [leth]enecc*lann*[333] o *dech*maid*h* a*m*mach. ⁊ nucun [ḟ]uil fiac*h* goiti na set fei*n*, u*air* is leis fei*n* iat. Masa oin can ci*n*niud*h* re, os[334] ni forna fuirmit*er* agge, is e age a timg*air*i.

Masa fe*ar*and tucustar i*n* duini *ar* fochraicc, ma ducuaid*h* air raisin re, cid *ar* daig*h*in a etarscar*t*ha ris uili, cid*h* *ar* daig*h*im cait*h*m*h*i a ḟeoir ł *ar*b*h*a, is lanfiach ł let*h*fiac*h* duinecaic*h*t*h*i an*n* C. [*CIH* 168.27–169.3]

G*n*é *aile:*[335] G*a*ch fuig*ell* cuir ⁊ cun*nar*rta, ona ⁊ aithne ⁊ *air*lic*the,* ⁊ g*a*ch ni is nesam*h* toisc*ide*, m*a*n*a* bé f*or* dil no *ar* sé*n*a, is t*r*iang*ill*e fri scu*r* t*r*oisce, ⁊ l*eth*g*ill*e ria mb*reith,* ⁊ lang*ill*e i*ar* mb*reith.*

330 The first ⟨a⟩ is written subscript.

331 I follow one of the emendations suggested by Binchy, *CIH* 168, n. g.

332 Binchy, *CIH* 168, n. h, queries whether the second ⟨re⟩ is a dittography mistake.

333 I follow the emendation suggested by Binchy, *CIH* 168, n. i.

334 Binchy, *CIH* 168, n. j, queries whether *os* should be emended to *is*. I take the form here and at *CIH* 2151.27 to be a form of the conjunction *ó* combined with the 3 sg. pres. of the copula; see *eDIL s.v. 2 ó*.

335 Written in *marg. dext.* by the scribe. The material in the first five paragraphs of this commentary is also found in *CIH* 1452.11–24; see Appendix 6.

i.e. the *séts* of interest and the *séts* of requisitioning and the *séts* of a commercial loan.

If a person took them back, if it is for the purpose of taking them from him [i.e. the borrower] entirely, there is a full fine or a half fine for theft then immediately.

If it is for the purpose of using their milk or labor, if the *séts* have milk, [there is a] full fine or a half fine for stealing the milk then. If the *séts* have labor, there is a full fine or a half fine for unauthorized use then up to ten days, | and full honor-price or half honor-price from ten days. f. 53b

The *séts* of rent and the *séts* of a loan with a fixed period of time: If a person took them back before the [fixed] time came, whether for the purpose of taking them from him entirely, or for the purpose of using their milk or their labor, there is a full fine or a half fine for stealing the milk, and a full fine or a half fine for unauthorized use of the labor up to ten days, and full honor-price or half honor-price from ten days onwards. And there is not a fine for stealing the *séts* themselves because they are his own. If it is a loan without a fixed period of time, when it is something for which a time is not fixed, its time is [when] it is demanded back.

If it is land the person gave for rent, if he went on it before the [fixed] time, whether for the purpose of taking it from him entirely, or for the purpose of consuming its grass or corn, there is a full fine or half fine of human-trespass then C.

Another version: Every judgment of contract and sale, loan and deposit and commercial loan, and every thing which is a necessity of life, if it may not be for discharging a debt or for denial,[336] a pledge of one-third is [given] to end fasting, and a pledge of half [is given] before a decision, and [the] full pledge [is given] after a decision.

---

336 The phrase *díl nó séna* is difficult to interpret. The commentary seems to be drawing a distinction between, on the one hand, situations where a debt has been paid (or will be) or the debt is being denied, and, on the other hand, all other cases. In cases where the debt has been paid (or a pledge is given to bring the case to resolution), the case is over. In situations where the debt is being denied, the case is ongoing and needs further investigation.

G*ac* fuig*ell* cuir ⁊ cun*nar*rta, ona ⁊ ait*h*ne ⁊ *air*lice, ⁊ g*ac* ni is nes*am* t*oi*-*scid*e, dia mbé f*or* dil ⁊ séna, is sm*achtgille sechtmai*d do scu*r* t*r*oisce, ⁊ t*r*ian-g*ill*e ria mbr*eith* br*eith*e, ⁊ lang*ill*e i*ar* mbr*eith* br*eith*e.

G*ac* fuig*ell cuir* ⁊ *cundartha, ona*[337] ⁊ ait*h*ne ⁊ *air*lice, ⁊ g*ach* ni is tan*ais*te nesam*h* t*oiscid*e na bid*h* f*or* dil na f*or* séna, is sm*achtgill*e *secht*m*ai*d do scu*r* t*r*oisce, ⁊ triang*ill*e ria mbr*eith*[338] br*eith*e, ⁊ lang*ill*e i*ar* mbr*eith* br*eith*e.

G*ach* fuig*ell cuir* ⁊ *cundartha*, *ona* ⁊ a*ithne*[339] ⁊ *air*ligthe,[340] ⁊[341] g*ac* ni is tan*ais*te nes*am* t*oiscide*,[342] mad*h* bid*h* f*or* díl ⁊ f*or* séna, is sm*achtgill*e éigcint*ech* dá screp*al déc* fri fuaslu*cud* t*r*oisce, ⁊ sm*achtgill*e *secht*m*ai*d ria mbr*eith*(e) br*eith*e, ⁊ la*ngill*e i*ar* mbr*eith* br*eith*e.

Breat*ha*[343] im gata ⁊ saraig*h*te ⁊ turoirgne sam*h*laib*h*, is sm*achtgill*e éicin*n*-t*ech* in da screp*al déc* [secht]air[344] ria mbr*eith*em*hnus*, ⁊ triang*ille* bí ite*r* chai*n* ⁊ urr*adus*.

Na s*éoit* gill ⁊ a*ithne* ⁊ urla*mh*ais, slán do*n*tí i tait [a] (i)[345] l*áim* [a lacht][346] ⁊ a ng*nim*rad do c*aith*em,[a] *acht* a*chtugud* ne*mcaithme*;[347] m*a* r*o*[348] a*ch*taig*h*, fiach g*ait*e isi*n* l*acht* ⁊ f*iach* foi*m*ri*m* isi*n* ngni*mhrad*.

[a] .i. gi*n* fiac*h* gaite ⁊ ni aithgi*n*[349] J. [*CIH* 2003.25–2004.2]

337 I follow the editorial suggestions made by Binchy, *CIH* 2003, n. j.

338 The scribe originally wrote an extra ⟨e⟩ at the end of the word which he expunged by placing a *punctum delens* under it; see also Binchy, *CIH* 2003, n. k.

339 I follow the editorial suggestion made by Binchy, *CIH* 2003, n. l.

340 The ⟨g⟩ was added above the line by the scribe; see also Binchy, *CIH*, 2003, n. m.

341 The ⟨⁊⟩ was added above the line by the scribe; see also Binchy, *CIH* 2003, n. d.

342 I follow the editorial suggestion made by Binchy, *CIH* 2003, n. n.

343 Along the *marg. dext.* is written 'anfuig*ell* si*n*' 'that is *Anfuigell*' by the scribe; see also Binchy, *CIH* 2003, n. p. Although the paragraph which follows this one is included in the series of commentaries in source A above, it is uncertain whether this paragraph or the preceeding paragraphs actually belong with the *Anfuigell* material, despite the MS ascription, because the material is different from what is found in the rest of the *Anfuigell*-related commentaries.

344 Cf. *CIH* 1452.22 edited in Appendix 6.

345 I follow the emendation suggested by Binchy, *CIH* 2003, n. q.

346 Cf. source A above; see also Binchy, *CIH* 2003, n. r.

347 Binchy, *CIH* 2004, n. b, queries the expansion of MS '.a.n.c.', but cf. source A above.

348 I follow the editorial suggestion made by Binchy, *CIH* 2004, n. c.

349 This interlinear gloss is written in the hand of the scribe; see also Binchy, *CIH* 2004, n. a.

Every judgment of contract and sale, loan and deposit and commercial loan, and every thing which is a necessity of life, if it may be for discharging a debt and denial, a penalty pledge of one-seventh[350] is [given] to end fasting, and a pledge of one-third [is given] before a decision of judgment, and [the] full pledge [is given] after a decision of judgment.

Every judgment of contract and sale, loan and deposit and commercial loan, and every thing which is almost[351] a necessity of life that may not be for discharging a debt or for denial, a pledge penalty of one-seventh is [given] to end fasting, and a pledge of one-third [is given] before a decision of judgment, and [the] full pledge [is given] after a decision of judgment.

Every judgment of contract and sale, loan and deposit and commercial loan, and every thing which is almost a necessity of life, if it may be for discharging a debt and for denial, an indefinite[352] pledge penalty of twelve scruples is [given] for the release of fasting, and a pledge penalty of one-seventh before a decision of judgment, and [the] full pledge after a decision of judgment.

Judgments regarding thefts and violations and plunderings similarly, an indefinite pledge penalty of twelve scruples as well is [given] before judgment, and a pledge of one-third is [given for] both promulgated law and customary law.

The *séts* of a pledge and deposit and custody, free for the one in whose hand they are to use their milk and their labor,[a] except [if] he stipulated not to use [them]; and if he [i.e. the lessor] stipulated [not to use them], [there is] a fine for stealing the milk and a fine for unauthorized use for the labor.

[a] i.e. without a fine for theft and no restitution J.

350 The precise meaning of *smacht* here is unclear, but it should be noted that according to the legal text *Cóic Conara Fugill* 'The Five Paths of Judgment', the third procedural 'path', *cert* 'justice', deals with unfair contracts and requires giving a *smachtgille* 'penalty pledge' normally worth one-seventh of a cow; *eDIL*, *s.v. smacht* II(b); GEIL, 192; Archan, *Cóic Conara Fugill* §12 and gloss 1 (294); Stacey, *The Road to Judgment*, 119–121; Jaqueline Bemmer, "Validity and Equality in Early Irish Contract Law: *Dliged* and *Cert* in the light of *Cóic Conara Fugill*," *Studia Celtica Fennica* 5 (2008): 12–16.

351 The sense of *tánaiste* seems to refer to anything which is close to being a necessity of life but is not actually necessary.

352 The precise sense of *éccintech* 'indefinite, undetermined' is obscure to me.

§13 Fiach con ⁊rl-

Cu c*ét*ci*n*tach i*n*dlig*thech* si*n*, ⁊ ait*h*gi*n* no ot*hrus* iss *ed* ata a*na*[353] ci*n*aid. ⁊ mada nd*ern*tar faill i*mon* othr*us*, reit*h*id s*macht* m*eth*a follaigt*h*e ot*hrus*a a*n*d coruici lancoirp*díre*[354] na cneidi *cona* f*er*tai*n* t*r*ia co*m*raite, uair is comr*ait*e i*n* folludu*d*. Cid fo*dera* co rethe*n*d sm*acht* m*eth*a a ci*n*aid a ruib f*or* nec*h* ⁊ na ret*h*e*n*d a ci*n*aid a dair? Is e i*n* fa*th*: Rosoic*h* a rob a comsl*ain*ti(i)*us* ris fei*n* ⁊ nocha roic*h* a dær A. [*CIH* 2151.31–36]

353 One or two letters have been erased after the first ⟨a⟩. The suspension mark over the first ⟨a⟩ and the second ⟨a⟩, written subscript, have been added in later by the scribe in a lighter colored ink.

354 The scribe originally wrote an ⟨f⟩ instead of a ⟨c⟩. He changed the ⟨f⟩ to a ⟨c⟩ by erasing the descender.

§13 Fine of a dog, etc.[355]

That is a dog's unlawful first crime,[356] and restitution or sick-maintenance[357] is what there is for its offense [i.e. the fine for the injury]. And if the sick-maintenance was neglected [by the culprit], a fine of failure for neglecting sick-maintenance accumulates then up to the full body-fine of the wound when it is intentionally inflicted, because the neglect is [reckoned to be the same as] intent. What is the reason that fine of failure accumulates for someone for the offense of his animal and the offense of his bondsman does not accumulate? The reason is: His animal has equal liability with him himself and his bondman does not A.

355 For a discussion of this section, see the Introduction, 19.

356 For offenses to and by dogs see *GEIL*, 143 and 146; *EIF*, 114–121; Liam Breatnach, "On the Glossing of Early Irish Law-texts, Fragmentary Texts, and Some Aspects of the Laws Relating to Dogs," in *Celtica Helsingiensia: Proceedings from a Symposium on Celtic Studies*, ed. Anders Ahlqvist et al. (Helsinki: Societas Scientiarum Fennica, 1996), 15–20; Paul Russell, "Poets, Power and Possessions in Medieval Ireland: Some Stories from *Sanas Cormaic*," in *Law, Literature and Society. CSANA Yearbook* 7. Ed. Joseph F. Eska (Dublin: Four Courts Press, 2008), 10, 24–26, and 37–39; and *Canones Hibernenses* VI, in *The Irish Penitentials.* Scriptores Latini Hiberniae 5. Ed. and trans. Ludwig Bieler (Dublin: The Dublin Insitute for Advanced Studies, 1975), 174 and 175. The commentary seems to deal with the liability of the dog's owner for any unlawful injuries, such as dog-bites, inflicted by the dog; see *eDIL s.v.* 1 *cú.*

357 For sick-maintenance and injury see *GEIL*, 130–134; and D.A. Binchy, "Sick-maintenance in Irish Law," *Ériu* 12 (1938): 78–134. If someone has been injured and needs to convalesce for longer than nine days, the victim is moved to the house of a neutral third party and the victim's medical expenses are paid by the culprit.

§14 Recht flatha ⁊rl-

In inbaid rocuirset i*n* tuat*h*[358] i*n* rig do den*am* besc*na* dligth*ig* doib, *acht* mas e i*n* besc*na*-si*n* dorigne ł besc*na* is co*m*dligth*ech* ris ł is dligth*ech*a i*n*das, noc*h*a dlegar dib-siu*m* a tu*r*brod. ⁊ da nd*er*nat, ic*ait* er*aic* ina tu*r*brod, ⁊ ic*ait* in l*eth*fiac*h* co *dechmaid*[359] ł in lanfiach i*ar* *dechm*aid.[360] Masa besc*na* is i*n*dligth*ech*a dori*n*de ina si*n*, noc*h*a dlegar deisiu*m* a de*n*um, ⁊ ic*aid* in ri i*n* l*eth*fiac*h* ł in lanfiach A. [*CIH* 2151.37–42]

358 The ⟨a⟩ is written subscript.

359 Cf. Binchy, *CIH* 2151, n. f.

360 The ⟨aid⟩ were added above the line by the scribe.

§14 A lord's law, etc.[361]

When the people had the king make a lawful regulation for them,[362] provided that he made that regulation or a regulation equally lawful to it or more lawful than it, they ought not to violate it. And if they do, they pay a fine for violating it, and they pay the half fine up to ten days or the full fine after ten days. If the regulation he made is more unlawful instead, he ought not to have made it, and the king pays the half fine or the full fine A.

361 For a discussion of this section, see the Introduction, 19.

362 Cf. §6 for those entitled to make lawful regulations.

§15 Cin fir mairb ⁊rl-

Cach ni *im*a rab*us* i faill ⁊ i n-etrebaire, ⁊ rofit*ir* in galur, ⁊ ni rocuindig a fia*cha*. ⁊ cac*h* ní na raibe f*or* treb*aire* ł f*or* sli*cht* el*oide*, is c*er*taithgi*n* gi*n* ass. Maine raib i faill im*murro*, ł ni feas[363] in g*alar*, ł ma robui f*or* sli*cht* el*oide*, is aithgi*n* co los ⁊ as A.[364] [*CIH* 2152.1–4]

Na[365] h-uili fech fa rab*us* i faill ⁊ i n-etreb*airi*, ⁊ rofes in gal*ar*, ⁊ n*ar* h-ac*r*a co tainic bas i*n* duine fei*n*, is [s]la*n* dona co*m*arbaib ci*n* ni d'ic intib *acht* c*er*taithg*in* gi*n* los, gin as, ci*n* in[ḟ]orb*airt*[366] M. [*CIH* 2142.40–42]

---

1 Source **M** does not contain any of the text.

---

363 The ⟨a⟩ is written subscript.

364 Before starting this section of the text, the scribe recut his pen. The effect is that the handwriting has a very different cast from what comes before it and what comes after the first few lines of the next section.

365 Although source M is from *Findśruth Fíthal*, the commentary shares some points with those of source A; the commentary in M continues with topics not directly related to *Anfuigell*. The extract of text associated with this commentary reads 'Co b*er* br*eith* it*er* biu ⁊ marb?' 'How will I pass judgment between the living and the dead?'

366 The ⟨or⟩ were inserted above the line by the scribe; see also Binchy, *CIH* 2142, n. k.

§15 Liability of a dead man, etc.[367]

Each thing that was neglected and without guarantee,[368] and he knew [about] the illness,[369] and he [i.e. the one owed] did not demand his fines [from the debtor]. And each thing that was not on security or as a result of evasion, it is exact restitution without interest.[370] Unless there was neglect, however, and the illness was not known, or if it was as a result of evasion, it is restitution with interest[371] A.

All that he saw that was neglected and without guarantee, and the illness was known, and it [i.e. the debt] was not sued until the person himself died. The heirs are exempt from legal liability and do not pay anything for them except exact restitution without interest[372] M.

---

367 For a discussion of this section, see the Introduction, 19. For liabilities associated with the dead and their heirs, see *GEIL*, 157.

368 The sense of *étrebaire* is that the item in question is not secured by a surety.

369 Although the Irish is ambiguous, the sense of the clause is that the person who was owed knew that the debtor was ill. This interpretation brings the commentary in A into agreement with the commentary in M.

370 Literally 'without milk'.

371 Literally 'with calves and with milk'; see also §4.

372 Literally 'without calves, without milk, without produce'.

§16 Maidm a crich ⁊rl-

Daine sin tangatar re fogail n-i*n*dlis isi*n* c*r*ich. Mas i*n*dethi*m* fastaide rug*ad* cuca no et*ar*scart*h*a a *sét* riu, (a)[i]s [s]l*an*[373] a marb*ad* ce*n* cæ*macht*ai*n* a fastaide ł ci*n* cæm*acht*ai*n* na *sét* do bei*n* dib. Ma ta cæ*macht*a [f]ast*aid*i im*murro* ł cæ*macht*u na *sét* do et*ar*(*ar*)scarad[374] friu gi*n* a m*ar*b*ad*, is co*mar*dug*ud* co frit*h*aig*id* it*er* in fog*ail* doro*n*sat ⁊ doro*n*ad friu.

Masa i*n*det*h*im m*ar*bt*h*a rug*ad* cuca, cia b*eth* cæ*macht*a fast*ada* ci*n*co be, is co*mar*dug*ud* co frit*haigid* i*n* n-uair denma na fog*l*a. Mai*n*ib i*n*d u*air* den*m*a na fog*l*a, is com*ardugud* ci*n* frith*aigid*, cia b*eth* cæm*achta* [f]ast*aidi* ci*n*co be, it*er* in fog*ail* doro*n*sat ⁊ doro*n*ad riu.

In lu*cht* dorigne i*n* fog*ail* si*n*, ⁊ ca*ch* æ*n* f*or*a roic*h* a ci*n* i*n*bl*eogain* in ta*n* na t*ar*thith*ar*[375] fei*n*, no cia rot*air*sit, dia*m* nesa*m* i*n*t i*n*bl*eogan* ...[376]

Masa nec*h* im*murro* f*or*na roi[c](t)*h*[377] ci*n* inbl*eogain*, is og[ṡ]lan[378] ci*n* cæm*acht*a fast*ada* a richt dilsig. Ma *conanagair* a fast*ad*, is l*eth*fiac*h* i*n*d ri*cht* dilsig beos A.[379] [*CIH* 2152.5–17]

---

1 cri*ch* II; the ⁊rl- is omitted from II.

---

373 I follow the emendation suggested by Binchy, *CIH* 2152, n. b.

374 I follow the emendation suggested by Binchy, *CIH* 2152, n. c.

375 Binchy, *CIH* 2152, n. d, queries whether this word should be emended to *tarthat*; the final syllable is ambiguous in the MS owing to a suspension mark. I have expanded the final syllable to reflect the pres. pass. sg. form of *do-airret*.

376 This sentence is corrupt. It appears as if the scribe has left out some material. Although *inbleogain* is listed in e*DIL* as a n. noun, the form of the def. art. here, *int*, indicates that the noun has switched genders from n. to m., which is common in the MI period.

377 I follow the suggestion of Binchy, *CIH* 2152, n. e.

378 I follow the suggestion of Binchy, *CIH* 2152, n. f.

379 For similar material from *Bretha Éitgid*, see *CIH* 288.21–289.15 and 1201.39–1204.18; and *AL* 3: 286.14–289.40.

§16 A rout in a territory, etc.[380]

Those people who came into the territory to [make] an unlawful attack.[381] If they [i.e. the locals] had intended on apprehending [the raiders] or of regaining their *sét*s, there is no liability for killing them [i.e. the raiders] [if] they cannot apprehend them or take the *sét*s from them. If [they, i.e. the locals] could apprehend [them, i.e. the raiders], however, or regain the *sét*s from them without killing them [i.e. the raiders], it is a balancing of liabilities with a counter-claim between the attack that they [i.e. the raiders] made and [what] was done to them [by the locals].

If they [i.e. the locals] had intended on killing them [i.e. the raiders], whether or not [they] could apprehend [them], it is a balancing of liabilities with a counter-claim at the time that the attack was made. If it is not at the time that the attack was made, it is a balancing of liabilities without a counter-claim, whether or not [they] could apprehend [them], between both the attack they [i.e. the raiders] made and [what] was done to them [by the locals].

The people who made that attack, and everyone who has his liability as a kinsman-surety when he himself [i.e. the raider] is not seized, or although they seized [him], if the kinsman-surety is necessary ...[382]

If it is someone, however, who does not have liability as a kinsman-surety, he is completely exempt from legal liability, [if he] cannot apprehend [him and kills him] in mistake for an outlaw. If he could have apprehended him, it is, moreover, a half fine for him [i.e. that he owes for killing him] in mistake for an outlaw A.[383]

---

380 For a discussion of this section, see the Introduction, 19–21.

381 For raiding and blood-feuds, see McLeod, "The Blood-Feud in Medieval Ireland," 114–133.

382 This paragraph is complicated by being incomplete. The substance of it is as follows: If the raiders are not apprehended, their nearest relatives who would be liable for their crimes are considered financially responsible for the damage done by the raiders. If the raiders are caught, but are not able to pay the fines that they owe, their relatives would be financially responsible instead.

383 For killing someone in mistake for a thief or outlaw, see CIH 1161.15–17 and 1067.30–31, respectively. Both of these passages are cited and discussed in McLeod, *Bloodshed and Compensation*, 17–18. The fine for killing an innocent man in mistake for an outlaw is half of that for murder. The fine for murder consists of two parts: 1), *wergeld* fixed at seven *cumals* for every free person and 2), the honor-price (or part thereof) of the victim's kin payable to members of the victim's kindred; GEIL, 125–127. Not all kinsmen are obligated to act as a kinsman-surety; for example, poets and churchmen were exempt; see *eDIL s.v. inbleoga(i)n, inableogain* and cf. §50.

.i. maid*hus* dib isi*n* cri*ch* iar ndenam fog*h*la, ⁊ is am*al* ci*n* druit*h* ł das*a*-*chta*[ig] léo iarna crud*h*.

Na h-uil*i* dæ*ine* tancad*ar* re marb*ad* isi*n* cri*ch* ⁊ na h-uil*i* dæ*ine* réna fog*ail* a nderrn*n*sat, is [s]l*an* g*o* t*r*ian iat doib g*o* cæmt*achta*i*n* a f*astada*,[384] ⁊ mana fuil roba (t*h*)sl*an* .i. dil*us* do gr*es* g*o* rodamt*ar* dlig*ed*, ł go t*r*ian f*or*cr*ada* ó damt*ar* .i. g*a*c uile fog*al* danea(n)t[h]*er*[385] aga tabairt fr*i* dlig*ed* II. [CIH 1202.32–37]

384 See also Binchy, *CIH* 1202, n. o.

385 Binchy, *CIH* 1202, n. s, notes that the first ⟨a⟩ is written subscript, but it is in fact the second ⟨a⟩ which is written subscript. *CIH* 1202.37 reads 'daneant*ar*', but Binchy, n. s, suggests that the form should perhaps be read as *donethar* or *da ndentar*. I suspect the form verb intended is a MI pres. pass. sg. of *do-gní*, i.e. *dogníther*.

i.e. they were routed in the territory after making an attack, and it is like a crime of an imbecile or of a madman for them regarding the payment.[386]

All the people who opposed the killing in the territory and all the people who opposed their attack which they [i.e. the raiders] made, they are exempt from legal liability up to a third [for killing] them [i.e. the raiders], [if] they could apprehend them, and if not [they] are exempt from legal liability, i.e. until they [i.e. the raiders] submit to law, there is never liability, or up to a third of the excess after they submitted to law, i.e. every injury that is made by bringing them to law II.

---

386 For the liability of crimes committed by those of unsound mind, see *GEIL*, 92–93. Generally speaking, the kindred is liable for any offenses committed by those of unsound mind as it would be their responsibility to look after and care for its mentally disabled family members.

§17 Crecha urr*ad*ais ⁊rl-

p. 11a .i. sl*an* co trian crech a nd-ag*aid* creiche; | ⁊ mana d*er*nt*ar* crech a nd-ag*aid* creche, *acht* ap*ad* ⁊ trosc*ad* do tab*air*t, ⁊ ma roleged a elod, is *cóic sét* ⁊ eneclann ⁊ diabl*ad* fia*ch* do a legud a n-elai.

In crech a nd-ag*aid* creiche: Ma dorigne i*n* *cét*fer crec*h* ⁊ ni t*ar*gaid dlig*ed*, ⁊ dori*n*ded crech air i*n*d, is sl*an* do*n* fir ded*en*ach co *trian* ⁊ co*mar*dugud it*er* da t*rian* dire na *cét* crec*h*e ⁊ dire na creic*h*e dedi*n*chi, ⁊ cidbe dib aca *m*be an i*m*arcraid, ic*aid* re celi. Ma targ*aid* in *cét*fer dlig*ed*, is co*m*ardugud ce*n* frith*aigid* eta*rr*u an*n*-sic.

Masa[387] feich dligis cach dib da celi, *acht* mas a n-æ*n*f*ec*ht tucsat a toich*id*, ac*h*t mas ui*m*e doc*h*uat*ar* docu*m* i*n* br*eithe*ma*n* da fis ci*ndus* icfati[s](t),[388] iss *ed* is coir do*n* bret*h*emai*n* a rrad:[389] ‘Co*m*ardug*ud* eta*rr*u ł co*m*lecud dib’. Mas ui*m*e docuat*ar* docu*m* in br*eithe*ma*n* da fis cia dib is taisec*h*a toich*id* a c*h*eli, iss *ed* is coir do*n* brethe*main* a feich do*n*ti is taisec*h*a toich*id*.

Masa feich beca dlig*es* in dara fer ⁊ feich mora dlig*es* in fer aili, noch[a]n i*n*dlig*thech* d’fir na fiach mbec ce*n*co h-ica na fia*ch*a mora[390] dlegar de no cu *r*ahict*h*ar[391] a feich beca ris A. [*CIH* 2152.18–32]

.i. i*n* creac i *n*-aig*h*id*h* creic*h*i, *acht* mai*n*e t*h*argaid*h* i*n* cetfe*ar* dlig*h*ed*h*, is [s]lan dun ḟir[392] ded*henach* cu t*r*ian, ⁊ ma t*har*gaid*h* is com*har*dugud*h* can [ḟ]rit*h*oig*h*id*h*.[393]

1 Creacha C, Crec*h* II. ‖ urrad*h*ais C, urr*adais* II; *CIH* 1202.38 reads ‘urr*ad* (?)’. ‖ ⁊rl- *om.* C and II.

387 The scribe originally wrote a ⟨d⟩ after this word, but it was erased later; see also Binchy, *CIH* 2152, n. g.

388 The verb has been emended to the 3 pl. cond. form of *íccaid* ‘pays’. A similar mistake appears in the C version of the commentary as well which has *icfaitit*.

389 The words *a rrad* were inserted above the line by the scribe; see also Binchy, *CIH* 2152, n. i.

390 Binchy, *CIH* 2152, n. j, notes that ⟨ra⟩ have been written above the line. The letters were written by the scribe.

391 The first ⟨a⟩ was written below the line by the scribe.

392 Binchy, *CIH* 168, n. e, states that the lenition mark was added later, but he gives no explanation as to how he arrived at this determination. The ink color of the lenition mark is the same as the scribe’s and does not appear to have been added later. Here and throughout, I respectfully disagree with all of Binchy’s assertions regarding the relative scribal chronology of the lenition marks in this MS.

393 I follow the emendation suggested by Binchy, *CIH* 168, n. c.

§17 Of a raid according to customary law, etc.[394]

i.e. a raid in retaliation for a raid[395] is exempt from legal liability up to a third [of the amount of the fines for injury]; | and if a raid has not been done in retaliation for a raid, but notice and fasting are given, and if they were evaded, it is five *sét*s and honor-price and doubling of fines for evading them. p. 11a

The raid in retaliation for a raid: If the first man made a raid and did not offer law, and a raid was made because of it, the second man is exempt from legal liability up to a third and [there is] a balancing of liabilities between [the remaining] two thirds of the first raid's fine and the second raid's fine, and whichever of them has the greater amount [i.e. fines still owed after their respective fines have been balanced], he pays the other. If the first man offers law, it is a balancing of liabilities without a counter-claim between them then.

If each of them owes fines to the other, and if it is the first time that they brought their suit, and if they went to the judge about it to find out how they should pay, it is proper for the judge to say: 'A balancing of liabilities between them or equal lapsing of them'.[396] If they went to the judge about it to find out which of them should first sue the other, it is proper for the judge [to grant] the fines to the one who should sue first.

If one of the two owes small fines and the other one owes large fines, it is not unlawful for the man who is owed the small fines not to pay the large fines that are owed by him until his small fines are paid to him A.[397]

i.e. a raid in retaliation for a raid, if the first man does not offer law, the second man is exempt from legal liability up to a third, and if [the first man] offers law, it is a balancing of liabilities without a counter-claim.

394 For a discussion of this section, see the Introduction, 21–22.

395 Cf. §16 for raiding across territories.

396 The sense of this clause is that the two parties either balance what is owed to each other, i.e. if an equal amount is owed to each other, nothing is paid, if one owes more than the other, the amount above what was considered equal is paid to the other. If they decide not to balance their liabilities, they can decide not to sue each other at all.

397 This paragraph seems to present an alternative payment method in a situation where the two parties do not consult a judge about the payment procedure.

Masa feich dlig*h*es ca*ch* dib*h* da *ch*eile, *acht* i *n*n-[a]enḟecht tucsat*ar* a toi*ch*id*h*, mas i*m*i da*ch*uad*ar ar* a*mmus* in breathem*h*an d'ḟi*ar*faig*h*id*h* do[398] ci*n*nas icfaiti[s](t)[399] is *ed* is *ch*oir do *a* rad*h*: 'Com*ar*dughudh et*arro* ł coim*h*le*ch*ud dib*h*'.

Mas ed*h* ra*ch*ursed*h* cuicci ne*ch* dib is toisci toi*ch*id*h* a *ch*eili, is ed*h* is *ch*oir a feic*h* dunti is taisci toichid.

Masa feic*h* becca dlig*h*es in d*ar*a fear ⁊ feic*h* mora dlig*h*es i*n* fe*ar* eile, nucun inddlig*thech* dunti (dlig*h*es)[400] na fiachu becca gengu tucca a feic*h* mora dun fir ele no cu tuct*har* a ḟeic*h* becca do C. [*CIH* 168.17–27]

i. mas a n-æn*acht* dorin*n*e cac*h* dib c*r*ec*h* ara ceil*e*, masa cut*r*um*a* iat, is a mb*eth* aid*h*e a nd-aig*h*i II. [*CIH* 1202.–38–39]

398 A suspension mark above the ⟨o⟩ has been erased; see also Binchy, *CIH* 168, n. f.

399 Cf. the verb form in source A above.

400 Cf. the commentary in source A.

If each of them owes fines to the other, and if it is the first time they brought their suit, if they went to the judge about it to ask how they should pay, it is proper for him [i.e. the judge] to say: 'A balancing of liabilities between them or equal lapsing of them'.

If they went to him [to find out] which of them should first sue the other, it is proper [to give] his fines to the one who should sue first.

If one man owes small fines and the other man owes large fines, it is not unlawful for the one who is owed the small fines not to pay his large fines to the other man until his small fines are given to him C.

i.e. if each of them made a raid against the other once, if they are equivalent [referring to the raids], they offset each other II.

§18 Enechruice rig ⁊rl-

.i. indi is luga ata do*n* rig, in æ*n*mad rann *fich*it[401] ata do a ndul co' mnai i*n*dlis; ⁊ ma roleced el*od* ime-side, is *cóic sét* ⁊ e*n*eclan*n* ⁊ diabl*ad* fiach do a leg*ud* a eloide A. [*CIH* 2152.33–35]

401 The ⟨it⟩ are written above the line.

§18 Compensation for dishonor[402] due to a king, etc.[403]

i.e. a twenty-first [part of the honor-price] is the smallest amount paid to the king for him[404] cohabitating with a *bé n-indles*; and if it is evaded, five *sét*s and honor-price and doubling of fines for evading it A.

402 The legal term *enechrucce* refers to the compensation due to someone for dishonor done to one's relative or tenant; see *eDIL s.v. enechrucce, ainechrucce*.

403 For a discussion of this section, see the Introduction, 22–23.

404 The pronoun refers to another man cohabiting with a kept woman. The *be n-indles* 'non-owned woman' is a type of concubine. In the legal texts she is depicted as married but cohabitating with another man, which she does with her husband's permission; see Power, "Classes of Women Described in the *Senchas Már*," 98–99; *Cáin Lánamna*, 272–273; and *Uraicecht Becc*, CIH 1607.16–18. The commentary here is problematic. If the *be n-indles* is cohabiting with another man with her husband's permission, it is unclear why the king is owed a fine, unless this situation is seen as a dishonor against the king as well. That being said, this fine would certainly be another way for the king to generate income. In a commentary dealing with honor-price in *Uraicecht Becc* 'Small Primer', CIH 1607.11–12, *AL*, 3: 72.6–7, it is stated that a man involved with a *be n-indles* receives a twenty-first of his honor-price for injury done to her.

§19 Recht sencairde ⁊rl-

Cairde robui acna dai*n*ib a*n*d si*n* ar d*us*, ⁊ tai*n*ic cai*n* cuca fui. Mas e frea*cra* 'fuill*em*' ar siat 'd'er*aic* ar cana re h-er*aic ar* cairde co roib er*aic* cana a*n*d; ⁊ i*n* u*air* rach*us* ar cai*n* uai*n*d, fogn*ad ar cair*de dui*n*d', *acht* ma roba*tar* fiadai*n* acu, ł ma robui co*m*aititiu co raibe i*n*t ac*h*tug*ud* a*n*d, is a mb*eth* aran a*cht*ug*ud*-si*n*. Mu*n*a rabat*ar* fiad*ain* a*n*d it*ir* no mu*n*a raibe co*m*aititiu, is lasi*n*ti dori*n*de i*n* fog*ail* fa deoid a se*n*a *con*ac*h* raibe i*n*t *achtugud*-si*n* a*n*d, ⁊ a mb*eth* can er*aic* ł co nd*er*nt*ar* besc*na* nua A. [*CIH* 2152.36–2153.2]

Ma rabai cairdi accu *ar* dus ⁊ tai*n*ic cai*n* c*h*ucu *acht* mas *ed* raac*h*taig*h*set 'tuilliu*mh*' *ar* siat 're h-eraicc *ar* cairdi d'eraicc ar cana gurab*h* eraicc chana and; ⁊ in tan rac*h*as *ar* cain uai*n*d biaid *ar cair*di acaind' is a beith amlaid-sei*n* *acht* masa co*mh*aittitiu [ḟ]uil[405] accu fein i*m*mi-sei*n*, ł ma tat fiad*h*ain accu is a beith aml*aid*-si*n*. Mai*n*e [ḟ]uil ni dib-sei*n* accu, is a ṡena dunti dari*n*ni in fogail na fuil i*n*t ac*h*tugud*h*-sein an*n*, ⁊ beit*h* can ic *no* cu nd*er*nt*ar* besgna eile accu N. [*CIH* 115.5–10]

1 None of the text is preserved in source **N.**

405 The ⟨uil⟩ were added above the line by the scribe with reference marks; see also Binchy, *CIH* 115, n. b.

§19 Authority of old laws, etc.[406]

A law[407] the people had in the first place in that case, and a *cáin*[408] impugned it. If they respond: 'An addition', they say, 'according to the compensation[409] of our *cáin* to the compensation of our law until it is [the same as the] compensation of the *cáin*; and when our *cáin* will leave us, our law serves us', provided that they had witnesses, or if there was mutual acknowledgement that there was the agreement then, they are to be according to that agreement. If there were no witnesses at all or if there was not a mutual agreement, the one who committed a crime afterwards has a right to deny that there was that agreement then, and they are to be without compensation until a new regulation is made A.

If they had a law in the first place and a *cáin* came to them, provided that they agreed: 'An addition' they say 'to the compensation of our law according to the compensation of our *cáin* until it is [the same as the] compensation of the *cáin*; and when our *cáin* will leave us, we will have our law', they are to be thus provided that they themselves have a mutual agreement regarding that, or if they have witnesses that they are to be thus. If they have none of these, the one who committed a crime [can] deny that that agreement exists then, and there will be no paying [for crimes] until another regulation is made by them N.[410]

406 For a discussion of this section, see the Introduction, 23.

407 Although *cairde* can refer to a treaty between two or more *túaths*, it can also be used more generally for any law or agreement within a *túath*; *eDIL s.v. cairde*.

408 For promulgated law, see *GEIL*, 21–22; and T.M. Charles-Edwards, *Early Christian Ireland* (Cambridge: Cambridge University Press, 2000), 559–569.

409 Although *éraic* can refer to *wergeld* specifically, in this section the word is being used more generally for 'payment, compensation, fine'; see *eDIL s.v. éric, éraic*.

410 The commentary in source N might derive from *SM* 31 *Bretha Cairdi* 'Treaty Judgments'; *CCIH*, 17 and 302–303.

§ 20 Saigid féchem[ain][a] **.i. ni saig[i] naidm *féchemain***[b] **cin fiadna dia *for*gell ł nadman*n* in*raici* e*cht*ran*n*[a] no rath*a* no aiti*re* in*nraic* inf*or*uis.**[c]

[a] .i. in*n*saige na fia*ch* do*n* *tre*bai*r*e *for*in cint*ach* J.

[b] .i. *noch*on in*n*saige do nasc*aire* t*ar* cen*n* in feich*em*an .i. nasc*aire* *aile* robat*ar* an*n* *ar* *air*d oc naidm dal*a* *aile*, ⁊ ni rob*h*at*ar* risi*n* dail-si*n* J.

[c] .i. aiti*re* co n-in*ne* *ar*ais robat*ar* im cai*n*gin *aile* is tig*h*. ⁊ is as gabt*ar* si*n*: *Con*a*ch* gab*h*an*n* nech greim a fiad*nais*e *aile* *acht* iman caing*in* risi tai*n*ic. Is laisin cint*a*c a sena na t*ar*d in treb*air*e re ni it*ir* t*ar*a cen*n* m*an*a b*et* fiad*ain*. ⁊ in baile a n-ab*air* *for*t*ach* [a]iti*re* nodogaib*h*,[411] im b*e*c adama*r* an*n*-side, ⁊ is leis i*m*de*n*am *con*a re mor tai*n*ic co ro log*h* ein*ech* J.

Raith adai*m* ⁊ na[d][412] atamar[413] si*n* .i. in t*re*b*air*e aca rad co ndech*aid* in*n* an*n* si*n*, ⁊ noc*h*on [ḟ]uilit[414] fiad*ain* aice ris, ⁊ ata i*n* bidbaid aca rad na*ch* dech*aid*. Is laisi*n* (i*n*) bidbaid a se*n*a, ⁊ ic*aid* i*n* raith fei*n* na fia*ch*u.

Gne *aile*: & i*n* bail a n-aib*er*:[415] F*or*toi*n*g aiti*r*e nodagaib,[416] im bec atama*r* an*n*-side, ⁊ is le i*m*den*am* *con*id re mor tai*n*ic gu ro log en*ech*.

Man atama*r* i*n* treb*air*i, ⁊ at*m*aid fei*n* ⁊ ni fuilit fiadai*n* aice, se*n*t*ar* de. ⁊ rait*h* adai*m* ⁊ nad atama*r* si*n*, ⁊ ic*aid* fei*n*. Ma tait fiad*ain* aice, ł mad atama*r*

---

1 Saiged **A** | [col. 550] Saige J. ‖ féchem **A** fechem J. Source A ends here. The remainder of the text is from source J; see also *CCIH*, 165. The three glosses are also only found in source J. ‖ Binchy, *CIH* 2030, n. n, queries whether the .f. of the MS should be expanded as *feichemain* or *fiach*; see also Thurneysen, "Aus dem irischen Recht V," 402 for an edition and translation (into German) of *CIH* 2030.34–35. Thurneysen amends the text of J as follows: *saigid feicheman .i. ní·saigh(e) naidhm fecheman cin fiadna dia foirgell no nadmann inraici*(?) *echtrann*[*a*] *no ratha no aitire innruic inforuis*. In the OI text, I have emended *féchem* and *.f.* to acc. sg. *féchemain*.

---

411 The form *nodogaibh* is probably for *dodagaib*; cf. *nodagaib* in A and the note below.

412 Cf. the following commentaries in sources A and J below.

413 The ⟨at⟩ were added above the line by the scribe; see also Binchy, *CIH* 2153, n. a.

414 *Fuilit* is a MI 3 pl. form of OI *fuil*.

415 The phrase 'a n-aib*er*' was added above the line by the scribe.

416 The form *nodagaib* is the pres. ind. 3 sg. of *do-gaib*, with the MI confusion of the preverbs *no*/*ro*/*do* (here the preverb should be *do-*), and a f. class C object agreement marker *-da-*; lit. 'he lessened it [i.e. his hand]'. The verb *do-gaib* 'lessens, diminishes' is frequently used in conjunction with *a láim* 'his hand' to refer to a surety entering into suretyship/fulfilling his obligations as a surety. The noun *lám* 'hand' is feminine.

§20 He sues a debtor,[a] i.e. the binding-surety does not sue a debtor[b] without witnesses to attest it or qualified external binding-sureties or paying-sureties or a qualified resident[c] hostage-surety.[417]

[a] i.e. the liable[418] party is sued for the debts by the surety J.

[b] i.e. the surety does not sue on behalf of the debtor, i.e. another surety [and] he were then present at the binding of the other contract, and they were not against that contract J.

[c] i.e. a hostage-surety with household wealth [and] they were there regarding another claim that he had entered [into suretyship]. And it is from that it is said: Someone does not take the place of another witness except for the claim for which he agreed. The liable party has a right to deny that the surety gave anything at all on his behalf if there were no witnesses. And where it says: Testifying of a hostage-surety lessens it [i.e. the surety testifies that he undertook to go surety for a smaller amount], a small amount is allowed then, and he [i.e. the defendant] has a right to prove that he agreed to a large amount up to [his] honor-price J.

The paying-surety who acknowledges [that he accepted to act as a surety] and who is not acknowledged, i.e. the surety says that he entered into suretyship in that case, and he does not have any witnesses for it, and the defendant says that he did not enter [into suretyship]. The defendant has a right to deny it, and the paying-surety himself pays the fines.

Another version: And where it says: A hostage-surety testifies that he went surety [lit. he lessens it], regarding a small amount [i.e. the surety testifies that he undertook to go surety for a smaller amount], which is acknowledged in that case, and it is up to him [i.e. the defendant] to prove that he [i.e. the surety] agreed to a large amount up to [his, the surety's] honor-price.

If the surety is not acknowledged, and he himself acknowledges [it] and he does not have any witnesses, it is denied by him [i.e. the defendant]. And a paying-surety who acknowledges [that he accepted to act as a surety] and

417 For a discussion of this section, see the Introduction, 23–24.

418 *Cintach* refers not only to someone who is guilty of a crime, but also to anyone who is liable for a debt, fine, etc.; *eDIL* s.v. *cintach*.

fei*n* e, dogni co log e*n*ech. ⁊ cia robui aice log e*nech* i *n*-ai*msir* cu*nnartha* ł ci*n*co raibe, mu*n*a fuil aice i *n*-ai*msir* ica,[419] ce adamt*ar* am bec, se*n*t*ar* de o si*n* amach A. [*CIH* 2153.3–11]

Gne *aile*:[420] Ma*n* atama*r* in trebaire ⁊ atm*aid* fei*n*, ⁊ ni fil fiad*ain* aice, sent*ar* de. ⁊ r*aith*[421] adai*m* ⁊ na n-adama*r*, ⁊ ic*aid* fein.

Ma[422] tait fiad*ain*, ł mad admaite*r* fein, dogni co log*h* eine*ch*. Cia robui aice log*h* eine*ch* i n-aimsir cunn*ar*ta ł ci*n*co roibe, m*an*a fuil i n-ai*m*sir ica, ce admaite*r* im beg, sent*ar* de o si*n* amac*h*.[423]

Rait*h* ataim ⁊ nad atama*r* .i. at*a* r*aith* aca atmail *co n*dech*aid* risna fiac*h*aib*h*, ⁊ at*a* in b*idba*[424] aca sena na t*uc* it*ir* t*ar*a cen*n* í, *acht* m*an*a fuil fiad*ain* aice *co n*dech*aid* an*n* í, is a sena do*n* b*idbaid*[425] *co*n*a* t*uc* t*ara* cen*n* í, ⁊ ic*aid* in r*aith* fein na fiach*u* o doatai*m*.[426] ⁊ cemad ail do*n* feich*emain* ca*ch* ní ag*ras* d'ic don r*aith*, *noch*o roich, *acht* sena do*n* rait*h* na dech*aid acht* risiní atmas.

& ce rob*eth* in b*idba* ⁊ in feichem*h*[427] t*oicheda*[428] i n-æ*n*inad, *noch*on indlig*thech* do*n* f*eichemain*[429] t*oicheda* ci*n*co h-in*n*saig*h*e *ar*in mbid*h*b*aid*. ⁊ is as-si*n* g*abar*:[430] *Conach* dir don cor fiach*a* d'ic uada b*u*dein *acht* ma*n* a*cht*aigter *air* a n-ic fo *cétóir*. ⁊ dia n-a*cht*aig*h*te*r*, dleg*air* de comin*n*saige re f*eichemain ar* b*idbaid* ⁊ comtob*ach* air, ⁊ *noch*o dleg*ar* de fei*n* a n-ic uad*ha* J. [*CIH* 2030.34–2031.18]

419 The ⟨c⟩ was added above the ⟨i⟩ by the scribe; see also Binchy, *CIH* 2153, n. b.

420 The phrase *gne .ii.* was written in *marg. sin.* by the scribe; see also Binchy, *CIH* 2031, n. b.

421 See also Binchy, *CIH* 2031, n. c.

422 See Thurneysen, *Bürgschaft*, 43 for an edition and translation (into German) of *CIH* 2030.7–13.

423 Cf. *CIH* 2153.7–11, source A above.

424 This is a later form of *bibdu*; see *eDIL s.v. bibdu* and the corresponding forms in A; and cf. Binchy, *CIH* 20131, n. d.

425 See also Binchy, *CIH* 2031, n. e.

426 For *roataim*; *doataim* shows the MI confusion of *ro*/*do*/*no*.

427 The word *feichemh* was added above line with reference marks by the scribe; see also Binchy, *CIH* 2031, n. f.

428 I follow the suggestion made by Binchy, *CIH* 2031, n. g.

429 I follow the suggestion made by Binchy, *CIH* 2031, n. h.

430 See Binchy, *CIH* 2031, n. i.

who is not acknowledged [by the defendant], and he himself [i.e. the surety] pays. If he has witnesses or if he himself is acknowledged, he goes [into suretyship] up to [the amount of his] honor-price. And whether or not he has possession [of the amount] of his honor-price at the time of the contract, if he does not have it at the time of payment, though a small amount is allowed, it is denied by him [i.e. the defendant] in such cases A.

Another version: If the surety is not acknowledged and he himself acknowledges [it], and he does not have a witness, it is denied by him [i.e. the defendant]. And a paying-surety who acknowledges and is not acknowledged, and he himself [i.e. the surety] pays.

If there are witnesses, or if he himself is acknowledged, he goes [into suretyship] up to [the amount of his] honor-price. Whether or not he has possession [of the amount] of his honor-price at the time of the contract, if he does not have it at the time of payment, though a small amount is allowed, it is denied by him [i.e. the defendant] in such cases.

A paying-surety who acknowledges and he is not acknowledged, i.e. the paying-surety acknowledges that he entered into suretyship for the fines, and the defendant denies that he [i.e. the surety] gave anything at all on his behalf, unless he has a witness that he entered suretyship for it, the defendant can deny that he gave [anything] on his behalf, and the paying-surety himself pays the fines since he acknowledged [them]. And though the claimant might want every thing that he sues to be paid by the paying-surety, he does not obtain [it], but the paying-surety denies that he went surety [for anything] except for that which he acknowledges.

And though the defendant and the plaintiff might be in the same place, it is not unlawful for the plaintiff though he does not sue the defendant. And it is from that it is said: It is not proper for the surety to pay penalties himself except if it is stipulated for him to pay immediately. And if it is stipulated, a joint suing is required against the plaintiff by the defendant and a counter-claim for him, and he is not required himself to pay them J.

§ 21 Fod[431] truig ⁊rl-. Is la cach lasa fot*h*aigth*er* is lais a t[h]uinide

.i. in*n*r*ai*c oc i*n*dr*ai*c [ḟ]uil su*nn* oc aidb*r*ig, ł esi*n*r*ai*c ac esi*n*r*ai*c, ł esi*n*r*ai*c oc i*nn*r*ai*c. Set si*n* roce*n*daig dui*ne*, ⁊ atat*har* aca fuaitr*ed* ui*me*, ⁊ is nesa do*n*ti
p. 11b roce*n*daig e i*n*as do*n*ti fuil aca*n* fuidr*ed*, | ł cid co*m*foc*us* doib, ł cid nesa do*n*ti ata aci*n* fuaidr*ed*, ⁊ ata i*n*a aitite*n* gi*n* a fuaidr*ed* re risbud diles uad he A. [*CIH* 2153.12–16]

431 *Fod* is a form of *foth*; see *eDIL s.v.* 1 *foth.*

§ 21 Claim of [the] shore, etc. It is the possession of each [person] by whom it is found[432]

i.e. a qualified person from a qualified person is claiming here, or an unqualified person from an unqualified person, or an unqualified person from a qualified person. That *sét* which a person purchased, and someone is opposing him about it, and it is more necessary [i.e. the item in dispute is more needful] for the one who purchased it than the one who is opposing [the purchase], | or whether it is equidistant [in terms of necessity] for them [both], p. 11b
or it is more necessary for the one who is opposing [the purchase], and there is recognition [of ownership] without opposing it for a time during which it might be forfeited by him [i.e. the original owner][433] A.

432 For a discussion of this section, see the Introduction, 24. I should like to thank Paul Russell for valuable suggestions regarding this section of text.

433 The sense of the passage is that the necessity or non-necessity of the disputed item is not a factor in determining rightful ownership in this case.

§ 22 Fod luinge

.i. b*ar*c dot*himair*c[434] ece*n*ta gait*h*e docu*m* tire an*n* si*n*, ⁊ comrai*n*d b*air*ce dligth*ige* f*ur*re .i. t*r*ia*n* do fir i*n* f*er*ai*n*d hi t*ar*la hi, ⁊ t*r*ia*n* do rig na tuait*he*, ⁊ tria*n* do lu*cht* na tuait*h*e uili. ⁊ i*n* *sét* is ferr i*n*dti do rig na tuait*he*, ⁊ fuill*ed* ris gorbo tria*n* do. ⁊ i*n* *sét* is[435] ferr a cuit rig tuait*h*e, a t*r*ia*n*-sec uad, ⁊ fuill*ed* ris cu*r*ub ceth*raimth*e a cota uad do rig *cóic*id.[436] ⁊ i*n* *sét* is ferr a cuit rig *cói*-cid,[437] a t*r*ia*n*-sec uad, ⁊ fuill*ed* ris cu*r*ub ceth*ramth*a a cota uad do rig Er*enn*. ⁊ t*r*ia*n* a cota o dær*mainch*aib ecl*ais*i [do eclais][438] ⁊ o dærcheili fl*ath*a do fl*aith* co rud ɫ ecma*cht* no diri*n*d, ⁊ aile[439] *déc* an*n*-seic. ⁊ nochon [f]uil ni o sær*ch*eli fl*ath*a do fl*aith*(a).[440]

Can asa ngabar i*n*d aili *déc*? Is as gab*ar*: Am*ail* as e t*r*ia*n* ata o dærma*n*caib ecl*as*a do ecl*ais* ⁊ o dær*ch*elib fl*ath*a do fl*aith* co rud ɫ ecma*cht* ɫ dir*ainn* ata uait*h*ib i rud .i. næ*m*ad, cub*aid* de-seic cia*m*ad he t*r*ian na ceth*ramth*a ata o dærma*n*caib ecl*as*a do eclais[441] co rud ɫ ecma*cht* no dir*ainn* dob*eth* uait*h*ib i rud .i. *aile déc*.

⁊ i*n*t ain*m*rai*n*de b*er*es ri *cóic*id[442] o rig tuait*h*e ⁊ rig Er*enn* o rig *cóic*id[443] di so*m*ai*n*e na b*air*ce curab e i*n*t ainmrai*n*de-si*n* ic*as* dona[444] *secht* cu*malaib* ata i*n*a ne*m*tochur.

---

1 While the commentary from Source **O** is relevant to *Anfuigell*, the text which accompanies the commentary is from *Bretha Éitgid*: *díles tochur do fir puirt* 'jetsam belongs to the owner of the shore'; see *CCIH*, 24; and *GEIL*, 108 and 276–277.

---

434 The form *dothimairc* appears to be the pres. ind. 3 sg. of *do-immoirg* 'drives, impels', with the preverbal particle *do*, which would have been perfective *ro* in OI; the preverbal particles *no*/*ro*/*do* are frequently confused in MI. The lenition of the ⟨t⟩ is a result of the relative clause with object antecedent.

435 The ⟨s⟩ was inserted above the line by the scribe.

436 The ⟨id⟩ were written above the line by the scribe.

437 The ⟨id⟩ were written above the line by the scribe.

438 I follow the emendation suggested by Binchy, *CIH* 2153, n. c; see further below.

439 The ⟨le⟩ were added above the line; cf. Binchy, *CIH* 2153, n. d.

440 I follow the emendation suggested by Binchy, *CIH* 2153, n. e.

441 Approximately six letters have been erased after this word.

442 The ⟨id⟩ were written above the line by the scribe.

443 The ⟨id⟩ were written above the line by the scribe.

444 The ⟨na⟩ were inserted above the line.

§22 Claim of a boat[445]

i.e. a ship which the force of the wind had drived towards the land in that case, and division of a lawful ship [is made] of her,[446] i.e. a third for the owner of the land in which she landed, and a third for the king of the *túath*, and a third for the people of the entire *túath*. And the best *sét* in her [is given] to the king of the *túath*, and it is added to until he has a third. And the best *sét* from the share of the king of the *túath*, a third of it [is given] by him, and it is added to until a fourth of his share [is given] by him to the king of the province. And the best *sét* from the share of the king of the province, a third of it [is given] by him, and it is added to until a fourth of his share [is given] by him to the king of Ireland. And a third of their share from a church's base monastic clients to [their] church and from a lord's base clients to [their] lord up to a wood or inaccessible place or wasteland, and [it is] a twelfth then. And there is nothing from a lord's free clients to [their] lord.

Whence is the twelfth derived? It is derived from this: Just as there is a third from base monastic clients to [their] church and from a lord's base clients to [their] lord up to a wood or inaccessible place or wasteland, that which is [due] from those [things found] in a wood, i.e. a ninth, it is appropriate from this that there should be a third of the fourth that is [due] from base monastic clients to a church up to a wood or inaccessible place or wasteland so that there should be [due] from those [things found] in a wood, i.e. a twelfth.[447]

And the proportion which a king of a province takes from a king of a *túath* and a king of Ireland [takes] from a king of a province from the profit of the ship, that is the proportion that he pays for the seven *cumal*s which are [due] when they are not jetsam.[448]

---

445 For a discussion of this section, see the Introduction, 24–25. For the laws relating to jetsam, see *GEIL*, 107–108; and Mac Niocaill, "Jetsam, Treasure Trove and the Lord's Share in Medieval Ireland," 103–110.

446 Here and throughout, I follow the English convention of referring to ships in the feminine. OI *barc* 'ship' happens to be grammatically feminine in gender.

447 For the relative portion of the value of an object found in various locations, see Mac Niocaill, "Jetsam, Treasure Trove and the Lord's Share," 105–108.

448 I interpret *nemtochur* as the negative prefix *nem-* and *tochor* 'jetsam', the vn. of *do-cuirithar*.

Gne *aile*: In ta*n* is fo to*mus* fl*ath*a urdalta tai*n*ic i*n* b*ar*c, *sét* fo*r*aice ui*n*gi d'fir tire, ⁊ l*eth* na b*air*ce do*n* fl*aith*, ⁊ in l*eth* aili do b*eth* acu fei*n* re ce*n*daige*cht*.

Mai*n*ib fo to*mus* fl*ath*a urdalta tai*n*ic *acht* re ce*n*daig*ech*t ce*n*a, is co*m*rai*n*d b*air*ce dl*igthige*[449] ara l*eth* ⁊ *in* l*eth* doib do ce*n*daig*echt* diles. Dia*m*a ferr leo te*cht* doib as gi*n* ni do fagbail, is fir tire ⁊ fl*ath*a a tui*n*ide .i. ł tui*n*ide a cota fei*n* do b*eth* ina lai*m*, no is fir tire a tui*n*ide co ti fl*aith* dia co*m*rai*n*d. Mane[450] *th*e*cht*a cura .i. b*ar*c fo*cher*d i*n*gra fo an*m*ai(*m*)[n] .i. it*er* dis .i. i*n*gell do tia*ch*tai*n* fo to*mus* fl*ath*a urdalta gi*n* treb*air*e *air* im tia*ch*tai*n*, no con*n*ar*th*a[451] .i. t*r*eb*air*e air im tia*ch*tai*n* d*ar* ce*n*d[452] A. [*CIH* 2153.17–40]

.i. is dil*es* d'fir puirt a tarla *ch*uici coruici *cóic séotu*; ⁊ o ra*ch*as tarrsu, is comrai*nn* bairci dlig*thige* air. I*n* tan tainic fo tom*us* tuait*h*e airit*h*i hi. ⁊ ni h-i*n*dti
p. 50a dorala hi, *acht* doseit gæt*h* | hi a c*r*ich aile dar ai*n*deoin, (⁊) [is][453] comrai*n*d bairce dlig*thige* uirre isi*n* c*r*ich i tarla.

⁊ is aml*aid* donit*er*-si*n*: In set is ferr i*n*dti do rig na tuait*h*i, ⁊ fuill*ed* ris co roib t*r*ian na bairci an*n*, ⁊ a t*r*ian do t*h*uait*h* ⁊ a t*r*ian d'fir puirt. ⁊ t*r*ian i*n séoit* is ferr rainic do rig tuait*h*i uad do rig *cóic*id, fuill*ed* ris co roib *cethrai*-*mth*i cotac*h* tuait*h*i and, ⁊ cethr*aimth*i na cethr*amth*an o rig *cóic*id[454] do rig Eiren*n*.

---

449 This was added *inter. col.* with reference marks possibly by another hand; see also Binchy, *CIH* 2153, n. h.

450 'mane t*h*e*ch*ta' against *CIH* 2153.37–38 'man ethechta'.

451 Binchy, *CIH* 2153, n. i, notes that the ⟨o⟩ was made over another letter, possibly the compendium for *ar*. I am unable to tell what is written under the ⟨o⟩. The scribe appears to have momentarily lost his place as the ⟨art*h*a⟩ are written in the script size he normally uses for the text and the inside of the first ⟨a⟩ has been painted.

452 The words 'd*ar* ce*n*d' were inserted above the line by the scribe.

453 I follow the emendation suggested by Binchy, *CIH* 315, n. a.

454 The ⟨id⟩ were written above the line by the scribe.

Another version: When the ship came seeking a specific lord, a *sét* worth an ounce[455] [is given] to the owner of the land [on which the ship landed], and half the [value] of the ship to the lord, and the other half they have themselves for commerce.

If she [i.e. the ship] did not come seeking a specific lord but rather for commerce, there is a division of a lawful ship for their half [i.e. for the *túath*] and the [other] half for them [the sailors] for lawful commerce. If it is preferable for them [i.e. the locals] for them [i.e. the sailors] to depart without obtaining anything, it is the possession of the owner of the land and of the lord, i.e. or possession of his own share to be in his hand, or it is the possession of the owner of the land until the lord comes to divide it. Unless it has guarantors, i.e. a ship casts anchor to stay, i.e. between two people, i.e. a promise to come seeking a specific lord without surety for him regarding coming, or contracts, i.e. a surety for him regarding coming in return A.

i.e.[456] the owner of the shore where she [i.e. the ship] landed owns up to [the amount of] five *séts*; and whenever it will go beyond them [i.e. anything worth above and beyond the five *séts*], it is a division of a lawful ship [that is made] of her. When she [i.e. the ship] came seeking a specific *túath*, and she did not land in it, but the wind | blew her into another territory by force, p. 50a
and division of a lawful ship of her in the territory in which she landed.

And it is thus that that is done: The best *sét* in her is [given] to the king of the *túath*, and it is added to until there is a third of the [value] of the ship then, and third of it [i.e. of the value of the ship] to the *túath* and a third of it to the owner of the shore. And a third of the best *sét* that the king of the *túath* received [is given] by him to the king of the province, it is added to until it is a fourth of the *túath*'s share then, and the fourth of the fourth from the king of the province [is given] to the king of Ireland.

455 An ounce was generally reckoned to be of silver; see *EIF*, 593.

456 For this commentary, see also *AL* 3: 424.13–426.26. Although the material from source O is embedded within *Bretha Éitgid*, it might ultimately derive from *Muirbretha*; *GEIL*, 277.

In t*r*ian rosoic*h* do t*h*uait*h*, a comroi*n*d doib et*ar*u a coitci*n*di do ca*ch* oen dib conic fuba ⁊ ruba[457] ⁊ biath*ad* ⁊ congbail ⁊ coi*m*et loc*h*ta na bairci. In t*r*ian rosoic*h* d'fir [puirt],[458] nocon [ḟ]uil ni uad do neoc*h*, *acht* mana fuil flait*h* daerait*h* air, *acht* in cut*r*uma be*r*es a ecl*ais* bunaid a dualg*us* cotac*h* f*r*it*h*i a manaig*h*.

Is and ata l*eth* a set uait*h*i ar cen*n*aig*echt* do denum ria don leit*h* aili: I*n* tan tainic fo tomus tuait*h*i airit*h*i hi, ⁊ is i*n*ti dorala hi; l*eth* a set uait*h*i don tuait*h* ar cen*n*aig*echt* do denu*m* ria don l*eth* aile. ⁊ *no*con urailend dlig*ed* uirri-si l*eth* a set uait*h*i doib-sium no co ndernat cen*n*aig*echt* ria. ⁊ *no*cun urailen*n* dlig*ed* ari*n* tuait*h* cen*n*aig*echt* do denu*m* ria *no* co tuca si l*eth* a sét doib a n-aiscid, ⁊ o dob*er*a is dlig*ed* cenda*ch*ta do denu*m* ria. Cid fo*dera* l*eth* a set uait*h*i ar cen*n*aig*echt* it*ir*? Is e fa*th* fo*dera*: Is ris doc*h*uaid men*m*a in udair co mb*er*dais-[s]ium d'i*m*arc*r*aid isin l*eth* recait ni is mo ina l*eth* dob*er*ait i n aiscid.

Is[459] an*n* ata *sét sé* screp*al* uait*h*i no *sét* foraici uingi: I*n* tan tainic fo t*ho*m*us* dui*ne* airit*h*i hi, ⁊ ni 'na [ḟ]lesc lama-sin fei*n* dorala iat *acht* a feran*n* dui*ne* aile 'na comoc*us*, ⁊ *sét sé* sc*r*ep*al* do ar con*n*ad ⁊ uisci do lecad di masa seic*h*ida ⁊ iaran*n* ⁊ saland ata i*n*dti, no *sét* foraici ui*n*gi masa cno gnae ⁊ cuirnd [buabaill],[460] ⁊ escup fi*n*a no mela ma ta fi*n* ł mil indti[461] O. [*CIH* 315.5–28]

457 For the military service owed by base clients to the lord, see the Introduction to §§ 24 and 29.

458 I follow the emendation suggested by Binchy, *CIH* 315, n. b.

459 Cf. § 29, source A, *CIH* 2155.21–26.

460 Cf. *CIH* 2155.22 and see Binchy, *CIH* 315, n. c.

461 The word *indti* was added above the line with reference marks by the scribe.

The third that the *túath* received, it is divided by them amongst them equally for each one of them who is capable of attack and defense and feeding and maintaining and guarding the ship's cargo.[462] The third that the owner of the shore received, he does not give anything to anyone, unless there is a lord of base clientship over him, but [it is] the equivalent that his family's church gets in respect to a share of its monastic client.

The case in which half of her *sét*s is [given] by her to conduct commerce with her [i.e. the ship] for the other half: When she came seeking a specific *túath*, and she landed in it [i.e. the territory she was seeking]; half of her *sét*s [is given] by her to the *túath* to conduct commerce with her for the other half. And law does not require her [to give] half of her *sét*s to them until they conduct commerce with her, and law does not require the *túath* to conduct commerce with her until she gives half her *sét*s to them gratis, and when she gives [them], it is lawful to conduct commerce with her. What is the reason that half of her *sét*s is [given] by her for commerce at all? The reason is: The idea of the author was that they would receive in addition more for the half that they sell than for the half that they give gratis.

The case in which a *sét* worth six scruples[463] is [given] by her or a *sét* worth an ounce: When she came seeking a specific person, and they did not land in his own domain but in the land of another person close to him, and a *sét* worth six scruples [is given] to him for allowing her firewood and fresh water if there are hides and iron and salt in her [i.e. the ship], or a *sét* worth an ounce if there are beautiful nuts[464] and drinking horns,[465] and a jar[466] of wine or honey, if there is wine or honey in her [i.e. the ship] O.

462 *Lochta* is the gen. sg. of *lucht*, which can refer both to the contents of the ship, i.e. its cargo, but also its crew. The passage here suggests that we understand *lochta* to refer to both the ship's crew (if they survive) and its cargo; see *eDIL s.v. lucht*.

463 A scruple is one twenty-fourth of an ounce; see EIF, 593.

464 The identification of these nuts remains problematic; see Kelly, "Drifting on the Ocean," 211–218; GEIL, 165; and, for a different opinion, Jonathan M. Wooding, *Communication and Commerce along the Western Sealanes AD 400–800*. British Archaeological Reports International Series 654 (Oxford: Tempvs Reparatvm, 1996), 70.

465 For drinking horns, see Proinsias Mac Cana, "Ir. *Buaball*, W. *Bual* 'Drinking Horn'," *Ériu* 44 (1993): 81–86. The amount due to the landowner increases with the value of the ship's cargo.

466 For *escop* as a jar used as a standard measure of wine and honey, see EIF, 581.

§23 Fod remdilsi ⁊rl-:

Du*in*e rorec*ustar* *sét* re celi ar d*us* a*nn* si*n*; ⁊ cia*ma*d ail les a reic re nech aili[467] asa h-ait*h*le, noc*ha* c*h*uim*g*ec*h* e, *acht* a b*eth* 'co*n*ti ris*ar* reca *ar* d*us* é.

Gne *aile*: .i. is diles do*n*ti ris*ar* raca(d)[468] na *séotu*, gid*ma*d[469] ail d'fir bu*n*aid a tait*h*mec*h* ł do*n* ci*nn* ł[470] do*n* fiur fi*n*e robui f*or* *air*d ł do neoc*h* aili a reicc ris A. [*CIH* 2154.1–5]

Is *ed* is foth c*reca* go remd*ílsi* an*n*: In tan is tasg*a* rocenuigh intí ogar h-aidhbr*ed* é na[471] tall*ad* in *sét* ontí fuil oga n-aidhbr*iud*. Is *ed* is f*oth* *creca* gi*n* remdilsi an*n*: In tan is taisc*e* tall*ad* in *sét* óntí fuil aga n-aidhbr*iud* na rocen*na*[i]dh antí ógar h-aidhbr*ed* é. Is *ed* is foth[472] n-inais an*n*: A br*eth* aige buden F. [*CIH* 1271.29–33]

1 Only source A contains the text for this section.

467 The sequence ⟨isa⟩ follows *aili* and is partially erased.

468 See also Binchy, *CIH* 2154, n. b. The verb *rec*(*c*)*aid* occasionally has the stem *rac*-; see *eDIL s.v.* 1 *rec*(*c*)*aid*.

469 *Gidmad* is a later form of *ciamad*.

470 The phrase *ł don cinn ł* was inserted *marg. sin.* with reference marks by the scribe; see also Binchy, *CIH* 2154, n. c.

471 This is a MI form of OI *indaas* 'than, than is'.

472 Here *foth* is neuter.

§23 Claim of prior right, etc.[473]

A person who sold a *sét* to another previously in that case; and although he wishes to sell it to someone else afterwards, he is not capable [of doing so], but it belongs to the one to whom he sold it in the first place.

Another version: i.e. the *séts* belong to the one to whom he sold [them], although the original owner wishes to dissolve it [i.e. the original contract of sale], or the chief, or the head of the kindred who was present, or someone else [wishes] to sell them to him[474] A.

This is a claim of purchase with prior right then:[475] When the one from whom it is claimed had bought it before the *sét* was taken from the one who is claiming it. This is a claim of purchase without prior right then: When the *sét* was taken from the one who is claiming it before the one from whom it is claimed had bought it.[476] This is a claim of growth then: It being born in his own possession[477] F.

473 For a discussion of this section, see the Introduction, 25.

474 The construction is rendered literally as 'their selling to him'.

475 For this commentary, see *eDIL s.v. remdílse.*

476 The first two conditions of this commentary deal with issues of when someone has a claim of purchase with or without prior right. In the first scenario, the person being sued for the *sét* had already purchased it before it was taken from the suer. In the second scenario, the person being sued for the *sét* had not yet paid for it before it was taken from the suer. The general concept seems to be that we have a scenario where person A sells a *sét* to person B, but then A later changes his mind and tries to sue person B for the *sét* he had just sold to person B.

477 In other words, the claim is that the animal was born while the mother was in his possession; *eDIL s.v. inás.*

§ 24 Riar forbfl*atha*[478] ⁊rl-

In celsi*ne* i*n*dligtec*h*:[479] Sl*an* cac*h* fog*al* doge*ntar* aca dich*ur*, ⁊ lanfiach i*n* ca*ch* fog*ail* doge*ntar* aca u*r*ail.

In celsi*ne* dligth*ech*: Sl*an* cac*h* fog*al* doge*ntar* aca u*r*ail, ⁊ lanfiac*h* i*n* cac*h* fog*ail* doge*ntar* aca dicu*r*.

Is *ed* is celsi*ne* i*n*dligth*ech* an*n*: Dærrat*h* do gab*ail* o fl*aith* budein, ł særrat*h* no dærrat*h* do gab*ail* o fl*aith* e*cht*ran*n*. Nocha*r* gab i*n* celi dærr*ath* o fl*aith* aile[480] a*n*d si*n*. ⁊ ma rogab, am*ail* is [s]l*an* in særr*ath* do u*r*ail air, is [s]l*an* in dærr*ath*.

p. 12a Cid fo*dera con*id mo dilsigit[481] | biada i*n* rat*h* do*n* celi i*n* ta*n* na t*u*c in fl*aith* seotu tu*r*claide [ná] (ł)[482] in ta*n* t*u*c? Iss e i*n* fa*th*: Dligth*ech*a i*n* fl*aith* in ta*n* dorat s*éo*tu tu*r*claide na i*n* ta*n* na tuc.

Gne *aile*: Masa nech dlig*es* celsi*ne*, is [f]astaide cid *ar* eci*n* cid *ar* ais ob*us* [d](s)ærcelsi*ne*[483] co tab*air*t i*n* rat*h*a ⁊ i*n* s*ét* tu*r*claide, cid *ar* nech da*na* bes giall*a ar* eci*n* gi*n*cob ed. Masa nec*h* na dligen*n* giall*a* do, nochan [ḟ]ast*aid*i ob*us ar* ecin, cid særceli cid dærceli, ⁊ icfaid[484] lanfiac*h* ca*ch*a cneide f*er*f*us*.

Masa[485] nech na dligen*n* celsi*ne*, *noch*an [ḟ]astad*a*[486] dærcel*sin*i *ar* eici*n*, *acht* ic*aid* er*aic* na n-uili cned rof*erus*t*ar* og u*r*ail na celsi*ne* ⁊ eric[487] gaite isi*n* mbiad A. [*CIH* 2154.6–20]

---

478 Although *forflaith* is the headword given in *eDIL*, the headword should probably be *forblaith*, which shows the regular development of */w/ > /β/ after lenited /r/. Spellings such as *forflaith* and *forbflaith* are based on anology with the simplex; see GOI § 201.

479 The ⟨t⟩ was inserted above the line by the scribe.

480 The word *aile* was inserted above the line by the scribe; see also Binchy, *CIH* 2154, n. d.

481 The ⟨sigit⟩ were written below the line by the scribe to finish the column of text. Although the form of the verb is the pres. ind. 3 pl. of *dílsigid* 'surrender, give up', one wonders whether a 3 sg. form was meant instead.

482 I follow the emendation suggested by Binchy, *CIH* 2154, n. f.

483 I follow the emendation suggested by Binchy, *CIH* 2154, n. g.

484 The ⟨c⟩ was added above the line by the scribe.

485 The scribe originally wrote *Mansa*, but he expunged the ⟨n⟩ with a *punctum delens* below the letter; see also Binchy, *CIH* 2154, n. h.

486 The ⟨t⟩ was inserted above the line by the scribe; see also Binchy, *CIH* 2154, n. i.

487 The phrase ⁊ *eric* was inserted above the line by the scribe; see also Binchy, *CIH* 2154, n. d.

§ 24 Stipulation of an overlord, etc.[488]

The unlawful clientship:[489] Exempt from legal liability is every injury that will be made rejecting it, and full fine [to be paid] for every injury that will be made enjoining it.

The lawful clientship: Exempt from legal liability is every injury that will be made enjoining it, and full fine [to be paid] for every injury that will be made rejecting it.

This is unlawful clientship then: To take a base fief from one's own lord, and[490] to take a free fief or base fief from an external lord. The client does not take a base fief from another lord in that case. And if he takes [it], just as he [i.e. the lord] is free to enjoin the free fief on him, he is free [to enjoin] the base fief on him.

What is the reason that the clients give greater | food renders[491] when the p. 12a
lord did not give *sét*s of subjection than when he did? The reason is: The lord is more lawful when he gave *sét*s of subjection than when he did not.

Another version: If it is someone who is owed clientship, it is binding, whether unwillingly or willingly, when it is a base client with giving of the fief and the *sét*s of subjection, whether on someone for whom there may be [owed] hostages willingly or not.[492] If it is someone who is not owed hostages by him, it is not binding when it is unwilling, whether a free client or a base client, and he [i.e. the lord] will pay the full fine of every injury that he will inflict.

If it is someone who is not owed clientship, base clientship unwillingly is not binding, but he [i.e. the lord] pays the fine of all the wounds that he has inflicted enjoining the clientship, and a fine of theft for the food A.

---

488 For a discussion of this section, see the Introduction, 25–26.

489 For detailed discussions of clientship, see *GEIL*, 29–33; and *EIWK*, 337–363.

490 It is difficult to reconcile *nó* in its usual meaning of 'or' here; 'and' makes better sense. There is nothing inherently illegal about being in more than one base clientship relationship as long as the fief advanced is less than that advanced by the first lord; *GEIL*, 32. It is difficult to determine whether the commentary is being ellipitical, or whether this is an example of a slightly different legal practice regarding clientship. The issue might be that the client is entering an arrangement with a lord outside of his own territory.

491 The clause *mo dilsigit biada in rath don celi*, literally 'they give greater food renders to the client' is problematic. Usually when the verb *dílsigid* is used with *do*, it means 'give to', but food renders are not given to clients, rather they are paid by clients to their lords. Free clients owe a proportionally larger food render than base clients because the lord does not pay them *sét*s of subjection; *GEIL*, 32.

492 The hostages mentioned here are not hostage-sureties, but rather political hostages; *GEIL*, 173–176.

§ 25 Fiach mna marbslabra ⁊rl-

A da sc*ar*ad deit*h*b*ir* mar*æn* ł a da scar*ad* *in*deit*h*b*ir* mar*æn*, is roi*n*d *ar* do na coibchi gi*n*mot*h*a *in*di ata ar scat*h* dilata ligi. Gi*n* comarba si*n*, ⁊ ma ta com*ar*ba, is a tab*airt*[493] i n-iarr*ad*, ma ta in iarr*ad* an*n*. ⁊ ma*n*a fuil, is tuil-l*ed* ris. ⁊ masa mo *in*das, is aisiuc na h-im*arcr*ada amuig aris f*or* cula. Masa scarad dethb*ir* '*con* dara de ⁊ scar*ad* *in*dethb*ir* 'c araile, in coibchi don det*h*b*ir*sech,[494] ⁊ int alt*r*am don indethb*ir*sec*h* A. [*CIH* 2154.21–26]

493 The first ⟨a⟩ is written subscript; see also Binchy, *CIH* 2154, n. j.

494 The ⟨d⟩ was inserted below the line by the scribe; see also Binchy, *CIH* 2154, n. k.

§ 25 Liability of a woman's dowry which consists of inanimate chattels,[495] etc.[496]

When their separation is justified for both or when their separation is unjustified for both, the *coibche* is divided in two except that which is for bed covering. That is without an heir, and if there is an heir, it [i.e. the *coibche*] is to be paid as fosterage-fee,[497] if it [amounts to] the fosterage-fee. And if it does not, it is added to. And if it is greater than it [i.e. the fosterage-fee], the surplus is returned back again. If the separation is justified for one of them and the separation is unjustified for the other, the *coibche* [is given] to the justified one, and the fosterage responsibility [is given] to the unjustified one[498] A.

495 For *marbslabra*, see *eDIL s.v. slabrae, slaibre*. The meaning is tentatively suggested by Plummer.

496 For a discussion of this section, see the Introduction, 26–27.

497 Discussions on fosterage can be found in GEIL, 86–90; and EIWK, 78–81. For the division of the fosterage-fee in the event of a divorce, see also § 37 in Kelly, *Marriage Disputes*.

498 For a slightly different edition and translation of this commentary, see Kathleen Mulchrone, "The Rights and Duties of Women with regard to the Education of their Children," in *Studies in Early Irish Law*, ed. R. Thurneysen et al. (Dublin: Royal Irish Academy, 1936), 200.

§26 Comfer tire tuinide[a] ⁊rl-[499]

[a].i. a tairise*m*[500] P.

Indraic roaidbriust*ar* an f*er*an*n* su*nn* ac i*n*dr*ai*c aile ł esin*n*r*ai*c oc indr*ai*c. Sl*an* di fo*m*ailt an f*er*aind co tair a imde*num*, cidbe daro. ł cid *séoit* oca ta l*acht* ł gnimr*ad* cea*n*a,[501] ł cid a n-*ur*lai*m* cena, is [s]lan di a l*acht* ⁊ a ngnim*rad* do caith*em* gi*n acht*ugud for necht*ar* de, .i. *for*intí ogar h-aidbriud ⁊ foran *ur*laim, a nemcaith*me* A. [*CIH* 2154.27–31]

air*m in*a tartaig*h*, is and a tuinig*h*[b] P. [*CIH* 712.12–14]

[b].i. imdena*m*[502] P.

1 tuinid **A.** ‖ *om.* P.

499 It is difficult to determine whether source P *CIH* 712.13–14 and Digest D (12) *CIH* 1961.17–23 belong with this section. *CIH* 712.13–14 overlaps with parts of *CIH* 1961.19–20, and *CIH* 1961.20–23 overlaps with parts of source A *CIH* 2154.26–31.

500 This is an interlinear gloss on the text.

501 The first ⟨a⟩ was inserted below the line by the scribe.

502 This is an interlinear gloss on the comments following the text.

§ 26 An occupier of the land has possession,[a] etc.[503]

[a] i.e. establishing it P.

A qualified person claimed the land here from another qualified person or an unqualified person [claimed the land] from a qualified person. He is free to use the land until it is proved [i.e. until the correct ownership is proved], whatever he will find [on the land]. Or whether *séts* which have milk or labor besides, or whether in possession besides, he is free to use their milk and their labor when there is not a stipulation on either of them, i.e. on the one who is suing and on the one in possession, not to use them A.

the place in which he finds it, it is there he [establishes] possession[b] P.

[b] i.e. proof P.

503 For a discussion of this section, see the Introduction, 27.

§ 27 Ecor aircell*a*[504] ⁊rl-

Duine so rore*cus*tar ferand ⁊ tug*ad* fola loigi do da cind. ⁊ ma *rucustar techt*u-*gud* ind asa h-aithli, is fia*ch techtaigthe* t*ire*[505] gin c*hu*n*d*, gin coibne uad i*n*d. ⁊ gid athgab*ail* gab*us*, biad fia*ch* i*n*dlig*id* athgab*al*a uad A. [*CIH* 2154.32–34]

504 The expansion of the final syllable of *aircella* is tentative; the reading at *CIH* 2154.32 is 'aircell*ach* (?)'. If we assume that Binchy thought *aircellach* was a form of *aircheltach* 'thief, robber', one would expect a gen. sg. form like *aircheltaig* or perhaps *aircellaig*. If *aircella* were from *airchellad* 'stealing', one would expect a gen. sg. form like *airchelta*. The form *aircella* is understood here to be a gen. sg. of *airchell*, vn. of *ar-cel*(*l*)*a* 'stealing, theft'. That being said, the suspension mark for the last syllable is ambiguous in the MS and one could just as easily justify emending to 'airchell*aig*'.

505 See also Binchy, *CIH* 2154, n. m.

§ 27 Making entry as a thief, etc.[506]

This person had sold land and the price was given to him for it. And if he [i.e. the seller] took possession of it afterwards, it is a fine of taking possession of land without a head [of kin], without a kinsman [due] from him for it. And though he takes distraint, there will be a fine of illegal distraint [due] from him A.

506 For a discussion of this section, see the Introduction, 27.

§28 Port fiach[507] ⁊rl-

.i. ni tiagait fine i fus fora f*er*and. Fer fine roleg el*od* in fir fine aili, ⁊ in fear fine isa h-el*od* roleg*ed* an*n* nocha dech*aid* arin fearand ⁊ noch*ur* leig do neoch aili dul air.[508] Is *ed* fo*dera* in uilidetu uili d'ic ris it*er* aithgi*n* co los ⁊ as ⁊ diabl*ad* co fia*ch* el*od*a cena. ⁊[509] ní a n-athgab*ail* rogab*ad* in ferand, uair damad ed, noragad lobad ina cend.

Deithb*ir* et*ar*ru-si*n* ⁊ in fal fine ic*us* a cinta; ni teit a n-aiream dó ferglith na mes na clais na h-it*h*, cid maith, *acht* ní roclan*n*a a lam fadesin fir besa cat*h*ac*h*.[510]

Is *ed* [f]uil an*n*-side: Fer fine rolec el*od fir fine*,[511] ⁊ i*n* fer fine isa h-el*od* roleg*ed* an*n* docuaid ari*n* feran*n* é, ⁊ fomailt in f*er*ai*n*d a ndag*aid* na *cóic sét* ⁊ na h-e*n*ecl*ainn*i ⁊ na lethgab*ala* diabulta. ⁊ in tan tic-sium re dlig*ed* ic*aid* aithgi*n* co los ⁊ as ⁊ inforb*air*t acht man*ar* facaib denta *ar*in f*er*and do neoch rocland a lam budein di neoch dilas in aithgi*n*. ⁊ ma rofacaib, a dul *ar* son na p. 12b h-aithge*n*a, ⁊ com*ar*dugu*d* | it*er* an aithg*in* ⁊ na denta, ⁊ cidbe dib aca *m*be an i*m*arc*r*aid ic*aid* re celi.

---

507 Binchy, *CIH* 2154 cites cross references at *CIH* 1876.9, 2056.7, and 2239.28, all mainly from the *SM* 15 text *Di Thúaslucud Rudrad* 'On the Dissolution of Prescriptions', but none of the citations are lengthy. An edition and translation of this text is currently in preparation.

508 'air' against *CIH* 2154.37 'an*n*'.

509 One letter might have been erased after ⟨⁊⟩.

510 This part of the commentary seems to be taken directly from *Di Thúaslucud Rudrad* 'On the Dissolution of Prescriptions'; cf. *CIH* 245.26–29: *Cis lir fala foran-iadat dilsi cacha sealba asna tindtaightear cid diubairt? Fal dine icas a caithe, co ro h-icar fris cach set ronic cona somaine na teid a n-aiream do fergle*[ith] *na meas na h-ith in tire, cidh maith, acht ni roclanda a lam fadesin fir asa cathach* ... 'How many [types of] legal barriers close the right of every property [and] which is not returned, though it is a fraud? Barrier of a kinsman who pays [for] his [i.e. another kinsman's] liabilities, until every *sét* is paid to him along with its profit, which does not take into account grazing the land's grass or mast or corn, however good, except what the hand of the man who is liable for trespass planted ...'; and see also *AL* 5: 500.9–16.

511 See also Binchy, *CIH* 2155, n. a.

§28 Bank of fines,[512] etc.[513]

i.e. the kinsmen here do not go on the land. A kinsman who evaded another kinsman, and the kinsman who had been evaded then did not go on the land, and he did not allow anyone else to go on it. This is the reason the entirety is to be paid to him both restitution with interest[514] and doubling up to [the amount of] the fine for evading besides. And the land was not taken in distraint, because if it were, it would be forfeited in addition.

There is a difference between this and the 'barrier of a kinsman' who pays his liabilities; it does not take into account grazing of the grass or mast or furrow or corn, however good, except that which the hand of the man who is liable for trespass [i.e. the evading kinsman] planted.

This is what there is in this case: A kinsman who evaded [another] kinsman, and the kinsman who was evaded then went onto the land, and [he made] use of the land as an offset to the five *sét*s and the honor-price and the double half-seizure[515] [that he is owed]. And when he [i.e. the absconder] submits to law he [the kinsman] pays restitution with interest[516] if he does not leave a structure on the land for someone that his own hand established as something set apart from the restitution. And if he did, it goes towards the restitution [i.e. it goes towards paying the restitution], and a balancing of claims | between the restitution and the building, and whichever one of p. 12b
them has the surplus, he pays to the other.

---

512 The phrase *port fiach* is problematic. The editors of e*DIL* cite a suggestion made in *AL* 5: 501 that the phrase is "probably the technical expression for the man who has become responsible for the accumulated debts arising out of the absconding of a fellow tribesman;" see also *eDIL s.v.* 1 *port*. For a different interpretation, see Eugene O'Curry, *On the Manners and Customs of the Ancient Irish: A Series of Lectures*, 3 vols (London: Williams and Norgate, 1873), 1: clxxxvii, n. 341 'outside the limit of pursuit'. The commentary deals with a situation in which a kinman has paid the debts of an absconding kinsman. If the kinsman does not take over the absconder's land, he is owed restitution with interest and a fine for evasion from the absconder. The kinsman can decide instead to take over the absconder's land to offset what he himself has paid. The absconding kinsman may, however, regain his land, but only after paying what he owes his kinsman. If the kinsman uses the absconder's land to offset what he has paid, there is a balancing of liabilities between the kinsman and the absconder, if the absconder wants his land back. If the kinsman has used more of the land in terms of value than what he paid for the absconder (including any other fines he is owed), the surplus is given to the absconder.

513 For a discussion of this section, see the Introduction, 27.

514 Literally 'with calves and milk'.

515 I am not certain exactly what is being specified by the term *na lethgabala diabulta*; see *eDIL s.v. leth*.

516 Literally 'with calves and milk and produce'.

Cid fo*dera cona* h-icth*ar* e*n*ecl*ann* risi*n* fer fi*n*e a Se*ncus* [Már] i*ar* ndul *arin* fera*nn*, ⁊ co n-ict*ar* risna[517] rathaib i Cor*us* Fi*n*e i*ar* ndul *arin* fera*n*n? Is e i*n* fa*th*: In dui*n*e budei*n* dochuaid ari*n* fer*and* sund. Iss *ed* fo*dera* ce*n* eneclainn[518] an*n*. Tall im*murro* a Cor*us* Fi*n*e nochan iat na rat*h*a budei*n* docuaid air tall *acht* in fi*n*e rotidnaic do*n*a rat*h*aib a ngill é, ⁊ iss *ed* fo*dera* e*n*ecl*ann* d'ic friu[519] A. [*CIH* 2154.34–2155.15]

517 The sequence ⟨ul *arin* fera*nn*, ⁊ co n-ict*ar* risna⟩ was added with reference marks partially *inter col.* and above the line of text by the scribe; see also Binchy, *CIH* 2155, n. b.

518 The ⟨ec⟩ were inserted above the line by the scribe; see also Binchy, *CIH* 2155, n. c.

519 One letter has been erased after this word.

What is the reason that honor-price is not paid to the kinsman in the *Senchas* [*Már*] after going on the land, and that it is paid to the paying-sureties in *Córus Fine*[520] after going on the land? The reason is: The person himself went on the land here. This is what causes there not to be honor-price then. There, however, in *Córus Fine* it is not the paying-sureties themselves who went on it there but the kinsman who granted it to the paying-sureties as a pledge, and this is the reason honor-price is paid to them A.

520 For this text, see *CCIH*, 235–239, especially 237 where this sentence is translated and discussed. The text is concerned, as the title ('The Ordering of the Kindred') suggests, with regulations between kinsmen.

§ 29 Fobraithe bairce ⁊rl-

.i. treic*he*a*m* fir lui*n*ge .i. t*r*eide tre*n*-cemnigth*er* do*n*ti atci i*n* lo*n*g .i. i*n* *sét* *sé*[521] screp*al* ɫ[522] i*n* *sét*[523] *for*aice ui*n*gi *ar* ernail ⁊ escob fine (f*or* er*n*ail[524] ⁊) a lan f*or* ernail *aile*. Dedi dlig*es* in rod*er*caid[525] atci ria cach: I*n* *sét* *sé*[526] screp*al* ɫ[527] in s*é*t foraice ui*n*gi *ar* er*n*ail ⁊ escob fi*n*e *con*a lan ar er*n*ail[528] *aile*. Is an*n* ata in s*ét* *sé* scr*e*p*al* do: I*n* tan is clu*m*a(n) ⁊ sechada ⁊ *iar*nach robui i*n*dti. Is an*n* ata i*n* *sét* araice ui*n*gi do: I*n* tan is or ⁊ *airgeth* ⁊ cno gnoei ⁊ cuir*n* buabaill robui i*n*dti. Is a*n*d ata escob fi*n*a do: I*n* tan is fi*n* robui i*n*dti.

Ma 'tcon*n*ic i*n* dui*n*e i*n* lo*n*g, ⁊ rofes a*n* raba i*n*dti, ⁊ is ci*n*dti co t*air*fida[529] f*uir*ri, is ait*h*gi*n* na lu*n*ga uad ⁊ aithg*in* a raba i*n*dti. Masa cun*n*tab*air*t in[530] tairfida f*uir*ri ɫ na t*air*fidea, is l*eth*ait*h*g*in* na lu*n*ga uad ⁊ l*eth*ait*hgin* a rab i*n*dti.

Masa ci*n*dti *con*a tairfida f*uir*ri, is sl*an*.

---

1 Forbr*ith*i KK. ‖ b*air*c KK. ‖ *om.* KK.

---

521 The ⟨i⟩ of the abbreviation for *sé*, '.ui.', looks like it was made over another letter which was erased; see also Binchy, CIH 2155, n. d.

522 Perhaps ⟨⁊⟩ should be read here instead of ⟨ɫ⟩ to bring this list of items into conformity with the similar list given in CIH 139.32–34: *set foraca* (⁊ *di*) *uinge* (*do* ɫ) *masa or* ɫ *airget* ɫ *allmhaire set* ⁊ *set foraicce se scripla do masa iarand* ɫ *sechadha* ⁊ *escub meala* ɫ *fina ma ta mil* ɫ *fin indte*.

523 The sequence ⟨ɫ in .s.⟩ was written *inter col.* with reference marks by the scribe; see also Binchy, CIH 2155, n. e.

524 Binchy, CIH 2155, n. f, suggests omitting the phrase *for ernail*.

525 Cf. CIH 139.32–140.8. CCIH, 18 suggests that the material here about the *dercaid* 'lookout man' might ultimately derive from SM 38, *Muirbretha* 'Sea-Judgments'. An edition and translation of *Muirbretha* is in preparation by the author.

526 It is possible that a minim was erased after the ⟨.ui.⟩ as there is an extra space before the ⟨.⟩.

527 The ⟨ɫ⟩ was added in above the line by the scribe.

528 The ⟨il⟩ were inserted above the line by the scribe; see also Binchy, CIH 2155, g.

529 I understand the form *tairfida* to be the sg. pass. cond. of the later simplex from *doairret*. It should be noted that the text does not refer to piracy or wrecking; it refers to boats which have been shipwrecked and the possibility (or not) of salvaging any of the cargo.

530 For the interrog. part. used in dependent questions to mean 'whether', see *eDIL s.v.* 2 *in* (ii) a; and GOI § 463. The same construction appears later in the commentary.

§ 29 Payment of a ship, etc.[531]

i.e. 'three-steps' for the man of a boat,[532] i.e. three things are 'strongly-advanced' to the one who sees the ship,[533] i.e. the *sét* worth six scruples or the *sét* worth an ounce[534] for a share and a full jar[535] of wine for another share. The watchman who sees [the ship] before anyone else is entitled to two things: The *sét* worth six scruples or the *sét* worth an ounce as a share and a full jar of wine as another share. It is in this case that he gets the *sét* worth six scruples:[536] When the cargo consists of feathers [i.e. down] and hides and iron [i.e. tools, utensils, etc.]. It is in this case that he gets the *sét* worth an ounce: When the cargo consists of gold or silver or beautiful nuts and drinking horns. It is in this case that he gets a jar of wine: When the cargo consists of wine.

If the person saw the boat, and it was known what was in her [i.e. the ship's cargo], and it is certain that she would be seized, it is restitution of the [value of the] boat [which is owed] from him and restitution of what was in her [i.e. the value of the cargo]. If there is doubt whether she would be seized or not, it is half-restitution of the [value of the] boat from him and half-restitution of what was in her [i.e. the cargo].

If it is certain that she would not be seized, he is exempt from legal liability.

---

531 For a discussion of this section, see the Introduction, 27–28. I take both *fobraithe* and *forbrithi*, from sources A and KK, respectively, to be forms of *fobrithe* 'a sub-award, payment'; see *eDIL s.v. fobrithe*.

532 The word *treicheam* seems to be for 'trí' 'three' and '*céim*' 'step, process, stage'; see *eDIL s.v. céim*.

533 The general sense is that the man who sees the boat is entitled to three things. That being said, the watchman really only gets at best two of the three items listed, i.e. a *sét* and a jar of wine, if the ship is carrying wine. The form *tren-cemnigther* is a quasi-etymological gloss on *treicheam*.

534 The value of the ounce is generally reckoned to be that of silver; see *EIF*, 593.

535 For the *escop* as a measure of wine and honey, see *EIF*, 581.

536 Cf. § 22, source O.

Ma 'tcon*n*raic i*n* dui*ne* i*n* lo*n*g, ⁊ no*chan* fes i*n* raba i*n*dti, ⁊ is ci*n*dti co t*air*fidea f*uir*ri, is *secht* cu*mala* uad co fia*ch*aib sellc*echt*a. ⁊ is iat na feich sellc*echt*a h-isi*n*: Cethr*aimth*i dire ⁊ *ocht*m*ad*[537] dire ⁊ *aile déc* .i. *cethraimth*e dire i*m*[538] s*ét*aib diabulta ⁊ i*m* dai*n*ib.

Masa cun*n*tab*air*t in t*air*fida f*uir*ri ł na t*air*fida, is l*eth*cu*m*al uad co l*eth*-fiachaib sellc*echt*a gaite. Is iat na l*eth*feich sellc*echt*a isi*n*: *Ocht*mad[539] dire ⁊ [in][540] *seiss*id[541] ra*n*d *déc* a dire ⁊ in *ceth*ram*ad* ra*n*d *fich*it[542] a dire, .i. *ocht*[mad][543] dire i*m* s*ét*aib diabalta ⁊[544] im dai*n*ib.

Masa ci*n*dti *cona* t*air*fida f*uir*ri, is [s]l*an* A. [CIH 2155.16–34]

.i. br*eth* bec b*erar*[545] KK. [CIH 1107.12]

537 I have emended '.uii.' to '.uiii.' here and below as the fractions do not work out otherwise.

538 Although the prep. *imm* regularly govens the accusative case, in late OI and MI it sometimes governs the dative case in the plural; *eDIL s.v.* 1 *imm.*

539 I have emended '.uii.' to '.uiii.' here and above as the fractions do not work out otherwise.

540 I follow the emendation suggested by Binchy, CIH 2155, n. h.

541 The ⟨id⟩ were added above the line by the scribe.

542 The ⟨it⟩ were added above the line by the scribe.

543 I follow the emendation suggested by Binchy, CIH 2155, n. i.

544 The ⟨⁊⟩ was inserted above the line with a reference mark by the scribe.

545 The gloss in KK seems to be a quasi-etymological gloss on *fobrithi* where the prep. *fo* 'under' is used in the sense of 'sub-'.

If the person saw the boat, and it was not known what was in her, and it is certain that she would be seized, it is seven *cumal*s [which are owed] from him with fines of culpable onlooking.[546] And these are the fines of culpable onlooking: One-fourth of [the] penalty and an eighth[547] of [the] penalty and a twelfth, i.e. a fourth of [the] penalty regarding double *sét*s and regarding crew.

If there is doubt whether she would be seized or not, it is half a *cumal* [which is owed] from him with half of the fines of culpable onlooking of theft. These are the half-fines of culpable onlooking: An eighth[548] of [the] penalty and the sixteenth of [the] penalty and the twenty-fourth of [the] penalty, i.e. an eighth of [the] penalty regarding double *sét*s and regarding crew.

If it is certain that she would not be seized, he is exempt from legal liability A.

i.e. a little judgement is judged KK.

546 On the crime of *sellach*, being a culpable onlooker, see *GEIL*, 154–156. In early Irish law, anyone who witnessed an offense without doing anything to prevent or stop it was responsible for some degree of liability. The watchman is obligated to report any shipwrecked boat which has even a possibility of being seized. He is charged with the fine of culpable onlooking if he is silent on the matter, except in cases where it is certain that neither the ship itself nor its cargo or crew could be reached. The fine seems to be a deterrent against the watchman spotting the shipwreck, but not telling anyone, and then taking the goods for himself. As seen in § 22, the value of the shipwreck's cargo is usually distributed amongst the community; not reporting a wreck deprives the wider community of valuable goods and constitutes a form of theft.

547 See note 537.

548 See note 539.

§ 30 **Br*eth* cen dilsi, cen arach; ní coir breath gin dilsi, gi*n* árach.**

.i. ci*n* fir-fæm*ad* do*n*a da fech*emnaib*, .i. da gell dob*er*ar[549] do*n* bre*th*emai*n* in tan teca*r* i*n*a reir fuigill cu*r* a reir t[e]ist*a*[550] *iar* tai*n*, ⁊ is langilli dob*er*ar an*n* fo c*ét*oir. ⁊ is iat na gella dob*er*ar risi*n* aile *déc* ł gell *aile* tara ce*n*d, .i.[551] ce*n* arach treb*air*i do tabairt d*ar*a ce*n*d do*n*a fech*em*naib, ł da gell f*r*i rer, da gell f*r*i brit*h*.

Ma tanca*tar* na fech*em*ai*n* d'i*n*dsaig*id* i*n* bre*th*ema*n*, ⁊ atmait a scela d'i*n*disi*n*, ⁊ atmait br*eith* do br*eith* doib, ⁊ at*at* *iar* tain aca rad na*ch* iad-siut sceol roi*n*dsetar ⁊ ni hi-siut br*eth* r*u*cad doib orra, a den*am* do*n* bre*th*em*ain* *con*id iat-siut sceoil roi*n*dset*ar* ⁊ *con*id hi-siut bre*th* r*u*cus*tar* doib orra, ⁊ i*n* da aili *déc* do br*eith* do i*ar* si*n*. ⁊ is as-si*n* gab*ar*: Cia f*or*toi*n*g, ni f*or*to*n*g*ar*.

Mu*n*a atmait na fec*h*emai*n* a scela d'i*n*disi*n* ⁊ in br*eith* do br*eith* doib, ł cia at*m*ait a sceoil[552] d'i*n*disi*n*, mu*n*a at*m*ait br*eith* do br*eith* doib, is a se*n*a doib na r*uc*-su*m* br*eith* doib, ⁊ a dul-su*m* ga*n* ni. Mass iat-s*um* adub*air*t risi*n* mbre*th*em*ain* br*eith* do br*eith* doib, ci*n*cu *air*isit uirre, is i*n* ail[i] *déc* do br*eith* do-su*m*. Mai*n*ib iat-su*m* adub*airt* ris it*ir* br*eith* do br*eith* doib, ⁊ r*uc*-su*m* i*n* br*eith*, *acht* ma *air*isit uirre, is i*n* aili *déc* do br*eith* do-s*um*. ⁊ mai*n*e *air*isit, is a dul-su*m* gan ni[553] A. [*CIH* 2155.35–2156.11]

---

1 Breath **Q**. ‖ gin **Q**, gi*n* **JJ**. ‖ Source **JJ** repeats the phrase 'gi*n* dilsi', but it should be omitted. In the MS, the phrase has a rectangle faintly penciled around it. ‖ gi*n* **Q**, **JJ**. ‖ *a*rach **Q**, *arach* **JJ**. The text in source **A** ends with ⁊rl-; source **JJ** ends with *arach*. Only Source **Q** contains the full passage from the text. Source Q does not contain any relevant commentary.

---

549 Although plural verbal forms are normally used with dual subjects in OI, there is a tendancy during the MI period for plural subjects to be used with singular verbal forms, especially in relative constructions: cf. *is iat na gella doberar* below; see *GOI* § 539; and McCone, *The Early Irish Verb*, 182.

550 The sequence *brethemain in tan tecar ina reir fuigill cur a reir t*[e]*ista* has been added by the scribe with reference marks two lines above where the text starts; see also Binchy, *CIH* 2155, n. j.

551 The scribe has inserted reference marks here matching those above *arach* in the text; see also Binchy, *CIH* 2155, n. k, who suggests that the reference marks indicate that *arach* is being glossed.

552 The ⟨i⟩ was added subscript by the scribe.

553 The sequence ⟨ulsu*m* gan ni⟩ was written under the column by the scribe.

§30 A judgment without security, without guarantee; a judgment without security, without guarantee is not correct.[554]

i.e. without the 'true-consent'[555] of the two claimants, i.e. two pledges which are given to the judge when they submit to proper judgment according to testimony afterwards, and full pledges are given then immediately. And they are the pledges given for the twelfth[556] or another pledge on their behalf, i.e. without giving a surety's guarantee on their behalf by the claimants,[557] or two pledges to obey [the decision], two pledges for a judgment.

If the claimants came to the judge, and they consent to tell their accounts [i.e. each agrees to give his version of events], and they consent [for] a judgment to be given to them, and afterwards they say that they are not the accounts that they had told, and this was not a judgment that was given to them for them [i.e. their accounts], the judge [needs] to prove that they are the accounts that they told and that this was a judgment that was given to them for it, and the twelfth is given to him [i.e. the judge] [as payment] for judgment after that. And it is from that that is derived: Whatever he proves by oath, it is not oversworn.

If the claimants do not consent to tell their accounts and the judgment to be given to them, or though they consent to tell their accounts, if they do not consent for a judgment to be given to them, they [can] deny that he [i.e. the judge] gave a judgment to them, and he gets nothing. If they told the judge to give a judgment to them, though they do not abide by it, the twelfth is given to him [as payment] for judgment. If they did not tell him at all to give a judgment to them, and he gives the judgment, but if they abide by it, the twelfth is given to him [as payment] for judgment. And if they do not abide, he [i.e. the judge] gets nothing A.

---

554 For a discussion of this section, see the Introduction, 28. This section of the text serves as a warning to judges not to give a judgment without sureties to witness it and to guarantee that the judgment will be followed. Even if the judge gives a correct judgment, he will not be paid his fee, if the claimants deny that he gave them a judgment, unless the judge can prove it.

555 Although *fír-fœmad* 'true-consent' appears to be a quasi-etymological gloss, I am not certain what it glosses. It is possible that it is glossing something in the previous clause of the OI text which is no longer extant.

556 The judge receives a fee equivalent to a twelfth of the amount involved in the case; *GEIL*, 53.

557 It is possible that 'i.e. without … the claimants' is meant to be a gloss on the first *arach* of the text in source A; see Binchy, *CIH* 2155, n. k.

.i. ma tangad*a*r na feich*emain* docu*m* an br*eithem*, ⁊ admuid a sce[oi](io)l[558] d'in*n*isi*n*, ⁊ adm*ait* br*eith* do br*eith* doib, ⁊ atait aga r*adh* i*ar* d*ain* ni hiatsiut n*a* sg*eoil* d'i*nnséta*r, ⁊ ní hi-siud br*eth* rug*ad* d*oib*, a de*n*am do*n* b*reithemain*[559] *con*a hí-siuit b*reth*[560] *rug*, ⁊ *con*a iat[561] sg*eoil* roi*nnsetar*, ⁊ i*n* [dá][562] *aili déc* do br*eith* d*ho*. ⁊ is as g*ab*t*ar* si*n*: Cia f*or*toi*n*g, ni f*or*t*on*g*ar*. ⁊ m*ana* admuid na feich*emain* a sg*eoil* ⁊ ní admuid br*eith* do br*eith* doib*h*, is a se*n*a doib n*a*car in*nsétar* a sg*eoil* ⁊ nac rug*ad* br*eth* doib*h*, ⁊ a d*h*ul-som*h* ce*n* ní JJ. [*CIH* 1314.36–1315.3]

558 See also Binchy, *CIH* 1314, n. p.
559 See also Binchy, *CIH* 1314, n. q.
560 See also Binchy, *CIH* 1314, n. r.
561 The ⟨t⟩ was inserted above the line by the scribe.
562 See also Binchy, *CIH* 1315, n. a, and source A above.

i.e. if the claimants came to the judge, and they consent to tell their accounts, and they consent [for] a judgment to be given, and afterwards they say that they are not the accounts that they had told, and this was not a judgment that was given to them, the judge [needs] to prove it was the judgment given, and they are the accounts that they had told, and the twelfth is given to him [as payment] for judgment. And it is from that that it is derived: Whatever he proves by oath, it is not oversworn. And if the claimants do not consent [to tell] their accounts, and they do not consent [for] a judgment to be given to them, they can deny that they told their accounts and that a judgment was given to them, and he [i.e. the judge] gets nothing JJ.

p. 13a § 31 Deindill[563] rathachais ⁊rl-

Du*in*e ata ag sena nach dech*aid* a rathach*us* in so,[564] ⁊ fiadain aga fast*ad* air. ⁊ ma*in*e betis, rose*n*fad. In dei*n*dill rath*achais*: 'Se fe*n* obr*us* tiachtai*n* fut*h*u, ⁊ nocha cu*maing* u*air* atait budei*n* aga den*am* co tangat*ar* na *ceth*ra h-u*air*e *fich*it.

In bail ata guugud rathaigis re*main*d at[a]m[aid][565] a*n*d-side: Co ndech*aid* i*n*d, ⁊ a dichu*r* de *tr*iallas[566] A. [*CIH* 2156.12–17]

.i. i*n* dei*nn*ell r*athaigis*:[567] É fei*n* obr*us* tia*cht*ai*n* fut*h*u, ⁊ *noch*u cui*m*gec*h* é u*air* atait fiadai*n* aca de*num* cu ta*n*gat*ar* na *ceithri* u*air fich*it. Du*in*e doc*h*uaidh a rat*h*aiges an*n* ⁊ ata 'ga se*n*a; u*air* atait fiadai*n* an*n* dob*era*[568] f*air* é, (⁊)[569] *noch*u les a se*n*a R. [*CIH* 1063.22–26]

---

1 Source **R** might contain a longer section of the text than that preserved in source **A**. It reads as follows: D*eth*b*ir* it*er* in dei*n*dell rathaiges (§ 31) ⁊ i*n* saigid feich*eman* (§ 20) ⁊ i*n* i*m*ded*h*ail ait*ire* (§ 10) ⁊ i*n* gu(d)ug*ud* rat*h*ac*h*ais (§ 4) ⁊ i*n* co*m*bac*h* nad*m*a (§ 2) 'The difference between annulling the paying-suretyship and suing the claimant, and protection of the hostage-surety, and [turning a promise] of paying-suretyship [into] a lie, and the breaking of a contract'. The passage then goes on to give explanations about each of these types of sureties, although the order given here does not follow the order presented in **A** and the commentaries (other than the one given in this section) are different. The whole passage, *CIH* 1063.22–1064.3, is edited and translated in Thurneysen, "Aus dem irischen Recht V," 400–402.

---

563 The ⟨e⟩ was written inside the bow of the ⟨d⟩.

564 The words '*sena ... inso*' are written on the line above the text. Two words, approximately seven letters, have been erased before this clause.

565 Cf. Binchy, *CIH* 2156, n. a.

566 Cf. § 2, source A, *CIH* 2147.22.

567 See also Binchy, *CIH* 1063, n. f.

568 The 3 pl. fut. form of *do-beir, do-bérat,* is expected rather than sg. *do-béra,* but this could be an example of the MI use of a sg. verbal form with a pl. subject in a relative construction; McCone, *The Early Irish Verb*, 182.

569 Without the emendation, the final clause does not make good sense in English.

§ 31 Annulling a paying-suretyship, etc.[570] p. 13a

This is a person who denies that he entered into paying-suretyship, and witnesses prove it. And unless there were [witnesses], he could deny [it]. The annulling of a paying-suretyship: He himself works[571] to impugn them [i.e. the witnesses], and he cannot because they themselves prove that the twenty-four hours [prescribed by law] have passed.

The place where '[turning a promise] of paying-suretyship [into] a lie' is that we mentioned above:[572] He entered into it, and he endeavors to get rid of it A.

i.e. the annulling of a paying-suretyship: He himself works to impugn them [i.e. the witnesses], and he cannot because witnesses prove that the twenty-four hours [prescribed by law] have passed. A person who entered into paying-suretyship then and he is denying it; when there are witnesses there who will prove it, he cannot deny it R.

570 For a discussion of this section, see the Introduction, 28.

571 The form *obrus* is a 3 sg. pres. act. rel. form of *opraid.*

572 See § 4.

§ 32 Coscrad uad ænaig ⁊rl-

Sm*acht* ar dærcele g*r*aid fene a ne*m*dul i*n*d ⁊ i tiachtain as. Diabl*ad* ngni*mraid* ar særceli g*r*aid fei*ne* i ne*m*dul i*n*d ⁊ a tiachtai*n*[573] as. (cid fo*dera*)[574] Sm*acht* ar dærceli g*r*aid fl*ath*a i ne*m*dul i*n*d ⁊ *e*necl*ann* orra a tiachtai*n* as. Diabl*ad* ngni*mraid* ar særceli g*r*aid *flath*a a ne*m*dul i*n*d ⁊ *e*necl*ann* orra a tia*cht*ai*n* as.

Cid fo*dera con*id mo[575] orra a tia*cht*ain as amuig n[a](o)[576] a ne*m*dul a*n*d amach fo *cét*oir? Is e i*n* fa*th*: Aicbeli[577] do dul leis amach ⁊ a [ḟ]acbail[578] amuig a c*r*ich ne*m*besc*na* na ne*m*dul les amach fo *cét*oir. Cid fo*dera con*id mo arna g*r*adaib fl*atha* ce*n* dula leis isi*n* sloig*ed* na arna[579] g*r*adaib fe*ne*? Is e i*n* fa*th*: Mo tic tu*r*b*r*od i*n* sloig*id* do*na* g*r*adaib fl*ath*a do b*eth* i*n*a ec*m*ais na do*na* g*r*adaib fe*ne*, ⁊ coir gia*m*ad mo *ar*na g*r*adaib fl*ath*a na arna[580] g*r*adaib fei*ne*.

---

1 Although source **S** [*CIH* 2218.33] does not contain any additional parts of the text, it is worth quoting in full the line from *Bretha Nemed Toísech* in which the text occurs: Coscrad uad aonuidh asa moum de dire co log enech aonan cingci(n)ge[s] (?) 'Disturbing by him of an assembly as a result of which he [pays] the largest fine up to honor-price, the same as for Pentecost (?)'. Sources **O** and **T** do not preserve any of the text from *Anfuigell*. The commentary from T (*CIH* 1169.19–1170.15) is printed and translated in Appendix 2 because it mostly repeats the material from sources **A** and **O**.

---

573 The second ⟨t⟩ was added above the line with a reference mark by the scribe; see also Binchy, *CIH* 2156, n. b.

574 I follow the emendation suggested by Binchy, *CIH* 2156, n. c. It would appear that the scribe miscopied the phrase from a few lines down.

575 The scribe initially wrote ⟨n⟩ but added another minim to change it to ⟨m⟩.

576 I follow the emendation suggested by Binchy, *CIH* 2156, n. d.

577 *Aicbeli* is the comp. of *aicbéil*.

578 See also Binchy, *CIH* 2156, n. e.

579 The ⟨na⟩ were inserted above the line by the scribe; see also Binchy, *CIH* 2156, n. f.

580 The ⟨na⟩ were inserted above the line by the scribe; see also Binchy, *CIH* 2156, n. f.

§ 32 Disturbing by him of an assembly,[581] etc.[582]

A fine[583] for a base client of the non-noble grades for not going to it [i.e. an assembly] and for coming away from it [i.e. an assembly]. A doubling of labor [that they owe their lord as a fine] for free clients of the non-noble grades for not going to it and for coming away from it. A fine for base clients of the noble grades for not going to it and honor-price for coming away from it. A doubling of labor for free clients of the noble grades for not going to it and honor-price for coming away from it.

What is the reason that [the fine] for them is larger for coming away from it outside[584] than not going out to it immediately? The reason is: It is more dangerous for him to go away and leave him [i.e. his lord] outside in a territory not covered by protocol[585] than for him not to go out immediately. What is the reason that [the fine] is larger for the noble grades not going with him [i.e. with their lord] to the hosting than for the non-noble grades? The reason is: It is a greater infringement of the hosting for the noble grades to be absent than for the non-noble grades, and [it is] right that there should be a larger [fine] for the noble grades than for the non-noble grades.

581 For 'disturbing' an assembly, see D.A. Binchy, "The Fair of Tailtiu and the Feast of Tara," *Ériu* 18 (1958): 117–122, who provides several examples of assemblies being disrupted for political purposes. M. Joseph Wolf, Harvard University, is currently preparing an article on this section of *Anfuigell*.

582 For a discussion of this section, see the Introduction, 28–29.

583 For this commentary, cf. also *AL*, 3: 494–499.

584 The sense of *amuig* here is that the client was already outside the territory when he left.

585 The phrase *crich nembescna* 'a territory not governed by a protocol' refers to a territory with whom another territory does not have a treaty; see Neil McLeod, "Review Article: A True Companion to the *Corpus Iuris Hibernici*," *Peritia* 19 (2005): 153, n. 33.

Mas e in grad fl*ath*a *con*a *ch*elib tai*n*ic as, in s*macht* no i*n* enecl*ann* [ḟ]uil a*n*d, a l*eth* d'ic do-so*m* ⁊ a l*eth* d'ic doib-siu*m*. ⁊ do neoch na fil do celib i*na* farrad, is e-siu*m* ic*us* a cuitig, daig is e rob*er*ad a cuitig trebdire. [⁊] (i)[586] comrai*n*d sm*acht*a cana acna bi fer c*r*ui air .i. a l*eth* do rig in *cóic*id,[587] ⁊ in l*eth aile* do roin*n*[588] a t*r*i .i. t*r*ian do fl*aith* is nesa uas do rig in *cói*cid,[589] ⁊ a t*r*ian do*n* fl*aith*(a)[590] is nesa sis do*n*ti ic*us*, ⁊ *in* t*r*ian eli do*n*a fl*ath*aib ⁊ dona h-et*ar*fl*ath*ib [ḟ]uil et*ar*ru. Mas e in grad fl*ath*a i medon ⁊ æ*n*celi tai*n*ic as, in cutr*um*a roicf*ad* int æ*n*celi *con*a tia*cht*ain uili as ⁊ gu*n*a b*eth* an*n*, curab ed ic*us* anosa. ⁊ in s*macht* no in enecl*ann* [ḟ]uil a*n*d d'ic do-so*m*. ⁊ comrai*n*d sm*acht*a cana acna bi fi*r*[591] c*r*ai air beos.

Mas iat na celida tai*n*ic as iarna rad do-som riu, i*n* sm*acht* no in enecl*ann* [ḟ]uil a*n*d is a ic do-so*m*. ⁊ co*m*rai*n*d sm*acht*a cana acna bi fir c*r*ui air beos.

Mas iat na celida tai*n*ic as ga*n* a rad do-so*m* riu, i*n* sm*acht* no i*n* enecl*ann* [ḟ]uil a*n*d is a ic doib. ⁊ co*m*rai*n*d sm*acht*a cana ac[n](*m*)a[592] bi fi*r*[593] c*r*ai air-side; a t*r*ian-side do-so*m*, ⁊ a t*r*ia*n* do rig in *cóic*id,[594] ⁊ in t*r*ia*n aile* do rai*n*d a t*r*i .i. a t*r*ian do*n* fl*aith* is nesa suas[595] do rig in *cóic*id, a t*r*ian do*n* fl*aith* is nesa sis do*n*ti ic*us* .i. ri na[596] tuait*h*e [ḟ]uil orra-so*m* tis, ⁊ a t*r*ian *aile* dona fl*ath*aib ⁊ do*n*a et*ar*fl*ath*aib [ḟ]uil et*ar*ru i medo*n*.

586 I follow the emendation suggested by Binchy, *CIH* 2156, n. g.

587 The ⟨id⟩ are written above the line.

588 The words 'do roin*n*' were inserted above the line with reference marks by the scribe; Binchy, *CIH* 2156, n. h, queries whether the correction was written by the scribe.

589 The ⟨id⟩ are written above the line.

590 See also Binchy, *CIH* 2156, n. i.

591 The scribe wrote 'fri'; Binchy, *CIH* 2156, n. j, queries whether this is a mistake for 'fer'.

592 See also Binchy, *CIH* 2157, n. a. A suspension mark for ⟨m⟩ was incorrectly added later over the second ⟨a⟩ by the scribe.

593 The scribe wrote 'fri'; Binchy, *CIH* 2157, n. b, queries whether this is a mistake for 'fer'.

594 The ⟨id⟩ are written above the line.

595 The ⟨a⟩ is written subscript.

596 This word was inserted above the line by the scribe; see also Binchy, *CIH* 2157, n. c.

If it is [someone] of the noble grades with his clients who came away from it, the fine or the honor-price is [determined] then, he pays half of it and half of it they [i.e. his clients] pay. And anyone who does not have clients along with him, it is he [i.e. the noble] who pays their [i.e. the clients'] share because he would receive their share of compensation for house-theft.[597] And dividing of the fine for [violating] promulgated law by he who does not have property,[598] i.e. half of it to the king of the province, and the other half is divided in three, i.e. a third to the lord who is nearest up to the king of the province, and a third of it to the lord who is nearest down to the one who pays, and the other third to the lords and to the intermediate lords who are between them. If it is [someone] of the intermediate noble grades and one client who came away from it, the share that the one client would pay [is the same as] their [i.e. the clients] all coming away from it and with his [i.e. his share that he owes] being in it [i.e. part of what is owed], that is what he [i.e. the client] pays now. And the fine or the honor-price is [determined] then, he [i.e. the noble] pays [it]. And dividing of the fine for [violating] promulgated law by he who does not have property moreover.

If the clients came away from it because he [i.e. the noble] told them [to do so], the fine or the honor-price is [determined] then and it is paid by him [i.e. the noble]. And dividing of the fine for [violating] promulgated law by he who does not have property moreover.

If the clients came away from it without him [i.e. the noble] telling them [to do so], the fine or honor-price is [determined] then [and] it is paid by them [i.e. the clients]. And dividing of the fine for [violating] promulgated law by he who does not have property; a third of it to him [i.e. his lord], and a third of it to the king of the province, and the other third is divided in three, i.e. a third of it to the lord who is nearest up to the king of the province, a third of it to the lord who is nearest down to the one who pays, i.e. the king of the *túath* who is over them [i.e. those who fled] below, and the other third of it to the lords and the intermediate lords who are between them in the middle.

---

597 The term *trebdíre* refers to the compensation due for theft from a house; see also Eoin MacNeill, "Ancient Irish Law: The Law of Status or Franchise," *Proceedings of the Royal Irish Academy* 36 C (1923): 290, n. 2; and McLeod, "Property and Honour-Price," 292.

598 The phrase *acna bi fer crui* is problematic as it is difficult to determine which of the several meanings of 1 *cró* is meant here; *eDIL s.v.* 1 *cró* 'bodyguard, inheritance, house, etc'. The interpretation adopted here is that anyone who does not own property is responsible for the *smacht*-fine rather than paying honor-price.

Ca*ch* u*air* is [s]m*acht* sin is fo aicn*ed* inti ic*us*. Ca*ch* u*air* is eneclann is fo aicn*ed* inti risi*n* n-icth*ar*.

Masa luc*ht* sm*achta* ⁊ enecl*ainni* tai*n*ic as, ait*h*fegth*ar* cuibdi*us* et*ar*ru-side .i. in luc*ht* is mo lan dib d'ic na h-i*mar*crada, ⁊ tecait a cuibdi*us* ar am*us* p. 13b i*n* lo*ch*ta | is luga lan ⁊ co*m*icat etaru.

Masa luc*ht* sm*achta* ⁊ diabulta ngni*mraid* no enecl*ainni* ⁊ diabulta ngnim*raid* tai*n*ic as, noc*h*an ait*h*fegt*ar* cuibdi*us* et*ar*ru, *acht* cac*h* dib d'ic a lana ara ag*aid*[599] budein, uair aithfegt*ar*[600] cuibdi*us* ite*r* luc*ht* sm*achta* ⁊ enecl*ainni*, ⁊ nochan aithfegt*ar* ite*r* luc*ht* sm*achta* ⁊ diabulta gni*mraid*, *acht* cach dib d'ic a lana ara ag*aid* budei*n* A. [*CIH* 2156.18–2157.15]

.i. smac*h*t ar daerceili g*r*aid fei*n*e i*n* nemdul i*n*d ⁊ i tia*chtain* as. Diab*ul* ngni*m*raid ar saerceilib g*r*aid fei*ne* i nemdul i*nd* ⁊ enecl*ann* a tia*cht*ain as. Masa g*r*ad fl*ath*a cona daerceilib tainic as, no cid iat na ceili tainic as, masa e-sum adubairt riu, is enecl*ann* d'ic an*n*. ⁊ co*m*rai*n*d s*machta* cana ocna[601] bi fer c*r*ai air; a l*eth* do rig in *cóic*id, a l*eth* aili do roi*n*d i t*r*i; a t*r*ian don rig is nesu suas do rig in *cóic*id, a t*r*ian do rig na tuait*he* [ḟ]uil orru-su*m* tṡis, ⁊ a t*r*ian dona flat*h*aib ⁊ dona et*ar*flat*h*aib [ḟ]uilet et*ar*u ar medon. Masa g*r*ad fl*ath*a ⁊ aenc*h*eile tainic as, enecl*ann* d'ic and fos. ⁊ i*n* cutru*m*a roicfad i*n* ceile co mbet*h* na celed uili an*n*, corob ed icas, ⁊ a fuil an*n* ot*h*a si*n* amac*h* d'ic dosu*m*. ⁊ i*n* comrai*n*d cetna air: a l*eth* do rig in *cóic*id, ⁊ in l*eth* aile do roi*n*d i t*r*i.

599 The first ⟨a⟩ was inserted below the line by the scribe; see also Binchy, *CIH* 2157, n. e.

600 The ⟨e⟩ was inserted above the line by the scribe; see also Binchy, *CIH* 2157, n. f.

601 The scribe has actually written 'cona', but cf. 'ocna' below; see Binchy, *CIH* 330, n. b.

Whenever it is a fine, it is according to [the status of] the one who pays. Whenever it is honor-price, it is according to [the status of] the one to whom it is paid.

If it is people [who owe] a fine and honor-price who came away from it, a joint payment between them is recognized, i.e. the people who are the most guilty of them pay the surplus [amount owed], and they come to a joint payment with the people | who are less guilty, and they pay equally between p. 13b
them.

If it is people [who owe] a fine and doubling of labor or honor-price and doubling of labor who came away from it, a joint payment between them is not recognized, but each of them pays [the amount of] his guilt of his own accord, because a joint payment is recognized between people [who owe] fine and honor-price, and it is not considered between people [who owe] fine and doubling of labor, but each of them pays [the amount] of his guilt of his own accord A.

i.e. a fine for base clients of the non-noble grades for not going to it [i.e. the assembly] and for coming away from it [i.e. the assembly]. Doubling of labor for free clients of the non-noble grades for not going to it and honor-price for coming away from it. If [someone of the] noble grades with his base clients came away from it, or though the clients came away from it, if it is he [i.e. the noble] who ordered them [to do so], honor-price is paid then. And dividing of the fine for [violating] promulgated law by he who does not have property; half of it to the king of the province, the other half of it is divided in three; a third of it to the king who is nearest up to the king of the province, a third of it to the king of the *túath* who is over them below, and a third of it to the lords and to the intermediate lords who are between them in the middle. If [someone of the] noble grades and one client came away from it, honor-price is paid now; and the share that the client should pay is [the same as for] all the clients then, this is what he pays, and that which is in it [i.e. owed] from that [amount] onwards is to be paid by him [i.e. the lord]; and the same division for it: Half of it to the king of the province, and the other half is divided in three.

Mas iat na ceilida fei*n* tainic as can deoi*n* do-sum, s*macht* no enecl*ann* and. ⁊ comrai*n*d s*macht*a cana ocna bi fer c*r*ai air: A t*r*ian do rig in *cóic*id, ⁊ a t*r*ian don g*r*ad fl*ath*a asa ceile tainic as, ⁊ a t*r*ian aile do roi*n*d i t*r*i; [.i. a t*r*ian do*n* fl*aith* is nesa suas do rig in *cóic*id, a t*r*ian do*n* fl*aith* is nesa sis do*n*ti ic*us* .i.][602] a t*r*ia*n* do rig na tuait*h*i [ḟ]uil orro-su*m* as, ⁊ a t*r*ian dona flat*h*aib ⁊ dona e*tar*flat*h*ib [ḟ]uil et*ar*u ar medon.

Ma tancat*ar* lu*cht* s*macht*a ⁊ enecl*ainne* as, can cuibdi*us* do gabail at*ar*u, *acht* cach dib d'ic a lana ara aig*h*id*h* budein; nocon gaba cuibdius it*er* lu*cht* s*macht*a ⁊ enecl*ainne*, nocon gaba it*er* lu*cht* diab*alta* nec*h* dib it*ir*.

Cach uair is [s]ma*cht* ict*ar* an*n*, is a ic fo aic*ned* inti icas; ⁊ ca*ch* uair is enecl*ann*, is a ic fo aic*ned* inti risi n-ict*ar*.

Cid fo*dera* con[id](ach)[603] mo arna g*r*adaib fl*ath*a an*n* na arna g*r*adaib fei*ne*? Is e fa*th* fo*dera*: Mo is turbrod dont sloiged ł don dunad na g*r*aid fl*ath*a 'na ecmais i*n*ait na g*r*aid feine, ⁊ mo recair a les iat, ⁊ coir ciamad mo nobeith orra. Cid fo*dera con*[i](a)d[604] mo orro i tia*cht*ain as i*n*a neamdul i*n*d? Is e fa*th* fo*dera*: Aicbeile don rig aa facbail amai*ch* a c*r*i*ch* neambescna[605] i*n*a nemdul leis amach fo *ch*etoir.

Cach uair is [s]ma*cht* si*n*, is fo aic*ned* inti icas. Ca*ch* uair is enecl*ann*, is fo aic*ned* inti risi n-ict*ar*.

Ma lu*cht* s*macht*a ⁊ enecl*ainn*i tanic as, at*h*fegt*air* cuibdius et*ar*u-side .i. in lu*cht* is mo lan d'ic na i*m*arcraidi, ⁊ tecait a cuibdes ar am*us* in lo*cht*a b*us* log*h*a lan, ⁊ comicat et*ar*u.

---

602 The scribe appears to have left out a line of text at *CIH* 330.22; cf. source A above.

603 I follow the emendation suggested by Binchy, *CIH* 330, n. c.

604 I follow the emendation suggested by Binchy, *CIH* 330, n. c.

605 See Binchy, *CIH* 330, n. d. At a later point a faint ⟨s⟩ was written above the ⟨e⟩.

If it is the clients themselves who came away from it without his [i.e. their lord's] consent, fine or honor-price then. And dividing of the fine for [violating] promulgated law by he who has no property; a third of it to the king of the province, and a third of it to the noble of the grade from which his client came away from it, and the other third of it is divided in three; [i.e. a third of it to the lord who is nearest up to the king of the province, a third of it to the lord who is nearest down to the one who pays, i.e.] a third of it to the king of the *túath* who is over those who came away, and a third of it to the lords and to the intermediate lords who are between them in the middle.

If people [who owe] a fine and honor-price came away from it, a joint payment does not apply between them, but each of them pays [the amount] of his guilt of his own accord. Joint payment does not apply between people [who owe] a fine or honor-price, it does not apply between people [who owe] double of any of them at all.[606]

Whenever it is a fine that is paid then, it is paid according to [the status] of the one who pays; and whenever it is honor-price, it is paid according to [the status] of the one to whom it is paid.

What is the reason that [the fine] is larger for the noble grades than for the non-noble grades? The reason is: It is a greater infringement on the hosting or on the army for the noble grades to be absent from the place than the non-noble grades, and they are needed more, and [it is] right that they should owe a larger [fine]. What is the reason that [the fine] for them is larger for coming away from it than for their not going to it? The reason is: It is more dangerous for the king to be left outside in a territory not covered by protocol than their not going out with him immediately.

Whenever it is a fine, it is according to [the status] of the one who pays. Whenever it is honor-price, it is according to [the status] of the one to whom it is paid.

If it is people [who owe] fine and honor-price who came away from it, a joint payment between them is recognized, i.e. the people who are the most guilty pay the surplus, and they come to a joint payment with the people who are less guilty and they pay equally between them.

606 This paragraph of the commentary contradicts the fine structure laid out in the last two paragraphs of source A and the last paragraph of source O below.

Masa luc*ht* s*macht*a ⁊ diabalta g*nimraid*[607] ⁊[608] enecl*ainne* ⁊ diabalta g*nimraid* tainic as, *no*con at*h*fegt*ar* cuibdes et*ar*ru *acht* cac*h* dib d'ic a lana ara ag*h*aid*h* budei*n*, uair at*h*fegt*air* cuibdes it*er* luc*ht* sma*cht*a ⁊ enecl*ainn*i, ⁊ nocon at*h*fegt*ar* it*er* luc*ht* s*macht*a ⁊ diabalta g*nimraid* no it*er* luc*ht* enecl*ainn*i ⁊ diabalta g*nimraid acht* cac*h* dib d'ic a lana ara agaid budein O. [CIH 330.9–42]

607 See also Binchy, CIH 330, n. e.

608 Cf. the reading with *nó* 'or' in source A.

If it is people [who owe] fine and doubling of labor and[609] honor-price and doubling of labor who came away from it, a joint payment between them is not recognized, but each of them pays [the amount] of his guilt of his own accord, because a joint payment is recognized between people [who owe] fine and honor-price, and it is not considered between people [who owe] fine and doubling of labor or between people [who owe] honor-price and doubling of labor, but each of them pays [the amount] of his guilt of his own accord O.

609 The similar passage in source A reads *nó* 'or', which might make better sense here.

§ 33 Uargalach[610] n-air ⁊rl-

.i. int ar[611] cu*r*tar i n-u*air* na gaile.[612] Cum*al* a nguin*n*[613] cui*r*p in cl*er*ig co taiselbad ɫ a mbuain a ci*n*d de (gi*n*) [go][614] taiselbad. L*eth*cum*al* i ngac*h* ni dib mu*n*a raib taiselb*ad*. L*eth*cum*al* a nguin cui*r*p i*n* tuata co taiselb*ad* no a mbuain a ci*n*d de co taiselb*ad*. Cethr*aimth*e cu*mail*e i*n* cach ni dib-si*n* mu*na*[615] [ḟ]uil taiselb*ad*. In l*eth*cu*mal* no in cum*al* ader ar son pei*n*de isi*n* cl*er*ech: Ma ta clerech da fine, is a br*eth* do, ⁊ mu*n*a fuil, is a br*eth* da ecl*ais* bu*n*aig.

⁊ sai*n*e fer dori*n*n*e* in marb*ad* ⁊ in dichendad a*n*d, ⁊ sai*n*e fe*cht* dori*n*ded he. ⁊ da*m*ad a n-æ*n*fe*cht*, nocha rach*ad* t*ar* lan i*n* marb*tha*. Ni de tai*n*ic in m*ar*b*ad* do*n* dichen*n*ad, ⁊ da*m*ad de, noc*h*a rach*ad* tar lan i*n* m*ar*b*tha*.[616] Ca*ch* ni is fog*al* risi*n* corp marb do g*re*s is a br*eth* do ecl*ais* bunaid.

Cid fo*dera cona* fuil *acht* l*eth*cum*al* no cethr*aimth*e cu*mail*e a*n*d seo, ⁊ i*n* bail ata tall: Fir ilaid ailed so*n* *secht*mad, .i. co fuil *secht*mad coirp*diri* an*n*seic?[617] Is e i*n* fa*th*: Ilach et*ar*scart*h*a cuirp fri h-an*m*ain [ḟ]uil a*n*d si*n*, ⁊ dichen*n*ad cuirp mairb [ḟ]uil a*n*d so ɫ guin cuirp mairb. ɫ d*ano* is re corp dilsig doro*n*ad i*n* gui*n*-seo ɫ in dic*h*en*n*ad, ⁊ i*n* sm*acht*-si*n* a*n*d don ecl*ais* *ar* ce*cht*ar de, ⁊ re h-i*n*dilsech dori*n*ded in buadug*ud* tall.

---

610 *Uargalach*, probably from the adj. *airgalach*, 'combative, warlike', *eDIL s.v. uargalach* (?), is also found as a personal name, e.g. Uargalach; T.M. Charles-Edwards, *The Chronicle of Ireland* (Liverpool: Liverpool University Press, 2006), *s.a.* 765. The following nasalization is probably a result of *uargalach* being in the acc. sg. case.

611 Although *ár* is not listed with a gender in *eDIL*, based on the form of the nom. sg. art., *int*, the word appears to be m. in this commentary.

612 This is a quasi-etymological gloss on *uargalach*.

613 One letter, possibly ⟨o⟩, has been erased after this word.

614 I follow the emendation suggested by Binchy, *CIH* 2157, n. g; cf. further below.

615 The ⟨a⟩ is written subscript.

616 'Ni de … m*ar*b*tha*' *om.* *CIH* 2157.24.

617 Cf. also *CIH* 1055.28–30, which is part of the text *Don aos fiachach sisanaigh*, the main version of which is found in *CIH* 2031.31–2033.16. The text has been edited by R.M. Smith, "A Tract on the *Áes Fíachach*," in *Irish Texts*, 4, ed. J. Fraser, P. Grosjean, J.G. O'Keefe (London: Sheed and Ward, 1934), 13–16; and discussed by Paul Russell, "*Y Naw Affaith*: Aiding and Abetting in Welsh Law," in *Tair Colofn Cyfraith*: *The Three Columns of Law in Medieval Wales*. The Welsh Legal History Society v (2005). Ed. T.M. Charles-Edwards and Paul Russell (Bangor: The Welsh Legal History Society, 2007), 160–162. Paul Russell is currently preparing an edition of this text.

§ 33 Warlike of slaughter, etc.[618]

i.e. the slaughter which is inflicted at the time of the conflict. A *cumal* for wounding the body of a cleric [and] exhibiting [it] or for cutting off his head [and] exhibiting [it as a trophy]. Half a *cumal* for each of these things if there is no exhibiting. Half a *cumal* for wounding the body of a layman [and] exhibiting [it] or for cutting off his head [and] exhibiting [it as a trophy]. A quarter of a *cumal* for each of these things if there is no exhibiting. The half *cumal* or the *cumal* it says [i.e. referring to the source of the legal judgment] as punishment[619] for [mutilating] the [dead] cleric: If [the] cleric has a kindred, it [i.e. the fine] is given to it [i.e. the kindred], and if he does not, it is given to his original church [lit. his church of origin].

And different men did the killing and the decapitation then, and it was done at different times. And if it were [done] at the same time, it would not exceed the full [penalty] of the killing. If the death did not result from the decapitation [i.e. the person was already dead before the decapitation], and if it were [to result] from it, it would not exceed the full [penalty] of the killing. Every injury that is done to the dead body is always given to [his] original church.

What is the reason that there is not but half a *cumal* or a quarter of a *cumal* here, and in the next passage there is: [If] men utter a cry of exultation [after the crime],[620] that requires a seventh [as a fine], i.e. there is a seventh of the body-fine here? The reason is: There is a cry of exultation [for] separating the body from the soul in that case, and there is beheading of a dead body in this case or wounding a dead body. Or, moreover, it is against the body of a criminal that this wound or the beheading was done, and that fine then [is] for the Church for each of them. And [it is] against an innocent person that the triumphing was done [referred to] elsewhere.

---

618 For a discussion of this section, see the Introduction, 29.

619 The sense of *pían* here is approaching the meaning of 'penance', i.e. atonement for mutilating and/or decapitating the dead body of the cleric.

620 *Ilach* refers to any shout or cry made in joy or triumph after a crime. Regardless of whether one participated in the crime, making such a shout incurred penalties as if one were an accessory to the crime; see *eDIL s.v. ilach*; and Smith, "A Tract on the *Áes Fíachach*," 15.

Gne *aile*:[621] Cu*mal* i nguin cui*r*p i*n* clei*rig* ł a mbein a ci*n*d de co taiselb*ad*. L*eth*cum*al* mad ci*n* t*aiselbad*. L*eth*cu*mal*[622] i ngui*n* cuirp i*n* tuata ł a mbein a ci*n*d de co taisilb*ad*. Ceth*raimth*e cu*mail*e mad ci*n* taiselb*ad*.

Dai*ne* ecsamla dorigne i*n* gui*n* ⁊ i*n* m*ar*b*ad* an*n* si*n*; ⁊ da*m*ad i*n*a*n*d dui*ne*, is n*echt*ar de fair, .i. fiac*h* m*ar*bt*h*a na*m*a ł gona nama, ⁊ co*m*ad [i n-]æ*n*-[fecht](dui*ne*)[623] dogne. Dia*m* i*ar* sai*ne* f*er*gi, nob*et*is a ndis uad, ⁊ a mbr*eth*-si*n* dia fine 'malle am*al* dib*ad* ł coirp*díre*, ł co*m*ad f*r*i h-ecl*ais* na fil *ar* so*n* pe*n*daite i*n* so A. [*CIH* 2157.16–36]

621 The phrase *gne .ii.* is written by the scribe in *marg. dext.*; see also Binchy, *CIH* 2157, n. i.

622 *Lethcumal* is followed by the sequence ⟨l⁊cu*m*⟩, a dittography mistake, which the scribe corrected by underlining; see also Binchy, *CIH* 2157, n. k.

623 I follow the emendation suggested by Binchy, *CIH* 2157, n. l.

Another version: A *cumal* for wounding the body of a cleric or for cutting off his head [and] exhibiting [it]. Half of a *cumal* if it is not exhibited. Half of a *cumal* for wounding the body of a layperson or for cutting off his head [and] exhibiting [it]. A quarter of a *cumal* if it is not exhibited.

Different people did the wounding and the killing in this case. And if it were the same person, either of the penalties is his responsibility, i.e. a fine for killing only or for wounding only, and it is at the same time that he does it. If it were after different outbursts of wrath [i.e. he wounds the body at one time and decapitates it at another time], there would be both of them [i.e. both fines due] from him, and those [i.e. the fines] would be given equally to his kindred [i.e. the kindred of the slain person] like an inheritance or like a body-fine, or this [fine] is [given] to a church to which he belongs as penance A.

§ 34 Arbach mbo da-ba ⁊rl-

Masa nech seg*ar* dia gui*n* no dia marb*ad* cin cinta, sl*an* do ca*ch* fog*al* dogena[624] aca dichu*r*, *acht* log cu*mail*e do pe*n*dait uad do denu*m* a sida re dia. Ma conai*n*ig [a díchur],[625] is co *tr*ian is [s]l*an*. ⁊ lanfiach on fir *aile* i*n* cach fog*ail* dogen*a* ri[s](u)-sum.[626] ⁊ comardug*ud* it*er* na da *tr*ian dleg*ar* de ⁊ in lan [ḟ]uil i*n*d-siu*m*, ⁊ cidbe dib aca *m*be an i*m*arc*r*aid, ic*aid* re ceili.

Masa nech seg*ar* dia gui*n* no dia[627] marb*ad* co ci*n*ta, sl*an* do*n*ti [ḟ]uil aci*nn* i*n*dsaig*id* ca*ch* fog*al* dogena ris-[s]iu*m*,[628] mu*n*a cæ*m*nacar a feich do tob*ach* de cena. Masa feich dlegar de, cid er*aic* fog*l*a cid feich cuir ł cun*n*ar*th*a, ma conai*n*ic cena ca*ch* ni dib-si*n*, is co *tr*ia*n* is [s]l*an*, ⁊ lanfiach onti rohi*n*dsaig*ed* a*n*d in[629] ca*ch* fog*ail* dogen*a* ris-[s]iu*m*.[630] ⁊ co*m*ardug*ud* it*er*
p. 14a in da *tr*ian [ḟ]uil | i*n*d-sui*m* ⁊ in lan uad, ⁊ cidbe dib aca mbe an i*m*arc*r*aid ic*aid* re cele A. [*CIH* 2157.37–2158.8]

1 None of the OI text is preserved in **O**.

624 The ⟨gena⟩ were inserted above the line by the scribe; see also Binchy, *CIH* 2157, n. n.

625 I follow the emendation suggested by Binchy, *CIH* 2157, n. o.

626 I follow the emendation suggested by Binchy, *CIH* 2158, n. a.

627 The ⟨i⟩ was mistakenly inserted above the line with a reference mark by the scribe after ⟨a⟩; see also Binchy, *CIH* 2158, n. b.

628 See also Binchy, *CIH* 2158, n. c.

629 *In* was inserted above the line with a reference mark by the scribe; see also Binchy, *CIH* 2158, n. e.

630 See Binchy, *CIH* 2158, n. c.

§ 34 Slaughter of cows which he recovers,[631] etc.[632]

If someone is sued for wounding him or for killing him even though he [i.e. the victim] has not [committed] a crime, exempt from legal liability is every injury he [i.e. the victim] will inflict warding him [i.e. his pursuer] off, except for the amount of a *cumal* for penance[633] from him to make his peace before God.[634] If he was able to ward him off, up to a third is exempt from legal liability. And [the] full fine from the other man for every injury he will do to him [i.e. the victim]. And a balancing of liabilities between the two-thirds owed from him [i.e. the victim] and the full [amount] that is [owed] to him [by the pursuer]. And whichever of them has the surplus, he pays the other.

If someone is sued for wounding him or for killing him after having committed a crime, exempt from legal liability is the one who is pursuing [for] every injury he will do to him, if he was not able to collect his fines from him, however. If fines are due from him, whether *wergeld* for injury or fines of contract or trade, if he was able, however, [to collect] each one of them, up to a third is exempt from legal liability. And [the] full fine [is due] from the one who is pursued then for every injury he will do to him [i.e. to the pursuer]. And a balancing of liabilities between the two-thirds that is | [owed] p. 14a
to him and the full [amount that is owed] from him [to the pursuer]. And whichever of them has the surplus, he pays the other A.

631 The meaning of the phrase *da ba* is uncertain due to the fragmentary nature of the text. I understand it to be the pres. subj. 3 sg. of *do-boing* 'wrests, exacts, levies, recovers' with a class A 3 sg. m. or n. object agreement marker. Although *arbach* is n. here (assuming the word appears in the nom. sg. in the OI text), it later switches genders to become a m. noun.

632 For a discussion of this section, see the Introduction, 29. This is an instance where the OI text, which (perhaps) deals with killing someone else's cows, is not actually the subject matter of the commentary, which deals with penalties for pursuing someone suspected of having committed a crime, which may, however, also include killing someone's livestock.

633 Cf. § 33, where a half *cumal* or a whole *cumal* is the amount of the fine for mutilating the body of a dead cleric, and § 35, where it is stated that the fine for killing in self-defense is that which is given in a penitential. Unfortunately, § 35 does not state the specific penitential being referenced, nor does it state what the penance listed in the penitential is.

634 This seems to be a reference to making a payment to the Church as a means of atonement for killing in self-defense. None of the Irish penitentials deal with the topic of killing in self-defense, although there is mention of killing someone in a brawl in the *Old-Irish Penitential*, Cap. v, § 4 where the penance is given as a year and a half or forty nights; cf. § 35; and *GEIL*, 128–129.

Ma ta caem*acht*u tobaig dlig*id* t*r*e toich*id* aile ac feich*emain* toich*eda* ⁊ ní [ḟ]uil caem*acht*u i*m*gabala ac bidb*aid*, am*al* nech segar dia guin no dia marb*ad* can ci*n*ta, no co ci*n*ta in bidb*a*.

Mana [ḟ]uil coem*acht*u tobaig dlig*id* tre toich*id* aile ac feich*emain* *toicheda* ⁊ ata coem*acht*u i*m*gab*al*a ac bidb*aid*, ⁊ mas e in bidb*a* romarb*ad* an*n*, is [s]lan. Mas e ro*m*arb nech, is lanfiach[635] O. [*CIH* 278.5–10]

635 Cf. source J, Digest D (33) *CIH* 2005.35–37.

If[636] the plaintiff has the ability to collect what he is owed by suing the other, and the defendant is not able to evade [him], [it is] like someone who is sued for wounding him or for killing him even though he has not [committed] a crime, or after having committed a crime [by] the defendant.

If the plaintiff does not have the ability to collect what he is owed by suing the other, and the defendant is able to evade [him], and if it is the defendant who was killed then, he [i.e. the plaintiff] is exempt from legal liability. If it is he [i.e. the defendant] who killed someone, [the] full fine is [owed by him] O.

636 Although source O contains very little of the commentary preserved in A, it is useful to include as it further explicates the material under discussion in source A.

§ 35 Is dilis frithguin

Sl*an* do a marb*ad* gi*n* cæ*mach*ta dula uad cena *acht* fir fo*n* coirp*díre* na cæ*m*nacair dul uad ⁊ *con*id (d)e[637] roi*n*dsaig, inni focl*us* pen*n*atoir do pen*n*ait uad.

Mai*ne* tard a coibse*na*-si*n* intí rom*ar*b*ad* an*n* na roi*n*dsaig, ⁊ ma rof*er*aid cneda f*or*inti [ḟ]uil i*na* beth*aid*, icfaith*er*-sid*he* o fine i*nn* fir rom*ar*b*ad* a*n*d. Ma dorat im*murro* a coibse*na* dia comarb*aib*, is leo-side a se*na* co lu*cht* a fira na roi*n*dsaig, ⁊ coirp*díre* d'ic ind an*n*-side, ⁊ lasi*n* fer [ḟ]uil a mbet*h*aig se*na* na roi*n*dsaig, ⁊ co*m*ardug*ud* gi*n* frith*aigid*[638] et*ar*ru.

Ma rof*er*ait[639] cneda ari*n*ti [ḟ]uil[640] i mb*eth*aig, ma atmait[641] ne*cht*ar de im*murro* an indsaig*id* ar d*us*, is [s]l*an* i*n*ti roindsaig ⁊ lanfia*ch* isi*n*ti na roi*n*dsaig A. [*CIH* 2158.9–18]

Slan d*ano* a marb*ad* mana caomnaca*ir* dul uad*ha*, a*cht* fir fon coirp*díre* uad*ha* na cæmnaga*ir* *con*ad é rohin*nsaig*, a*cht* aní [ḟ]ocl*us*[642] pen*n*adoir do pen*n*ait uad*ha*.[643]

---

1 Source LL does not preserve any of the text from *Anfuigell*, but is does preserve the following, which appears to be from a different legal text: Dil*us* gac frit*h*gui*n* gac frithai*n*me 'Lawful is every counter-wounding, every retaliatory name-calling'; see also *CIH* 866.34: Dil*es* gac frithgui*n*. *Frithainme* refers to a pejorative nickname; see *eDIL s.v. frithainme*; GEIL, 137; and McLaughlin, *Early Irish Satire*, 15–22.

---

637 I follow the emendation suggested by Binchy, *CIH* 2158, n. f.

638 The ⟨r⟩ was inserted above the line by the scribe; see also Binchy, *CIH* 2158, n. h.

639 For 3 sg. *roferaid*; cf. previous paragraph of commentary.

640 The sequence ⟨uil⟩ was inserted above the line by the scribe; see also Binchy, *CIH* 2158, n. e.

641 For 3 sg. *atmaid*; cf. the last paragraph of LL below.

642 I follow the emendation suggested by Binchy, *CIH* 1200, n. m.

643 The first part of the commentary is part of a larger commentary written *marg. inf.* with reference marks above *airech* at *CIH* 1200.24.

§ 35 Counter-wounding is lawful[644]

He is exempt from legal liability for killing him [i.e. his pursuer] [when he] does not have the ability to escape from him, however, but proof [must be provided] up to [the value of] the body-fine that he was not able to escape from him [i.e. the pursuer] and that it is he [i.e. the attacker] who pursued, and that which a penitential states as penance from him [for killing his attacker].[645]

If the person who was killed had not made his confession then that he had not pursued, and if he had inflicted wounds on the one who is alive, it [i.e. the fine] will be paid by the kindred of the man who was killed then. If, however, he made his confession to his heirs, they have a right to deny with compurgators [saying] that he pursued, and body-fine is to be paid for him [i.e. for the one who was killed] in this case, and the man who is alive has a right to deny that he [i.e. the deceased] did not pursue [him], and a balancing of liabilities without a counter-plea between them.

If he inflicted wounds on the one who is alive, if either of them admits, however, to pursuing first, the one who pursued is exempt from legal liability [i.e. there is no liability for wounding the pursuer] and [the] full fine [is owed] for the one who did not pursue A.

Exempt from legal liability then for killing him [i.e. the pursuer] if he did not have the ability to escape from him, but proof up to [the value of] the body-fine [must be provided] by him [i.e. the victim] that he was not able [to escape from the pursuer and] that it was he [i.e. the attacker] who pursued, but that which a penitential states as penance from him [for killing his attacker].

---

644 For a discussion of this section, see the Introduction, 30. For a discussion of killing in self-defense, see *GEIL*, 128–129. Cf. § 34.

645 Although none of the Irish penitentials deal specifically with the topic of self-defense, the *Old-Irish Penitential*, Cap. v, § 10 gives a penance of one year for accidentally killing a kinsman, and § 4 states that the penance for killing someone in a battle or brawl is a year and a half or forty nights. The *Penitential of Cummean*, Cap. iv.8 states that the penance for accidental killing is one year; *The Irish Penitentials*, ed. Ludwig Bieler.

Ni t*ar*d a coibsi*n* intí romarb*ad* an*n* na roin*n*saig*h*, ⁊ ma rofera a cn*eid* *ar*in fer fuil ina beat*h*a, ic*aid* fine i*n* lo*cht*a rom*ar*b*ad* an*n*. ⁊ ma dorat a coibsi*ne* dia co*m*arb*aib*, is leo-sid*h*eig a s*en*a g*o* lu*cht* fir*a* na roin*n*saig*h*, ⁊ corp*díre* d*h*'ic an*n*, ⁊ is laisi*n* fer fuil ina beath*aid* a s*en*a na roin*n*saig*h*, ⁊ com*ar*d*ad* gi*n* fri*thaigid* et*ar*a.

Ma atm*aid* n*echtar* d*h*e an in*n*saig*h* ar tus, is [s]lan i*n*tí roin*n*saig*h*, ⁊ lanfia*ch* isi*n*tí na roin*n*saig*h* LL. [*CIH* 1200.28–37]

The person who was killed had not made his confession then that he had not pursued, and if he inflicted wounds on the man who is alive, the kindred of the person who was killed pays [the fine] then. And if he made his confession to his heirs, they have a right to deny with compurgators [saying] that he did not pursue, and body-fine is to be paid then, and the man who is alive has a right to deny that he did not pursue, and a balancing of liabilities without a counter-plea between them.

If either of them admits to pursuing first, the one who pursued is exempt from legal liability [i.e. there is no liability for wounding the pursuer], and [the] full fine [is owed] for the one who did not pursue LL.

§36 **Burach n-*in*draig ⁊rl-**

.i. inan*n* beos ⁊ i*n* bl*a* tuath t*r*eag. Daine si*n* tangat*ar* re fog*ail* n-i*n*dlis ł re forloscad isi*n* c*r*ich, ⁊ *ru*csat seotu na c*r*ichi leo. ⁊ sl*an* a marb*ad* ce*n* sloi*n*ded, ce*n* aichni, ce*n* cæ*macht*a astaide a n-u*air* de*n*ma na fog*l*a fo *cét*oir. ⁊ sl*an* ca*ch* dui*n*e muirbfith*er* i*n*a ric*h*t. ⁊ i*n*de*th*em fast*aid*e *ru*cad cuca(d) a*n*d, ⁊ ni raibe cæ*macht*a [ḟ]ast*aid*e ⁊rl-

Is dil*es* do cach ⁊rl-

Do*n* g*r*ad isa fer*ann*, cid ed, ⁊ ni[646] do rig

Cia rogona nec*h* ⁊rl-

.i. sl*an* co t*r*ia*n* iat do*n* lu*cht* tall risi*n* ndernad fog*ail* ⁊ do ca*ch* æ*n* dia fuil fo[d](g)*ail*[647] *e*necl*ainn*i isi*n* fog*ail* dori*n*set. ⁊ it sl*an*a uile iat ce*n* cæ*macht*a a fast*aide*. & lanfia*ch* i*n*tib o*n* rig mai*n*e dlig fo[d](g)*ail*[648] enecl*ainn*i isi*n* fog*ail* dori*n*set .i. særceli ł dærceli do m*ar*b*ad*, ⁊ ni fil ni i*n*a *sét*aib A. [*CIH* 2158.19–28]

---

1 buirach J buir*ech* LL. ‖ n-in*nraic* J and LL. Sources J [*CIH* 2005.29–30] and LL [*CIH* 1201.22] only preserve the first two words of the OI text.

---

646 The word *ni* was inserted above the line with a reference mark by the scribe.

647 I follow the emendation suggested by Binchy, *CIH* 2158, n. i.

648 I follow the emendation suggested by Binchy, *CIH* 2158, n. i.

§36 A lawful attack, etc.[649]

i.e. the same still as the exemption of *túath*s for three attacks.[650] Those people who came to unlawfully attack or to commit arson in the territory, and they took away with them the territory's *sét*s. And killing them without naming, without recognition, without being able to restrain [them] immediately at the time of committing the attack is exempt from legal liability. And exempt from legal liability is [i.e. no one is liable for] each person who will be killed in mistake for them [i.e. the attackers]. And [they, i.e. those pursuing] had the intention of restraining them then, and there was not the ability to restrain [them], etc.

It is lawful for each, etc.

For the rank whose land it is, however, and not for a king[651]

Although he may have wounded someone, etc.[652]

i.e. exempt from legal liability up to a third for the people there against whom an attack was made and for each one for whom there is [due] a share of honor-price for the attack they made. And they are exempt from all legal liability [when they are] not able to restrain them. And full fine for them from the king unless he is entitled to a share of honor-price for the attack they had made, i.e. a free client or base client was killed, and there is nothing for their *sét*s A.

649 For a discussion of this section, see the Introduction, 30. Cf. §16 for similar subject matter.

650 Cf. *Bretha Éitgid*, CIH 288.21–289.15, *AL* 3: 286.14; and CIH 1201.39–1202.27. Based on the commentary in *Bretha Éitgid*, *treág* seems to be a compound of *trí* 'three' and *ág* 'attack'; *eDIL s.v.* ? *treág*.

651 The interpretation of this clause is obscure to me.

652 The Irish is ambiguous and could also be translated as 'Although someone wounded, etc.'

§ 37 Ni h-erenar *sét* ona ⁊rl-

na rat*h*a .i. dob*er*ar isi*n* rath ⁊ a ci*n*aid na fl*ath*a

na h-iarraid

i. dob*er*ar lesi*n* lenu*m* ⁊ a ci*n*aid ath*ar* in lei*n*b.

Masa fis a tia*cht*ana a*m*uig ⁊ a*n*fis a tia*cht*[an]a[653] tall, ⁊ ruc*ad* amac*h* ar daigi*n* a coi*m*eta, *acht* ma m*air*it na *séoit* tall, is ait*h*gi*n*. Mu*n*a m*air*end *acht* ni dib, is l*eth*ait*h*gi*n*. ⁊ mu*n*a m*air*end ni dib it*ir*, is [s]l*an*. Masa fis a tia*cht*a*n*a tall ⁊ fis a tia*cht*[an]a amuig, ł anfis a tia*cht*[an]a tall ⁊ a*n*fis a tia*cht*[an]a amuig, ⁊ *ru*cad amach *ar* daigi*n* a coimeta, is [s]l*an* A. [*CIH* 2158.29–35]

653 Binchy, *CIH* 2158, n. j, suggests that the scribe omitted the suspension mark here and below.

§ 37 **A *sét* of a loan is not paid, etc.**[654]

nor for fiefs,[655] i.e. it is given for the fief and for the lord's liability

nor for a fosterage-fee

i.e. it is given with the child and for the liability of the child's father.

If there is knowledge of their [i.e. the *sét*s] coming from outside and ignorance of their arrival inside, and they [i.e. the *sét*s] were taken away for the purpose of guarding them, but if the *sét*s remain [alive] there,[656] it is restitution [of the *sét*s]. If only some of them remain [alive], it is half restitution. And if none of them remain at all, he is exempt from legal liability.[657] If there is knowledge of their [i.e. the *sét*s] arrival inside and knowledge of their coming from outside, or ignorance of their arrival inside and ignorance of their coming [from] outside, and they were taken away for the purpose of guarding them, he is exempt from legal liability[658] A.

---

654 For a discussion of this section, see the Introduction, 30.

655 It is likely that the phrase *na ratha* belongs with the OI text. If that is the case, then loaned *sét*s should not be given by a lord as a fief for a client.

656 *Tall* can refer to location generally as well as 'inside', as opposed to *immaig* 'outside'. In this case, it is hard to determine whether the meaning of *tall* refers specifically to 'inside' or more generally to wherever the *sét*s were taken.

657 The reason that he owes nothing if the *sét*s do not remain alive is because they were taken with the intent of keeping them safe.

658 This commentary is difficult to interpret. It seems to deal with the child's fosterage-fee being paid to the foster-parents. The main text on fosterage, *Cáin Íarraith* 'The Regulation of Fosterage-Fee', does not contain this commentary; CCIH, 288; CIH 852.13–25, 901.34–902.14, and 1759.6–1770.14; and AL 2: 146–193.

§ 38 Inderb n-allmuire ⁊rl-

Da *sét* roba co*m*ait*h* i llo[659] in cu*n*dart*h*a, ⁊ secaini*m* isi*n* dara *sét* ⁊ i*n sét aile ar* bisech. ⁊ ce*m*ad ail do*n* dara fir a diub*air*t d'ac*r*a ari*n* fer *aile*, nocho roich, uair roba co*m*ait*h* a lo i*n* cu*n*dart*h*a iat.

Damna eich roce*n*daig dui*ne* a*n*d si*n*, ⁊ cid *m*esa i*ar* dain he i*n*a 'nni doratad dia ci*n*d, nochan [ḟ]uil fuill*ed* ris. ⁊ cid ferr he, noc*h*an [ḟ]uil a br*eth* for culu A. [*CIH* 2158.36–2159.2]

.i. damna eich rocen*n*aig dui*ne* an*n* si*n*, ⁊ comaith hí ⁊ in log dorat dia cind, *nochon* fuil tuill*ed* ris. ⁊ cid ferr he, *nocon* [ḟ]uil a br*eth* f*or cu*la

p. 55b .i. commaith na *séoit* i lo in cun*nar*ta | an*n* si*n*, ⁊ ata in darna *sét* dib ar bisech o si*n* amach ⁊ ata i*n sét aile* ar do*m*bisech. ⁊ ce*m*ad ris dised[660] menma in fir i*m*uig*h* diub*air*t d'agra an*n* no[661] in *sét* d'at*h*chur, ce nofasad secgni*m*-*rad*[662] aige fein ann, *no*c[h]o cu*m*aing, uair robu comaith i lo in cundarta iad I. [*CIH* 1556.38–1557.4]

1 allmaire **A.**

659 The words *i llo* were added in *marg. dext.* by the scribe; see also Binchy, *CIH* 2158, n. k.

660 The form *dised* is the 3 sg. imp. subj. of *téit* 'goes' where the nasalized /t/ is written ⟨d⟩; see *eDIL s.v.* 1 *téit*, and *GOI* § 501.

661 The ⟨n⟩ was inserted below the line by the scribe; see also Binchy, *CIH* 1557, n. a.

662 I take this form to be a mistake for *secainim*; see *eDIL s.v. seicgnímrad.*

§ 38 Uncertainty of imported goods,[663] etc.[664]

Two *sét*s are equally good on the day of the contract, and [there is] depreciation of one *sét* and the other *sét* increasing [in value]. And although one man might wish to sue the other man for his loss, he is not able to, because they were equally good on the day of the contract.

The matter of a horse that a person bought in that case, and though afterwards it may be worse [i.e. turn out to be less in value] than that which he had given for it, there is not an addition for it [i.e. nothing else is given for it to make up the loss]. And though it may be better [in value than when he bought it], it is not returned A.

i.e. the matter of a horse that a person bought in that case, and it was as good as the price he paid for it, there is not an addition for it.[665] And though it may be better, it is not returned

i.e. the *sét*s are equally good on the day of the contract | in that case, and p. 55b
one *sét* of them increases [in value] afterwards and the other *sét* decreases. And though it might be the desire of the plaintiff to sue the other one for [his] loss then or to return the *sét*, though the depreciation increases for the owner, he is not able to, because they were equally good on the day of the sale I.

663 The case and number of *inderb* 'uncertain' is ambiguous. Based on the nasalization, it seems to be being used here as an acc. sg. or gen. pl. substantive; both case forms are identical in the m. and n. genders.

664 For a discussion of this section, see the Introduction, 30–31.

665 It appears as if some of the commentary from source I has been left out.

§ 39 Ailgesach dunaid ⁊rl-

Lan*e*necl*ann* do*n* rig a n-ailges do gab*ail* de a sloig*ed* ł a ndu*n*ad i*ar* n-esc*air*i a ne*m*gab*ala*. ⁊ lan do i*n*a gab*ail* do[666] ca*ch* dui*ne*,[667] ⁊ lan do ca*ch* dui*ne* i*n*a gab*ail* de fei*n*, ⁊ lan da*no* i*n*a gab*ail* do*n* rig.

Mas re n-esc*air*i im*murro*, *cethramthu* do*n* rig i*n*a gab*ail* de fei*n*. ⁊ iss *ed* do da*no* i*n*a gab*ail* do ga*ch* dui*ne*, ⁊ iss *ed* da*no* do ca*ch* dui*ne* ina gab*ail* de fei*n* ⁊ i*n*a gab*ail* do*n* rig.

Ailges[668] bu dligth*ech* do gab*ail* a n-i*n*ad *aile* si*n*. Og dul do*n* fil*id* i ce*n*d (s)*cúarta*,[669] is and[670] gab*us* an ailgi*us*, ⁊ a n-ar*m* ł a n-etach gaib*us* i*n*t ailgi*us*,
p. 14b | ⁊ cutr*u*mas *sechtm*ad[671] loigi en*ech* in g*r*aid dia ngab*ar* iss *ed* gab*us*.

Mas ailgi*us* i*n*dlig*thech*, is lan*e*necl*ann* do ca*ch* dui*ne* i*n*a gab*ail* de fei*n*, ⁊ no*ch*an [ḟ]uil ni do neo*ch* dib i*n*a gab*ail* diaraile, mai*n*ib i sloig*ed* no i *n*du*n*ad, la*n*enecl*ann* an*n*-side.

Ailges .i. geis guide, is *ar* ail di*diu* dobe*r*ar i*n* guide-si*n* ⁊ ni *ar* mol*ad*. *Secht*m*ad*[672] loigi e*n*ech i*n*ti c*us*a cuin*n*eg*ar* in ailges, is [s]i an ailges te*ch*ta.[673]

In ailges i*n*dlig*thech*: Cidbe i*n*ad i *n*gab*ar* he ata lan*e*necl*ann* i*n*a gabail. Iss *ed* is ailges i*n*dlig*thech* an*n* a gabail i ndu*n*ad ł a sloig*ed*, no ani is *mo* na *sechtm*ad[674] loigi en*ech* inti dia ngab*ar*, ł fili e*cht*arc*r*ichi, ł[675] mainip dul a ce*n*d cuarta, ł mainip a n-ar*m* no a n-etach.

---

666 Although *de* is expected here, this is an example of the common confusion of *do* for *de*.

667 The idiom *gaibid áilges de* 'demands' is the underlying construction in this and the following clauses; *eDIL s.v. áilges*.

668 *Áilges* (and related *áilgesach*) is a poorly undertood legal term. The sense in the commentaries is that it refers to more than just a poet making a request for payment, but rather to an excessive request with the accompanying threat of satire if the request is not responded to. The commentaries present scenarios where the *áilges* is deemed lawful and unlawful; when lawful a payment of a seventh of the honor-price is required, when unlawful the fine is the full honor-price.

669 I follow the emendation suggested by Binchy, *CIH* 2159, n. b; cf. below.

670 The words *is and* were inserted above the line by the scribe; see also Binchy, *CIH* 2159, n. c.

671 The ⟨ad⟩ were written above the line by the scribe.

672 The ⟨ad⟩ were written above the line by the scribe.

673 This explanation of *áilges* is taken from *Sanas Cormaic*; *Sanas Cormaic*, no. 62 in Meyer's edition; see also the Early Irish Glossaries Database for editions of all the versions of this entry and the related entry from *Dúil Dromma Cetta*; http://www.asnc.cam.ac.uk/irishglossaries/texts.php?versionID=1&readingID=15601#15601. Accessed August 29, 2018. I should like to thank Paul Russell for bringing this entry to my attention.

674 The ⟨ad⟩ were written above the line by the scribe.

675 The ⟨ł⟩ was inserted above the line with a reference mark by the scribe.

§ 39 Importunate [request] of a fort, etc.[676]

Full honor-price for the king for demanding a request from him during a hosting or in a fort after notice [that] it could not be obtained. And full [honor-price] for him [i.e. the king] for each person who demands it, and full [honor-price] for each person for demanding it from him himself [i.e. each person from whom an unreasonable demand is made is owed their honor-price], and full [honor-price] moreover [is owed] to the king for demanding it.

If it is before notice, however, a fourth to the king for demanding it from him himself. And it [i.e. the fine] is [due] to him [i.e. the king] moreover for each person demanding it, and it is [due] moreover for each person for demanding it from him himself, and for demanding it from the king.

This was a request that was lawful to demand in another place. A poet going on a circuit, this is the request that he demands, and in arms or in clothes he obtains the request, | and [the] equivalent of a seventh of the p. 14b honor-price of the rank from whom it is demanded is what he takes.

If it is an unlawful request, full honor-price for each person for demanding it from him himself, and there is not anything [due] to any of them for demanding it from another, unless it may be during a hosting or in a fort, full honor-price then.

A request, i.e. *geis* [means] 'request', it is for disgracing then that request is made and not for praising. A seventh of the honor-price of the one from whom the request is demanded, that is the lawful request.

The unlawful request: Wherever it may be demanded, there is full honor-price for demanding it. This is the unlawful request then, demanding it in a fort or during a hosting, or for that which is greater than a seventh of the honor-price of the one from whom it is demanded, or a poet from a foreign territory, or unless he is going on a circuit, or unless it may be in arms or in clothes.

676 For a discussion of this section, see the Introduction, 31.

In ail*ges* dlig*thech* im*murro*, fili na c*r*ichi gab*us* he i*n* tan teit se dari*n* crich imac*h*, ⁊ i n-ar*m* ⁊ i n-etac*h* gab*us* he. ⁊ *sechtm*ad[677] loigi en*ech* in g*r*aid dia ngab*ar* he, iss *ed* gab*us* in ailgi*us* (indlig*thech*),[678] ⁊ fer fine gaibes he da cele. ⁊ ailges indlig*thech* mainib aml*aid*-si*n* beas A. [CIH 2159.3–21]

677 The ⟨ad⟩ were written above the line by the scribe.

678 Binchy, CIH 2159, n. e, remarks that the phrase *in ailgius indligthech* seems out of place here and that the last word has been erased almost completely. While the clause makes sense without the phrase, it is only *indligthech* that needs to be omitted.

The lawful request, however, a poet of the territory that demands it when he goes outside the territory, and in arms or in clothes he demands it. And a seventh of the honor-price of the rank from whom it is demanded is what he demands as the request, and a kinsman may demand it from another. And furthermore it is an unlawful request if it may not be like this A.[679]

679 The overlapping and repetitive nature of the commentary suggests that the material in source A was collected from a variety of different sources.

§ 40 Dasachtach nadma

T*r*eb*air*e roi*n*dsaig for bidbaid an*n* sin riasiu tai*n*ic uide icæ na fia*ch*. Mas ap*ad* tuc*us*t*ar*, is *cóic sét* uada, ⁊ masa t*r*oscad, is *cóic sét* uada ⁊ dilsi a fia*ch* gi*n* ac*r*a do g*r*es.

⁊ iar *cét*faid *con*a toibged di fe*n* ł do neoch *aile* do g*r*es na fia*ch*u-si*n*, no da*no* cena co toibget di fe*n* iar tia*cht*ain uide icce na fiach, u*air* no*ch*a di fe*n* dori*n*de i*n*dlig*ed* umpu o*n* *cét* lo A. [*CIH* 2159.22–26]

§40 Imprudence of a binding-surety[680]

A surety had sued a defendant [i.e. the other party to the contract] in that case before the appointed time for paying the debt came. If he gave notice, it is five *séts* [due] from him, and if it is fasting,[681] it is five *séts* [due] from him and forfeiture of his debt without ever suing.[682]

And according to the opinion [of others] they never recover from him himself [i.e. the defendant] or from someone else those debts, or others [say] that they recover [it] from him himself [i.e. the defendant] after the time appointed for paying the debt has arrived because it was not he himself who committed an illegality regarding them [i.e. the debts] from the first day [of the contract] A.

680 For a discussion of this section, see the Introduction, 31.

681 For fasting, see *GEIL*, 182–183 and the Introduction to §17.

682 The plaintiff's surety owes the defendant fines for suing for the debts before the appointed time.

§ 41 Naidm meisce ⁊rl-

Ni mesc it*ir* ma cu*m*ain leis ar matain a dala o aidc*he* (am*ail* don*eth con*a ceill).[683] Na h-uili soch*ur* dorigne f*or* mesci is fast*aid*i am*ail* don*eth con*a ceill. Ca*ch* doch*ur* im*murro* dorigne nocha fast*aidi* ɫ co raib *ceithri* u*aire* *fichit* i*n*a aititi*n* i*ar* tia*cht*ain ceille codnaig*h* do.

Na h-uile sochur ⁊ doch*ur* naid*m*ter ar dui*ne* *ar* meisci: No*ch*an [ḟ]ast*aid*i air iat ɫ co raib re re cet*r*i n-uaire *fich*it[684] i*n*a aititi*n* iar taid*echt* ceille codnaig*h* do. ɫ co*m*ad fast*aid*i i*n* soch*ur* ar *ceithri* u*aire* *fich*it,[685] ⁊ as [ḟ]ast*aid*i na dochair air ot*h*a si*n* amach. ⁊ conegat a ci*n*d ⁊ a coibdelaig [a taithmech][686] ari*n* re ari*n* dir doib. ⁊ is iat na soch*uir* cor*us* rait*h*, cor*us* co*m*ic*h*ius[a],[687] cor*us*[688] co*m*air cir*t*.

Gne *aile*:[689] Dilsi na h-urandigi ⁊ i*n* rath tar *air*dig. ⁊ na h-uili soch*ar* is do*ch*anta do neoch, gid co meisci gid gan meisce fonaisct*er* air. Is fast*aid*i air iat fo[690] *cét*oir. Na h-uile soch*ur* is [s]ocanta do neoch, no*ch*an fast*aid*i air iat no co raib se 'na aititi*n* re re cet*r*i n-u*aire* *fich*it i*ar* taid*echt* ceille do A. [*CIH* 2159.27–39]

683 Binchy, *CIH* 2159, n. f, comments that the phrase *amail doneth cona ceill* seems to be out of place and queries whether it should be omitted. As the phrase appears in the next line, this seems to be a result of eye-skip to the next line.

684 The ⟨it⟩ were written above the line by the scribe.

685 The ⟨it⟩ were written above the line by the scribe.

686 I follow the emendation suggested by Binchy, *CIH* 2159, n. g.

687 Binchy, *CIH* 2159, n. h, suggests emending to *comaithchesa*, but the form as it stands in the text is a later form of the gen. sg. of *comaithches*; see also *eDIL s.v. comaithches*.

688 *Corus* was written in *marg. dext.* with reference marks by the scribe; see also Binchy, *CIH* 2159, n. i.

689 '*gne .ii.*' was written in *marg. sin.* by the scribe; see also Binchy, *CIH* 2159, n. j.

690 The ⟨o⟩ was added above the line with reference marks probably by the scribe.

§41 A contract of drunkenness, etc.[691]

He is not [considered] drunk at all if he remembers in the morning his contracts from the night [before]. Every advantageous contract that he made drunk is binding as he would make in full command of his senses. Every disadvantageous contract, however, that he made is not binding until he acknowledges it twenty-four hours after coming to his senses.

Every advantageous and disadvantageous contract bound on a drunk person: They are not binding on him until he acknowledges it within a period of twenty-four hours after coming to his senses. Or the advantageous contract may be binding from twenty-four hours, and the disadvantageous contracts are binding on him from then onwards. And his chiefs and his kinsmen can seek to dissolve it during the time that is proper for them. And the advantageous contracts are an agreement of clientship,[692] a neighborhood agreement, and an agreement of proper joint-plowing.[693]

A different version: Forfeiture of the excess and the grant for extra services.[694] And every advantageous contract that is prejudicial for someone, whether in drunkenness or sober, is bound on him. They are binding on him immediately. Every advantageous contract that is advantageous for someone, they are not binding on him until he acknowledges it within a period of twenty-four hours after coming to his senses A.

691 For a discussion of this section, see the Introduction, 31–32. For the validity of contracts made while intoxicated, see McLeod, *Early Irish Contract Law*, 56–58; and GEIL, 154.

692 *Rath* is the term for the fief consisting of stock or land advanced by a lord as part of a clientship arrangement; *eDIL s.v.* 2 *rath*; see also §37.

693 For these three types of valid contracts, see McLeod, *Early Irish Contract Law*, 57; and *Di Astud Chor*, 148 (§21).

694 The phrase *rath tar airdig* is problematic. According to Binchy, who follows Thurneysen, the phrase might refer to "an additional amount of capital advanced by the lord to cover any rent or service the client might render which went beyond the legal amount due from him;" D.A. Binchy, "*Coibnes Uisci Thairidne*," *Ériu* 17 (1955): 66 (§7) and 80; Rudolf Thurneysen, "Aus dem irischen Recht I," ZCP 14 (1923): 362–363. and 393; and *idem*, "Aus dem irischen Recht IV," ZCP 16 (1927): 210.

§ 42 **Mescbuide fl*ath*a ⁊rl-.**

.i. mescad na fl*ath*a a buid*h*ec .i. li*n*d re ca*ch* mbiat*h*ad di.[695] Br*eth*ea*m*(ai)n*us*[696] ⁊ i*m*de*n*am ⁊ fiad*naise* do*n* fl*aith* f*or*a dærcele,[697] ⁊ nochan [ḟ]uil f*or*a særceli *acht* br*eth*emnus nama in ta*n* is air acart*ar* A. [*CIH* 2160.1–3]

695 The gloss, '*.i. mescad … di*', is written in *marg. sin.* by the scribe without reference marks; see also Binchy, *CIH* 2160, n. a. The gloss is a quasi-etymological gloss on the word *mescbuide.*

696 I follow the emendation suggested by Binchy, *CIH* 2160, n. c.

697 The ⟨c⟩ was inserted above the line by the scribe with a reference mark; see also Binchy, *CIH* 2160, n. d.

§ 42 Of the intoxication[698] of a lord, etc.[699]

i.e. intoxicating the lord with pleasure,[700] i.e. a drink before every meal for it. Judgment and proof and testimony by the lord for his base client, and there is nothing for his free client except only judgment when it is he [i.e. the free client] who is sued A.

698 The precise meaning of *mescbuide* here is uncertain; *eDIL s.v. mescbaid* 'disturbance, confusion, dissension'.

699 For a discussion of this section, see the Introduction, 32.

700 The phrase *a buidhec* is unclear here, but it appears to be a quasi-etymological gloss on the *buide* element of *mescbuide*. The adjective *buidech* has a range of meanings including 'pleased, grateful, satisfied, thankful'; *eDIL s.v.* 2 *buidech*. The phrase might refer to making the lord pleasantly drunk.

§ 43 Forbflaithe senaid ⁊rl-

Imde*n*um don ecl*ais* f*or*in lu*cht* dia ndlige*n*d ca*ch* ni dib-so uile, mane be ecl*ais* aile 'ga testug*ud*. Dia *m*be, is le a se*n*a na dlegar na fei*ch* it*ir* A. [CIH 2160.4–6]

§ 43 Of [the] overlordship of a synod, etc.[701]

The Church proves against the people from whom each thing is owed in every case,[702] unless there may be another church testifying on their [i.e. the people's] behalf. If there may be, it [i.e. the other church] has the right to deny that the debts are owed at all A.

701 For a discussion of this section, see the Introduction, 32.

702 In other words, the evidence provided by the Church is accepted as final proof of what is owed to it as a fine unless the evidence is contested by another church. For a discussion of ecclesiastical jurisdiction, see Etchingham, *Church Organisation in Ireland*, 63–83 and 130–148; and *GEIL*, 200.

§ 44 **Saru*gud* ordan**

Int uasal: Ma roleg*ad* a elod, is *cóic sét* ⁊ *e*necl*ann* ⁊ diabl*ad* fiach do a lec*ud*
p. 15a a elaid. ⁊ dui*ne* arna dlige*n*n a dul a rat*h* | rolecast*ar* a el*od* an*n* si*n*, ⁊ da ndle-
sid,[703] is a rat*h* dorec*h*ad[704] do he, ł da*no* cena is a roga na fl*ath*a a feic*h* A.
[*CIH* 2160.7–10]

---

703 I understand the verb to be the past. subj. 3 sg. of *dligid* 'owes, deserves, must, is bound to'.

704 I understand the verb to be the cond. ind. 3 sg. of *do-tét* 'comes, comes to, accrues to'.

§44 Flouting[705] noblemen[706]

The nobleman: If he was evaded, it is five *sét*s and honor-price and doubling of fines [which are owed] to him for evading him. And the person who is not obligated to act as his paying-surety | evaded him in that case [i.e. the other party to the contract evaded him], and if he were obligated [to act as his paying-surety],[707] it is his paying-surety to whom it [the debts] would come [i.e. the surety would be responsible for paying the nobleman's debts], or else, moreover, the lord can choose his [i.e. the surety's] fine A. p. 15a

705 Although *sárugud* usually means 'vioalting, outraging', the sense here seems to be closer to 'disregarding' or 'flouting' responsibilities.

706 For a discussion of this section, see the Introduction, 32.

707 In other words, if it were the paying-surety who evaded the nobleman, the surety would be responsible for paying the nobleman's debts.

§ 45 Slog cen urnaidm

In dui*n*e rotairgest*ar* na deorada leis isi*n* crich re dena*m* fog*l*a airit*h*i isi*n* crich, iss *ed* dleg*ar* luigi, .i. ar achtugud[708] arna h-urradaib ⁊ treb*aire* dar ce*n*d na ndeor*ad* na dernat fog*ail* isi*n* cric*h* *acht* in fog*al* risa ndec*hatar*. ⁊ o degenat aml*aid*-si*n*, sl*an* do ca*ch* fog*al* aile doge*n*at *acht* in fog*al* risar tairce*star* iad. Mane de*r*na aml*aid*-si*n* it*ir*, is am*al* fer tairct*h*i e-siu*m* u*m* ca*ch* fog*ail* doge*n*at isi*n* crich as taircest*ar* iat, ⁊ ca*ch* ni na tarraith*er* do*n*a deor*ad*aib is a ic do-s*om*.

Mas e i*n*det*h*em *ru*csat leo ca*ch* fog*al* uili do denum, is am*al* fer tairct*hi* he re ca*ch* fog*ail* doge*n*t*ar* isi*n* cric*h*. ⁊ nocho mo is fer co*m*gnima e u*mon* fog*ail* aca raibe de*n*um na u*m* fog*ail* acna[709] raibe de*n*um.

Mai*n*e *ru*csat leo *acht* i*n*dethe*m* æ*n*fog*l*a, *noch*an fer co*m*gni*m*a neach dib u*m* fog*ail* aile *acht* umu*n* fog*ail* aca raibe de*n*um.

Mas re fog*ail* dil*is* rotairget i*n* slog gi*n* treb*aire* tara ce*n*d *acht* luigi, is [s]l*an* doib i*n* fog*al*-sin gin cæm*acht*ain aice fei*n* a denma. ⁊ an u*r*ain fog*l*a icat fei*n* dia tairsith*er*, no[710] ica[d](t)-s*um*[711] mai*n*e tairsith*er*.

Mas re fog*ail* n-i*n*dlis im*murro*, is am*al* fer tairc[t]*h*i eisiu*m* imun fog*ail*-si*n*. In u*r*ain fog*l*a-si*n* icat fei*n* dia tairsith*er*; (⁊)[712] ł ica[d](t)-s*um* mai*n*e tairsit*er*, ⁊ icat-s*um*[713] ris-[s]iu*m*[714] i*ar* tain.

Cen treb*aire* sin i[715] ce*ch*tar de, uair dia *m*b*eth*, is e noicfad[716] i*n* tan na tarthith*er*-siu*m*[717] fei*n*, ⁊ ica-so*m* fris i*ar* tai*n* A. [*CIH* 2160.11–27]

---

1 Slog*h* C. ‖ ce*n* C. ‖ urnaid*m* C.

---

708 The phrase *.i. ar achtugud* was written by the scribe in *marg. sin.* with reference marks to the text; see also Binchy, *CIH* 2160, n. e.

709 The ⟨n⟩ was added in *marg. dext.* by the scribe; see also Binchy, *CIH* 2160, n. f.

710 The ⟨o⟩ was inserted above the line by the scribe; see also Binchy, *CIH* 2160, n. h.

711 The ⟨c⟩ was inserted above the line by the scribe. Binchy, *CIH* 2160, n. i, suggests emending *icat* to either *icaid* or *icad*.

712 I follow the emendation suggested by Binchy, *CIH* 2160, n. j.

713 The ⟨c⟩ was inserted above the line by the scribe.

714 I follow the emendation suggested by Binchy, *CIH* 2160, n. k.

715 The ⟨i⟩ was inserted above the line by the scribe; see also Binchy, *CIH* 2160, n. l.

716 The ⟨c⟩ was inserted above the line by the scribe.

717 Binchy, *CIH* 2160, n. m, notes that the suspension mark over the first ⟨h⟩ was made in error.

§45 A host without guarantee[718]

The person who had brought the mercenaries with him into the territory in order to make a particular attack in the territory, an oath is required, i.e. by stipulation of the people of the *túath* and a surety on behalf of the mercenaries that they will not make an attack in the territory except the attack for which they had gone. And when they will do thus, exempt from legal liability [is the instigator] for every other attack that they [i.e. the mercenaries] will make except the attack for which he had brought them. If he does not do thus at all, he is as an inciter regarding every attack that they will make in the territory to which he brought them. And everything that was not seized from the mercenaries is to be paid by him.

If they [i.e. the mercenaries] intended to make many attacks, he is as an inciter for every attack that will be done in the territory. And he is not a greater accomplice regarding the attack that he carries out than regarding an attack that he did not carry out.

If they intended only one attack, none of them is an accomplice regarding the other attack except regarding the attack which he carried out.

If they brought the host for a lawful attack without surety on their behalf except an oath, that attack is exempt from legal liability for them [when] he himself [i.e. the person who hired them] cannot himself do it. And the excess injury [i.e. what is owed for additional damage] let them pay themselves if they are seized, or let him pay if they are not seized.

If it was for an unlawful attack, however, he is as an inciter regarding that attack. That excess injury let them pay themselves if they are seized; or let him pay if they are not seized, and let them pay [the amount back] to him afterwards.

That is without surety for each of them, because if there were [a surety], it is he [i.e. the surety] who should pay when he himself was not seized, and [each] paying to him afterwards A.

718 For a discussion of this section, see the Introduction, 32–33.

In duini rat*hair*cest*ar* na daim*h*i leis isi*n* c*r*ich re denum*h* fogla *air*ithi, is *ed* dleg*h*ar de luig*h*i arna h-urrad*h*aib*h* ⁊ trebairi d*ar* cend na *n*deorad*h* na dinġnet[719] fog*h*ail isin c*r*ich *acht* in fog*h*al rise ndec*h*atar. ⁊ o dagena amlaid*h*-sei*n* is [s]lan do cid fogla ele danet.

Maini d*er*na amlaid*h*-si*n* eitir, is amail fe*ar* tairct*h*i eisium*h* in cac*h* fog*h*ail dagenat. ⁊ cac*h* ni na t*ar*thith*er* duna deorad*h*aib*h* uili is a ic do-su*m*h.

Mas e i*n*nit*h*ium*h* ruccsat leo cac*h* fog*h*al uili cu ticcfaitis du denum*h*, is fear tairct*h*i eisiu*m*h re cac*h* fog*h*ail dagentar isi*n* c*r*ich. ⁊ nuccu mo is fe*ar* coi*m*gni*m*ha nec*h* dib*h* risi*n* fog*h*ail aca raibi denu*m*h i*n*na risin fog*h*ail acna raib*h*i denum*h*.

Maini ruccsat leo *acht* i*n*nit*h*iu*m*h ænfogla, nucun fe*ar* t*air*cthi eisium*h* i*m*mo fog*h*ail eile *acht* imi*n* fog*h*ail-si*n*, ⁊ nucun fe*ar* coi*m*hgni*m*ha neac*h* dib*h* i*m* fog*h*ail eile *acht* imi*n* fog*h*ail acca raibi denu*m*h C. [*CIH* 169.4–16]

719 The *punctum* over the ⟨g⟩ here indicates nasalization; see also Binchy, *CIH* 169, n. a.

The person who brought the parties with him into the territory to make a particular attack, an oath is required for the people of the *túath* and a surety on behalf of the mercenaries that they will not make an attack in the territory except the attack for which they went. And if he will do thus, he is exempt from legal liability though they will make other attacks.

If he will not do thus at all, he is as an inciter regarding every attack that they will make. And everything that was not seized from all the mercenaries is to be paid by him.

If they intended to make other attacks when they came, he is [as] an inciter for every attack that they will make in the territory. And any of them is not a greater accomplice regarding the attack that he carries out than regarding the attack that he does not carry out.

If they intended only one attack, he is not [considered] an inciter regarding the other attack, only that attack [i.e. the one they were hired to do], and none of them is an accomplice regarding the other attack only regarding the attack that he carries out C.

§46 Aurnaidm cen forus

.i. dui*ne* docuaid a rat*h*ach*us* a*n*d sin ⁊ ata aga se*na*. U*air* na fuil*eth* fiadai*n* a*n*d, is les a se*na* co nech dia*m*bi log en*ech* ina diad*h*. ⁊ mai*ne* raibe co*m*aititi(*n*)u[720] dlig*id* it*er* na fech*em*naib et*ar*ru fei*n*, noc*h*an e-siu*m* at*m*as doib e.

G*ne* *aile*:[721] Co*m*airli t*u*cad do*n* fech*emain* toich*eda* an*n* si*n* ce*n* t*r*eb*air*e do gab*ail* re lai*m* co mb*eth*is fiadai*n* aigi na rose*n*ad[722] i*n* t*r*eb*air*e he. ⁊ is si a dethbir-seo ⁊ i*n* saig*id* feche*m*an tuas, .i. don t*r*eb*air*e t*u*cad co*m*airle tuas,[723] ⁊ do*n* feche*m*ain toich*eda* t*u*cad com*air*li[724] su*n*d A. [*CIH* 2160.28–34]

---

720 The scribe placed a suspension mark over the ⟨i⟩ in error; see also Binchy, *CIH* 2160, n. n.

721 The ⟨.ii.⟩ was added above the line with reference marks by the scribe.

722 The ⟨a⟩ was added below the line by the scribe; see also Binchy, *CIH* 2160, n. o.

723 The ⟨a⟩ was added below the line by the scribe; see also Binchy, *CIH* 2160, n. o. A suspension mark above the ⟨s⟩ has been partially erased.

724 The word *comairli* was added above the line by the scribe with a reference mark; see also Binchy, *CIH* 2160, n. l. Just past the word, the scribe has added in smaller letters ⟨air⟩ perhaps indicating the correct expansion of the second syllable.

§46 A bond without enforcement[725]

i.e. a person has gone into paying-suretyship in that case and he is denying it. When there are no witnesses then, he has the right to deny it with someone who has an honor-price afterwards.[726] And if there is not mutual acknowledgement of law between the claimants themselves, it is not he who declares it for them.

Another version: Advice had been given to the plaintiff in that case not to accept a surety until he would have witnesses that the surety could not deny it [i.e. agreeing to enter into suretyship for him]. And the difference here and the suing of a claimant[727] above is, i.e. to the surety advice was given above, and to the plaintiff advice was given here A.

725 For a discussion of this section, see the Introduction, 33–34.

726 In other words, he can deny it with a proper compurgator.

727 Cf. §20, *CIH* 2153.3.

§ 47 Fuasnad iar n-aititin

ł fuaitre*d* in ferai*n*d[728] .i. re re rudart*h*a. Dui*n*e robui i-naititi*n* a ferai*n*d a*n*d si*n* (⁊)[729] no go[730] dech*aid* i rudr*ad* ⁊ ata 'ga fuaitre*d* anosa. ⁊ nocha coi*m*gech é i*n*gi mad aititiu ai*n*fis ł mad aititiu mna no mic ł d*ochuinn*[731] ł d*ruith*[732] ł d*asachtaig*.[733] Nochan ferdi[734] ria*m* ana aititi*n*-side *acht* dobe*r*ar amuigh e, .i. no nochan fastaidthe[735] a fera*n*d arin lucht-si*n* co rabat ina aititi*n* re re rudart*h*a iar tia*cht*ain ceille codn*aig*[736] doib A. [*CIH* 2160.35–2161.3]

---

728 It is difficult to determine whether this clause is a gloss on the OI text or originally formed part of the text itelf. In the MS, it is written in the smaller script size used for writing commentary.

729 I follow the emendation suggested by Binchy, *CIH* 2160, n. j.

730 The word *go* has been added to the very end of the line in fainter ink. It is possible that this correction was not made by the scribe.

731 I follow the expansion suggested by Binchy, *CIH* 2161, n. a.

732 I follow the expansion suggested by Binchy, *CIH* 2161, n. b.

733 I follow the expansion suggested by Binchy, *CIH* 2161, n. c.

734 The form *ferdi* is for OI *ferr de.*

735 The ⟨i⟩ and ⟨the⟩ were added below the line by the scribe; see also Binchy, *CIH* 2161, n. d.

736 The word *codnaig* was added above the line by the scribe with a reference mark; see also Binchy, *CIH* 2161, n. e.

§47 Objection after acknowledgement[737]

Or claiming the land, i.e. before the time of usucaption.[738] A person who was in acknowledgment of the land in that case until it went into usucaption and he [i.e. the original owner] is claiming it now. And he is not able to except if there is acknowledgment of ignorance or acknowledgment of a woman or child or simpleton or fool or violent lunatic.[739] Their previous acknowledgement is of no gain,[740] but it is taken away, i.e. or the land is not to be secured by those people until they are in acknowledgment of it before the time of usucaption after the reason of a sensible adult comes to them A.

---

737 For a discussion of this section, see the Introduction, 34.

738 For acquiring land by usucaption, see *GEIL*, 109. Although it was an offense to settle on someone else's land, if the settler's presence is uncontested for a period of time (the length of time varies depending on the circumstances), the settler is able to make a claim to ownership of the land due to uncontested use of it.

739 For a discussion of the medieval Irish vocabulary used to describe those mentally disabled and their legal rights, see *GEIL*, 91–94.

740 None of the people listed in the previous clause are normally able to alientate land; they are not considered legally qualified to do so, or they must have the consent of their kindred. Even though they might be aware that someone has illegally settled on the land, their acknowledgment of this fact has no legal standing, and, thus, does not help the settler to establish ownership due to uncontested use of the land.

§48 Athgait imna

Gach uair is a n-udb*air*t t*u*cus*tar* in du*in*e na *séot*u don ecl*ais*, mas iat a seoit fe*in*, is a ndilsi di o uair na h-udb*ar*ta amach. ⁊ cid i cu*n*dr*ad* dob*er*ad di, is a ndilsi di o u*air* i*n* cu*n*d*arth*a amac*h*, ce b*eth* treb*air*e ce*n*co be, ar uaislideta na h-ecails*i*.

Masa seoit neich *aile* roudbrast*ar* i*n* du*in*e do*n* ecl*ais*, no cid i cor ł i cu*n*-
p. 15b drad, noch(b)a diles | a seoit onti isa seoit iad o doge*n*a a fuaidr*ed*[741] ari*n* re ari *n*dlegar de. A*n*focul do*n*ti t*uc* na *séot*u don ecl*ais* ma rofit*ir* narba leis.

Athgait imna .i. a*n*focul seoit gaite dorigne i*n* du*in*e *for*in ecl*ais* an*n* sin, ⁊ diabl*ad* in [n]eich dobiad*h* do tuait*h* di an*n* .i. ceth*ar*diabl*ad*[742] itir pen*n*ait ⁊ er*aic*. ⁊ mas ar tuata dorigne he, is diabl*ad* do-seic.

A fiachaib t*u*cad di a*n*d si*n* é, ⁊ mas *ar* dia, is [s]l*an* *acht* aisiuc *séoit* a co*m*aice*n*ta di. ł da*no* cena, uair dodligest*ar* a tab*air*t, cid *ar* fiachaib cid ar dia dob*er*ta di he, co mb*eth* ceth*ar*diabl*ad* di an*n* it*er* pen*n*ait ⁊ er*aic*.

Athgait imna[743] .i. in du*in*e roti*m*ain na *séot*u don ecl*ais*, ma r*u*c uait*he* aris iat, is *ocht*diabl*ad* air a*n*d mai*n*e torsat[744] na *séotu* budei*n*. ⁊ da toirset, is *ceth*ardiabl*ad*, no co*m*ad trediabl*ad*, ł a n-anfoc*al*[745] rob*eth* sin di .i. i*n*[746] *ceth*ardiabl*ad*.

---

1 None of the OI text for this section is preserved in C or E.

---

741 The ⟨i⟩ is written subscript.

742 The sequence ⟨diabl-⟩ was written in *marg. dext.* with reference marks by the scribe; see also Binchy, *CIH* 2161, n. g.

743 Although the OI text is repeated here, it is not written in the larger sized letters normally used for the text. In §51 source A, the scribe repeats the OI text within the commentary, but writes it in larger letters. The MSS are not consistent on this point.

744 The forms *-torset* and *-toirset* both appear to be past subj. 3 sg. forms of *do-roich* 'arrives, comes, returns'.

745 Although *anfocal* is not listed with a gender in *eDIL*, based on the form of the def. art. used here, the word would appear to be n.

746 The ⟨ī⟩ was inserted above the line by the scribe.

§48 Revoking[747] a legacy[748]

Whenever the person had given the *sét*s to the Church as an offering, if they are his own *sét*s, they are forfeit to it [i.e. the Church] from the time of the offering onwards. And though it is for sale[749] that he would give [them] to it [i.e. the Church], they are forfeit to it from the time of the sale onwards, whether there might be a surety or not, for the ennobling of the Church.

If the person had given *sét*s belonging to someone else to the Church, or whether in contract or for sale, the *sét*s are not forfeit | from the one whose p. 15b
*sét*s they are [i.e. from the owner] when he will claim them during the time which he is entitled to. A misrepresentation by the one who gave the *sét*s to the Church if he knew that [they] were not his.

Revoking a legacy, i.e. the person made a misrepresentation of a stolen *sét* against the Church in this case [i.e. the person intentionally did not state that the goods given to the Church were stolen], and doubling of that which would be [due] for a *túath* [is due] to it [i.e. the Church][750] then, i.e. four doubles, both penance and a fine. And if he did it against a layman, it is double for him.

It was given to it [i.e. the Church] for fines in that case, and if it may be for God,[751] he is exempt from legal liability except for restitution of a *sét* of the same value to it [i.e. the Church]. Or moreover, because it [i.e. the Church] was entitled to what was given, whether for fines or for God they were given to it [i.e. the Church], so that there would be four doubles for it [i.e. the Church] then, both penance and a fine.

Revoking a legacy, i.e. the person who bequeathed the *sét*s to the Church, if he took them back from it [i.e. the Church], it is eight doubles [due] from him then unless he returned the *sét*s themselves. And if he returned [them], it is four doubles, or until there are three doubles, or that would be [as the fine for] misrepresenting them for it [i.e. the Church], i.e. the four doubles.

---

747 The meaning of *athgait* is largely determined by the following commentary. The meaning 'revoking, withholding a legacy' was suggested by Plummer; *eDIL s.v. athgait.*

748 For a discussion of this section, see the Introduction, 34–35. *Imna* refers to a "testamentary disposition ... made in full (bodily) health;" see Charles Plummer, "Notes on Some Passages in the Brehon Laws," *Ériu* 9 (1923): 31.

749 In other words, he sells the items to the Church.

750 As in previous sections dealing with fines due to the Church, the fines due are double those that would be due to the laity.

751 The sense of this phrase seems to be that these are items which would be part of the laity's or monastic client's normal obligations to the Church; GEIL, 33; Etchingham, *Church Organisation in Ireland*, 249–271; and *Córus Bésgnai*, §38.

Mas do tuaith roti*m*nad na *séotu*, ma r*u*c uait*he* iat, is *ceth*ardiabl*ad air* a*n*d mai*n*e toirset na *séotu* fei*n*.[752] ⁊ da toirset, is diabl*ad* A. [*CIH* 2161.4–21]

Ma du dia i*m*mnait*er ar* d*us* .i. mas i n-udb*air*t tuc*ustar* in duini na seotu
f. 53c dun ecclais, is cetfaid*h con*abad*h* ece*n* | do a n-aithgen d'ic mai*n*e [ḟ]uil aici,
⁊ da *m*beith aici is ecen do. Eraicc i*n* anfoccail im*murro* du gres.

Mas i cor ł i cun*n*rud*h* im*murro*, is ece*n* in ai*th*gei*n* d'ic an*n*-sid*he* m*ar*æn re h-eraicc i*n* anḟoccail C. [*CIH* 169.17–21]

p. 456a Mana *th*oirset [na séotu] budéin, ⁊ da ṫoirset,[753] is ceit*h*irdiablad*h*, no comadh *th*rediablad*h*, no comad*h* fiac*h* anfocail robeit*h* sin.

M*adh* do *th*uata rot*h*imnast*ar* iat, ma rucustar uad*h*a iat, is ceit*h*irdiabladh eir ind, mani *th*oirset na *séotu* budein. ⁊ da ṫoirseat, is diablad E. [*CIH* 1017.1–4]

752 After *fein*, '⁊ datoirset na .s. fei*n*' has been erased; Binchy, *CIH* 2161, n. i, suggests that sixteen letters have been erased.

753 The *punctum* over ⟨t⟩ here and following is used to indicate nasalization.

If he bequeathed the *séts* to a layman, if he took them back from him, it is four doubles [due] from him [i.e. the layman] then unless he returned the *séts* themselves. And if he returned [them], it is doubling A.

If it is bequeathed to God first, i.e. if the person had given the *séts* to the Church as an offering, it is the opinion [of others] that it is not necessary | f. 53c
for him to pay for their restitution if he does not have it, and if he does [have it], he must [pay]. A fine for misrepresentation [must] always, however, [be paid].

If it is for a contract or for sale, however, it is necessary to pay the restitution in this case only as a fine for misrepresentation C.

Unless he returned the *séts* themselves,[754] and if he returned [them], it is p. 456a
four doubles, or until there is three doubles, or until that would be [as] a fine for misrepresentation.

If he bequeathed them to a layman, if he took them from him, it is four doubles [due] from him then, unless he returned the *séts* themselves. And if he returned [them], it is doubling E.

754 Although the beginning of the commentary is missing, it concerns offering goods to the Church, taking them back, and then returning them; cf. the same set of conditions and the fine structure given in the last two paragraphs of source A.

§ 49 **Indilsi duaise**[755]

.i. ima*n* fili, ⁊ is ce*r*tduais hi, ł duais[756] dut*h*rac*h*tach .i. fo*r*c*r*aid ara g*r*ad ⁊ *ara* mai*n*e.

.i. in fil*i*, ma roti*n*cell[757] *air* ic [c]ui*n*cid[758] im*ar*c*r*ada loigid*echt*a a aisdi, is fia*ch* gaite na h-im*ar*c*r*ada uad.

Ingnad si*n*, ⁊ i*n*t aire e*cht*a, i*n* ta*n* *rucustar* im*ar*c*r*aid d*ar*a biad coir, co fuil fia*ch* gaite na h-uilidetud uada. Iss *ed* fil a*n*d-seic: Taisce rocaith-seic i*n* biad na doroi*n*e in digail. Cub*aid* in ta*n* *rucustar* im*ar*c*r*aid*h* d*ar*a biad coir co fuil fia*ch* gaite na h-uilidetud[759] uad. I*n* dui*n*e-so[760] im*murro*, taisce doroi*n*e-sec i*n* mol*ad* na roti*n*cell air ac [c]ui*n*cid i*m*a*r*c*r*ada i loigid*echt* a aiste. ⁊ gia nob*er*ad i*m*a*r*c*r*aid a loigid*echt* a aisdi, cub*aid* go*n*a b*eth* *acht* fia*ch* gaite na h-ima*r*c*r*aid uada.[761]

Mass *ed* ader-siu*m* na roti*n*cell air, ⁊[762] ader i*n* fer amuig is ar ecla a ært*h*a doratsat*ar* [*recte* doratastar] ni do, a se*n*a do-so*m* na roti*n*cell *air*, ⁊ a de*n*am do*n* fir amuig cu*r*ub ar ecla a ært*h*a doratast*ar* ni do. Is [s]l*an* *acht* aisiuc na h-i*m*a*r*c*r*ada fo*r* culu.

Mas i comlog*ud* doratad[763] do cena he, is a b*eth* am*al* cu*n*dtabairt. & ma romait*h*est*ar* in fil*i* loigid*echt*[764] a aisde, is a b*eth* am*al* cu*nn*tab*air*t. Masa br*eth* *ru*cad cuigi, is er*aic* a gubr*eith*e fair i*n* tan is gubr*eth* *ruc* A. [*CIH* 2161.22–37]

1 None of the OI text is preserved for this section in source **M**.

755 See also the section of *Gúbretha Caratniad* beginning *Rucus indilsi nduais*, *CIH* 2192.20.

756 This is a later nom. sg. form of *dúas*; *eDIL s.v.* 1 *dúas*.

757 The verbal form *rotincell* appears to be the perf. 3 sg. from the verb **to-ind-*(*ad-*)*cell*; see *eDIL s.v.* ? *tincell*.

758 I follow the emendation suggested by Binchy, *CIH* 2161, n. k.

759 The ⟨id⟩ were added above the line by the scribe; see also Binchy, *CIH* 2161, n. l.

760 The ⟨so⟩ were added below the line by the scribe; see also Binchy, *CIH* 2161, n. m.

761 Approximately three letters have been erased following *uada*; see also Binchy, *CIH* 2161, n. n.

762 The ⟨⁊⟩ was added later by the scribe; see also Binchy, *CIH* 2161, n. o.

763 'doratad' against *CIH* 2161.35 'dorata'.

764 The ⟨id⟩ were added above the line by the scribe; see also Binchy, *CIH* 2161, n. q.

§ 49 An unlawful reward[765]

i.e. regarding the poet, and it is a proper reward, or a generous reward, i.e. an addition to his rank and his possessions.

i.e. the poet, if he threatened satire [after] requesting an excess of payment for his performance,[766] a fine of theft for the excess is due from him.

That is remarkable, and the lord of slaughter, when he took an excess of his proper share of food, a fine of theft for the total amount is due from him. This is what is there [i.e. this is the reason]: He consumed the food before he carried out the vengeance. It is proper when he took an excess of his proper share of food that there is a fine of theft for the totality due from him.[767] This person [i.e. the poet], however, he performed the praise [poem] before he threatened satire [after] requesting an excess in payment for his performance. And whoever got an excess in payment for his performance, it is fitting that there should be only a fine of theft of the excess due from him.

If he [i.e. the poet] says that he did not threaten satire, and the plaintiff says that it is from fear of being satirized that he had given anything to him [i.e. to the poet], he [i.e. the poet] denies that he threatened satire, and it must be proved by the plaintiff that it is from fear of being satirized that he had given anything to him. He [i.e. the poet] is exempt from legal liability except for giving back the excess.

If it is for balancing of mutual liabilities that it [i.e. the payment] was given to him, moreover, it is to be as [in cases of] uncertainty. And if the poet has forgiven payment for his performance, it is to be as [in cases of] uncertainty. If a judgment was given to him,[768] he [i.e. the judge, owes a] fine for his false judgement since [i.e. because][769] he has made a false judgment A.

765 For a discussion of this section, see the Introduction, 35–36.

766 The sense is that the poet threatened to satirize his patron (or whomever else was responsible for his payment) if he was not paid a larger amount for his performance than he was legally entitled. See also § 39. This is clearly an abuse of the poet's power.

767 For the *aire échta* 'lord of slughter', see McLeod, "The Lord of Slaughter," 101–114.

768 The Irish is ambiguous here; presumably the faulty judgment applies to either the plaintiff or the poet if there are no witnesses, as seems to be the case here. See the Introduction for a longer discussion on this paragraph.

769 For the causal use of *in tan*, see *eDIL s.v. tan, tain* 2 (b) (iii).

Int aire e*cht*a: Ma r*ucus*t*ar* imarc*r*aid t*ar*a biatha, is fia*ch* gaiti. I*n*gnad si*n*, ⁊ in fil*i* in tan rotincell air, *con*a fuil ac*h* fia*ch* gaiti na imarc*r*ad*h*a uad. Is *ed* fil an*n*-seic: Taisci dori*n*di in mol*ad* na roti*n*cell air a[c] cui*n*cid[770] imarcraid loigid*echt* a aisti, ⁊ cub*aid* *con*a b*eth*[771] *acht* fiach gaiti na imarc*r*ada uada. In duine-so im*murro*, taisce rocait*h*est*har* i*n* biad na dorigne i*n* dig*ail*, ⁊ cub*aid* in tan r*ucus*t*ar* im*ar*c*r*aid t*ar*a biath*ad* co mb*eth* fiach gaiti[772] na h-uilidetu uad M. [*CIH* 2141.15–20]

770 The words *a cuincid* were written *in rasura* by the scribe; see also Binchy, *CIH* 2141, n. i.

771 It is possible that one letter has been erased after *beth*.

772 The scribe wrote *gaiti* a second time and partially erased it; see also Binchy, *CIH* 2141, n. j.

The lord of slaughter: If he took an excess of his share of food, it is a fine of theft. That is remarkable, and the poet when he threatened satire, there is nothing except a fine of theft of the excess due from him. This is what there is: He performed the praise [poem] before he threatened satire [after] requesting an excess of payment for his performance, and it is fitting that there should be only a fine of theft of the excess due from him. This person [i.e. the lord of slaughter], however, he consumed the food before he carried out the vengeance, and it is fitting when he took an excess of his share of food that there should be a fine of theft of the totality due from him M.

§50 Doerad[773] fil*ed*[774]

In fil*i* o dag*en*a tein*m* læda ⁊ im*us* for*o*sna ⁊ dicetal do cen*n*aib, (⁊)[775] is sær ar ci*n*taib inbleogan e, ⁊ ata enecl*ann* do A. [CIH 2161.38–39]

773 *Doerad* is the vn. of *doíraid* 'enslaves, takes captive'.

774 The commentary concerns the method by which a foreign poet proves that he is a poet and maintains his own honor-price in a different territory.

775 I follow the emendation suggested by Binchy, CIH 2161, n. r.

§50 Taking a poet captive[776]

The poet when he will perform *teinm láeda* and *imbas forosna* and *díchetal di chennaib*,[777] he is exempt from [the] liabilities of [his] kinsmen,[778] and he has [his own] honor-price A.

776 For a discussion of this section, see the Introduction, 36–38.

777 An explanation of these three forms of divination can be found in *Sanas Cormaic*, no. 756. The citation from *Sanas Cormaic* is translated in Ford, *The Celtic Poets*, 47. See also *GEIL*, 45; and Carey, "The Three Things Required of a Poet," 41–58. The Introduction contains the relevant text from Meyer's edition of *Sanas Cormaic* along with Ford's translation.

778 In other words, he would not have to act as a kinsman-surety. Certain classes of people, including poets, were not liable for the crimes of their kinsmen; see *eDIL s.v. inbleoga(i)n, inableogain*; and generally McLeod, "The Blood-Feud in Medieval Ireland," 116–118.

§51 Fedb do thogais

Mas[779] da deoi*n* *ru*cad[780] a seoit do*n* mnai a*m*uig, cid ar ais cid ar eci*n* *ru*cad amach hi, is [s]l*an* ce*n* ni di fei*n* i*n*dtib, ⁊ l*eth*dire do*n* fi*n*e 'na s*ét*aib-si. ⁊ is e-si*n* æ*n*inad a fuil dire a s*ét* o dui*n*e do neoch el*e* ⁊ se fei*n* ar aird. & is e in fa*th* ara tab*airt*[781] l*eth*dire do*n* fi*n*e a s*ét*aib na mna foxu[i]l:[782] Ar doch*us* mui*n*dt*er*ais do b*eth* et*ar*ru i*ar* tai*n*. ⁊ is le fei*n* na s*éoit* an*n*.

Mas *ar* eci*n* *ru*cad imach hi ⁊ ar egi*n* *ru*cad a s*éoit*, is la*n*dire ⁊ la*n*enecl*ann* di budei*n* i*n*a s*ét*aib.

Mas da deoi*n* *ru*cad imach hi ⁊ *ar* eci*n* *ru*cad a s*éoit* uait*h*e, is[783] la*n*dire ⁊ l*eth*enecl*ann*. ⁊ toch*us* et*ar*scarac*h* fuil aicce an*n* si*n*, *co* *n*den*am* mait*h*i*us*a p. 16a de. ⁊ masa toch*us* ne*m*et*ar*scartach[784] fuil aice, ł cid toch*us* | et*ar*scarach, mai*n*e dena*nn* mait*h* de, nochon [ḟ]uil ni di *acht* ait*h*gi*n*.

Mas ar eci*n* *ru*cad amach hi ⁊ ar eci*n* *ru*cad s*éoit* na fi*n*e uait*h*e, is la*n*e*n*e-cl*ann* di an*n*.

Mas da deoi*n* *ru*cad imach hi ⁊ ar eci*n* *ru*cad s*éoit* na fine, l*eth*enecl*ann* di, ⁊ toch*us* et*ar*scart*h*ach [ḟ]uil aice an*n*.[785]

1 feadb **A**, feadb*h* **C**. ‖ togais **A**, t*h*og*h*ais **C**, tog*h*ais **E**. None of the OI text for this section is preserved in **D** or **T**. Source **T** duplicates the material from sources **A**, **C**, and **E**; it is edited and translated in Appendix 3.

779 See *Bretha Éitgid*, (source T) *CIH* 1178.34–1180.11 for similar commentary.

780 The 3 pl. perf. pass. form of *beirid*, i.e. *ro-uctha*, is expected rather than the later sg. form *rucad*, but this is an example of the MI use of a sg. verbal form with a pl. subject in a relative construction; McCone, *The Early Irish Verb*, 182.

781 Binchy, *CIH* 2162, n. b, queries whether this form should be expanded as *tabarr*.

782 I follow the editorial suggestion made by Binchy, *CIH* 2162, n. c.

783 The ⟨i⟩ was inserted above the line by the scribe.

784 As Binchy, *CIH* 2162, n. d, notes, ⟨et⟩ are added below the line.

785 The word an*n* was added above the line by the scribe.

§ 51 Defrauding a widow[786]

If[787] it is with her consent that her *séts* were taken from the woman [while she was] away [from her kindred],[788] whether she was taken willingly or by force, no one is liable [to pay] anything to her herself for them, and half compensation [is to be paid] to the kindred for the *séts*. And that is the one instance in which there is compensation of his *séts* from one person to someone else, and he himself is present. And this is the reason for his giving half compensation to the kindred for the *séts* of the abducted woman: On account of the likelihood of a household being between them after that. And [the kindred?][789] itself has the *séts* then.

If it is by force that she was taken away and by force that her *séts* were taken, it is full compensation and full honor-price for her herself for her *séts*.

If it is with her consent that she was taken away and by force that her *séts* were taken from her, it is full compensation and half honor-price. And she has property sufficient for independence[790] in that case, and she makes good use of it. And if she has property insufficient for independence, or though [she has] property sufficient for independence, | if she does not make good use of it, there is nothing for her except restitution. p. 16a

If it is by force that she was taken away and by force that the kindred's *séts* were taken from her, it is full honor-price for her then.

If it is with her consent that she was taken away and by force that the kindred's *séts* were taken, half honor-price for her, and she has property sufficient for independence then.

786 For a discussion of this section, see the Introduction, 38–41. Although the OI text refers specifically to widows, the commentary applies to women more generally.

787 For a discussion and translation of a similar commentary from *Bretha Éitgid*, CIH 1179.36–1180.11, see McLeod, "Property and Honour-Price," 285–286; the commentary printed in McLeod is from source T. The commentaries from sources A and C are noted by McLeod, 285, n. 28. See also *AL* 3: 540–547 for this and the commentary discussed in source E below.

788 I follow McLeod's interpretation of the passage; McLeod, "Property and Honour-Price," 285.

789 The referent here is obscure to me.

790 As discussed by McLeod, *etarscarthach* property is the amount of property necessary for a person to maintain their own social status. *Nemetarscarthach* property is property which does not amount to enough for someone to maintain their social status in their own right; McLeod, "Property and Honour-Price," 284.

Mas do deoi*n* *ru*cad na *séoit* uait*h*i, cid ar ais gid ar eci*n* *ru*gad amach hi, nochan [ḟ]uil ni di, ⁊ la*n*dire ⁊ lane*n*ecl*ann* do*n* fi*n*e i*m* ga*ch* ni dib-si*n*.

Fedb do t[h]ogais

In be*n*: Ma t*ucu*st*ar* ni do *sét*aib imach da fir i n-ai*n*fis da fi*n*e, tic[f]a fi*n*e fo coraib, ⁊ l*eth*dire imailli riu amuig*h*. ⁊ mas iat *séoit* na fi*n*e t*uc* si a*mach*, is la*n*dire do ic risi*n* fi*n*e 'na *sét*aib. Inc*r*echad[791] si*n* ar, M*a*c Cat*h*an, i*n*ni dobe*r*ad i*n* be*n* da deoi*n* da fir dire do ic ria a*n*d. *Con*id ed is coir an*n*-side: Is go l*eth*dire asre*n*ar .i. is go*na* ...[792] am*al* i*n*ni ata do*n* dara l*eth* re dire roernith*er* di i*n*dtib .i. ait*h*gi*n*. ⁊ cubaid, mas iat *séoit* na fi*n*e t*uc* si amac*h*, dire do ic risi*n* fi*n*e 'na *sét*aib; no da*no* cena is foxul ata fuirre, ⁊ ni h-i*n*crech*ad* de-side A. [*CIH* 2162.1–24]

.i. mas asa deoi*n* ruccait[793] a seoit on m*h*nai amac*h*, gid*h* ar ais gid*h* *ar* eic-ci*n* ruccad*h* amac*h* hi, is slan ca*n* ni di budein intib, ⁊ let*h*diri dun fini i*na* setaib-si. ⁊ is e-sin æ*n*inad*h* isin be*r*la ata diri set dui*n*e ele du neoc*h*.

Mas ar ecin ruccad*h* i*m*ach hi, gid*h* [ar ais gid][794] *ar* [e]cin[795] ruccait a seoit uaithi, is laneneclan*n* ⁊ landiri di budein ina setaib*h*.

3 The OI text is only repeated in source **A**.

791 The ⟨d⟩ was inserted above the line by the scribe.

792 Binchy, *CIH* 2162, n. f, notes that some words have been dropped, but he offers no details.

793 *Ruccait* is a later 3 pl. perf. pass form of *beirid*. The commentary in C switches back and forth between using this later pl. verbal form and the sg. form, *rucad*, with a pl. subject.

794 I follow the emendation suggested by Binchy, *CIH* 169, n. d.

795 I follow the emendation suggested by Binchy, *CIH* 169, n. e.

If it is with consent that the *sét*s were taken from her, whether she was taken away willingly or by force, there is nothing [to be paid] to her, and full compensation and full honor-price [to be paid] to the kindred for every one of them [i.e. for everything which was taken].

Defrauding a widow

The woman: If anything of the *sét*s were given away to her spouse without her kindred knowing, the kindred will impugn the contracts, and half compensation in the same manner for them so long as they are apart from each other. And if they are the kindred's *sét*s that she gave away, full compensation is paid to the kindred for their *sét*s. That is faulty, according to Mac Cathán,[796] what the woman might give with her consent to her spouse, for her to pay compensation for it [i.e. the woman should not have to pay compensation for what she freely gave to her spouse of her own chattels]. This is what is proper then: It is up to half compensation that is paid, i.e. so that not ... [part of the text is missing] as for what there is on the other side [i.e. the opposite] regarding compensation it can be paid by her for them, i.e. restitution. And [it is] proper, if they are the kindred's *sét*s that she gave away, to pay compensation to the kindred for their *sét*s; or else she was abducted, and it is not a fault because of it A.[797]

i.e. if it is with her consent that her *sét*s were taken from the woman [while she was] away [from her kindred], whether she was taken willingly or by force, no one is liable [to pay] anything to her herself for them, and half compensation [is to be paid] to the kindred for the *sét*s. And that is the one instance in which there is compensation of [his own] *sét*s from one person to someone else.

If it is by force that she was taken away, whether her *sét*s were taken from her willingly or by force, it is full honor-price and full compensation for her herself for her *sét*s.

796 This figure has not been identified; he may or may not be the Mac Cathán mentioned in *Cáin Lánamna* § 36, second commentary from source B, or the Cathán mentioned in two other commentaries in *Cáin Lánamna*, i.e. § 11 source B, and § 15 source A.

797 Cf. *Cáin Lánamna* § 36 second commentary from source B 278–279; and CCIH, 369.

Mas da deoin ruccad*h* amach hi ⁊ *ar* ecin ruccad*h* a seoit uaithi, is landiri di ⁊ let*h*eneclan*n*. ⁊ tothc*hus* et*ar*sc*ar*t*h*a [ḟ]uil aicci and si*n* *co* *n*denum*h* mathi*us*a de. Masa t*h*ochus ne*mh*et*ar*sc*ar*tha [ḟ]uil aicci, ł cid*h* tot*h*c*hus* et*ar*scart*h*ach, mai*n*e de*n*and mait*h* de, nucu*n*n [f]uil ni di *acht* aithg*h*ein.

Mas *ar* ecin ruccad*h* amach hi ⁊ *ar* eci*n* ruccad*h* seoit na fini uait*h*i, is laneneclan*n* di an*n*.

Mas da deoin ruccad*h* amach hi ⁊ *ar* ecin ruccad*h* seoit na fini uaithi, is letheneclan*n* di, ⁊ tothc*hus* et*ar*scartha [ḟ]uil aicci an*n* fos.

Mas da deoin ruccait na seoit uaithi, gid*h* *ar* ais gid*h* *ar* ecin ruccad*h* amach hi, nucu*n*n [ḟ]uil [ni][798] di; ⁊ landiri ⁊ laneneclan*n* dun fini im*murro* i*n* cac*h* inud*h* dib*h* C. [*CIH* 169.22–37]

p. 439a … fi firi ⁊ ni h-i*n*crechaid deiside[799] D. [*CIH* 984.16]

.i. in ben focsail: Mas ar eici*n* rucad amac*h* hi, enecl*ann* d'ic ria budein ⁊ enecl*ann* d'ic re fi*n*e.

Mas da deoin rucad*h* amach hi, slan gan ní d'ic ria budein ⁊ enecl*ann* d'ic re fi*n*e. Cipe aid*h*ead*h* gnait*h* [ł][800] ingnait*h* beires im*m*uich hi risin mís ⁊ re re i*n* mís, corpdire ⁊ enecl*ann* d'ic re' fi*n*e-si.

⁊ i*n* clan*n* dorig*h*nead ria risi*n* mís ⁊ re re i*n* m*h*is, is a dilsi d'[ḟ]i*n*e[801] a m*h*at*har* no co tuct*h*ar log amac*h* dara ceand, ⁊ o dab*er*ar, is iat-si*n* is cland cetmuindt*ir*e urnadmand no ad*h*alt*r*aig urnadma.

798 I follow the emendation suggested by Binchy, *CIH* 169, n. f.

799 For this fragment of text, see the MS introduction, 49.

800 I follow the editorial suggestion made by Binchy, *CIH* 1017, n. b.

801 The emendation is suggested by Binchy, *CIH* 1017, n. c.

If it is with her consent that she was taken away and by force that her *sét*s were taken from her, it is full compensation and half honor-price. And she has property sufficient for independence in that case and she makes good use of it. If she has property insufficient for independence, or though [she has] property sufficient for independence, if she does not make good use of it, there is nothing for her except restitution.

If it is by force that she was taken away and by force that the kindred's *sét*s were taken from her, it is full honor-price for her then.

If it is with her consent that she was taken away and by force that the kindred's *sét*s were taken from her, it is half honor-price for her, and she has property sufficient for independence then still.

If it is with her consent that the *sét*s were taken from her, whether she was taken away willingly or by force, there is nothing [to be paid] to her; and full compensation and full honor-price [to be paid] to the kindred for every one of them [i.e. for everything thing which was taken] C.

… on her and it is not a fault because of it D. p. 439a

i.e. the abducted woman: If it is by force that she was taken away, honor-price is to be paid to her herself and honor-price is to be paid to [her] kindred.

If it is with her consent that she was taken away, no one is liable to pay anything to her herself and honor-price to pay to [her] kindred. Whatever death, usual or unusual, takes her [while she is] away before the [end of the first] month and within the space of the month, body-fine and honor-price are paid to her kindred.[802]

And the child begotten on her before the month and within the space of the month, it belongs to the kindred of his mother or until a price may be given on his behalf, and when it is given, they are considered as the children of a betrothed spouse[803] or a betrothed concubine.

802 See Myles Dillon, "The Relationship of Mother and Son, of Father and Daughter, and the Law of Inheritance with regard to Women," in *Studies in Early Irish Law*, ed. R. Thurneysen et al. (Dublin: Royal Irish Academy, 1936), 172–176.

803 For translating *cétmuinter* as 'spouse', see Liam Breatnach, "On Old Irish Collective and Abstract Nouns, the Meaning of *cétmuinter*, and Marriage in Early Mediaeval Ireland," *Ériu* 66 (2016): 6–26.

Cach u*air* is ar eicin rucad*h* amach í, is a roga na fine ata in[804] racfat[805] in cland no na racfat. ⁊ da racat, urailidh dlig*ed* aran ath*air* a cendach.

Cach uair is da deoin rucad*h* amach, a rog*h*a i*n* ath*ar* ata i*n* cendeog*h*a[806] in chland no na cen*n*eog*h*a. ⁊ da cen*n*aid*h*e, urailid*h* dlig*ed* aran fi*n*e a reic f*r*is. ⁊ da dardais[807] i*n* fine i *n*-aiscid do iat, furailid*h* dlig*ed* ari*n* aith*air* a gabail, uair is [s]ochar do a gabail. No d*ano* che*n*a, gid ar ais gid ar ecai*n* rucad*h* amach hi, urailig*h* dlig*ed* aran ath*air* a gabail. Am*ail* ad*eir* isna Mac[ṡ]le*cht*aib:[808] Ma baitsech nabi tuailaing toiscid ⁊ folach a c*h*inad, is a suid*h*iu is teachta athc*h*ur mac sula ⁊ mac sanaise. *Acht* c*h*ean*a* cac*h* uir
p. 456b is ar eici*n* rucadh ama*ch* hi, | ciamad hé roga i*n*n athar a c*h*ean*n*ach, nocon uraileanh*n* dliged aran fine a reic ris manap ail doib budein.

In c*h*lan*n* dorignead*h* ria iarsi*n* mís, ⁊ cu tisseat ar urnaidm dligt*h*each, iss iat-sain is cland cetmuint*ir*e foxail and no adaltraige foxail. ⁊ is orro beanas foxail t*r*ian a cotta.

Mas ar eicin rucad amach hi, ⁊ ar maithib re fi*n*e rogab coibc*h*i, sm*acht* c*ét*muint*ir*e d'ic ria ⁊ sm*acht* ad*h*altraig d'ic uaithi mana tistar fo coraib. ⁊ [ma] tecar fo coraib[809] co*n*[a] icand na[ch ní] (meic),[810] ⁊ sm*acht* cetmuin*tir*e d'ic ria.

---

804 For the interrog. part. used in dependent questions to mean 'whether', see *eDIL s.v.* 2 *in* (ii) a; and *GOI* § 463. The same construction appears in the next paragraph of the commentary.

805 This is the 3 pl. fut. ind. conjunct form of *reccaid* 'sells, barters, exchanges'.

806 This is the 3 sg. pres. ind. conjunct form of *cennaigid* 'buys, purchases'.

807 This is a 3 pl. past subj. pass. form of *do-beir*, i.e. *tartais*, with ⟨d⟩ representing a nasalized /t/.

808 The emendation is suggested by Binchy, *CIH* 1017, n. f.

809 The ⟨co⟩ were inserted above the line with reference marks by the scribe; see also Binchy, *CIH* 1017, n. g.

810 Cf. the reading at *CIH* 1179.25 'cona hicun*n* na*ch* ní'. The reading in source E, 'co *n*icand na meic', makes little sense linguistically or legally. It looks like the scribe incorrectly interpreted the three minims of 'ni' as an abbreviation for 'meic'.

Whenever it is by force that she was taken away, it is the kindred's choice whether they will sell[811] the child or not. And if they sell [the child], law requires the father to buy him.

Whenever it is with her consent that she was taken away, the father has the choice whether to buy the child or not. And if he buys [the child], law requires the kindred to sell him [i.e. the child] to him. And if the kindred might give them[812] to him for free, law requires the father to take them because it is an advantageous contract for him to take them. Or else [i.e. alternatively], whether willingly or by force that she was taken away, law requires the father to take them. As it says in the *Macślechta*:[813] If a woman of indiscriminate morals is not capable of [providing] food and bearing his liabilities, thus it is proper to return the 'children of sunlight' [i.e. legitimate children] and the 'children of secrecy' [i.e. illegitimate children]. But in any case whenever it is by force that she was taken away, | though it may be the p. 456b
father's choice to buy him [i.e. the child], law does not require the kindred to sell him to him [i.e. the father] unless they themselves [i.e. the kindred] wish [to do so].

The child begotten on her after the month, until they [i.e. the parents] are lawfully betrothed, they are [considered] as children of an abducted spouse then or an abducted concubine. And [the] abduction deprives them of a third of their share.

If it is by force that she was taken away, and for the good of the kindred that she took [i.e. accepted] a bride-price, the fine of a spouse is to be paid to her and the fine of a concubine is to be paid by her if the contract may not be opposed. And [if] it is opposed she pays nothing, and the fine of a spouse is paid to her.

---

811 Although the verbs used in relation to the child are 'selling' and 'buying', the child is not literally being sold or bought. Rather, it is the legal rights to the child which are being sold or bought.

812 The commentary switches back and forth between referring to one child and more than one.

813 Only a handful of glossed fragments of this text survive; see *GEIL*, 270; and *CCIH*, 300–301. Breatnach gives the tract the title *Bretha for Macślechtaib* 'Judgments on Categories of Sons'. The tract is the twenty-eighth in the *Senchas Már* legal tradition and belongs to the final third of it. Other than source T (Appendix 3), I have not been able to identify another instance of this citation.

Mas da deoin rucad amach hí, ⁊ ar mait*h*ib re fi*n*e rogab coibche, no cid ar eici*n* rucad ama*ch* hi manap ar maithib re fine rogab coibc*h*e, sm*acht* adaltraigi d'ic ria ⁊ sm*acht* ad*h*altraigi d'ic uait*h*i mana tistar fo coraib. ⁊ [ma] tecar fo coraib con[a] ícand na*ch* ni ⁊ sm*acht* ad*h*altraigi d'ic ria. ⁊ a roga na fi*n*e ata fo*n* comairet re robui imuich i*n* bean rachas doib ar son ait*h*gena na gni*m*raid no i*n* isi rachas a gni*m*rad a fir, ⁊ ga*n* a fe*ar* do dul i*n*a gni*m*rad. ⁊ is cetbaid gu meidis aræ*n* di, bean *ar* son aithg*ena* gni*m*raid ⁊ issi do dul a gni*m*rad a fir, ⁊ is gan a fe*ar* do dul i*n*a gni*m*rad. ⁊ noco*n* [ḟ]uil ait*h*ḟegad ḟog*h*ul lain na leit*h*e na cet*h*ra*m*t*h*a*n* na dartaid et*ar*ru risi*n* re-sin, am*al* ca*ch* lanamain dligt*h*ig, no co ria fogail a n-airillnig*h*ther enecl*ann*. ⁊ o rasia, a fegad*h* cia dib risar foglaidaed and.

p. 457a Mas risi*n* fear rofoglad*h* and, noco*n*n [ḟ]uil ni d'ic ris. ⁊ mas re neach eile roḟog*h*laig*h*ead*h* and, is a ic don ḟir am*ail* ícas in gataig*h*e cin na seoit ngaitte E. [*CIH* 1017.5–39]

If it is with her consent that she was taken away, and she took [i.e. accepted] a bride-price for the good of the kindred, or although she was taken away by force [and] if it was not for the good of the kindred that she took a bride-price, the fine of a concubine is to be paid to her and the fine of a concubine is to be paid by her if the contract may not be opposed. And [if] it is opposed she pays nothing and the fine of a concubine is paid to her. And the kindred has the choice for the same length [of time] that she was away [from them whether] a woman will go to them as compensation for the work [they lost from her while she was away] or she will perform the work of her husband, and without her husband performing her work. And it is the opinion [of others] that assigns both to the kindred, a woman as compensation for the work and her performing the work of her husband, and it is without her husband performing her work. And there is no reckoning of injury [paid with] full [fine] nor half nor one-fourth nor a heifer between them during that time, like every lawful marriage, or as far as an injury that merits honor-price [to be paid]. And if it will happen, it will be taken into account which of them will have received [the] injuries then.

If it is the husband who was injured then [by the woman], she does not p. 457a
pay anything to him. And if it is someone else who was injured then, it is paid by the husband just as the thief pays for the crime [committed by] stolen chattels E.

§ 52 Turrtugud for cill ⁊rl-

Mad dorigne i*n* dui*n*e co*m*airci borblachais ari*n* ecl*ais* no *arin* cill, is diabl*ad* in neich ata do tuata it*er* pen*n*ait ⁊ er*aic* an*n* A. [*CIH* 2162.25–26]

.i. co*m*airce .i. indlig*thech* don ri tu*r*tug*ud* f*or* cill na f*or*a co*m*arbad ge*n* na cen*n*aichthi do ic f*r*isi*n* cill. ł ni dlig*thech* don ri turr*thugud* f*or*a [cill] (tuaith) ge*n* *dech*m*a*da ⁊ p*r*imide ⁊ almsana do ic f*r*ia.

Ma dorigne i*n* dui*n*e co*m*airce borbl*ach*ais f*or*an ecl*ais*, is diabl*ad* i[n] neich dobiad do thuata di a*n*d it*er* pen*n*aid ⁊ eraic D. [*CIH* 984.17–22]

1 turrugud A. || ⁊rl- *om.* A.

§52 Sanctuary from a monastic community, etc.[814]

If the person sought sanctuary by violence from the Church or from the monastic community, it is double of that which is [due as a fine] to a layman both penance and fine[815] then A.

i.e. sanctuary, i.e. it is unlawful for the king [to seek] sanctuary from a monastic community or from its coarb without paying bequests to the monastic community. Or it is not lawful for the king [to seek] sanctuary from [a church] without paying tithes and first fruits and alms to it [i.e. the Church].

If the person sought sanctuary by violence from the Church, it is double that which would be [due] to a layman for it [i.e. for the Church] then both penance and fine D.

---

814 For a discussion of this section, see the Introduction, 42.

815 In other words, the Church would be due double the amount of both penance and fine. In this section *éraic* could mean either a general fine for injury or *wergeld* in the case of death; cf. §§48 and 56.

§53 Cetmuindter do ḟretech

C*ét*muin*nter* si*n*: ⁊ nocho dleg*ar* a at*h*chu*r* no co ti fog*al* imscair. ⁊ o ticfad, is i*m*sc*ar* fo aicn*ed* na fog*l*a A. [*CIH* 2162.27–28]

.i. d[an]o[816] dir athchu*r* .i. in c*ét*mui*n*dter, *no*cho dir a h-athchur ɫ go ti fog*ail* i*m*sgair di. ⁊ o tiucfas, is i*m*sgar fo aic*ned* na fogla D. [*CIH* 984.22–23]

.i. i*n* cetmuinter: Mas a n-i*n*deit*h*berus, a dilsi d*h*i o uair a freitig amach ⁊ coibc*hi* ⁊ enecl*ann*. ⁊ is cetfaid*h* comad tre easpa dob*er*thea a freiteach co mbeth a dilsi di o uair a freitig amach ⁊ coibc*hi* ⁊ enecl*ann* E. [*CIH* 1017.40–43]

1 Cetmuinntir E. || fretech **A**, freitech **D**, ḟreiteach E.

816 Binchy, *CIH* 984, n. h, queries whether *do* is for *dō*; the use of reagent makes it impossible to see whether there is a suspension mark or not. *Dano* makes better sense linguistically than *do*.

§53 Repudiating a wife[817]

That is [regarding] a wife: It is not right to expel her until a wrong justifying separation[818] is committed. And if it should be committed, it is a separation according to the nature of the injury A.[819]

i.e. moreover proper expelling, i.e. the wife, it is not proper to expel her until she commits a wrong justifying separation. And if she will commit [such a wrong], it is a separation according to the nature of the injury D.

i.e. the wife: If it is unjustified, bride-price and honor-price are forfeited to her from the time of her repudiation onwards. And it is the opinion [of others] that though it might be through folly that her repudiation was done, bride-price and honor-price are forfeited to her from the time of her repudiation onwards E.

817 For a discussion of this section, see the Introduction, 42. While *cétmuinter* can refer generally to a spouse, it can also refer specifically to a husband or wife; *eDIL s.v. cétmuinter*. Based on the commentaries to D and E, it is clear that the word should be taken to mean 'wife' here; see also Breatnach, "On Old Irish Collective and Abstract Nouns," 14.

818 *Fogal* refers generally to any attack, insult, trespass, or injury. The phrase *fogal imscair*, according to Plummer's notes, refers specifically to a 'wrong justifying separation'; *eDIL s.v. imscar*.

819 Early Irish law recognized a variety of reasons for separating from a spouse; see *GEIL*, 73–75; and Kelly, *Marriage Disputes*, 4–6.

§ 54 Fodb do æsclad[820]

.i. nemnesam i*n*t et*ach* no co nigth*er*, ⁊ o nig*h*t*er* he is nesa*m*, u*air* nesa*m* tes*t*a de a b*eth* gi*n* nigi dia*m*ad i n-at*h*gab*ail* rogabt*ha*. Mas *ar* daigi*n* fog*la* rofocail-siu*m* i*n*t et*ach* ari*n* f*er* amuig gen a nige, *acht*[821] ma rofas fog*al* de, is l*an*fia*ch* na fog*la* rofas de d'ic and.[822] Mu*nar* fas fog*al* de it*ir*, is [s]l*an*, no co*m*a[d] fia*ch* maigne na fog*la* rob ail leis-[s]iu*m* do tia*chtain* de. Mas do dichu*r* fia*ch* de (rob ail) rofocail[823] doib ce*n* a nigi, is am*al* i*n*det*h*b*ir* torba u*m* ait*h*gi*n*, no co*m*ad am*al* anfot i*n*det*h*bir um la*n*fia*ch*.

Fodb do æsclad

.i. (a)[e]tach[824] i*n* m*air*b: Ma ronig*ed* he, is a*n*ad n-ai*ne* f*or*in at*h*gab*ail* rogab*ad* ui*m*e, ⁊ dit*h*im t*r*ese fuirre. Ma*n* ronig*ed* it*ir* he, is a*n*ad t*r*ese fuirre ⁊ dit*h*im *cóic*t*h*i. ł d*an*o cena is i*n*t etach budei*n* ar *treisi* ⁊ *in* bo ce*n*dadaig ar *cóic*t*h*i ⁊ i*n* *secht*bairge*n* ar *sechtmaid* ⁊ *in* fled c*r*oligi ar mis.

⁊ ma tall*ad* uait*h*ib e, mas for *conair* tall*ad* uait*h*ib e, ⁊ mai*n*e rai*n*ic in toch*us*[825] don ecl*ais* e, ⁊ noc*ha*[826] fuil ni do*n* ecl*ais* an*n* *acht* mane raib a dualg*us* fog*la* i*n*dilsig[827] a maigi*n* ł a *sechtarmaigin* *acht* enecl*ann* ⁊ dire ⁊ ait*h*gi*n* do*n*ti a raba lai*m*. ⁊ ma rai*n*ic in toch*us*[828] don ecl*ais* e, enecl*ann* ⁊ d*íre* ⁊ ait*h*gi*n* don ecl*ais* an*n*, ⁊ enecl*ann*[829] do*n*ti a raba lai*m* A. [*CIH* 2162.29–2163.5]

---

1 faesculad **D**, foesclad **E**. 9 The text is repeated only in source **A**.

---

820 The ⟨c⟩ was inserted below the line by the scribe.

821 The phrase 'gen a nige s̄' was written below the line with reference marks by the scribe; see also Binchy, *CIH* 2162, n. h.

822 The word *and* was inserted below the line by the scribe; see also Binchy, *CIH* 2162, n. i.

823 The phrase *ł rofocail* was inserted above the line of text by the scribe as a correction for *rob ail*; see also Binchy, *CIH* 2162, n. k. The ⟨ł⟩, as is common in medieval Irish manuscripts, indicates that the material which follows it is a correction to the text rather than an alternate reading.

824 I follow Binchy's editorial emendation at *CIH* 2162, n. l.

825 The ⟨t⟩ was inserted below the line by the scribe; see also Binchy, *CIH* 2163, n. a.

826 The ⟨o⟩ was written over two letters which have been erased. The ⟨a⟩ is written subscript.

827 Binchy, *CIH* 2163.2 prints 'i*n* dilsig', but cf. the form 'in*n*dilsi' in source D at *CIH* 984.29.

828 The ⟨t⟩ was inserted below the line by the scribe; see also Binchy, *CIH* 2163, n. a.

829 The ⟨c⟩ was inserted below the line by the scribe; see also Binchy, *CIH* 2163, n. c.

§ 54 Washing the spoils of the dead[830]

i.e. the clothing is not necessary[831] until it is washed, and when it is washed, it is necessary, because it lacks necessity on account of its not being washed if it might have been taken in distraint. If it is for the purpose of [causing] injury that he had awarded the clothing to the plaintiff without washing it, but if injury resulted from it, it is the full fine of the injury that resulted from it [that is] to be paid then. If injury did not result from it at all, he is exempt from legal liability, or there might be a fine in respect of place[832] for the injury that he desired to result from it. If it is to remove a fine from him that he had awarded [it] to them without washing it, it is [treated] like a careless act of social utility regarding [the payment of] restitution, or it might be [treated] like an injury due to negligence regarding [the payment of the] full fine.

Washing the spoils of the dead

i.e. the clothing of the dead person: If it was washed, it is a delay of one day for the distraint that was taken regarding it, and a delay in pound of three days for it. If it was not washed at all, it is a delay of three days for it and a delay in pound of five days. Or else then it is the clothing itself after three days and the heriot cow after five days and the seven loaves after seven days and the funeral feast after a month.[833]

And if it was stolen from them, if it was taken from them on the road, if the property was not due to the Church, the Church does not get anything in that case unless it may be on account of unlawful injury in [the] precinct or outside [the] precinct, but honor-price and compensation and restitution to the one in whose hand it [i.e. the property] was. And if the property was due to the Church, honor-price and compensation and restitution to the Church, and honor-price to the one in whose hand it [i.e. the property] was A.

---

830 For a discussion of this section, see the Introduction, 42–44.

831 See the Introduction to § 54 for a discussion of *nesam* 'indispensable, necessary'.

832 It is possible that the scribe meant to write *imraid* 'intent' instead of *maigne* 'place'.

833 *CIH* 2162.38–39 is translated and discussed in Kelly, *Marriage Disputes*, 118–121; see also § 35 therein for a similar passage. These items are what is due to the Church for burial of the deceased and related expenses; a lord's clients were also expected to contribute towards the cost of the funeral feast. What, exactly, the seven loaves consisted of/represented is unclear.

.i. etach in mairb: Ma roniged he, is anad n-aine f*or*an athg*abail* rogob*ad* ime ⁊ dithi*m* t*r*esi .i. manar niged it*ir*, is anad t*r*eisi f*u*rri ⁊ dithi*m* *cóic*thi. ł d*ano* cena is i*n*t etach budei*n* ar t*r*eisi ⁊ i*n* bo cen*n*adaig ar *cóic*thi ⁊ i*n*t ṡechtbairgi*n* ar *secht*main ⁊ i*n* fle(g)[dh][834] c*r*olighi ar mis.

⁊ ma tallad uaithib he, mas ar conair tall*ad* uaithib he, muna rainic in[ḟ]iachus don eclais he, nochon [f]uil ni don ecl*ais* and, *acht* muna raib a dualgus fog*la* in*n*dilsi a maigin no a *secht*armaigin, *acht* enecl*ann* ⁊ dire ⁊ aithg*in* donti a raba laim. Et mas a ci*n*[n] cilli tall*ad* uaithib hé, laneneel*ann* do*n* ecl*ais* an, uair is fogail in*n*diles a cin*n* cille, ⁊ enecl*ann* ⁊ dire ⁊ aithgi*n* donti a raibe laim. ⁊ ma rainic in[ḟ]iachus don ecl*ais* he, enecl*ann* ⁊ dire ⁊ aithgin don ecl*ais* and ⁊ enecl*ann* donti a raibe laim D. [*CIH* 984.24–985.]

.i. nemneasam i*n*t etach no co nig*h*th*er* he, ⁊ o nigfith*er*, is neasum. Mas ar daigi*n* fog*h*la roḟoclat int etach gan a nigi, ma rofas fogail de, is lanfiach na fogla rofasatar d'ic an*n*. Manar fas fogail de eitir, is diablad i*n* etaig i n-anfocul. Mas da dichur a ḟiach de cheana rofoclat i*n*t etach, is am*al* i*n*deit*h*b*ir* *th*orba i*m* ait*h*gein E. [*CIH* 1018.1–5]

Aescl*ad* .i. nig*he* ł gl*anadh*, ut *est* fodb d'æscl*ad* .i. e*etach*[835] in m*air*b do uisge-luag*h*, do luad*h* *ar*in uisce O'Dav.[836] [*CIH* 1473.1–2]

834 I follow the emendation suggested by Binchy, *CIH* 984, n. i.

835 The MS reads 'e⁊aċ' for *étach*; see also Binchy, *CIH* 1473, n. a. The doubling of ⟨e⟩ seems to be a way to indicate /eː/.

836 O'Dav no. 170; the text presented here differs slightly from that in Stokes' edition.

i.e. the clothing of the dead person: If it was washed, it is a delay of one day for the distraint that was taken regarding it, and a delay in pound of three days, i.e. if it was not washed at all, it is a delay of three days for it and a delay in pound of five days. Or else then it is the clothing itself after three days and the heriot cow after five days and the seven loaves after a week and the funeral feast after a month.[837]

And if it was taken from them, if it was taken from them on the road, if it was not a debt due to the Church, the Church does not get anything in that case, except if it may be on account of unlawful injury in [the] precinct or outside [the] precinct, but honor-price and compensation and restitution to the one in whose hand it was. And if [it] was taken from them [for the purpose of committing a crime] against a church, full honor-price for the Church then because it is an unlawful injury against a Church, and honor-price and compensation and restitution to the one in whose hand it was. And if it was a debt due to the Church, honor-price and penalty and restitution to the church then, and honor-price to the one in whose hand it was D.

i.e. the clothing is not necessary until it is washed, and when it will be washed, it is necessary. If it is for the purpose of [causing] injury that they awarded the clothing without washing it, if injury resulted from it, the full fine of the injury that resulted [from it is] to be paid then. If no injury resulted from it at all, double [the value of] the clothing [is to be paid] for deception. If it is to remove a fine from him moreover that they were awarded the clothing, it is [treated] like a careless act of social utility regarding [the payment of] restitution E.

Aesclad 'washing', i.e. washing or cleaning, *ut est* 'to wash [the] spoils', i.e. to wash in water the dead man's clothing, to move on the water O'Dav.[838]

837 The beginning part of this commentary is translated and discussed in Etchingham, *Church Organisation in Ireland*, 440–441.

838 Stokes, "O'Davoren's Glossary," 225–226.

§ 55 Aire[839] eisc flatha

Masa leis in port a(n)diu ⁊ anall, a roga do i*n seiss*ed doge*n*a d'i*m*e ce*cht*arde i*n* da l*eth*i ł in t*r*ia*n* d'æ*n*l*eth*. Mu*n*ab leis *acht* æ*n*lea*th*, de*n*ad *seiss*id do*n* l*eth* p. 16b is leis; ⁊ da nd*er*nad ni is *mo* na si*n*, da t*r*ia*n* na h-i*mar*c*r*ada uad | do*n* lu*cht* na sod sis ⁊ suas, cidbe co*n*air dib tic i*n*t iasc A. [*CIH* 2163.6–9]

i.e. mas re h-æ*n*duine i*n*n ab*h*an*n* illiu ⁊ anall, i*m*met t*r*ian den lei*th* no seisid cea*ch*tard*he* na d*h*a lei*th*e. Manap leis it*ir*, i[m](*n*)meit[840] seisid i*n* lei*th*e is leis. Ma raæmast*ar*[841] ní is m*h*o ana si*n*, da trian imarcra i*n*n eisc do*n*a c*h*or*th*aib uad*h*a sis, massa iasc t*h*ic anuas, no d*h*a trian i*m*marcra i*n* eisc do*n*a c*h*ort*h*aib uad*h*a suas, masa iasc tic anis E. [*CIH* 1018.6–10]

Aire .i. ime ł fal ut *est* aire eisc(i) fl*at*ha .i. ime do denam *ar* cinn eisc na fla*tha*. ⁊ ad*eir* sé: Ni te*cht*a ni bes [mó][842] no t*r*ian i*n*n uisce do aire .i. do ime[843] O'Dav.[844] [*CIH* 1468.8–9]

---

1 fl*ath*a A.

---

839 The ⟨e⟩ was inserted below the line by the scribe; see also Binchy, *CIH* 2163, n. d.

840 I follow the emendation suggested by Binchy, *CIH* 1018, n. a.

841 An ⟨ḟ⟩ was erased after the first ⟨a⟩; see also Binchy, *CIH* 1018, n. b.

842 I follow the emendation suggested by Binchy, *CIH* 1468, n. c; see also Stokes, "O'Davoren's Glossary," 206.

843 The phrase *.i. do ime* is a gloss written above the line by the scribe; see also Binchy, *CIH* 1468, n. d.

844 O'Dav no. 60. I have made minor editorial changes to Stokes' text.

§ 55 A lord's fishing weir[845]

If he owns the bank on both sides [of the river], he can choose the sixth that he will make for damming each of the two sides or the third from one side. If he only owns one side, he will make a sixth from the side that he owns. And if he should make anything greater than that, two-thirds of the surplus is due from him | to the people who have a weir above and below, whichever p. 16b
way the fish comes to them A.

i.e. if one person owns [the bank] on both sides of the river, the wealth of a third from the one side or a sixth from each of the two sides [is his]. If he does not own them both at all, the wealth of a sixth of the side he owns. If he received anything greater than that, two-thirds of the surplus of the fish is due from him to those who own weirs below [his], if the fish come from above. Or two-thirds of the surplus of the fish is due from him to those who own weirs above [his], if fish come from below E.

Aire 'weir', i.e. a dam or fence, *ut est* 'a lord's fishing weir', i.e. to make a dam against the lord's fish. And it says: 'It is not lawful to dam, i.e. *ime* 'to dam', more than a third of the water' O'Dav.[846]

845 For a discussion of this section, see the Introduction, 45.

846 Stokes, "O'Davoren's Glossary," 206.

§56 Etla dithli ⁊rl-

.i. ma doro*n*ad i*n*ni-si*n* risi*n* ecl*ais*, is diabl*ad* ind [ḟ]eit*h*[847] dobiad do tuata di, it*er* pen*n*ait ⁊ er*aic* A. [*CIH* 2163.10–11]

.i. ma doronad ini-si*n* risi*n* ecl*ais*, is diabl*ad* in feich dobiad do tuata and, it*er* pen*n*ait ⁊ eraic D. [*CIH* 985.5–6]

---

1 ndithli A, dithle D. ⁊rl- *om.* A.

---

847 The ⟨e⟩ was inserted below the line by the scribe; see also Binchy, *CIH* 2163, n. e. MS *indeith* is for *ind feich*; cf. source D below.

§ 56 Penance[848] for theft[849]

i.e. if that thing had been done against the Church, it is double of the fine that would be due to a layman for it [i.e. for the Church], both penance and fine[850] A.

i.e. if that thing had been done against the Church, it is double of the fine that would be due to a layman then, both penance and fine D.

848 There is so little of the text that it is difficult to determine which meaning to assign to the form *etla*; see *eDIL s.vv.* 1 *etla*, 2 *etla*, *étla*, *étlód*, and *étla(id)*. The commentary, however, deals with penalties for any offenses done against the Church, which is why the meaning given in 1 *etla* was chosen here. Penance appears as a fine in §§ 34, 35, 48, and 52.

849 For a discussion of this section, see the Introduction, 45.

850 For this fine structure, see also §§ 48 and 52.

§ 57 Díguin digona: Ní snaig*hi*[851] deor*ad ar*aile, ní dlig*h*[852] nech fiac*h* i ndiguin a am*us*

Deor*ad* si*n* robui ar[853] comairce, ⁊ tarla deor*ad* neich *aile* ric a leas a comairgi do, ⁊ cu*r* saraig*ed* uime he, ⁊ cu*r* raibe i*n*t uasal aca rad dlig*id* ni i*n*d. ⁊ noc*h*a dlig*enn* ni i*n*d, u*air* na*ch* he roerb i*n* com*airci* ⁊ na*ch* asa baile dochuaid ⁊ na*ch* ara fer*an*d dorin*n*ed i*n* sarug*ud* an*n*.

⁊ l*etheneclann* do neoch a sarug*ud* a p*r*im-[m]na[854] ⁊ a m*eic* gor, t*r*ia*n* n-e*necl*a*inn*i do a sarug*ud* a m*eic* særlece ⁊ ca*ch* dui*ne* dia mui*n*dt*ir* æ*n*tigi. ⁊ ni he roerb[855] doib i*n* com*airci* an*n* si*n*, ⁊ da*m*ad he, robiad lan n-e*necl*a*inn*i a sarug*ud* ga*ch* dui*ne* dib A. [*CIH* 2163.12–19]

1 diguin A, D, E, díg*u*i*n* H, *om.* C. ‖ digo*n*a H, *om.* C. ‖ ní … arail*e om.* A, C, D, and E. ‖ ní … amus *om.* A, D, E, ni C. ‖ dl*ig* H, written in *marg. sin.* with a reference mark by the scribe; see also Binchy, *CIH* 1432, n. h. ‖ nec*h* H. ‖ *om.* C. ‖ a H. 2 ndig*uin* H. ‖ *om.* H. ‖ amais C. Both readings make sense in the context of the passage. See also *CCIH*, 165.

851 For *snaidhi*; see also Binchy, *CIH* 1432, n. g.

852 This form is followed by a space for two letters in source C; see also Binchy, *CIH*, 169, n. g.

853 The ⟨a⟩ is written subscript.

854 I follow the emendation suggested by Binchy, *CIH* 2163, n. f.

855 A letter was erased between ⟨r⟩ and ⟨b⟩; see also Binchy, *CIH* 2163, n. g.

§57 Violation of protection of a person who himself is under the protection of a third party:[856] An outsider[857] does not protect another, no one is entitled to a fine for the violation of protection of his hirelings.[858]

That is an outsider who was under protection, and an outsider of someone else [i.e. someone from a different territory] who needed his protection came to him, and he [i.e. the person who offered the protection] was violated regarding it [i.e. the protection], and the noble said he is entitled to something for it [i.e. for the protection being violated]. And he [i.e. the noble] is not entitled to anything for it because it was not he [i.e. the noble] who ordered the protection, and he [i.e. the person in need of protection] did not come from his [i.e. the lord's] settlement, and the violation then was not done on his land.

And half honor-price to anyone for violating[859] [the protection of] his wife[860] and his dutiful son, a third of honor-price [is] due to him for violating [the protection of] his independent son[861] and each person from his resident household. And it is not he who ordered them [i.e. the members of his household to undertake] the protection in that case, and if it were he, there would be [i.e. he would have] full honor-price for violating [the protection of] each one of them A.

856 The phrase *díguin dígona* is the term for a person who is under the protection of a person who himself is under the protection of a third party; see *eDIL s.v. díguin*.

857 *Deorad* refers to anyone from outside a community who does not have full legal rights, including exiles and outlaws; see *eDIL s.v. deorad*; and GEIL, 5–6.

858 For a discussion of this section, see the Introduction, 45–46. The final clause refers to protection offered not by the person in question himself, but by his attendants.

859 Although *sáragud* can refer to committing physical violence against someone, within the context of the commentary, I understand it to refer to the protection offered by the wife and various dependents being violated, rather than physical harm being done to the members of the household.

860 Although Breatnach, "On Old Irish Collective and Abstract Nouns," does not deal explicitly with the compound *prím-ben* (although it is mentioned in passing (25 and n. 90)), it is another term for a married woman rather than a 'chief wife'.

861 For the *macc sóerléicthe* 'son allowed independence', see GEIL, 81 and 317, *s.v. mac(c)*.

.i. let*h*eneclan*n* du neoc*h* i s*a*rug*h*ud*h* *a* [ph]*rim*-[m]na[862] ⁊ a meicc goir, *t*rian n-eneclai*n*ne do i s*a*rug*h*ud*h* a meicc særleict*h*i ⁊ cach duini da mui*nd*tir [a]entig*h*i. ⁊ ni e raerb i*n* comargi and-sein, ⁊ damad*h* he nabiad*h* lanenecl*ann* do i s*a*rug*h*ud*h* cac*h* duine dib. ⁊ do-s*omh* darindset hi, ⁊ nucun [ḟ]uil ni daib*h*-sium*h* an*n* C. [*CIH* 169.38–170.]

.i. na h-uile daine docuir in ri amach di*n* cumairce: Cid deoraid cid urr*aid* iat, ⁊ is [s]i cumairci i*n* righ roairb*er*tnaigest*ar*, la*n*enecl*ann* do*n* ri 'na sarug*ud*; ⁊ mas e in ri docuir amach iat ⁊ ni hi cu*m*airce in rig roairb*er*tnaiget*ar*, noch[a]n [ḟ]uil nach ni doib fein na do*n* rig i*n*a sarudha[d].

Manab e i*n* ri docuir amach it*ir* iat, ⁊ is [s]i comairce i*n* rig roairb*er*tnaiget*ar*, masa dai*n*e cusna fuil cae*m*achtai*n* imsgair risi*n* ri iat, ata t*r*ia*n* n-e*n*ecl*ainn*e do*n* ri i*n*a sarug*ud*. ⁊ masa daine aca fuil cae*m*achtai*n* imsgair risi*n* ri iat, nochan [ḟ]uil nach ni doib fein na do*n* ri i*n*a sarug*ud*. ⁊ mas [s]i a co*m*airce bodei*n* roairb*er*tnaiget*ar*, ata enecl*ann* doib fein ina sarug*ud*, ⁊ nochan [ḟ]uil nach ní do*n* ri.

.i. lethe*n*ecl*ann* do neoch a sarug*ud* a p*r*im-[m]na ⁊ a mic goir, *t*rian enecl*ainn*i do a sarug*ud* a mic sairleicthi ⁊ ca*ch* dui*n*e da mui*n*tir ae*n*tighe. ⁊ ni he roarb doib i*n* cumairce, ⁊ da*m*adh e, robo la*n*enecl*ann* do-so*m* a sarug*ud* ca*ch* dui*n*e dib. ⁊ do-s*om* doro*n*sat hí, ⁊ nochan [ḟ]uil ní doib-siu*m* an*n* D. [*CIH* 985.7–19]

862 I follow the emendation suggested by Binchy, *CIH* 169, n. h.

i.e. half honor-price for anyone for violating [the protection of] his wife and his dutiful son, a third of honor-price for him for violating [the protection of] his independent son and each person from his resident household. And it is not he who ordered the protection in that case, and if it were he, there would be full honor-price due to him for each one of them being violated. And [if] they had done it for him, (and) there is nothing due to them [i.e. the members of his household] then C.

i.e. all of the people whom the king sent out with the protection [i.e. under his protection]: Whether they are outsiders or native freemen, and it is the protection of the king that they pleaded, full honor-price [is] due to the king for violating[863] them. And if it is the king who sent them out and it is not the protection of the king that they pleaded, there is nothing due to them themselves or to the king for violating them.

If it is not the king who sent them away at all, and it is the protection of the king that they pleaded, if they are people who do not have the ability to part from the king, there is a third of honor-price due to the king for violating them. And if they are people who have the ability to part from the king, there is nothing due to them themselves or to the king for violating them. And if it was their own protection that they pleaded, there is honor-price due to them themselves for violating them, and there is nothing for the king.

i.e. half honor-price for anyone for violating [the protection of] his wife and his dutiful son, a third of honor-price [is] due to him for violating [the protection of] his independent son and each person from his resident household. And it is not he himself who ordered them [to provide] the protection, and if it were he, there would be full honor-price due to him for violating [the protection of] each one of them. And [if] they had done it for him, (and) there is nothing due to them then D.

863 Here and in the next paragraph, it is unclear whether those under the king's protection have been physically harmed themselves, or whether it is the protection that they provided which has been violated.

.i. duine si*n* ata ar c*h*umairc*he*: ⁊ rog*h*ab-san ni c*h*uici for a c*h*omairce ⁊ se fein *ar* comairc*he*. ⁊ mas a dualgus budein dorigni se i*n* c*h*omairc*he*, is [s]lan a sarug*h*ud*h*. Mas a dualgus i*n*ti ara ta co*m*airce, is laneneccl*ann* do-san asa sarug*h*ud*h*.

p. 457b ł letheneccl*ann* do a sarugu[d] a p*r*i[m]-m*h*na | ⁊ a meic gair, t*r*ian n-enecl*ainne* do a sarugudh[864] a meic sǽrleice ⁊ ca*ch* dui*n*e da mui*n*tir æntig*he*. ⁊ ni he-seam*h* roerbast*ar* doib i*n* comairce do de*nam*, ⁊ da*m*ad*h* he, robiadh laneneccl*ann* do-sa*m* and E. [*CIH* 1018.10–17]

Mas a dualg*us* intí *ar*a fuil com*airci* doní sé a com*airci*, is l*eth*enec*lann* do ina ts*a*rug*h*[ud].

⁊ l*eth*en*eclann* do a s*a*rug*h*[ud] a pri*m*-mna ⁊ a mic gor, ⁊ t*r*ian n-en*ecla*-*inn*e do a s*a*rug*h*[ud] a mic sæorleic*thi* ⁊ g*a*c dui*n*e dia mui*n*ti*r* aontig*h*i. ⁊ *no*chan eisu*m* roearb[865] riu an com*airci* do de*n*am an*n* sin, ⁊ *damad* é, dob*eth* lanen*eclann* do-s*om* un*n*t*a*-sid*h*e H. [*CIH* 1432.20–26]

864 Binchy, *CIH* 1018, n. e, notes that two letters, possibly ⟨ug⟩, have been written above ⟨udh⟩. I was not able to confirm the reading as the letters are illegible.

865 The ⟨a⟩ is written subscript.

i.e. that person who is under protection: And he took someone[866] to him under his protection and he himself [is] under protection. And if it is by his own right that he provided the protection, violating it [i.e. the protection] is exempt from legal liability. If it is by right of the one under whom he has protection, full honor-price is due to him [i.e. to the one under whom he himself has protection] for violating it [i.e. the protection].

Or half honor-price [is] due to him for violating [the protection of] his wife | and his dutiful son, a third of honor-price [is] due to him for violating p. 457b [the protection of] his independent son and each person from his resident household. And it is not he who had ordered them to provide the protection, and if it were he, there would be full honor-price due to him then E.

If it is by right of the one under whom he has protection that he provides the protection, half honor-price is due to him for violating it [i.e. the protection].

And half honor-price [is] due to him for violating [the protection of] his wife and his dutiful son, and a third of honor-price [is] due to him for violating [the protection of] his independent son and each person from his resident household. And it is not he who ordered them to provide the protection in that case, and if it were he, there would be full honor-price due to him for them H.[867]

866 The text's *ní* 'anything, something' is hard to reconcile here. The sense seems to be *nech* 'someone'.

867 See also *AL* 4: 230.2–12.

§58 Mesdar[868] ainmi

Na *séoit* rober*th*a i cor no i cu*n*drad: I*n* ai*n*im robiad orro .i. ciamad ris digsed a m*en*ma i*n*ni bud esbadach dib *tr*ia fog*ail* do de*n*um riu cu*m*ad esbadac*h* dib i cor ł i cu*n*drad do den*am* dib, nochan ed bias orro *acht* airdmes co*m*ai*th*ec*h*.

Measdar[869] ainme. I cor ł i cundr*ad* duratad i*n* set and si*n*, ma ta aird*m*es na co*m*ai*th*ech *air*.

Is and ata aithgi*n* inic*h* ⁊ i*n* dire inich: In tan tallad i*n* set ⁊ se co inic*h*, ⁊ dogab*t*ar amuig é ⁊ se ḟon i*n*andas cetna, no ni maire*n*n it*ir* é, ⁊ aithgi*n* inic*h* an*n* sin ⁊ dire i*n*ic*h*.

Is an*n* ata i*n*d aithgi*n* easbad*h*ac*h* ⁊ i*n* dire i*n*ic*h*: In tan tallad i*n* sed ⁊ sé inic*h*, ⁊ raloitead acan fir amuig, ⁊ urailid dlig*ed* a ngab*ail* cid*h* caech cid*h* lec*h*olb[870] am*ar* tarraid é co*n*a i*m*tuill*ed* leis. ⁊ dire inich les and.

Is and ata ind aithgi*n* inic*h* ⁊ i*n* dire easbadac*h*: In ta*n* roba c*h*æc*h* no c*r*in no bacac*h* i*n* set aca b*r*eit*h* a*m*ach, ⁊ mai*n*e m*air*end amuic*h* é, ait*h*gin inic*h* ⁊ dire easbadach uair ait*h*ginet*ar* olc i n-olc. ⁊ dire easbad*h*ac*h* leis A. [*CIH* 2163.20–32]

1 measdar A. ‖ ainme D. None of the text is preserved in C or P.

868 The form *mesdar* is ambiguous because the passage lacks sufficient linguistic context. It is probably the pres. subj. pass. rel. sg. of *midithir* 'judges', giving a translation of 'that defects may be judged'.

869 The rest of this part of the commentary was written in *marg. sup.* by the scribe; see also Binchy, *CIH* 2163, n. h.

870 Read *lethcolb*.

§58 That defects may be judged[871]

The *séts*[872] were given in contract or in a sale: The defect that they might have, i.e. though they agreed that which may be lacking from them as a result of an injury done to them renders them defective to consider them in contract or for sale,[873] it will not be [estimated] for them [i.e. they will not make the estimation themselves], but [the] calculation [will be made based on the opinion] of neighbors.[874]

That defects may be judged. In contract or in sale the *sét* was given in that case, if it is the opinion of another regarding it.

It is here that there is full restitution and the full compensation: When the *sét* was taken and it was perfect, and it is taken outside [i.e. to another place] and it is in the same state, or it does not survive at all, and full restitution in that case and full compensation.

It is here that there is the incomplete restitution and the full compensation: When the *sét* was taken and it was perfect, and it was injured in the plaintiff's possession,[875] and law requires taking it whether one-eyed or half-shanked as he finds it with its increase.[876] And he has full compensation then.

It is here that there is the full restitution and the incomplete compensation: When the *sét* was one-eyed or withered or lame when it was taken way, and if it does not survive away at all, full restitution and incomplete compensation because bad is restored for bad.[877] And he has incomplete compensation A.[878]

871 For a discussion of this section, see the Introduction, 46.

872 In this section, *séts* refer specifically to cattle or other livestock.

873 In other words, both parties agree that the defect to the cattle resulted from an injury, and thus, that because the cattle are now considered defective, they cannot be exchanged as part of the original terms of the contract.

874 For the sake of fairness, neutral thirds parties are brought to assess the value of the defective cattle.

875 The sense seems to be that the defect was discovered after it was in the plaintiff's possession.

876 The sense of the clause is that, if the defect in the goods was discovered after it was in the plaintiff's possession, then he has to take the damaged goods as they are, but he is entitled to have the value of the damaged goods estimated, and is he entitled to anything additional by way of compensation after the valuation.

877 See source P below for the opposite reasoning. It is possible that a negative particle is missing here.

878 The commentaries for this section of the text are concerned with defects which are only discovered after the goods have been purchased. For compensation for defects in purchased goods, see McLeod, *Early Irish Contract Law*, 39–43.

f. 53d O duini i cor ɫ cun*n*rad*h* ruccait na seoit a*n*meacha[879] and sin, ⁊ cia*m*ad*h* | ail dunti rucc na seotu i*n* cutruma bad esbad*hach* dib*h* guna fe*arth*ai*n* orru tre fog*h*ail cumad*h* ed na h-ictha ris, nu[cu]n[880] ed*h* icfar[881] ac*h*t ardmeas comait*h*each C. [*CIH* 170.4–6]

p. 439b .i. ni mes is dir f*air* o bis ai*n*im and *acht* ardamus .i. cema coibeis l*ethe* ɫ t*r*in isi*n* set 'ga ic ris, [.i. fer] amuig, a foglaib in ain*m*i dobiad f*air*. Nochan [ḟ]uil a esbaig-sid*he* a cor no a cun*n*rad, *acht ar*damus doch*us*a na co*m*ait*h*ec*h* fair. F*init* a*men* fi*nit*[882] D. [*CIH* 985.20–23]

Is and ata i*n* aith(i)g*in* i*nich* ⁊ i*n* dire i*nich*: I*n* tan talla[d] i*n* set ⁊ se i*nich*, ⁊ dog*h*ab*ar* a*muich* é fon inich*us* cetna, ɫ ni mairi*n*d it*ir* é, aithgi*n* i*n*ich an*n* si*n* an*n* ⁊ dire[883] i*nich*.

Is an*n* ata i*n* aithgi*n* esb*adach* ⁊ in dire[884] inic*h*: I*n* tan tall*ad* i*n* set ⁊ se

p. 191Bb i*nich*, ⁊ roloited i*n* set | aci*n* fir amuig, furailid dlig*ed* a gabail mar ta é *con*a imt*h*uill*ed* leis. ⁊ dire i*n*ic*h* leis an*n*.

Is an*n* ata i*n* aithgi*n* i*nich* ⁊ i*n* dire esb*ad*ach: I*n* ta*n* ropo caec*h* ɫ ropo c*r*i*n* no ropo l*eth*colb i*n* *sét* oca bret*h* i*m*ac*h*, ⁊ ni mairi*n*d a*muich* é, aith*gin* i*n*ic*h* an*n* uair ni ait*h*gei*nter* olc i *n*-olc, .i. olcaith*gin* i *n*-olcaith*gin aile*, ader isi*n* inad *aile*, ⁊ dire esb*adach* leis P. [*CIH* 715.32–41]

---

879 Binchy, *CIH* 170, n. a, queries the resolution of the suspension mark over the three minims following the ⟨a⟩. He comments that the word looks more like 'ai*n*neacha' and suggests the possibility that the exemplar had 'ain*m*eacha'.

880 I follow the emendation suggested by Binchy, *CIH* 170, n. b.

881 The verb appears to be a 3 sg. fut. pass. form of *íccaid*, although a form such as *íccfaider* would be expected.

882 See also Binchy, *CIH* 985, n. d. The remainder of this column and the verso of the folio have been left blank.

883 Binchy, *CIH* 715, n. t, notes the suspension mark over the ⟨r⟩, which appears to be an error.

884 Binchy, *CIH* 715, n. t, notes the suspension mark over the ⟨r⟩, which appears to be an error.

The defective *sét*s obtained from a person in contract or in a sale in that case, and although | the one who obtained the *sét*s may wish the amount f. 53d
which might be deficient from them [resulting from] wounds inflicted on them through injury not to be paid by him [i.e. the purchaser], it will not be paid except [according to the] calculation of neighbors C.

i.e. it is not a judgment that is proper for it when there is a defect in it except p. 439b
opinion,[885] i.e. without its equivalent of a half or a third of the *sét* to be paid to him, i.e. [the] plaintiff, for the types of defect that it might have. It is not useless in contract or for sale, but [it will be paid according to] the calculation that had been given for it by the neighbors. It finishes, amen, it finishes. D.

It is here that there is the full restitution and the full compensation: When the *sét* was removed and it was perfect, and it is taken outside [i.e. it was taken to another place] in the same state, or it does not survive at all, full restitution in that case for it and full compensation.

It is here that there is incomplete restitution and full compensation: When the *sét* was removed and it was perfect, and the *sét* | was injured in p. 191Bb
the plaintiff's possession, law requires taking it as it is with its increase. And he has full compensation for it.

It is here that there is the full restitution and the incomplete compensation: When the *sét* was one-eyed or withered or half-shanked when it was taken away, and it does not survive away, full restitution for it because bad is not restored for bad, i.e. bad restitution for another bad restitution, it says in the other place,[886] and he has incomplete compensation P.

---

885 The beginning of the commentary is a quasi-etymological gloss on *mesdar*.

886 Cf. source A above.

APPENDIX 1

Text and Commentary from Source C [CIH 167.30–38]

As noted in CCIH, 21, the material from source C [CIH 167.30–38] concerns stampeding cattle. This material is found within the series of extracts from *Anfuigell*. Although the material in C does not correspond to anything similar in the rest of the *Anfuigell* material, it is possible that the text in C represents part of the text and commentary from *Anfuigell* which is not attested elsewhere. For that reason, it is edited and translated below. A similar commentary is also found at CIH 1327.3 as part of a series of commentaries.[1]

In fub*h*tad*h* n-eis(i*n*)li*n*d:[2] In bel(c)oc*h* uat*h*a ł bodba, cibe fat*h* *ar*a nd*e*rnad*h* he, is lanfiac*h* cac*h*a fog*h*la raasat*ar* de uili d'ic an*n* .i. landiri isna setaib ⁊ lancoirp*dir*i isna cned*h*aib*h*, ⁊ enecclan*n* indtib*h* aræn.

Mad*h* *sechtar* beloc*h* uat*h*a ł bodba, *acht* mas *ar* daigin fogla, is lanfiac*h* cac*h*a fog*h*la raas de.

Mas *ar* daig*h*in esba, is lethfiac*h* cac*h*a fogla raas de.

Mani d*e*rnsat na daini i*n* fub*h*tud it*ir*, cid*h* teced daneitis na daini eile reompu, is [s]lan daib-siu*mh* *acht* na rucat a seotu. ⁊ da ruccat ...[3] Mas *ar* daig*h*in a t*h*ec*h*taig*h*thi, i[s][4] fiac*h* goitti. Mas *ar* daig*h*in a leasaig*h*t*h*i, is [s]eoit i*m*luaidi daib and ł cutig*h*i tobaig*h*.

The dangerous scaring:[5] The terrible or dangerous pass [e.g. between hills], whatever reason for which it was done [i.e. scaring the cattle], [the] full fine for each injury that had resulted from it entirely is to be paid, i.e. full fine for the *sét*s and full body-fine for the wounds, and honor-price for them both.[6]

1 See also CCIH, 60.
2 The first three words of the commentary might be part of the OI text of *Anfuigell*.
3 It is possible that a clause is missing from the commentary at this point.
4 I follow the emendation suggested by Binchy, CIH 167, n. i.
5 As mentioned above, this commentary deals with frightening cattle so as to cause them to stampede.
6 The fines are higher for scaring the cattle through a narrow and/or dangerous pass because it would be far more dangerous to both the animals and any nearby people than frightening the cattle in an open field.

 | DOI:10.1163/9789004391987_009

If it is outside the terrible or dangerous pass, but if it is for the purpose of causing injury, it is full fine for each injury that resulted from it.

If it is on account of folly, it is half-fine for each injury that resulted from it.

If the people did not cause the scaring [of the cattle] at all, although all the people fled before them, they are exempt from legal liability provided that they did not bring their *sét*s. And if they brought ... If it is for the purpose of taking possession of it, it is a fine of theft. If it is for the purpose of preserving it [from harm], they have [as a reward] *sét*s for driving then or a share for rescuing.

APPENDIX 2

Commentary from § 32 Source T [*CIH* 1169.19–1170.15]

.i. sm*acht ar* dærceil*ib* grai*dh* fei*n*e i*n* ne*m*dul i*n*d ⁊ i tia*chtai*n as. Dubl*ad* ngni*mraid ar* sær*ch*eil*ib* graid ḟene i*m* ne*m*dul i*n*d ⁊ i tia*chtai*n as. Sma*cht* ar dær*ch*eil*ib* grai*dh* fl*ath*a i ne*m*dul i*n*d ⁊ ene*clann* orr*a* i tia*chtai*n ass. Dubl*ad* ngni*mraid* o sær*cheil*ib grai*dh* fl*ath*a i*m* nemdul i*n*d ⁊ en*n*ecl*ann* orr*a* i tia*chtai*n as.

Ci*dh* fo*dera con*ad*h* mo orr*a* i tia*chtai*n as amuig*h* (ɫ) [ná] a nemdul an*n* amach fo *cét*oir? Is e in fa*th* fo*dera*: Aicmeile dul leis amach ⁊ a facb*ail* imuig*h* i c*r*ich nembescna (ɫ) [ná] ne*m*dul leis amach fo *cét*oir. Ci*dh* fo*dera con*ad*h* mo *ar*na grad*h*aib fl*ath*a ce*n* dul isi*n* sloig*heth* na *ar*na gradaib*h* feine? Is e in fa*th* fo*dera*: Mo t*h*ic tu*r*brod*h* int sloig*id* do*n*a grad[aib][1] fl*ath*a do b*heth* ’na h-ecm*uis* na do*n*a gradaib fene, ⁊ coir[2] gemad*h* mo *ar*na grad*aib* fl*ath*a na *ar*na grab*aib* fene.

Mas e in grad*h* fl*ath*a *con*a *ch*eil*ib* ta*n*ic as, i*n* sm*acht* ɫ in ene*clann* [ḟ]uil an*n*, a l*eth* d’ic do-som ⁊ a l*eth* d’ic doib-siu*m*. ⁊ do neoch na fuil da ceilid*h*ib i*n*a farad, is eisiu*m* ic*us* a cuidig*h*, daig*h* is e rob*er*ad*h* cuitig*h* t*r*eibdire. ⁊ c*o*mroi*n*d sm*acht*a cana icna bi fer c*r*ai air[3] .i. a l*eth* do rig*h* in *cóic*id*h* ⁊ in l*eth aile* do roi*n*d a t*r*i .i. a t*r*ian do*n* fl*aith* is n[e](u)sa[4] suas do rig*h* a*n cóic*id*hi*, ⁊ a t*r*ia*n* do*n* fl*aith* is nesa sis donti ic*us*, ⁊ in t*r*ian *aile* do*n*a fl*aith*ib ⁊ do*n*a h-eta*r*fl*aith*ib [ḟ]uil eta*r*a i med*h*on.

Mas e an grad*h* fl*ath*a ⁊ a æonceile ta*n*ic as, in cutr*um*a roicfad*h* int aonceil*e con*a t*h*i-a*cht*iun | uil*i* as gu*r*ab ed ic*us* anosa, ⁊ in sm*acht* (⁊) [ɫ][5] in*n* enecl*ann* [ḟ]uil an*n* d’ic p. 26a
do-s*um*, ⁊ comroind sm*acht*a cana acna bi fer crui air beos.

Mad siat na ceil*i* tai*n*ic as i*ar*na rad do-sum riu, in sm*acht* ⁊ in enecl*ann* [ḟ]uil an*n*, is a ic do-sum. ⁊ c*o*mroi*nn* sm*acht*a cana acna bi fer c*r*ai air[6] beos.[7]

Mas iat na ceil*eda*[8] tai*n*ic as gan rad do-sum riu, in sm*acht* (⁊) [ɫ] in enecl*ann* [ḟ]uil an*n* is a ic doib. ⁊ c*o*mroi*nn* s*macht*a cana oc[n]a (m)bi[9] fer c*r*ai air-side; a t*r*ian do-sum,

---

1 I follow the emendation suggested by Binchy, *CIH* 1169, n. f.

2 The word *coir* was written twice by the scribe, but he crossed out the second one; see Binchy, *CIH* 1169, n. g.

3 The ⟨i⟩ is written subscript; see also Binchy, *CIH* 1169, n. h.

4 I follow the emendation suggested by Binchy, *CIH* 1169, n. i.

5 Cf. the fine structure in A.

6 The word *air* was added *marg. sin.* with reference marks; see Binchy, *CIH* 1170, n. a.

7 The ⟨s⟩ was added above the line by the scribe.

8 The scribe wrote ⟨n⟩ after this but expunged it with a *punctum* written underneath it; see also Binchy, *CIH* 1170, n. b.

9 I follow the emendations suggested by Binchy, *CIH* 1170, n. c.

 | DOI:10.1163/9789004391987_010

⁊ a trian do ri in *cóic*id, ⁊ in trian *aile* do roin*n* i tri .i. a trian don fl*aith* is n[e](u)sa[10] suas do rig*h* in *cóic*id*h*, ⁊ a trian don fl*aith* is nesa sis donti ic*us* .i. rig na tuait*h*i fuil orr*a*-sum tis, ⁊ in trian *aile* dona fl*ath*aib ⁊ dona h-et*ar*fl*aith*ib fuil et*aru* i medon.

Ca*ch* u*air* is [s]m*acht* sin is fo aicn*ed* inti ic*us*. Ca*ch* u*air* is enecl*ann* is fo aic*ned* inti risi n-ict*ar*.

Masa lu*cht* sm*achta* ł lu*cht* ene*clainn*e tai*n*ic as, atfegt*ar* cuib*us* et*aru*-side .i. in lu*cht* is mo lan d'ic na h-im*arc*raide, ⁊ teca*r* a cuib*us* ar am*us* in lo*cht*a is luga lan dib*h*, ⁊ comicait et*aru*.

Masa lu*cht* sm*achta*[11] ⁊ dub*alta* ngnimrad[12] tainic as, (⁊)[13] *noch*on ait*h*fega*r* cuib*us* *etaru* *acht* cach dib d'ic a lain *ar'* aig*ed* budein, u*air* aitḟegt*ar* cuibdi*us* *etar* lu*cht* sm*acht*a ⁊ ene*clainne*, ⁊ *noch*on at*h*fegt*ar* *etar* lu*cht* sm*acht*a ⁊ dub*al*ta ngni*mraid* ł it*er* lu*cht* ene*clainn*i ⁊ dub*al*ta ngnimrad, *acht* ca*ch* dib d'ic a lai*n* *ar'* ag*aid* buden.

i.e. a fine for base clients of the non-noble grades for not going to it [i.e. the assembly] and for coming away from it [i.e. the assembly]. Doubling of labor [that they owe their lord as a fine] for free clients of the non-noble grades for not going to it and for coming away from it. A fine for base clients of the noble grades for not going to it and honor-price for them for coming away from it. Doubling of labor from free clients of the noble grades for not going to it and honor-price for them for coming away from it.

What is the reason that [the fine] is greater for them for coming away from it outside[14] than for not going out to it immediately? This is the reason: It is more dangerous for him to go away and leave him [i.e. his lord] outside in a territory not covered by protocol than for him not to go out immediately. What is the reason that [the fine] is larger for the noble grades not going to the mustering than for the non-noble grades? The reason is: It is a greater infringement of the hosting for the noble grades to be absent than for the non-noble grades, and [it is] right that there should be a larger [fine] for the noble grades than for the non-noble grades.

If it is [someone] of the noble grades with his clients who came away from it, the fine or the honor-price is [determined] then, and he [i.e. the noble] pays half of it and they [i.e. the clients] pay half of it. And anyone who does not have his clients along with him, it is he who pays their share, because it is he who would receive a share of compensation for house-theft. And dividing of the fine for [violating] promulgated law by

10 I follow the emendation suggested by Binchy, *CIH* 1170, n. d.

11 'smachta' is followed by '⁊ dub*alta* ngnimrad' which was later erased; see also Binchy, *CIH* 1170, n. f.

12 The ⟨r⟩ was inserted above the line by the scribe; see also Binchy, *CIH* 1170, n. g.

13 I follow the emendation suggested by Binchy, *CIH* 1170, n. h, although the overall sense of the passage does not change without the emendation.

14 The sense of *amuigh* is that the client was already outside the territory when he left.

he who does not have property, i.e. half of it to the king of the province, and the other half is divided into three, i.e. a third of it to the lord who is nearest up to the king of the province, and a third of it to the lord who is nearest down to the one who pays, and the other third to the lords and the intermediate lords who are between them in the middle.

If it is [someone] of the noble grades and his one client who came away from it, the share that the one client would pay [is the same as] their [i.e. the clients] all coming | p. 26a
away from it, that is what he pays now, and the fine or the honor-price is [determined] then to be paid by him [i.e. the noble]. And dividing of the fine for [violating] promulgated law by he who does not have property moreover.

If the clients came away from it because he [i.e. their lord] told them [to do so], the fine or the honor-price is [determined] then [and] it is paid by him [i.e. the lord]. And dividing of the fine for [violating] promulgated law by he who does not have property moreover.

If the clients came away from it without him telling them [to do so], the fine or the honor-price is [determined] then [and] it is paid by them [i.e. the cleints]. And dividing of the fine for [violating] promulgated law by he who does not have property; a third of it to him [i.e. his lord], and a third of it to the king of the province, and the other third is divided into three, i.e. a third of it to the lord who is nearest up to the king of the province, a third of it to the lord who is nearest down to the one who pays, i.e. the king of the *túath* who is over them below, and the other third to the lords and to the intermediate lords who are between them in the middle.

Whenever it is a fine, it is according to [the status] of the one who pays. Whenever it is honor-price, it is according to [the status] of the one to whom it is paid.

If it is people [who owe] a fine or people [who owe] honor-price who came away from it, a joint payment between them is considered, i.e. the people who are the most guilty pay the surplus, and their joint payment is reached with the people of them who are less guilty, and they pay equally between them.

If it is people [who owe] a fine and doubling of labor who came away from it, a joint payment is not considered between them, but each of them pays [the amount] of his guilt of his own accord, because a joint payment is considered between people [who owe] fine and honor-price, and it is not considered between people [who owe] fine and doubling of labor or between people [who owe] honor-price and doubling of labor, but each of them pays [the amount] of his guilt of his own accord.

APPENDIX 3

Commentary from § 51 Source T [*CIH* 1178.34–1180.11]

Fuatach dichmairce[1] .i. in be*n* ḟuataig*h*, *acht* mas ar eci*n* ruca*d* amac*h* hí, ene*clann* d'íc re budei*n* ⁊ ene*clann* d'ic re cen*n*aib*h* ⁊ re coibdelch*aib* fo aic*ned* a coib*h*delch*ius* ríu, ⁊ coirp*dír*e d'íc in*n*ti. Cid*h*be ag*ed* [read *aighed*][2] gnat*h* ɫ i*n*gnat*h* tair[3] amuig*h* hí, cid*h* gala*r* cid*h* do t*h*oirrc*hius*, is coirp*dír*e ⁊ enecl*ann* d'ic re f[i](í)ne. ⁊ munab marb it*ir* hí, is ene*clann* d'íc re b[u](ú)dei*n*, ⁊ ene*clann* d'íc re fine. Mas tall docúas i*na* gnais ar eici*n* ɫ *ar* el*ud*, masa marb tall hi, mas do*n* toirrchi*us* is marb hí, is coirp*díre* ⁊ ene*clann* d'íc re fine, ⁊ mas da gala*r aile*, is [s]l*an*.

Mas da deoin ruca*d* am[a](u)ch hí, *noch*an ict*har* ní ria budei*n*, ⁊ ene*clann* d'ic re cen*n*aib*h* ⁊ re coib*h*dealch*aib*,[4] ⁊ cid*h*be aig*h*id*h* gnat*h* ɫ ingnat*h* be*rus* amuig*h* hí risi*n* mís ⁊ re re i*n* mis, is coirp*díre* ⁊ ene*clann* d'íc rea fi*ne*.

In cl*ann* dogent*ar* re amuig*h* resi*n* mís ⁊ re re in mís, a dilsi do fine math*ar*, ⁊ m*ad* ail doib*h* recat ⁊ mad ail doip na recat. ⁊ da recat, *nocon* urailin*n* dlig*ed* a reic ɫ co tuct*ar* a lanlog*h* a mbraig*h*et doib tara *cend*.[5] ⁊ o rob*er*ait, is iat is cl*ann* c*ét*muin*n*t*ir*i urnad*ma* an*n* ɫ ad*h*altraid*he* u*r*nad*ma*.

Cac*h* u*air* is ar eicin ruc*ad* amac*h* hí, is *a* rog*h*a na finec*h*aire ata in[6] recf*ad* ɫ na recf*ad* iat. ⁊ da recat, u*r*ail*id* dlig*ed* ara n-aithrech*aib* a cen*nach*.

Mas da deoi*n* ruc*ad* amach hí, is a rog*h*a in ath*ar* ata in cei*n*deg*h*a iat ɫ na cin*n*eg*h*da. ⁊ da c*endaig*i,[7] urail*id* dlig*ed* ari*n* fine a rec ris. ⁊ da tuct*ar* do i n-aisc*id* iat, urail*id* dl*iged* air a lesug*ud* daig*h* is [s]ocha*r* dó. ɫ d*ano* che*n*a cid*h ar* ais cid *ar* eci*n* ruc*ad* amach hí, urail*id* dl*iged* arin ath*air* a cen*nach*. Is as gaba*r* eiside:[8] .i. ma baítsec nabí tualai*ng* a toiscide ⁊ foluc*h* a cin*adh*, is i suig*h*iug*ud* [perhaps read *suidiu*][9] is tec*ht*a at*h*cor m*aic*

1 This fragment of text is from *Bretha Éitgid*.
2 See also Binchy, *CIH* 1178, n. p.
3 The verbal form *tair* is the pres. subj. 3 sg. of *do-airicc* 'comes, finds'.
4 The first ⟨a⟩ is written subscript.
5 The scribe abbreviated ⟨end⟩ as ⟨⁊̄⟩; see also Binchy, *CIH* 1179, n. c.
6 For the interrog. part. used in dependent questions to mean 'whether', see *eDIL s.v.* 2 *in* (ii) a; and *GOI* § 463. The same construction appears in the next paragraph of the commentary.
7 The scribe abbreviated ⟨endaig⟩ as ⟨⁊̄⟩; see also Binchy, *CIH* 1179, n. d.
8 Although the source of the following legal principle is not identified, § 51E identifies the source as *Bretha for Macślechtaib*.
9 The emended reading is suggested by Binchy, *CIH* 1179, n. f.

 | DOI:10.1163/9789004391987_011

sula ⁊ san*uise*. *Acht* ch*en*a namá cac*h* uair is ar eicin ruc*ad* amac*h* hí, ge*m*ad*h* he rog*h*a an ath*ar* a gc*en*d*ac*, noco urailen*n* dl*iged* arin fi*n*e a reic ris iat *acht* munub ail doib budei*n*.

In cl*ann* dogent*ar* iarsa*n* mís, ⁊ co tisat ar u*r*naid*m* ndlig*thech*, is iat-sid*he* is cl*ann* c*ét*mu*in*t*ir*e foxail an*n* ł ad*h*altraid*he* foxail. ⁊ is dib scuir*us* foxal t*r*ian a cotac*h*.

Mas ar eicin ruc*ad* amach hí, ar mait*hi* re fine rogab coibc*hi*, sm*acht* *cét*mu*in*- p. 15b
tire ł ad*h*al*traig*i d'ic ria, ⁊ sm*acht* ad*h*al*traigh*i d'ic uait*hi* mana tist*ar* fo cor*aib*. ⁊ [ma][10] teca*r* fo cor*aib*, *con*a ican*n* nac*h* ní, ⁊ s*macht* c*ét*mu*in*t*ire* ł ad*h*al*traig*i d'ic ria.

Mas da deoi*n* *r*ucad hí, cid *ar* maiti ci*n*cob *ar* mait*h*i re fine r[o](ó)g*a*b coibqe, ł mas ar eici*n* ⁊ ní h-*ar* mait*h*i re fine rog*a*b coibqe, s*mach*t ad*h*al*traigh*i d'íc ria ⁊ s*macht* ad*h*al*traigh*i d'ic uaithe mana tist*ar* fo cor*aib*. ⁊ [ma][11] teca*r* fo cor*aib*, *con*a h-icun*n* nac*h* ní, [⁊][12] s*macht* ad*h*al*traigh*i d'ic ria. Manar gab coibqe it*ir* amuig*h*, ⁊ *ar* mait*h*i re fei*n* ł re fine, coirp*díre* a cn*eid*i d'íc ria am*ail* rohicfait*h*ea re dui*n*e nac*h* lana*m*anda. ⁊ is a rog*h*a na fine ata in co*m*fat robuí [amuig][13] hí in ben i*n* *ar* son ai*thgena* a gnim*raid* bías doib, ł in a dul-si a ngmi*m*ra*d* ḟir, ⁊ gan fer do dul ina gni*mradh*-si. ⁊ is *cét*f*aid* co *m*b*et*is araen doib*h* .i. b*en* ar son ai*thgen*a a gnimr*aid*-si ⁊ a dul-si a ngni*mrad* ḟir, ⁊ gan fer do dul ina gni*mrad*[-si][14] ł co tisat araen re dlig*ed*. *Nocon* fuil ait*h*fegad*h* fog*h*la láin no l*ethe* ł dairte ł *cet*raman et*ar*u, am*al* cac*h* lanamai*n* dlig*thig*, ł co ría fog*ail* i n-*air*iltnigt*er* ene*clann*. ⁊ ó rosía fog*ail*, a feg*h*ad*h* cia risi ndenud f*ogail*. *Acht* mas in fer, noc*h*on icun*n* nac*h* ní. Mas re nec*h* *aile*, is a íc do*n* ḟir am*ail* ícus in gat*aig*i cintu na s*ét* ngaiti[15] gei*n* bit aice amuig*h*.

Mas[16] da deoi*n* ruc*ad* a seoit fei*n* [uait]hí[17] amuig*h*, cid*h* ar ais cid *ar* eici*n* ruc*ad* amac*h* hí, is [s]l*an* gan ní d'íc re fen[18] an*n*, ⁊ l*eth*dire ⁊ l*eth*ene*clann* d'íc re fine isna s*ét*aib. ⁊ is é-si*n* æ*nineth* isi*n* berla a fuil dire a seoit fei*n* o dui*n*e do neoc*h* *aile*, ⁊ se fei*n* ar aird.

Mas *ar* eici*n* ruc*ad* amac*h* hí, ⁊ ar eici*n* ruc*ad* a s*éoit* uaithi amuig*h*, is ai*thgin* ⁊ lanene*clann* ⁊ la*n*dire d'íc ré fei*n* an*n*, ⁊ ene*clann* d'íc re fine.

---

10 I follow the emendation suggested by Binchy, *CIH* 1179, n. h.

11 I follow the emendation suggested by Binchy, *CIH* 1179, n. h.

12 I follow the emendation suggested by Binchy, *CIH* 1179, n. j.

13 I follow the emendation suggested by Binchy, *CIH* 1179, n. k.

14 I follow the emendation suggested by Binchy, *CIH* 1179, n. l.

15 The scribe originally wrote a second ⟨n⟩ after the ⟨g⟩ but expunged it with a *punctum delens* underneath it; see also Binchy, *CIH* 1179, n. n.

16 The commentary from here to the end has been edited and translated by McLeod, "Property and Honour-Price," 285–286.

17 I follow the emendation suggested by Binchy, *CIH* 1179, n. o.

18 The scribe originally wrote the word *fine*, but he corrected his mistake by erasing the ⟨e⟩ and turning the ⟨i⟩ into a tall ⟨e⟩.

Mas da deoi*n* *rucadh* amac*h* hí, ⁊ ar eici*n* ruc*ad* a *séoit* uaithí amuig*h*, ene*clann* d'íc re fine an*n*, ⁊ ai*thgin* ⁊ landire ⁊ lanene*clann* d'íc ria-si fein. ⁊ toc*hus* et*ar*scartach[19] [f]uil aice an*n* si*n*, *co n*denu*m* mait*hus*a dé. ⁊ masa toc*hus* ne*met*arscartac*h* [f]uil aice, ł cid*h* tóc*hus* et*ar*scart*ac* muna déna mait*h* dé, noc*h*an [f]uil nach ní dí *acht* ai*thgin* cer*t*.

Mas da deoi*n* ruc*ad* *séoit* na fine uait*h*i amuig*h*, cid*h* ar ais cid*h ar* eici*n* ruc*ad* a*m*ach hí, [is][20] slan gan ní d'íc ria-si an*n*, ⁊ ai*thgin* ⁊ land*íre* ⁊ lanene*clann* d'íc re fine.

Mas ar eici*n* ruc*ad* amach hí, ⁊ ar eici*n* ruc*ad* *séoit* na fine uaithi amuig*h*, is ene*clann* d'íc ria-si, ⁊ ai*thgin* ⁊ land*íre* ⁊ lanene*clann* d'ic re fine.

Mas da deoi*n* ruc*ad* amach hí, ⁊ ar eici*n* ruc*ad* *séoit* na fine uaithi amuig*h*, ai*thgin* ⁊ d*íre* ⁊ ene*clann* d'íc risi*n* fine an*n*, ⁊ l*eth*ene*clann* d'íc ria-si, masa toch*us etarscarthach* [f]uil aice *co n*denu*m* mait*hius*a dé. Masa t*ochus* ne*metar*sc*arthach* [f]uil aici, ł cid*h* t*ochus* et*arscarthach*, maine deni mait*h* dé, *nochon* fuil nac*h* ní dí.

Abduction without consent, i.e. the abducted woman, but if it is by force that she was taken away, honor-price is to be paid to her herself, and honor-price is to be paid to her heads [of kindred] and to her relatives according to the nature of her relationship to them. And body-fine is to be paid to her. Whatever death, usual or unusual, finds her [while she is] away, whether [by] illness or by pregnancy, body-fine and honor-price are to be paid to her kindred. And if she does not die at all, honor-price is to be paid to her herself, and honor-price is to be paid to her kindred. If she was known[21] there by force or by elopement, if she dies there, if the pregnancy kills her, body-fine and honor-price are to be paid to her kindred. And if [death] is by another illness, he [i.e. the abductor] is exempt from legal liability.

If it is with her consent that she was taken away, nothing is paid to her herself, and honor-price is to be paid to her heads [of kindred] and to her relatives. Whatever death, usual or unusual, takes her [while she is] away before the [end of the first] month and within the space of the month, body-fine and honor-price are to be paid to her kindred.

The child who will be begotten on her [while she is] away before the [end of the first month] and within the space of the month, it belongs to the mother's kindred, and whether they wish to sell [the legal rights to the child], or they do not wish to sell. And if they sell, law does not require them to sell it [i.e. the legal rights to the child] until [the] full amount of a hostage is given to them on its behalf. And when they give [it],[22] they[23] are [considered] as children of a betrothed spouse then or of a betrothed concubine.

19 The ⟨c⟩ was inserted below the line by the scribe.

20 I follow the editorial emendation by McLeod, "Property and Honour-Price," 285.

21 *Gnás* refers to the abductor having intercourse with the abducted woman; *eDIL s.v. gnás*.

22 The verbal form *roberait* is obscure to me. It could be a 3 pl. pres. subj. with the *ro* of potential.

23 The commentary switches between sg. and pl. when referring to the offspring.

Whenever it is by force that she was taken away, it is the family group's choice whether they will or will not sell sell them. And if they sell [them], law requires their fathers to buy them.

If it is with her consent that she was taken away, it is the father's choice whether he buys them or not. And if he buys [them] law requires the kindred to sell them to him. And if they are given to him for free, law requires him to care for them because it is an advantageous contract for him. Or else [i.e. alternatively], whether willingly or by force that she was taken away, law requires the father to purchase them. That is taken from: i.e. if a woman of indiscriminate morals is not capable of providing their food and bearing their liabilities, thus it is proper to return the 'child of sunlight' and '[the child] of secrecy'. But in any case, only whenever it is by force that she was taken away, though it may be the father's choice to buy them, law does not require the kindred to sell them to him unless they themselves wish [to do so].

The child who will be begotten after the month, until they [i.e. the parents] are lawfully betrothed, they are [considered] as children of an abducted spouse then or of an abducted concubine. And [the] abduction deprives them of a third of their share.

If it is by force that she was taken away, [and] for the good of the kindred that she p. 15 b
took [i.e. accepted] a bride-price, [the] fine of a spouse or of a concubine is to be paid to her, and [the] fine of a concubine is to be paid from her unless the contract be opposed. And if it is opposed, she pays nothing, and [the] fine of a spouse or of a concubine is to be paid to her.

If it is with her consent that she was taken away, whether or not for the good of the kindred that she accepted a bride-price, or it is by force [that she was taken away] and it is not for the good of the kindred that she accepted a bride-price, [the] fine of a concubine is to be paid to her, and [the] fine of a concubine is to be paid by her unless the contract be opposed. And if the contract is opposed, she does not pay anything, and [the] fine of a concubine is to be paid to her. If she did not accept a bride-price at all [while she was] away, and [it is] for the good of herself or her kindred, [the] body-fine of her wounds is to be paid to her as it would be paid to a person not [in] a relationship. And it is the kindred's choice whether for the same length [of time] she was away they will have the woman [i.e. another woman] as compensation of her work [which they would normally have had were she not away], or she will perform the work of [her] husband, and without [her] husband performing her work. And it is the opinion [of others] that assigns both to them, i.e. a women as compsensation for her work and her performing the work of [her] husband, and without [her] husband performing her work until they both submit to law. There is no reckoning of injury [paid with] full [fine] or a half or of a heifer or of one-fourth between them like every lawful relationship, or as far an injury which merits honor-price [to be paid]. And if an injury will happen, it will be taken into account against whom [the] injury was made. And if it is [against] the husband, she pays nothing. If [the injury is made] aginst someone else, it is paid by the husband just as the thief pays for the crimes of the stolen *sét*s while they are away in his possession.

If it is with her consent that her own *sét*s were taken from her [while she was] away [from her kindred], whether willingly or by force she was taken away, no one is liable to pay anything to her herself then, and half compensation and half honor-price are to be paid to her kindred for the *sét*s. And that is the one instance in the law in which there is compensation of his own *sét*s from a person to someone else, and he himself is present.

If it is by force she was taken away, and by force that her *sét*s were taken from her [while she was] away, restitution and full honor-price and full compensation are to be paid to her herself then, and honor-price is to be paid to her kindred.

If it is with her consent that she was taken away, and by force that her *sét*s were taken from her [while she was] away, honor-price is to be paid to her kindred then, and restitution and full compensation and full honor-price are to be paid to her herself. And she has property sufficient for independence in that case, and she makes good use of it. And if she has property insufficient for independence, or though she has property sufficient for independence, unless she makes good use of it, there is nothing for her except exact restitution.

If it is with her consent that her kindred's *sét*s were taken from her [while she was] away, whether willingly or by force that she was taken away, no one is liable to pay anything to her then, and restitution and full compensation and full honor-price are to be paid to her kindred.

If it is by force that she was taken away, and by force that her kindred's *sét*s were taken from her [while she was] away, honor-price is to be paid to her, and restitution and full compensation and full honor-price are to be paid to her kindred.

If it is with her consent that she was taken away, and by force that her kindred's *sét*s were taken from her [while she was] away, restitution and compensation and honor-price are to be paid to the kindred then, and half honor-price is to be paid to her, if she has property sufficient for independence, and she makes good use of it. If she has property insufficient for independence, or though she has property sufficient for independence, unless she makes good use of it, there is nothing for her.

APPENDIX 4

List of Variant MS Readings against *CIH*

The following is a concordance of the variant readings in the edited texts against those found in *CIH*. Differences which arise as a result of different editorial decisions regarding the indication (or not) of the expansion of common MS abbreviations, e.g. § 3 *CIH* 2147.11 'lucht' for 'lu*cht*' in the edition, are not given below. The variants are listed by section, page, and line number.

Heading 64.3 'do' against *CIH* 979.23 'dó'.
64.6 'foglann' against *CIH* 979.26 'foglaim'. The end of the word consists of four minims. Binchy, *CIH* 979, n. h, suggests *foglann* as a possible reading.

§ 1 66.3 'comarleict*hi*' against *CIH* 2146.18 'comarleicti'.
66.4 'in br*eith*eman' against *CIH* 2146.19 'mbr*eith*eman'.
70.7 '-seo' *om.* *CIH* 2146.33
72.2 'anfuig*ell*' against *CIH* 1477.14 'an fuig*ell*'.

§ 2 74.1n1 'tait*h*mig*h*' against *CIH* 2146.39 'taithmig'.
74.2 'nasc*airecht*[*a*]' against *CIH* 2146.40 'nascair*echt*'.
74.9 'rotoc*h*ait*h*sed*ar*' against *CIH* 2147.6 'rotocaithsedar'.

§ 4 88.12 'ní' against *CIH* 2026.29 'ni'.

§ 5 94.3 'ḟ*er*t' against *CIH* 2147.40 'f*er*t'.

§ 6 96.1 'tuathe' against *CIH* 167.39 'tuaithe'.

§ 7 102.4 Source A does not contain the sequence ⟨ł a⟩ as printed in *CIH* 2148.18. Binchy counted the last two syllables (the first of which is suspended) of *eclasa* twice.
104.14 'fei*n*' *om.* *CIH* 2026.12.

§ 8 106.1 '⁊rl-' *om.* *CIH* 980.12.
106.5 'ni' against *CIH* 2148.29 'in'; cf. *CIH* 1436.22–23 'Ni digui*n* nabi do maig*in* nabi do guaire gaibhus gin'.
108.2 'ciama[d]' against *CIH* 2148.34 'ciamad'.
'*secht*ir' against *CIH* 2149.17 '.uii.ar'.
112.17 Although Binchy prints 'ní' *CIH* 1558.4, I doubt that the mark in the MS is truly a length mark.

 | DOI:10.1163/9789004391987_012

112.19 'oc indilsich' against *CIH* 1558.6 'ocon dilsich'.

112.22 Although Binchy prints 'ní' *CIH* 1558.8 (twice), I doubt the mark in the MS is truly a length mark.

114.2 '*ar*illnith*er*' against *CIH* 1431.18 'airillnith*er*'.

114.4 '*arr*illnit*er*' against *CIH* 1431.20 'airillnit*er*'.

114.6 't*ar*gsi*n*' against *CIH* 1431.22 'tairgsi*n*'.

114.7 't*ar*gsi*n*' against *CIH* 1431.23 'tairgsi*n*'.

114.8 't*ar*g[s]i*nn*' against *CIH* 1431.24 'tairgi*nn*'.

116.8 'cleit*he*' against *CIH* 139.7 'chleithe'. The lenition mark Binchy thought he saw above the ⟨c⟩ is actually a lenition mark from f. 40rb27 which has partially bled through the vellum.

116.24 'ruccad' against *CIH* 139.22 'ruccad*h*'.

116.24 '*ar*' against *CIH* 139.22 'a'.

§ 9 **120.3** 'fiall*aig*' as against *CIH* 2149.28 'fiall*ach*'.

§ 10 **126.5** 'isa' against *CIH* 2150.15 'asa'.

128.3 '*m*b*eth*' against *CIH* 2150.23 'beth'.

128.16 'ní' against *CIH* 2027.17 'ni'.

128.16 '.⁊rl-.' *om. CIH* 2027.17.

§ 11 **130.11** 'do' against *CIH* 2150.32 'de'.

132.10 'c*h*ind*h*' against *CIH* 168.15 'chind'.

§ 12 **134.6** 'foi*m*rimi' against *CIH* 2151.3 'foi*m*rim'.

134.11 'reie' against *CIH* 2151.8 'rei el*e* (?)'.

136.12 'ci*nn*iud' against *CIH* 2151.21 'ci*nn*id'.

§ 13 **142.6** 'comsl*ain*ti(i)*us*' against *CIH* 2151.36 'co*m*sl*ain*tius'.

§ 16 **150.2** 'léo' against *CIH* 1202.33 'leó'.

150.4 'nderrn*n*sat' against *CIH* 1202.35 'nderrn*a*sat (?)' where Binchy seems to query his expansion of the suspension mark over the ⟨n⟩.

150.5 'dlig*ed*' against *CIH* 1202.36 'dligh*ed*'.

§ 17 **154.3** 'com*ar*dughudh' against *CIH* 168.22 'comardugud'.

§ 20 **160.14** 'i*n*' *om. CIH* 2153.5.

162.10 'í' against *CIH* 2031.11 'i'.

162.11 'í' *om. CIH* 2031.12.

162.11 'í' against *CIH* 2031.12 'i'.
162.14 'feichem*h*' against *CIH* 2031.15 'feichem'.

§ **21 164.2** '⁊ esin*raic* oc in*nraic*' *om. CIH* 2153.13.

§ **22 166.2** 'dot*himairc*' against *CIH* 2153.17 'doti*m*airc'.
166.6 'ceth*ramth*a' against *CIH* 2153.22 'ceth*ramtha*'.
166.13 'cia*m*ad' against *CIH* 2153.27 'cu*m*ad'.
168.6 'is' against *CIH* 2153.36 'as'.
168.8 'mane *thechta*' against *CIH* 2153.37–38 'man ethechta'.

§ **23 172.3** 'ris*ar*' against *CIH* 2154.3 'risa'.

§ **24 174.2** 'i*n*dligtec*h*' against *CIH* 2154.6 'i*n*dlighech'.

§ **26 178.5** 'an' against *CIH* 2154.29 'a'.

§ **27 180.1** 'aircell*a*' against *CIH* 2154.32 'aircell*ach* (?)'.

§ **28 182.3** 'noch*ur*' against *CIH* 2154.37 'nochar'.
182.4 'air' against *CIH* 2154.37 'an*n*'.
182.7 'dó' against *CIH* 2155.3 'do'.

§ **30 190.3** 't[e]ist*a*' against *CIH* 2155.37 'tist*is* (?)'.

§ **32 200.2** 'risi*n*' against *CIH* 2157.7 'risi'.

§ **33 206.10–11** 'Ni de … m*arbtha*' *om. CIH* 2157.24.
208.8 'pe*n*daite' against *CIH* 2157.36 'pe*n*daiti'.

§ **34 210.3** 'uad' against *CIH* 2157.38 'uada'.
212.1 'ní' against *CIH* 278.6 'ni'.

§ **35 214.6** 'sid*he*' against *CIH* 2158.13 'side'.
214.9 'roi*n*dsaig'; Binchy, *CIH* 2158.16 queries the expansion of the final syllable of this word as 'roi*n*dsaig*e*', however, based on a comparison of the gen. sg. form of this word in sources A and LL, the suspension mark over the ⟨g⟩ would appear to be a mistake.

§ **36 218.1** 'n-in*nraic*' against *CIH* 1202.22 and 2005.30 'nin*nraid*' although Binchy, *CIH* 1201, n. i, queries the correct expansion of the final syllable. He also queries the same expansion at *CIH* 2005.30.

218.2 'ꝉ' against *CIH* 2158.20 '⁊'.
218.7 'do' against *CIH* 2158.23 'di'.

§ 38 222.13 '*no*c[h]o' against *CIH* 1556.4 'ɫcho'.

§ 39 224.8 'ce*n*d' against *CIH* 2159.8 'cen*n*'.

§ 48 246.10 'itir' against *CIH* 2161.12 'it*er*'.
246.12 'é' against *CIH* 2161.14 'e'.
248.10 'rot*h*imnast*ar*' against *CIH* 1017.3 'rotimnast*ar*'.

§ 49 250.17 'doratad' against *CIH* 2161.35 'dorata'.

§ 51 258.4 'tic[f]a' against *CIH* 2162.18 'ticfa'.
258.8 'roernith*er*' against *CIH* 2162.22 'roeirnith*er*'.
262.12 'cu tisseat' against *CIH* 1017.22 'cutisseat'.
264.9 'ḟog*h*ul' against *CIH* 1017.34 'foghul'.

§ 54 270.2 'nig*h*t*er*' against *CIH* 2162.29 'nigt*er*'.
270.15 '*acht*' against *CIH* 2163.2 'si*n*'.
270.15 'mane' against *CIH* 2163.2 'maine'.

§ 57 278.3 'ar' against *CIH* 2163.12 'in'.
278.8 'a' *om.* *CIH* 2163.17.

§ 58 284.1 'ainmi' against *CIH* 2163.20 'ainim'. Although the word contains seven minims in a row, the scribe starts each new letter with a much larger serif on the first minim.
284.4 'airdmes' against *CIH* 2163.23 'ardmes'.
284.9 'é' against *CIH* 2163.26 'e'.
284.9 'é' against *CIH* 2163.26 'e'.
284.11 'easbad*h*ac*h*' against *CIH* 2163.27 'easbad*ac*'.
284.11 'sé' against *CIH* 2163.28 'se'.
284.12 'cid*h*' against *CIH* 2163.29 'cid'.
284.12 'cid*h*' against *CIH* 2163.29 'cid'.
284.13 'lec*h*olb' against *CIH* 2163.29 'leccolb'.
284.13 'é' against *CIH* 2163.29 'e'.
284.15 'é' against *CIH* 2163.31 'e'.
284.16 'easbad*h*ac*h*' against *CIH* 2163.32 'easbadach'.
286.10 'dog*h*ab*ar*' against *CIH* 715.33 'dogabar'.

Appendix 2 292.11 'aitfegt*ar*' against CIH 1170.13 'aithfegt*ar*'.

Appendix 3 296.2 '⁊ ai*thgin*' *om.* at CIH 1179.42.

APPENDIX 5

Regarding *Aidbred* 'Claiming'

As mentioned in the Introduction, it had been thought that *Anfuigell* was a much larger tract than it actually is. During the course of editing *Anfuigell*, it became apparent that a new text had begun.[1] Following the end of § 58 in the main MS source, TCD 1387, *olim* H.5.15, on p. 16b21 there is a large decorated initial letter of the size and ornamentation only used in this MS for the start of new texts (see Plate 2 and cf. Plate 1). The decorated initial is the start of a fragment of OI text beginning *Aidbriud ardnemed fola di maigin*, *CIH* 2163.33. *Anfuigell* covers a wide range of subject matter, but starting with the word *aidbriud* and continuing on in TCD MS 1387 to p. 22a5, *CIH* 2173.37, the subject matter is consistently about the legal process of regaining lost or stolen property, and the MS source attestation pattern changes dramatically from *Anfuigell*'s. What we have here is the legal text *Aidbred* 'Claiming'.[2]

The title of a legal text known as *Aidbred* was given in Lynch's 1662 *Cambrensis Eversus*. In chapter 20 Lynch responds to charges made by Gerald of Wales that '*Hibernos "gentem exlegem"*'[3] 'the Irish were a "nation without laws"',[4] and to prove Gerald wrong, Lynch helpfully provides the names and descriptions of several Irish legal texts. One of the titles he gives is *Aidbreatha*, and he tells us that the text is about theft.[5] *Aidbred* is the verbal noun of *ad-fíri* 'claims, sues', but it is also a legal term for the process by which one's stolen property can be regained if found in someone else's possession. Matthew Kelly's translation of Lynch from 1850 is noteworthy for the fact that some of the footnotes in chapter 20 were written by John O'Donovan, who produced a transcription of TCD MS 1387. The footnotes written by O'Donovan have his initials after them. O'Donovan has a footnote on *Aidbreatha* which simply says "copy in H.3.17 and H.3. 18,"[6] which refers, of course, to two of the composite legal manuscripts owned by Trinity College, Dublin. He does not tell us where in these two manuscripts the text can be found.

1 I am currently in the process of preparing a critical edition and translation of the text.

2 The text as we have it in all of the MS sources consists only of fragments of the OI text, but it is accompanied by copious legal commentaries, much like *Anfuigell*.

3 Lynch, *Cambrensis Eversus*, quoted in Kelly's translation, 2: 362.

4 Translated in Kelly, *Cambrensis Eversus*, 2: 363.

5 Kelly, *Cambrensis Eversus*, 2: 369. Lynch appends *breatha* 'judgments' to the end of other titles of legal texts, i.e. *Anfuighilbreatha* = *Anfuigell* and *Ainteachtbreatha* = *Ántéchtae* (*Breth*); the former immediately precedes *Aidbred* in the main MS source, TCD MS 1387, and the latter comes immediately after it.

6 Kelly, *Cambrensis Eversus*, 2: 369, n. k.

 | DOI:10.1163/9789004391987_013

The next mention of *Aidbred* is in 2005 in *CCIH*. Breatnach is aware of Lynch (and Kelly's translation) as he refers to both several times in *CCIH*. In chapter five Breatnach discusses the attested titles of the early Irish legal texts, and he says the following in reference to Lynch's list of legal texts, of which all but two have a separate discussion in his chapter: "the remaining two appear to be corrupt, and since it is unclear what they might be corruptions of they may be noted here."[7] He then quotes Lynch and Kelly on *Aidbred* and says that "the only suggestion I can make is that *Aidbhreatha* might be a corruption of *Gaitbretha*, an otherwise unattested variant of *Bretha im Gatta*, tract 24 of *Senchas Már*."[8] The other title refers to a text on maritime law, which has not been identified or may not even be extant.

To sum up so far, we have a title of a legal text mentioned by Lynch in 1662, O'Donovan in 1850 refers to two MSS which have the text, and Breatnach in 2005 says that the title in Lynch is a corruption. Let us take a closer look at Lynch's list of legal texts. The list contains the following titles found in this order: *Meillbreatha, Fiondsuth, Ainteachtbreatha, Anfuighilbreatha, Fotha mór, Fotha beag, Aidbreatha, Corus fine, Eidgheadh, Dula, Cain Fuithribhe, Cui drubhartaigh bearro, Cain lanamna mór, Cain lanamna beag, Fuidfeinchais*, and *Cain borachtu*. The spellings are those given in Lynch. He mentions other texts in passing, but this is the main list. As Breatnach mentions, we can identify more or less all of these.[9] The question then is: What is Lynch's source for these texts? Where did he get his information? He tells us, in fact, that his source was the antiquary Dubhaltach Mac Fhirbhisigh:

> Vidi ego è plura è pergameno spissa legume Hibernicarum volumina, et in illis textum charactere grandiori conscriptum lineis modice disjunctis faciliori vocum interpretatione minutioribus literis inserta. Uberiora commentaria per paginam diffusa textum obibant eadem omninò ratione qua textum et glossam in libris utriusque juris aspicimus. Ex his superiores titulos ante aliquot annos decerpsit Duvaldus Virbisius.[10]

> I saw a great number of thick volumes of Irish laws, with the text written in large characters, and a large space between the lines, to admit more conveniently in smaller letters a glossary on the meaning of the words. The pages were covered over with copious commentaries, inserted between the text, as are usually seen in compilations of canon or civil law. Some years ago, Duvald Mac Firbis transcribed from these books the titles I have given.[11]

---

7 *CCIH*, 161.

8 *CCIH*, 161–162.

9 *CCIH*, 161.

10 Lynch's text as printed in Kelly, *Cambrensis Eversus*, 2: 374.

11 Kelly, *Cambrensis Eversus*, 2: 375.

Lynch could not have had a better source for his information because Dubhaltach at one point owned all the main manuscripts (other than Egerton 88) where *Aidbred* is found,[12] and O'Donovan is correct that parts of the text are found in H.3.17 and H.3.18.[13]

A list of the main sources for *Anfuigell* 'Wrong Judgment' according to *CCIH*, 164 follows; the numbers refer to pages in *CIH*.

A 2146.15–2173.41, TCD MS 1387 [H.5.15]
B 979.23–980.17, TCD MS 1337 [H.3.18]
C 167.19–170.6, Oxford University, Bodleian Library MS Rawl. B 506
D 984.16–985.23, TCD MS 1337 [H.3.18]
E 1017.1–1018.25, TCD MS 1337 [H.3.18]
F 1269.21–1276.17, BL MS Egerton 88
G 2069.43–2076.20, TCD MS 1336 [H.3.17]

Anfuigell actually has the following main sources:

A 2146.15–2163.32, TCD MS 1387 [H.5.15]
B 979.23–980.17, TCD MS 1337 [H.3.18]
C 167.19–170.6, Oxford University, Bodleian Library MS Rawl. B 506
D 984.16–985.23, TCD MS 1337 [H.3.18]
E 1017.1–1018.25, TCD MS 1337 [H.3.18]

Aidbred 'Claiming' has the following main sources, using the same MS sigla as given in *CCIH*:[14]

A 2163.33–2173.41, TCD MS 1387 [H.5.15]
F 1269.21–1276.17, BL MS Egerton 88
G 2069.43–2076.20, TCD MS 1336 [H.3.17]

12 O'Sullivan, "The Book of Domhnall Ó Duibhdábhoireann," 277; and *idem*, "The Manuscript Collection of Dubhaltach Mac Fhirbhisigh," 439–447.

13 For example, TCD MS 1336 [H.3.17] = *CIH* 2069.43–2076.20 and TCD MS 1337 [H.3.18] = *CIH* 713.4–9.

14 Just as there are many more MS sources for *Anfuigell* than are listed here, there are at least fifteen more sources for material related to *Aidbred*.

O'Davoren's Glossay no. 862(3) and *CIH* 1452.11–24

1) This appendix consists of two citations. The first is no. 862(3) from O'Davoren's Glossary; the text given below is from the BL MS Egerton 88 version, f. 86vb,[1] *CIH* 1499.14–15. *CCIH*, 164 notes that this entry contains a reference to *Anfuigell*. While the other citations from *Anfuigell* from O'Davoren's Glossary have been able to be matched up with the relevant fragment of text, this citation has not.

CIH 1499.14–15. The headword for O'Dav no. 862 is *fuilngenn* 'supporting'.

ł fuilgenn .i. inas na colla, ł ai*thgh*in, am*ail* ader Anfuige*ll*: Fuill*em* ⁊ fuilleth ⁊ fuillgen*n*.[2]

Or *fuilgenn* 'support', i.e. increase of the item pledged, or equivalent, as *Anfuigell* says: Interest and addition and support.

2) The second citation, *CIH* 1452.11–24, is mentioned in *CCIH*, 164 (*CIH* 2003.25–2004.2) and is found in source J, Digest D (32), TCD MS 1336;[3] it is edited as part of §12. The citation at *CIH* 2003.25–2004.2 is included with the *Anfuigell* material because the phrase *Anfuigell sin* 'that is *Anfuigell*' has been written crosswise in the *marg. dext.*[4] Of the six paragraphs of commentary, which are marked at the beginning by the phrase *gné aile* 'another version', only the last paragraph, *CIH* 2003.40–2004.2, is found in the other commentaries in §12 (source A, *CIH* 2152.12–14); the same material is also found at *CIH* 2002.20–21 as part of a marginal note.[5] Despite the material being ascribed to *Anfuigell* in the MS, there is still a degree of uncertainly as to whether all six paragraphs of commentary belong with the other *Anfuigell*-related material. The material from Digest D (32), aside from the last paragraph, is also found in BL MS Egerton 88 embedded within a series of citations with commentaries mainly concerned with distraint (*CIH* 1452.11–24, BL MS Eg. 88, ff. 59vb–60ra).[6] The commentary printed below is in

---

1 The entry is in Maghnus II's hand; O'Sullivan, "The Book of Domhnall Ó Duibhdábhoireann," 292.

2 The text printed here varies from that given in Stokes, "O'Davoren's Glossary," 341. He does not attempt to translate this part of the entry due to its lack of context. The words *fuillgenn* and *fuilngenn* both look like the vn. formed from a later simplex verb derived from *fo-loing* 'supports, maintains, endures, is liable for'. In O'Dav no. 862(1), *fuilgnenn* is glossed by *fo-loing*.

3 Digest D (32) concerns judgments on pledges; *CCIH*, 81.

4 As noted by Binchy, *CIH* 2003, n. p.

5 Binchy, *CIH* 2002, n. h.

6 *CCIH*, 65; and *AL* 1: 276.28–278.14.

 | DOI:10.1163/9789004391987_014

Domhnall's hand.[7] Due to the uncertainty surrounding which text the commentary belongs with, it is edited and translated here.

2) *CIH* 1452.11–24.

G*ach* fuig*ell* cuir ⁊ *conn*art*h*a, ón[a](u) ⁊ ait*h*ní ⁊ airlict*h*i, ⁊ g*ac* ní is nesam toisc*eda*, m*ana* be f*or* diol na sena, is t*r*iang*ille* fri scu*r* troisc*the*, ⁊ l*ethgille* ria mbr*eith*, ⁊ langill*e* iar mbr*eith*.

G*ach* fuig*ell* cuir ⁊ con*nart*ha, ona ⁊ aic*h*ni ⁊ airlict*h*i, ⁊ g*ach* ní nesam toisci, dia mbe f*or* diol ⁊ sena, is sm*acht*gill*e sechtmaid* do scur t*roiscthe*, ⁊ triang*ille* ria mbr*eith*, ⁊ langill*e* iar mbr*eith* br*eit*h*i*.

G*ach* fuig*ell* cuir ⁊ con*n*art*h*a, ona [⁊] aic*h*ni [⁊] airlic*the*, ⁊ gac*h* ni is tan*ais*i nesaim toisci na bi f*or* diol na sena, is sm*achtgille sechtmaid* fri særadh t*roiscthe*, ⁊ triang*ille* ria mbr*eith*, ⁊ l*ethgille* iar mbr*eith*.

G*ach* fuig*ell cuir* ⁊ *cundartha*, *ona* ⁊ a*ithni* ⁊ a*irlicthe*,[8] ⁊ cach ní is tan*ais*e nesaim t*oisceda*,[9] ma bi f*or* diol ⁊ sena, is sm*achtgille* ecin*n*tec*h* da scr*epal déc* fria fuasl*uca* t*roiscthe*, ⁊ sm*achtgille sechtmaid* ria mbr*eith*, ⁊ lang*ille* iar mbr*eith*emn*us*.[10]

Br*eth*a im gad*a* ⁊ tu*r*oirgni ⁊ saraig*h*t*h*i, is aml*aid* is sm*achtgille* ecindtec in da screp*ail déc secht*air ria mbr*eith*em*nus*, ⁊ tria*n*gille bid*h* ite*r* cain ⁊ urr*adus*.

Every judgment of contract and sale, loan and deposit and commercial loan, and every thing which is a necessity of life, if it may not be for discharging a debt or denial, a pledge of one-third is [given] to end fasting, and a pledge of half [is given] before a decision, and [the] full pledge [is given] after a decision.

Every judgment of contract and sale, loan and deposit and commercial loan, and every thing which is a necessity of life, if it may be for discharge of a debt and denial, a penalty pledge of one-seventh is [given] to end fasting, and a pledge of one-third [is given] before a decision, and [the] full pledge after a decision of judgment.

Every judgment of contract and sale, loan and deposit and commercial loan, and every thing which is almost a necessity of life which is not for discharging a debt or denial, a penalty pledge of one-seventh is [given] for freeing from fasting [i.e. to end fasting], and a pledge of one-third [is given] before a decision, and [the] full pledge after a decision.

Every judgment of contract and sale, loan and deposit and commercial loan, and every thing which is almost a necessity of life, if it may be for discharging a debt or

---

7 O'Sullivan, "The Book of Domhnall Ó Duibhdábhoireann," 291.

8 See also Binchy, *CIH* 1452, nn. h–l.

9 I follow the editorial suggestion made by Binchy, *CIH* 1452, n. m.

10 The scribe has made an erroneous suspension mark for ⟨n⟩ over the second ⟨m⟩; see also Binchy, *CIH* 1452, n. n.

denial, an indefinite penalty pledge of twelve scruples is [given] for releasing him from fasting, and a penalty pledge of one-seventh [is given] before a decision, and [the] full pledge after judgment.

Judgments regarding thefts and plunderings and violations, it is the same as an indefinite penalty pledge of twelve scruples [given] as well before judgment, and a pledge of one-third is for both promulgated law and customary law.

Glossary

The organization of the following glossary is modeled on that in Fergus Kelly's *Marriage Disputes*, which, like *Anfuigell*, is a fragmentary OI legal text with copious commentaries. Due to the fragmentary nature of the OI text of *Anfuigell*, it is not always possible to determine a word's part of speech with certainty. The headwords (and most definitions) are given as they appear in *eDIL*, when present. Otherwise, they are given in the nom. sg. for nouns. The nom. sg. form is not given when it is orthographically identical to the headword. The words themselves are listed as found in the text and/or commentary. The numbers refer to the sections of text. The glossary contains all of the words found in the OI text along with words of legal or linguistic interest; the glossary is not comprehensive for the commentaries. For each noun, the OI gender is given, when known. When a word is found in the OI text, the section number is given in **bold**; when it is found in the commentary, the section number is followed by the MS siglum.

.i. *ed ón* 'that is': 20

ł *nó* 'or': 20

⁊ *ocus* 'and': *passim*

1 a poss. pron.: 3 sg. m./n. leniting **4**, **21**, **57**

2 a prep. with dat. 'out of, from': with 3 sg. m./n. affixed object agreement marker *as* **1**

ab f. 'river': gen. sg. *abhann* 55E

achtaigid 'stipulates as a condition': perf. ind. 3 sg. *roachtaiged* 10A, 10J, 12A, *roachtaigh* 10J, *nar achtaiged* 10A, *nar achtaigh*[ed] 10J, *manar achtaiged* 12A; perf. ind. 3 pl. *roachtaigit* 10A

adaltrach f. 'concubine': gen. sg. *adhaltraig* 51E, *adaltraige* 51E, *adaltraigi* 51E, *adhaltraigi* 51E, 51T, *adhaltraidhe* 51T, *adhaltraighi* 51T

ad-fíri 'sues, claims': pres. ind. pass. sg. *-aidhbred* 23F: later simplex *aidbrid*, perf. ind. 3 sg. *roaidbriustar* 26A

ad-gair 'sues, prosecutes, accuses': pres. ind. pass. sg. *-acairther* **1**; past subj. pass. sg. -[a]*carthi* 1A

áer f. 'satire': acc. sg. *air* 49A, 49M

áerad vn. of *áeraid* 'satirizing': gen. sg. *ærtha* 49A

áesclad 'cleansing, washing': nom. sg. *aesclad* 54O'Dav; dat. sg. *æsclad* **54**, *aesclad* 54O'Dav

aidbred m. vn. of *ad-fíri* 'suing, claiming': dat. sg. *aidbrig* 21A, *aidhbriud* 23F, *aidbriud* 26A

aigne m. 'advocate, lawyer': nom. sg. *aighne* 6B

aile adj. 'other, another': m. acc. sg. subst. *araile* **57**

áilges f. 'request, demand': nom. sg. *ailges* 39A, *ailgius* 39A; acc. sg. *ailgius* 39A; dat. sg. *ailges* 39A

áilgesach adj. 'importunate': nom. sg. *ailgesach* **39**

ainfine 'stranger kindred': acc. sg. *ainfine* 7A, 7J, *anfine* 7A; acc. du. *anfine* 7A, 7J, *ainfine* 7J

ainim f. 'blemish, defect': nom. sg. 58A, 58D; gen. sg. *ainmi* 58D; acc. pl. *ainmi* 58, *ainme* 58A

ainmrainde m. 'designated fraction, proportion, fixed amount': nom. sg. 1A, 22A, *ainmrainne* 8HH

airbertnaigid 'pleads': perf. ind. 3 pl. rel. *roairbertnaigestar* 57D, *roairbertnaigetar* 57D

airchell vn. of *ar-cel(l)a* 'taking away, stealing, theft, robbery': gen. sg. *aircella* 27

airchinnech m. 'monastic superior': nom. sg. *airchindeach* 6B

aircsiu vn. of *ar-aicci* 'culpable looking on, looking for legal protection': nom. sg. *aircsi* 8A, 8I, *airgsi* 8A, *aircse* 8B, *airicsi* 8I, *aircsiu* 8HH; acc. sg. *airgsi* 8A

1 **aire** m. 'noble, lord': **aire échta** 'lord of slaughter': nom. sg. *aire echta* 49A, 49M: **aire forgill** 'lord of superior testimony': nom. sg. 6B

2 **aire** n. vn. of *ar-fen* 'dam, weir': nom. sg. 55, 55O'Dav; dat. sg. *aire* 55O'Dav

airgalach adj. 'combative, warlike': acc. sg. *uargalach* 33

airlámas m. 'custody, possession': gen. sg. *urlamais* 12A, *urlamhais* 12J

airlicud m. vn. of *ar-léici* 'borrowing, commercial loan': acc. sg. *airlegud* 12A; gen. sg. *airlicthi* 1A, 12A, *airliccthi* 12C, *airlicthe* 12J, *airlice* 12J, *airligthe* 12J

airnaidm n. vn. of *air-naisc* 'binding, guarantee, bond': nom. sg. *aurnaidm* 46; acc. sg. *urnaidm* 45

airrach n. 'forced loan, requisition': gen. sg. *erraig* 12A, *errigh* 12C

aiscid f. vn. of *ad-saig* 'gift, present, gratis': dat. sg. *aiscid* 22O, 51E, 51T

aithne n./f. 'depositing, entrusting': dat. sg. *aithne*, *athne* 1A; gen. sg. *aithne* 1A, 12A, 12J, *aithni* 1A; dat. pl. *aithnedaib* 1A

aitire f. 'hostage-suretyship, hostage-surety': nom. sg. 10A, 10J, 11A, 20 A, 20J; acc. sg. *aitire* 10a, 10J, 20; gen. sg. *aitire* 10, 10A, 10J, 20J

aitires 'hostage-suretyship': acc. sg. *aitirius* 10A

aititiu f. vn. of *ad-daim* 'acknowledgement': nom. sg. 47A; dat. sg. *aititin* 47, 47A

allmuir m. '(in pl.) imported goods': gen. pl. *allmuire* 38

almsa f. 'alms': acc. pl. *almsana* 52D

altóir f. 'altar': dat. sg. *altoir* 8A

altram(m) m. vn. of *ailid* 'nurturing, fosterage': nom. sg. *altram* 25A

amus m. 'attendant, hireling': gen. pl. *amus* 57

anfocal n. 'misrepresentation': nom. sg. 48A, *anfocul* 48A; dat. sg. *anfocul* 54E; gen. sg. *anfoccail* 48C, *anḟoccail* 48C

anfót m. 'negligence, inadvertence': nom. sg. *anfoit* 3E, *anfot* 54A

anfuigell 'wrong judgment, wrong decision, wrong submitting to judgment, non-judgment':[1] nom. sg. 1, 1O'Dav; dat. sg. heading B

anmain f. vn. of *anaid* 'staying, waiting': acc. sg. *anmai(m)*[n] 22A

1 The definition 'wrong submitting to judgment' is suggested in *CCIH*, 164.

anurrad 'outlaw': nom. pl. *anurraid* 9A

ár m. 'slaughter, destruction': nom. sg. *ar* 33A; gen. sg. *air* 33

árach n. 'binding, guarantee': acc. sg. 30, *arach* 30, 30A

árbach n. 'slaughter, carnage': nom. sg. *arbach* 34

argat n. 'silver': nom. sg. *airgeth* 29A

as-ren 'pays': pres. ind. 3 pl. with class B n. object agreement marker *atrenat* 9AA; pres. ind. pass. sg. *isrenur* 8

astaithe vbl. of nec. from *ad-suidi* 'to be secured': *fastaithi* 2R, *fastaidthe* 47A

athgabáil f. vn. of *ad-gaib* 'distraint': acc./dat. *athgabail* 54A, 54D;[2] dat. sg. *athgabail* 54A

athgait 'revoking, withholding a legacy (?)': nom. sg. 48, 48A

at-tá substantive verb 'there is': pres. ind. imper. sg. *atathar* 21A

attach n./m. vn. of *ad-teich* 'pleading, refuge': nom. sg. *atach* 8A, 8B, 8I, 8HH; acc. sg. *attach* 8A

aurradus m. 'native law, customary law': acc. sg. *urradus* 12J; gen. sg. *urradais* 17

aurrae, aurrad 'a person native to a particular area, native freeman': nom. pl. *urraid* 57D

baccach adj. 'lame': nom. sg. *bacach* 58A

bach vn. of *boingid* 'breaking': nom. sg. 2A

baítsech f. 'harlot, woman of indiscriminate morals': nom. sg. 51E, *baítsec* 51T

barc f. 'ship': nom. sg. 22A; gen. sg. *bairce* 22A, 22O, 29, *bairci* 22O

bé n-indles 'kept woman': dat. sg. *mnai indlis* 18A

beirid 'carries, brings, judges': pres. subj. 3 pl. with class C n. object agreement affix *nodberat* 9AA

belach n. 'gap, pass (between hills)': nom. sg. *beloch* App1C

bélrae n. 'law, legal enactments, (language of the) law': dat. sg. *berla* 51T

ben f. 'woman': nom. sg. 51A, 51E, 51T; dat. sg. *mnai* 51A, 51C; gen. sg. *mna* 25, 47A

bésgnae 'custom, law, protocol': nom. sg. *besgna* 6C

bibdu m. 'defendant, other party to a contract': nom. sg. *bidba* 2A, 20J, 34O, *biudbad* 2I, *bidbaid* 20A; acc. sg. *bidbaid* 20A; dat. sg. *bidbaid* 2A, 4J, 20J, 34O, 40A,[3] *biudbad* 2I, *bidhbaid* 20J

blaí f. 'exemption, immunity': nom. sg. *bla* 1A

blíadain f. 'year': dat. sg. *bliadna* 7

bó f. 'cow': gen. pl. *bo* 34

borblachas m. 'violence': gen. sg. *borblachais* 8A, 8I, 52A, 52D

brága 'hostage, prisoner, captive': dat. sg. *braighet* 51T

bran m. 'raven': nom. sg. 1O'Dav

brangaire 'raven's cry': nom. sg. 1, 1O'Dav

breth f. vn. of *beirid* 'judgment, judging, legal ruling, decision': nom. sg.

2 The case is ambiguous following the prep. *for*, which governs both the acc. and dat. cases.

3 This form could be the acc. sg. as well because the prep. *for* governs both the acc. and dat. cases, and the form of *bibdu* would be the same in either.

30, 49A, *breath* 30; dat. sg. *breith* 12J; gen. sg. *breithe* 12J; nom. pl. *breatha* 12J; gen. pl. *breath* 1, *breth* 1O'Dav

breithem m. 'judge': dat. sg. *brethemain* 30A, 30JJ; gen. sg. *breitheman* 1A, *bretheman* 30A, *breithem* 30JJ

breithemnas m. 'judgment': nom. sg. *bretheamnus* 42A; acc. sg. *brethemnus* 42A; dat. sg. *breithemhnus* 12J

briugu m. 'hospitaller': nom. sg. 6B

bris(s)ed m. vn. of *bris(s)id* 'breaking': nom. sg. *brised* 2A

buidech adj. 'pleasing, sated': dat. sg. *buidhec* 42A

búrach n. 'attack': nom. sg. *burach* 36

cach pronominal adj. 'each, every': m. nom. sg. 21; dat. sg. *cach* 36; gen. sg. *caich* 8

cáech adj. 'blind in one eye': nom. sg. *caech* 58A, 58P

cáin f. 'promulgated law': nom. sg. *cain* 19A, 19N; acc. sg. *cain* 12J; gen. sg. *cana* 19A, 19N

caíned m. vn. of *caínid* 'keening, lamenting, wake': dat. sg. *cainiud* 3A, *cained* 3A, *cainudh* 3C, *cainiudh* 3C; gen. sg. *cainti* 3A

cairde n. 'pact, covenant, general law': nom. sg. 19A, *cairdi* 19N; gen. sg. *cairde* 19A, *cairdi* 19N

cath m. 'battle, fight': acc. sg. *cath* 1; gen. sg. *catha* 1, 1O'Dav

céilsine f. 'clientship': nom. sg. *celsine* 24A

cell f. 'church, monastic community': acc./dat. *cill* 52, 52D;[4] acc. sg. *cill* 52D; gen. sg. *cilli* 54D, *cille* 54D

cen prep. with acc., leniting, 'without': 30, 45, 46, *cin* 20, *gin* 30

certdúas 'proper reward': nom. sg. *certduais* 49A

cethracha num. m. 'forty': gen. pl. *cethorchat* 7

cétmuinter 'spouse, wife': nom. sg. *cetmuindter* 53, *cétmuinnter* 53A, *cétmuindter* 53D, *cetmuinter* 53E; gen. sg. *cetmuindtire* 51E, *cetmuintire* 51E, 51T, *cetmuinntiri* 51T

1 cía indef. pron. 'whatever': 1, 5

2 cía conj. 'though, although': 8, 36

cin m. 'guilt, crime, liability, payment': nom. sg. 15; acc. sg. *cin* 51E; acc. pl. *cintu* 51T; dat. pl. *cintaib* 50A; gen pl. *cinad* 51E, *cinadh* 51T

clann f. 'offspring, child': nom. sg. 51E, 51T, *cland* 51E; acc. sg. *cland* 51E

clúm f. 'feathers, down': nom. pl. *cluma* 29A

cnú f. 'nut': nom. pl. *cno* 22O, 29A

codnach m. 'sensible adult, legally competent person': nom. sg. 3A, *codhnach* 3C; gen. sg. *codnaig* 47A; nom. pl. *codnaig* 3A, *codhnaidh* 3E; gen. pl. *codnach* 3C

coibche f. 'bride-price': nom. sg. *coibchi* 25A, 53E; acc. sg. *coibchi* 51E, 51T, *coibche* 51E, *coibqe* 51T; gen. sg. *coibchi* 25A

coibdelach m./f. 'relative': dat. pl. *coibdelchaib* 51T, *coibhdealchaib* 51T

coibdelachus n. 'relationship': gen. sg. *coibhdelchius* 51T

cóictach adj. 'having fifties, in fifty, fifty-fold': gen. pl. *coecdach* 7

4 The case could be either acc. or dat. sg.; the prep. *for* governs both cases.

cóir adj. 'proper, correct, just': m. nom. sg. *coir* 4, 30

collud vn. of *coillid* 'violating, infringing': nom. sg. 8

comaithches m. 'neighborhood relationship': gen. sg. *comichius*[a] 41A

comaithech adj. 'belonging to a neighbor': m. gen. pl. subst. *comaithech* 58A, 58D, *comaitheach* 58C

comar m. 'joint-plowing': gen. sg. *comair* 41A

comardad vn. of *comardaid* 'balancing of liabilities': nom. sg. 35LL, *comarda*[d] 10A

comardugud m. vn. of *comardaigid* 'balancing of claims': nom. sg. 8A, 10J, 16A, 17A, 28A, 34A, 35A, *comhardugudh* 17C, *comardughugh* 17C

combach n. vn. of *con-boing* 'breaking, cutting, destroying': nom. sg. 2, 2A, 2I

combrised m. vn. of *combrisid* 'mutual breaking': nom. sg. *combrissed* 2A

comḟer 'partner, companion, occupier (?)': nom. sg. *comfer* 26

comlécad 'lapse equally (?)': nom. sg. *comlecud* 17A, *coimhlechud* 17C

comlogad 'mutual concession, balancing of mutual liabilities': dat. sg. *comlogud* 49A

commaín 'exchange, hire': acc. sg. *comain* 12A; gen. sg. *comaine* 12A

commairge f. 'protection, sanctuary': nom. sg. *comairce* 52D, 57D, 57E, *cumairci* 57D; acc. sg. *comairci* 52A, 57A, 57H, *comairce* 52D, 57D, 57E, *comargi* 57C, *comairche* 57E; acc./dat. *comairce* 57A, 57E, *cumairche* 57E, *comairche* 57E;[5] dat. sg. *cumairce* 57D; gen. sg. *comairgi* 57A

condall m. 'assembly (?)': nom. sg. 7

connad n. 'firewood': acc. sg. *connad* 22O

cora f. 'fence, weir': dat. pl. *corthaib* 55E

corn m. 'horn, drinking horn': nom. pl. *cuirnd* 22O, *cuirn* 29A

coscrad m. vn. of *con-scara* 'disturbing, breaking apart, destroying': nom. sg. 32

crech f. 'plundering expedition, raid': nom. sg. 17A, *creac* 17C; acc. sg. *crech* 17A, 17II; gen. sg. *crecha* 17, *creiche* 17A, *creche* 17A, *creichi* 17C

cre(i)cc f. 'buying, selling': gen. sg. *creca* 23F

crích f. 'territory': dat. sg. *crich* 16

crín adj. 'old, withered, decrepit': nom. sg. *crin* 58A, 58P

cú m. 'hound, dog': gen. sg. *con* 13

cundrad m. 'condition, contract, commerce, sale': acc. sg. 2A, *cundradh* 2B, *cunnrad* 2I; gen. sg. *cunnarta* 12A, *cunnarrta* 12J

dám f. 'retinue, company, party': acc. pl. *daimhi* 45C

dásachtach adj. 'foolish, imprudent': m. nom. sg. subst. 'violent lunatic' *dasachtach* 40; m. gen. sg. subst. *dasachtaig* 47A

dechmad f. 'tithe': acc. pl. *dechmada* 52D

deithbires m. 'just or reasonable cause, necessity': nom. sg. *dethbirius* 12A

5 The case is ambiguous because the prep. *ar* (for *for*) can govern either case.

deorad m. 'exile, outlaw, stranger, outsider, pilgrim, mercenary': nom. sg. 57, 57A; nom. pl. *deoraid* 57D; acc. pl. *deorada* 45A; dat. pl. *deoradaib* 45A, *deoradhaibh* 45C; gen. pl. *deorad* 45A, *deoradh* 45C: **deorad Dé** 'exile of God': nom. sg. 5A, 5B

derbḟine f. 'true kin': acc. sg. *derbfine* 7A, 7J, *derbhfine* 7J, *deirbhfine* 7K

díanṡárugud 'forcible violation': nom. sg. *diansarugud* 8A, 8I

díchennad m. vn. of *díchennaid* 'beheading, decapitation': nom. sg. *dichennad* 33A; acc. sg. *dichennad* 33A; dat. sg. *dichennad* 33A

díchmairc 'without permission': gen. sg. *dichmairce* 51T

dígal f. vn. of *do-fich* 'revenge, vengeance': acc. sg. *digail* 49A, 49M

díguin n. vn. of *do-guin* 'violation of a man's protection through the wounding or slaying of another': nom. sg. *diguin* 8A, 57; dat. sg. *diguin* 8, 57; gen. sg. *digona* 57

díl m. vn. of *do-lá* 'discharging, satisfying a debt, recompense': acc. sg. *dil* 12J, *díl* 12J

díles adj. 'forfeited to (*do*), forfeited by (*ó*), not liable to penalty, immune from legal consequences, appropriate, proper, lawful': m. nom. sg. *diles* 1, 1A, 5, 9AA, 9JJ, 36, *dilis* 35

dílse f. 'property, right, claim, forfeiture, security': nom. sg. *dilsi* 1A, 8, 12A; acc. sg. *dilsi* 2A, 2I, 30

dílsech m. 'outlaw, culprit': nom. sg. 8A, *dilsec* 8L; dat. sg. *dilsech* 8A, *dilsich* 8I; gen. sg. *dilsig* 16A; nom. pl. *dilsig* 8A, *dilsigh* 8HH

dílsigid 'makes forfeit, gives up, hands over to': pres. ind. 3 pl. *dilsigit* 24A

dindell 'annulling, canceling': nom. sg. *deindill* 31, 31A, *deinnell* 31R

díthle n. vn. of *do-tlen* 'theft, stealing': gen. sg. *dithli* 56

dligid 'is entitled to, is owed, deserves, is bound to': pres. ind. 3 sg. *-dlig* 57; past. subj. 3 sg. *-dlesid* 44A

do prep. with dat., leniting, 'to, for': 4, 7, 8, 36, 51, 53, 54; with art. sg.: *don* **heading** (here confused with the prep. *di* 'of, from'); with poss. 3 sg. pron.[6] *dia* 20

do-áirci 'induces, brings about, leads, conducts': perf. ind. 3 sg. *rotairgestar* 3A, *rathairgestar* 3C

do-airret 'overtakes, catches, seizes': pres. ind. pass. sg. *-tarthithar* 16A; perf. ind. 3 pl. *rotairsit* 16A; cond. ind. pass. sg. *-tairfida* 29A, *-tairfidea* 29A: from later simplex *tar(r)thid*: pres. ind. 3 sg. *tartaigh* 26P, *tarraid* 58A

do-alla 'steals, takes away, removes': later simplex *tallaid*: pret. ind. pass. sg. *tallad* 23F, 58A, 58P, *talla*[d] 58P

do-beir 'gives, places, brings, gets, takes out': pres. ind. pass. sg. *-tucthar* 1

do-boing 'exacts, wrests, levies, recovers, takes': pres. subj. 3 sg. with class

---

6 The gender of the poss. pron. is ambiguous; the m. and f. forms are identical, and there is no obvious antecedent in the clause.

A 3 sg m. or n. object agreement marker *da-ba* 34[7]

dochonn m. 'simpleton': gen. sg. *dochiunn* 47A

dochor m. 'unfair or disadvantageous contract': nom. sg. *dochur* 41A; nom. pl. *dochair* 41A

do-ecmaing 'happens, occurs': imp. subj. 3 sg. *-tecmad* 3A, *-teccmadh* 3C

do-fairget 'proffers, offers': from later simplex *tairсid*: perf. ind. 3 sg. *rotaircedh* 3E

do-gní 'does': perf. ind. pass. rel. 3 sg. *-dernaiter* 4

do-guin 'violates, outrages': pres. ind. pass. sg. *-digonur* 8

do-icc 'comes': pres. ind. imper. pass. 3 sg. *-teacar* 4R; imp. subj. 3 pl. *dotisdais* 2A

do-immoirg 'compels, enforces, drive': pres. ind. 3 sg. *-timairgind* 12A; perf. ind. 3 sg. *dothimairc* [for *ro-thimairc*] 22A

do-indnaig 'grants, bestows, delivers': perf. ind. 3 sg. *rotidnaic* 28A

doírad m. vn. of *doíraid* 'taking captive': nom. sg. *doerad* 50

do-roich 'arrives, comes, returns': past. subj. 3 sg. *-torsat* 48A, *-toirset* 48A, 48E, *-toirseat* 48E

do-slí 'deserves, merits, is entitled to': pres. ind. 3 sg. *dosli* 8

do-tét 'comes, comes to, accrues to': cond. ind. 3 sg. *dorechad* 44A

do-tuit 'falls, perishes, is killed': pres. ind. 3 sg. *dotuit* 1; pres. ind. 3 sg. rel. *toites* (from later simplex *tuitid*) 1A

drúth m. 'imbecile, fool': gen. sg. *druith* 47A

dúas f. 'gift, reward (especially given to a poet)': nom. sg. *duais* 49A; gen. sg. *duaise* 49

duine m. 'person': nom. sg. 3

duine-chaithig 'trespass committed by a person, human-trespass': gen. sg. *dunacaithe* 11A, *duinechaichthi* 11C, *duinechaithe* 12A, *duinecaichthi* 12C

dúnad m. 'fort, residence': gen. sg. *dunaid* 39

éccodnach m. 'non-sensible adult, legally incompetent person': nom. sg. *ecodnach* 3A, *ecodhnach* 3C; nom. pl. *ecodnaig* 3A, *eccodnaig* 3E

ech m. 'horse': gen sg. *eich* 38A, 38I

echtrann adj. 'strange, foreign, external': n. acc. pl. *echtrann*[a] 20

ecor m. vn. of *in-cuirethar* 'making entry': nom. sg. 11, 27

eisinnraic adj. 'untrustworthy, not qualified to perform certain legal functions': m. nom. sg. subst. *esinraic* 21A; m. dat. sg. subst. *esinraic* 21A

éislinn adj. 'unsafe, dangerous': m. acc. sg. *eis(in)lind* App1C

élúd m. 'evasion, elopement': nom. sg. *elud* 4; acc. sg. *elod* 2A, 2I; dat. sg. *elud* 51T

en 'water': gen. sg. *ena* 5

enechrucce m. 'compensation for dishonor done to a relative or tenant': nom. sg. *enechruice* 18

7 The identification of this verbal form is uncertain.

eneclann m./f. 'honor-price, compensation for insult, loss or injury':[8] nom. sg. 8L, 9A, 17A, 18A, 28A, 32A, 32O, 32T, 44A, 50A, 51E, 51T, 53E, 54A, 54D, 57D, App1C; acc. sg. *ineclainn* 2A, *eneclainn* 2I, 28A, *eneclann* 51E; dat. sg. *eneclainn* 8HH, *enecclainn* 8HH, *eneclann* 8HH; gen. sg. *eneclainne* 8L, 8HH, 32O, 32T, 57C, 57D, 57E, 57H, *eneclainni* 9A, 28A, 32A, 32O, 32T, 36A, 57A, 57D

epscop m. 'bishop': nom. sg. 6B

éric, éraic f. '*wergeld*, fine, penalty': nom. sg. *eraic* 34A, 49A, *eraicc* 48C; acc. sg. *eraic* 1A, 3A, 24A, 48A, 52, 52D, 56A, 56D, *eraicc* 48C

ernaid 'pays': pres. ind. pass. 3 sg. *-erenar* 37

esba(e) m. 'uselessness, folly': acc. sg. *easpa* 53E; dat. sg. *espa* 9A; gen. sg. *espa* 9A, *esba* App1C

escop 'a large vessel or measure for wine': nom. sg. *escup* 22O, *escob* 29A

etarscarthach adj. 'separable, property sufficient for independence': nom. sg. 51A, 51C, 51T, *etarscarach* 51A, *etarscartach* 51T, *etarscartac* 51T

etarscarthae adj. 'separated': nom. sg. *etarscartha* 51C

etla f. 'repentance, penance': nom. sg. 56

étrebaire f. 'non-security, without guarantee': dat. sg. *etrebaire* 15A, *etrebairi* 15M

fál m. 'fence, legal barrier': nom. sg. *fal* 28A, 55O'Dav

féchem m. 'claimant, debtor': acc. sg. *féchem*[ain] 20, *féchemain* 20, *feichemain* 20J; gen. sg. *feicheman* 20J; dat. du. *fechemnaib* 30A; dat. pl. *fechemnaib* 2A: **féchem toicheda** 'plaintiff': nom. sg. *fechem toicheda* 2A, *feichem toicheda* 2I, *feichemh toicheda* 20J; dat. sg. *fechemain toicheda* 2A, 46A, *feichemain toicheda* 2I, 20J, 34O

fedb f. 'widow': nom. sg. 51

fénechas m. 'native customary law': acc. sg. *fen*[e]*chus* heading B

fer m. 'man': gen. sg. *fir* 15: **fer amuig** 'plaintiff': nom. sg. 49A; acc. sg. *fer amuig* 54A; dat. sg. *fir amuig* 49A, 58P: **fer comgníma** 'accomplice': nom. sg. *fer comgnima* 45A, *fear coimgnimha* 45C: **fer léiginn** 'lector, head of a monastic school': nom. sg. *fer leighind* 6B: **fer táircthe** 'inciter': nom. sg. *fer taircthi* 45A, *fer tairc*[t]*hi* 45A, *fear taircthi* 45C

feraid 'provides, performs, does': fut. ind. rel. 3 sg. *ferfus* 24A; pret./perf. ind. pass. sg. *roferustar* 24A

fíach m. 'fine, penalty, liability': nom. sg. *fiach* 1O'Dav, 13, 25; acc. sg. *fiach* 57; gen. pl. *fiach* 28

fíada m. 'witness': acc. pl. *fiadna* 20

fíanlach, fíallach m. 'warband, troop of warriors, *fían*-band': nom. sg. *fiallach* 1A; nom. pl. *fiallaig* 9A

fili m. 'poet': nom. sg. 6B, 50A; gen. sg. *filed* 50

fín m. 'wine': nom. sg. *fin* 22O, 29A; gen. sg. *fina* 22O, 29A, *fine* 29A

8 Compounds such as *láneneclann* 'full honor-price' and *letheneclann* 'half honor-price' are not included in the Glossary.

fiurt m. 'miracle': acc. sg. *fert* 5A; acc. du. *fert* 5A; acc. pl. *ferta* 5A, 5B

flaith f. 'ruler, lord': gen. sg. *flatha* 42, 55, 55O'Dav

fo-ácaib 'leaves, relinquishes': pres. ind. pass. sg. -*facabar* 1, -*fagabar* 5

fobrithe 'sub-award, payment': nom. sg. *fobraithe* 29

fochraic f. vn. of *fo-cren* 'rent, payment, compensation': acc. sg. *focraic* 12A, *fochraicc* 12C; gen. sg. *focraice* 12A, *focreca* 12A, *focrecca* 12A, *fochraicce* 12C

fochsal m. vn. of *fo-coisle* 'abduction': nom. sg. *foxul* 51A, *foxail* 51E, *foxal* 51T; gen. sg. *foxu*[i]*l* 51A, *focsail* 51E, *foxail* 51E

fodail f. vn. of *fo-dáli* 'part, share, portion, category': gen. sg. *fogla* 9A; dat. pl. *foglaib* 58D

fodb n. 'spoils, generally of clothing or equipment, taken from the dead': nom. sg. 54, 54O'Dav.

folud n./m. 'substance, wealth, property': acc. sg. *folaid* 11

for prep. with acc. or dat. 'on, among, by': 52

forcor m. vn. of *for-cuirethar* 'rape by violence': nom. sg. *forcur* 8HH

forflaith f. 'ruler, overlord, overlordship': gen. sg. *forbflatha* 24, *forbflaithe* 43

forgell m. vn. of *for-gella* 'bearing witness, testimony': dat. sg. *forgell* 20

forloscud m. vn. of *for-loisci* 'burning, committing arson': acc. sg. *forloscad* 36A

fortacht f. vn. of *for-tét* 'help, benefit': nom. sg. 12

for-toing 'proves by oath, over-swears, attests': pres. ind. 3 sg. *fortoing* 30A, 30JJ; pres. ind. pass. sg. -*fortongar* 30A, 30JJ

foth n./m. 'right, title, claim': nom. sg. *fod* 21, 22, 23, *foth* 23F

fothaigid 'proves, finds, establishes': pres. ind. pass. sg. -*fothaigther* 21

forus n. 'enforcement': acc. sg. *forus* 46

fretech n. vn. of *fris-toing* 'repudiate': nom. sg. *freiteach* 53E; dat. sg. *fretech* 53; gen. sg. *freitig* 53E

frithaigid vn. of *fris-saig* 'counter-plea': acc. sg. *frithaigid* 16A, 17A, 35A, 35LL, [ḟ]*rithoighidh* 17C; dat. sg. *frithaigid* 16A

frithguin m. 'counter-wounding, counter-slaying, resisting an attack, attacking in retaliation': nom. sg. 35

fúaitriud m. vn. of *fúaitrid* 'impugn, claim': nom. sg. *fuaitred* 47A;[9] dat. sg. *fuaitred* 47A, *fuaidred* 48A

fúaslucad m. vn. of *fúaslaici* 'redeeming, releasing': dat. sg. *fuaslucud* 12J

fúasnad m. vn. of *fo-fúasna* 'objection': nom. sg. *fuasnad* 47

fúatach n. vn. of **fuataing* 'carrying off, abducting': nom. sg. *fuatach* 51T; gen. sg. *fuataigh* 51T

9 If this word originally formed part of the OI text, it would be in the dat. sg.; the form *fuaitred* is attested for the nom. sg. elsewhere; *eDIL s.v. fúaitriud.*

fubthad m. vn. of *fo-botha* 'scare away, frighten': acc. sg. *fubhtadh* App1C, *fubhtad* App1C

fuigell m. 'decision, judgment, sentence': nom. sg. 12J; dat. sg. *fuigell* 1A; gen. sg. *fuigill* 30A

fuillem m. vn. of *fo-slí* 'profit, interest': acc. sg. *fuillem* 12A; dat. sg. *fuillem* 12A; gen. sg. *fuillmeda* 12A, *fuilliuma* 12C

gáir f. 'call, shout, cry': dat. sg. *gair* 8

gait f. vn. of *gataid* 'theft, stealing, that which is stolen': gen. sg. *gaite* 9A, 12A, 12J, 24A, 29A, 48A, 49A, *gaide* 9A, *goti* 9C, 12C, *goiti* 12C, *gaiti* 49M, 51T, *gaitte* 51E, *goitti* App1C; acc. pl. *gada* 12J

galar n. 'sickness, disease': nom. sg. 15A, 15M, 51T, *galur* 15A; dat. sg. *galar* 3A; gen. sg. *galair* 3C

gataige m. 'thief': nom. sg. *gataighe* 51E, *gataigi* 51T

gáu f. 'falsehood, misstatement': nom. sg. *guugud* 4

gelḟine f. 'bright kindred': nom. sg. *gelfine* 7A, 7J; acc. sg. 7A, *gelfine* 7A, 7J, *gelḟini* 7A, *geilfine* 7J, 7K, *gelfini* 7J; acc. du. *gelfine* 7A, 7J, *gelfini* 7A, *geilfine* 7J, *geilfini* 7K

gell n. 'pledge': nom. sg. 9; dat. sg. *gill* 28A; gen. sg. *gill* 12A, 12J; nom. du. 30A; nom. pl. *gella* 30A

gíall m. 'hostage, pledge': acc. pl. *gialla* 24A

gnás f. 'intercourse': dat. sg. *gnais* 51T

gonaid 'kills, wounds': pres. subj. 3 sg. *rogona* 36

gúairiugud vn. of *ar-íada* 'false imprisonment': nom. sg. *guaire* 8A

guba m./n. 'lamenting, mourning': nom. sg. 3A; dat. sg. *guba* 3E, gen. sg. *guba* 3

gúbreth 'false judgement': nom. sg. *gubreth* 49A; gen. sg. *gubreithe* 49A

i prep. with acc. or dat., nasalizing, 'into, in, for, regarding': with acc. *a* 1, 4; with dat. 15, 57; with 3 sg. m./n. object agreement marker *ann* 'in it, there, then' 1, 5, 8

íar prep. with dat., nasalizing, 'after, according to': 8, 47

íarfine f. 'after-kin': acc. sg. *iarfine* 7A, 7J, 7K

íarn m. 'iron': nom. sg. *iarnn* 22O

íarnach adj. 'made of iron': m. nom. sg. *iarnach* 29A

íarrath m. 'fosterage-fee': nom. sg. *iarrad* 25A; acc. sg. *iarraid* 37; dat. sg. *iarrad* 25A

íasc m. 'fish': nom. sg. *iasc* 55A, 55E; gen. sg. *eisc* 55, 55E, 55O'Dav, *eisci* 55O'Dav

imbe n. vn. of *imm-fen* 'fencing': nom. sg. *ime* 55O'Dav; dat. sg. *ime* 55A, 55O'Dav

imdegail f. vn. of *imm-dích* 'protection, defense, protecting': nom. sg. 10

imm prep. with acc., leniting, 'regarding': with rel. pron. *ima* 8

immarchor n. vn. of *imm-archuirethar* 'carrying, removal': dat. sg. *imarchur* 3A, 3E, *imarcur* 3A, *imcur* 3C, *imuchur* 3C

immarsloinned m. 'misnaming, wrong designation': nom. sg. *imor*[ṡ]*lonn*[ed] 9A, *imar*[ṡ]*lonned* 9A, *imar*[ṡ]*lonn*[ed] 9A; acc. sg. *imarsloinned* 9AA

imna n. vn. of *imm-ánai* 'gift, bequest, technical term for a testamentary disposition made in full bodily health': gen. sg. *imna* 48, 48A

imraichne f. 'error, mistake': nom. sg. 9A; acc. sg. *imraichne* 9AA

imthuillid vn. of *imm-tuilli* 'increasing': dat. sg. *imtuilled* 58A, *imthuilled* 58P

1 **in** def. art. 'the': m. gen. sg. *in* 8

2 **in** interrog. part.: used in dependent questions, 'whether': 29A, 51E, 51T

inás m. 'growth, increase in cattle': gen. sg. *inais* 23F

inbleoga(i)n n./m. vn. of *in-omblig* 'kinsman, kinsman-surety': m. nom. sg. 16A; gen. sg. *inbleogain* 16A; gen. pl. *inbleogan* 50A

indeithbir adj. 'unnecessary, inexcusable, preventable, improper, unjustified': m. nom. sg. *indethbir* 1A, 3A, 3E, 9A, 54A, 54E, *indeithbeir* 3C; gen. sg. *indethbir* 3E

indeithbirius m. 'an unnecessary circumstance or event, non-necessity': nom. sg. *indethbirius* 12A; acc. sg. *indethbirus* 9A; dat. sg. *indethbirius* 9A, *indetbirius* 12A

inderb adj. 'uncertain': acc. sg. or gen. pl. subst. *inderb* 38

indílse f. 'unlawfulness, inappropriateness': nom. sg. *indilsi* 49

indraic adj. 'trustworthy, qualified to perform a certain legal function, lawful': m. nom. sg. subst. 26A, *innraic* 21A; m. dat. sg. subst. *indraic* 21A, 26A, *innraic* 21A: f. acc. sg. adj. *innraic* 20; n. nom. sg. adj. *indraig* 36; n. acc. pl. adj. *inraici* 20

indḟine f. 'end kin': acc. sg. *indfine* 7A, 7K, *innfine* 7J

inḟorais adj. 'resident': f. acc. sg. *inforuis* 20

is copula 'is': pres. ind. 3 sg. *is* 1, 5, 21, 35, 36; pres. ind. rel. sg. *is* 21; neg. pres. ind. 3 sg. *ni* 4, *ní* 30

la prep. with acc. 'with, by, belong to': 21; with m. 3 sg. poss. pron. *lais* 21; with rel. pron. *lasa* 21

lánamain f. 'marriage, partnership': nom. sg. *lanamain* 51E, 51T; gen. sg. *lanamanda* 51T

lebor m. 'book': dat. sg. *liubar* **heading**

léigenn n. vn. of *légaid* 'studying, reading, written law, ecclesiastical learning': dat. sg. *leighind* heading B

lethcolb adj. 'half-shanked': nom. sg. 58P, *leccolb* 58A

loc m. 'place': nom. sg. *locc* **heading**

loittid 'injures, damages, destroys': pret. ind. pass. sg. *roloitead* 58A, *roloited* 58P

long f. 'boat': acc. sg. *long* 29A; gen. sg. *luinge* 22, 29A, *lunga* 29A

lú adj. 'something small, something of little value': m. nom. sg. *lu* 8HH

mac m. 'child, boy, son': gen. sg. *mic* 47A: **mac gor** 'dutiful son': gen. sg. *meic gor* 57A, *meicc goir* 57C, *mic goir* 57D, *meic gair* 57E, *mic gor* 57H: **mac sóerléicthe** 'independent son': gen. sg. *meic særlece* 57A, *meicc særleicthi* 57C, *mic sairleicthi* 57D, *meic sǽrleice* 57E, *mic sœleicthi* 57H: **mac sanaise** 'child of secrecy, illegitimate child': gen. sg. [maic] *sanuise* 51T; gen. pl. *mac sanaise* 51E: **mac sula** 'child of sunlight, legitimate child': gen. sg. *maic sula* 51T; gen. pl. *mac sula* 51E

maidm m./n. 'battle, rout, defeat': nom. sg. 16

maigen f. 'place, precinct': **maigen díg-ona** 'area in a precinct within which everything and everyone is under the owner's protection': nom. sg. *maighen dighona* 8HH

marb adj. 'dead': m. gen. sg. *mairb* 15

marbslabrae 'inanimate chattels, the part of a woman's dowry which consists of inanimate chattels': gen. pl. *marbslabra* 25

mesc adj. 'drunk, intoxicated': nom. sg. 41A

mescad m. vn. of *mescaid* 'confusing, intoxicating': nom. sg. 42A

mescae f. 'intoxication, drunkenness': acc./dat. *mesci* 41A, *meisci* 41A;[10] acc. sg. *meisce* 41A; dat. sg. *meisci* 41A; gen. sg. *meisce* 41

mescbaid f. 'confusion, intoxication (?)': gen. sg. *mescbuide* 42

midithir 'judges': pres. subj. pass. rel. sg. *mesdar* 58, *measdar* 58A

mil f. 'honey': nom. sg. 22O; gen. sg. *mela* 22O

ná conj. 'nor': 37

naidm(m) n. vn. of *naiscid* 'binding, pledge, contract, a surety who guarantees a contract with his honor, *naidm*-surety, binding-surety': nom. sg. 20, 41; gen. sg. *nadma* 2, 2A, 2I, 40; acc. pl. *nadmann* 20

nascaire 'surety': nom. sg. 20J; dat. sg. *nascaire* 20J

nascairecht f. 'suretyship': gen sg. *nascairecht*[a] 2A

nech indef. pron. 'anyone, someone': nom. sg. 1, 57; acc. sg. *nech* 36; dat. sg. *neoch* 4

neimed m. 'privilege, sanctity, person possessing legal status or privileges': nom. sg. *nemed* 3, 3A

nemacrae n. 'unjust suing': dat. sg. *nemagra* 2A, *nemacra* 2I

nembésgnae 'not covered by protocol': gen. sg. *nembescna* 32A, 32T, *neambescna* 32O

nemetarscarthach adj. 'non-separable, property insufficient for independence': nom. sg. 51A, 51T

nemetarscarthae adj. 'non-separated': nom. sg. *nemetarscartha* 51C

nemgabál 'that which cannot be obtained': gen. sg. *nemgabala* 39A

nemnesam adj. 'not necessary': m. nom. sg. 54A, *nemneasam* 54E

nemtochor m. 'not jetsam': dat. sg. *nemtochur* 22A

nesam adj., superl. of *nes(s)a* 'necessary': m. nom. sg. 12J, 54A, *nesamh* 12J, *neasum* 54E

1 **ní** n. indef. pron. 'anything, something': nom. sg. *ni* 4

2 **ní** neg. 'not': 1, 20, 37, 57

nó conj. 'or': *no* 20

nós m. 'custom, procedure, tradition, precedent, ordinance': nom. sg. 6, 6A, 6B, 6C

ó prep. with dat., leniting, 'from, by': with 3 sg. m. affixed object agreement marker *uad* 32

ocus conj. 'and': *is* 7

oenach m./n. 'assembly, gathering, fair': gen. sg. *œnaig* 32

10 The case could be either acc. or dat. because the prep. *for* governs both.

ollam m. 'highest grade of poet': nom. sg. 6B

ón f. vn. of *oidid* 'loan, private loan, lending': nom. sg. *oin* 12A, 12C; acc. sg. *oin* 12A; gen. sg. *ona* 1A, 12A, 12C, 12J, 37

ór m. 'gold': nom. sg. *or* 29A

ord(d)an m. 'nobility': gen. pl. *ordan* 44

pennait f. 'penance, penalty': acc. sg. *pennait* 48A, 52A, 56A, 56D, *pennaid* 52D; dat. sg. *pendait* 34A, *pennait* 35A, 35LL

pennatóir m. 'a penitential, manual of penance': nom. sg. *pennatoir* 35A, *pennadoir* 35LL

pían f. 'punishment': gen. sg. *peinde* 33A

prím-ben f. 'wife': gen. sg. *prim-*[m]*na* 57A, 57D, [ph]*rim-*[m]*na* 57C, *pri*[m]*-mhna* 57E, *prim-mna* 57H

prímit f. pl. 'first fruits': acc. pl. *primide* 52D

port m. 'place, spot, bank, shore': nom. sg. 28, 55A

rath m. 'fief': nom. sg. 41A; acc. sg. *rath* 37A; gen. sg. *raith* 41A; acc. pl. *ratha* 37A

ráth m./f. 'suretyship, *ráth*-surety, paying-surety': nom. sg. *raith* 4A, 4B, 4J, 20A, 20J; acc. sg. *raith* 4A, 4B, 4J, *rath* 44A; dat. sg. *raith* 20J; gen. sg. *raithe* 4; nom. pl. *ratha* 28A; acc. pl. *ratha* 20; dat. pl. *rathaib* 28A

ráthaiges, ráthachas m. 'guaranteeing, suretyship, paying-suretyship': acc. sg. *rathighus* 4, *rathachas* 4A, *rathaighes* 4B, 31R, *rathaighus* 4J, *rathachus* 31A, 46A; gen. sg. *rathachais* 4, 31, 31A, *rathaigis* 31A, 31R

ré n./f. 'space, interval, time': gen. sg. *re* 12

recht m. 'authority': nom. sg. 19

réim(m) n. vn. of *réidid* 'movement, course, manner': nom. sg. *reim* 5

remdílse f. 'prior right, pre-ownership': acc. sg. *remdilsi* 23F; dat. sg. *remdilsi* 23F; gen. sg. *remdilsi* 23

rí m. 'king': nom. sg. 6B, *ri* 57D; acc. sg. *ri* 57D, dat. sg. *rig* 22A, 22O, *ri* 57D, *rig* 57D; gen. sg. *rig* 18, 57D

ríar f. 'demand, rule, stipulation': nom. sg. *riar* 24

rodercaid m. 'watchman': nom. sg. 29A

rudrad m. 'lapse of legal right, usucaption': acc. sg. *rudrad* 47A; gen. sg. *rudartha* 47A

saigid 'sues': pres. ind. 3 sg. *saigid* 20; pres. ind. 3 sg. *-saig*[i] 20

salann 'salt': nom. sg. *saland* 22O

sárugud m. vn. of *sáraigid* 'violating, outraging, disobeying, flouting': nom. sg. *sarugud* 44, *sarughudh* 57E; acc. sg. *sarugud* 8L, 57A, *sarugh*[ud] 8L; dat. sg. *sarugud* 57A, 57D, *sarughudh* 57C, 57E, *sarudha*[d] 57D, *sarugu*[d] 57E, *sarugudh* 57E, *sarugh*[ud] 57H; acc. pl. *saraighte* 12J

seiche f. 'hide of an animal': nom. pl. *seichida* 22O, *secheda* 29A

sellc(h)echt f. 'looking on, witnessing': gen. sg. *sellcechta* 29A; nom. pl. *sellcechta* 29A

senad 'assembly, synod': gen. sg. *senaid* 43

sénaid 'denies, reject': pres. ind. pass. sg. *sentar* 20A

sencairde n. 'old law': gen. pl. *sencairde* 19

sét[11] m. 'object of value, chattel': nom. sg. 37: **sét turchlaide** '*sét* of subjection': acc. pl. *seotu turclaide* 24A; gen. pl. *sét turclaide* 24A

síd n. 'peace': nom. sg. *sidh* 8; gen. sg. *sida* 8

sleith f. vn. of **selid* 'rape by stealth': nom. sg. *sleth* 8HH; acc. sg. *slethedh* 8HH

slóg m. 'army, host': nom. sg. 45; acc. sg. *slog* 45A

slógad n. 'hosting, military expedition': acc. sg. *sloiged* 32A, *sloigheth* 32T; dat. sg. *sloiged* 32O, 39A; gen. sg. *sloigid* 32A, 32T

snáidid 'protects': pres. ind. 3 sg. *-snaighi* 57

snádud m. vn. of *snáidid* 'legal protection, safe conduct': nom. sg. *snadhad* 8

sochar m. 'good or valid contract': nom. sg. *sochur* 41A, *sochar* 41A, [s]*ochar* 51E, 51T; nom. pl. *sochuir* 41A

sochonn m. 'legally competent person': gen. du. *sochonn* 2R

sod 'weir': gen. sg. *sod* 55A

-som *nota augens*: *-sa* **heading**

taircsiu f. vn. of *do-fargaid* 'offering': nom. sg. *tairgsi* 8A; acc. sg. *taircsi* 8A; dat. sg. *tairgsin* 8A, *taircsin* 8I: **taircsiu dligid** 'offering appeal to law, legal settlement': nom. sg. *tairgsi dligid* 8A, 8I, *taircse dligid* 8B, *tairigsi dligid* 8I, *taircsi dligid* 8I, *taircsiu dlighidh* 8HH, *taircsiu dlighid* 8HH; acc. sg. *tairgsin dligid* 8A, *tairgsi dligid* 8A, *tairg*[s]*enn dliged* 8A, *tairc*[s]*i dligi* 8I, *targsin dlighi* 8L, *targ*[s]*inn dlighi* 8L; gen. sg. *tiargsi dligid* 8A

tar prep. with acc. 'over, across, on': 11

tárcud m. vn. of *do-áirci* 'causing, bringing about': nom. sg. *targaud* 3A

teist f. 'testimony, witness, evidence' (from Latin *testis*): gen. sg. *t*[e]*ista* 30A

téit 'goes': pres. ind. rel. 3 sg. *tet* 4

tincell pret. 3 sg. of **to-ind-(ad-)cell* 'extorts by threats of satire': perf. ind. 3 sg. *-rotincell* 49A, 49M

tír n. 'land': gen. sg. *tire* 26

togáes f. 'deceiving, beguiling, defrauding': dat. sg. *togais* 51

toichid f. vn. of *do-saig* 'suing': gen. sg. *toicheda* 2A, 2I

toirrches m. 'pregnancy': dat. sg. *toirrchius* 51T

toisc(h)id f. vn. of **to-ad- saig* 'need, maintaining, sustenance': gen. sg. *toiscide* 12J

torbae n. vn. of *do-rorban* 'profit, benefit, usefulness': dat. sg. *torba* 9A; gen. sg. *torba* 3A, 3E, 54A, 54E *torbha* 3A

tráig m./f. 'shore, strand': gen. sg. *truig* 21

trebaire f. 'surety, guarantee': nom. sg. 11A; acc. sg. *trenaire* 2A, 2I, *trebairi* 4R; gen sg. *trebaire* 2A, 2I, *trebairi* 4J, 4R

trebdíre 'compensation for stealing from a house': gen. sg. *trebdire* 32A, *treibdire* 32T

---

11 For discussion of this word, see the Introduction, 12n8.

troscad m. vn. of *troiscid* 'fasting': nom. sg. 17A, 40A; gen sg. *troisce* 12J

túath f. 'community, people, territory': gen. sg. *tuaithe* 6

tugad late vn. of *do-beir* 'giving': nom. sg. 27A

tuinide f. vn. of **do-neith* 'possession, ownership': nom. sg. 21, *tuinigh* 26P; gen. sg. *tuinide* 26

turbród m. vn. of **to-air-brúi* 'legal violation, repudiation a of law': dat. sg. *turbrod* 6A, 6B, 6C

tuitim n. vn. of *do-tuit* 'falling in battle, death': dat. sg. *toitim* 1A

turorgain f. vn. of **to-air-(fo?)-oirg* 'plundering': acc. pl. *turoirgne* 12J

turtugud m. 'protection, sanctuary': nom. sg. 52D, *turrtugud* 52, *turrthugud* 52D

úasal adj. 'noble': m. nom. sg. subst. *uasal* 57A

úathbás m. 'terror': acc. sg. *uathbas* 9AA, 9JJ; gen. sg. *uathbais* 9

udbairt 'offering': dat. sg. *udbairt* 48A, 48C; gen. sg. *udbarta* 48A

People

Cumain m.: acc. sg. *Cumain* heading B

Finguine mac Cú-cen-máthair m.: gen. sg. *Findguine meic Con Gen Mathair* heading B

Mac Cathán m.: acc. or dat. sg. *Mac Cathan* 51A[12]

Places

Áine Cliach dat. sg. *Aine Cliach* heading B

Ériu f. 'Ireland': dat. sg. *Eirinn* 5B; gen. sg. *Erenn* 22A, *Eirenn* 22O

Fuithirbe Cormaic, Fuithrime Cormaic gen. sg. *Fuithribe Cormaic, Fuithrime Cormaic* **heading**, heading B

Texts

Bretha for Macṡlechtaib 'Judgments on Categories of Sons': dat. pl. *Mac*[ṡ]*lechtaib* 51E

Córus Fine 'The Ordering of the Kindred': dat. sg. *Corus Fine* 28A; gen. sg. *Corusa Fine* 4A, 4J

Senchas Már 'Great Tradition': dat. sg. *Sencus* [Már] 28A

12 The case is ambiguous because the prep. *ar* governs both the acc. and dat.

Bibliography

Manuscripts

Early Manuscripts at Oxford University http://image.ox.ac.uk/list?collection=bodleian
Dublin, Royal Irish Academy MS 1243 [23 Q 6]
Dublin, Trinity College MS 1336 [H.3.17]
Dublin, Trinity College MS 1337 [H.3.18]
Dublin, Trinity College MS 1363 [H.4.22]
Dublin, Trinity College MS 1387 [H.5.15]
Dublin, Trinity College MS 1433 [E.3.5]
Irish Script on Screen https://www.isos.dias.ie/
London, British Library MS Cotton Nero A7
London, British Library MS Egerton 88
O'Donovan, John. Brehon Law transcripts O'D 1586–1630 and translation 1849–1917, Royal Irish Academy Library, Dublin
Oxford, Bodleian Library MS Rawl. B. 506

Printed and Digital Sources

Ancient Laws of Ireland, eds. and trans. W.N. Hancock et al., 6 vols. Dublin: His Majesty's Stationery Office, 1865–1901.

Bechbretha, eds. and trans. Thomas Charles-Edwards and Fergus Kelly. Early Irish Law Series 1. Dublin: Dublin Institute for Advanced Studies, 1983.

Breudwyt Ronabwy: Allan o'r Llyfr Coch o Hergest, ed. G. Melville Richards. Caerdydd: Gwasg Prifysgol Cymru, 1948.

Cáin Fhuithirbe, ed. and trans. Liam Breatnach in "The Ecclesiastical Element in the Old-Irish Legal Tract *Cáin Fhuithirbe*." *Peritia* 5 (1986): 36–52.

Cáin Lánamna: *An Old Irish Tract on Marriage and Divorce Law*, ed. and trans. Charlene M. Eska. Medieval Law and Its Practice 5. Leiden: Brill, 2010.

"*Cáin Ónae*: An Old Irish Law Text on Lending," ed. and trans. Liam Breatnach. In *Mír Cúrad*: *Studies in Honor of Calvert Watkins*, eds. Jay Jasanoff, H. Craig Melchert, and Lisi Oliver, 29–46. Innsbruck: Institut für Sprachwissenschaft der Universität, 1998.

Canones Hibernenses, ed. and trans. Ludwig Bieler. In *The Irish Penitentials*. Scriptores Latini Hiberniae 5. Ed. Ludwig Bieler, 160–175. Dublin: The Dublin Insitute for Advanced Studies, 1975.

"*Coibnes Uisci Thairidne*," ed. and trans. D.A. Binchy. *Ériu* 17 (1955): 52–85.

Cóic Conara Fugill, ed. and trans. Rudolf Thurneysen. In *Cóic Conara Fugill: Die fünf Wege zum Urteil*. Abhandlungen der Preussischen Akademie der Wissenschaften. Phil.-hist. Klasse; Nr. 7. Berlin: Verlag der Akademie der Wissenschaften, 1926.

Cóic Conara Fugill, ed. and trans. Christophe Archan. In *Les Chemins du Jugement: Procédure et Science du Droit dans l'Irlande médiévale*. Paris: De Boccard, 2007.

Cormac's Glossary, trans. John O'Donovan and ed. Whitley Stokes. Calcutta: Irish Archaeolgoical and Celtic Society, 1868.

Corpus Iuris Hibernici, ed. D.A. Binchy. 6 vols. paginated consecutively. Dublin: Dublin Institute for Advanced Studies, 1978.

Córus Bésgnai: An Old Irish Tract on the Church and Society, ed. and trans. Liam Breatnach. Early Irish Law Series 7. Dublin: School of Celtic Studies, Dublin Institute for Advanced Studies, 2017.

Críth Gablach, ed. D.A. Binchy. Medieval and Modern Irish Series 11. Dublin: Stationery Office, 1941.

Di Astud Cor, ed. and trans. Neil McLeod. In *Early Irish Contract Law*. Sydney Series in Celtic Studies 1. Sydney: University of Sydney, 1992.

"*Di Ércib Fola*," ed. and trans. Neil McLeod. *Ériu* 52 (2002): 123–216.

Dúil Dromma Cetta, ed. Whitley Stokes. In "Irish glosses, edited by a member of the Council from a manuscript in the library of Trinity College, Dublin [H. 3. 18, p. 61, col. 1]." *Transactions of the Philological Society* 6 (1859): 168–215.

Early Irish Glossaries Database, eds. Paul Russell, Sharon Arbuthnot, and Pádraic Moran. 2nd ed. (Cambridge: ASNC, 2009) http://www.asnc.cam.ac.uk/irishglossaries.

Foclóir nó Sanasán nua: A new Vocabulary or Glossary, ed. Mícheál Ó Cléirigh. Louvain, 1643.

Gúbretha Caratniad, ed. and trans. Rudolf Thurneysen. In "Aus dem irischen Recht III." *Zeitschrift für celtische Philologie* 15 (1925): 302–370.

"The Lecan Glossary," ed. and trans. Whitley Stokes. In *Archiv für celtische Lexikographie* 1, eds. Whitley Stokes and Kuno Meyer, 50–100. Halle: Niemeyer, 1898.

"The Monastery of Tallaght," eds. and trans. E.J. Gwynn and W.J. Purton. *Proceedings of the Royal Irish Academy* 29 C (1911): 115–179.

O'Clery's Glossary, ed. and trans. Arthur W.K. Miller. In "O'Clery's Irish Glossary," *Revue celtique* 4 (1879–1880): 349–428 and 479–480 and *Revue celtique* 5 (1881–1883): 1–69.

"O'Davoren's Glossary," ed. and trans. Whitley Stokes. In *Archiv für celtische Lexikographie* 2, eds. Whitley Stokes and Kuno Meyer, 197–504. Halle: Niemeyer, 1904.

"The Old-Irish Penitential," trans. D.A. Binchy. In *The Irish Penitentials*. Scriptores Latini Hiberniae 5. Ed. Ludwig Bieler, 258–277. Dublin: Dublin Institute for Advanced Studies, 1975.

"Penitential of Cummean," ed. and trans. Ludwig Bieler. In *The Irish Penitentials*. Scriptores Latini Hiberniae 5. Ed. Ludwig Bieler, 108–135. Dublin: Dublin Institute for Advanced Studies, 1975.

Pseudo-historical Prologue to the Senchas Már, ed. and trans. John Carey. In "An Edition of the Pseudo-historical Prologue to the *Senchas Már*," *Ériu* 45 (1994): 1–32.
Sanas Cormaic, ed. Kuno Meyer. In "*Sanas Cormaic*: An Old Irish Glossary," in *Anecdota from Irish Manuscripts* 4, eds. O.J. Bergin, R.I. Best, K. Meyer, and J.G. O'Keefe, 1–128. Halle: M. Niemeyer, 1912.
Talland Étair: *A Critical Edition with Introduction, Translation, Textual Notes, Bibliography and Vocabulary*, ed. and trans. Caoimhín Ó Dónaill. Maynooth Medieval Irish Texts 4. Maynooth: Department of Old and Middle Irish, 2005.
Three Irish Glossaries, ed. Whitley Stokes. London: Williams & Norgate, 1862.
"A Tract on the *Áes Fíachach*," ed. R.M. Smith. In *Irish Texts* 4, eds. J. Fraser, P. Grosjean, J.G. O'Keefe, 13–16. London: Sheed and Ward, 1934.
Uraicecht na Ríar: *The Poetic Grades in Early Irish Law*, ed. and trans. Liam Breatnach. Early Irish Law Series 2. Dublin: Dublin Institute for Advanced Studies, 1987.
Urcuilte Bretheman, ed. Rudolf Thurneysen. In "Aus dem irischen Recht V," *Zeitschrift für celtische Philologie* 18 (1930): 362–364.
Urcuilte Bretheman, ed. Roland M. Smith. In "Urchuillti Bretheman," in *Irish Texts* 4, eds. J. Fraser, P. Grosjean, J.G. O'Keefe, 24–27. London: Sheed and Ward, 1934.

Secondary Sources

Abbott, T.K. and E.J. Gwynn. *Catalogue of the Irish Manuscripts in the Library of Trinity College, Dublin*. Dublin: Hodges, Figgis, & Co., 1921.
Bemmer, Jaqueline. "Validity and Equality in Early Irish Contract Law: *Dliged* and *Cert* in the light of *Cóic Conara Fugill*." *Studia Celtica Fennica* 5 (2008): 5–18.
Binchy, D.A. "Sick-maintenance in Irish Law." *Ériu* 12 (1938): 78–134.
Binchy, D.A. "The Linguistic and Historical Value of the Irish Law Tracts." *Proceedings of the British Academy* 29 (1943): 195–227, and also separately paginated 3–35.
Binchy, D.A. "The Fair of Tailtiu and the Feast of Tara." *Ériu* 18 (1958): 113–138.
Binchy, D.A. "Distraint in Irish Law." *Celtica* 10 (1973): 22–71.
Binchy, D.A. "The Pseudo-historical Prologue to the *Senchas Már*." *Studia Celtica* 10–11 (1975–1976): 15–28.
Breatnach, Liam. "An Mheán-Ghaeilge." In *Stair na Gaeilge*, ed. Kim McCone et al., 221–333. Maigh Nuad: Roinn na Sean-Ghaeilge, Coláiste Phádraig, 1994.
Breatnach, Liam. "On the Glossing of Early Irish Law-texts, Fragmentary Texts, and Some Aspects of the Laws Relating to Dogs." In *Celtica Helsingiensia*: *Proceedings from a Symposium on Celtic Studies*, eds. Anders Ahlqvist, Glyn Welden Banks, Riita Latvio, Harri Nyberg, and Tom Sjöblom, 11–20. Helsinki: Societas Scientiarum Fennica, 1996.
Breatnach, Liam. *A Companion to the Corpus Iuris Hibernici*. Early Irish Law Series 5. Dublin: School of Celtic Studies, Dublin Institute for Advanced Studies, 2005.

Breatnach, Liam. "On Old Irish Collective and Abstract Nouns, the Meaning of *cétmuinter*, and Marriage in Early Mediaeval Ireland." *Ériu* 66 (2016): 1–29.

Breatnach, Liam. "The Glossing of the Early Irish Law Tracts." In *Grammatica, Gramadach and Gramadeg: Vernacular grammar and grammarians in medieval Ireland and Wales*, eds. Deborah Hayden and Paul Russell, 113–132. Amsterdam: John Benjamins Publishing Company, 2016.

Byrne, Francis John. *A Thousand Years of Irish Script*. Oxford: The Bodleian Library, 1979.

Byrne, Mary E. "On the Punishment of Setting Adrift." *Ériu* 11 (1932): 97–102.

Carey, John. "An Edition of the Pseudo-historical Prologue to the *Senchas Már*." *Ériu* 45 (1994): 1–32.

Carey, John. "The Three Things Required of a Poet." *Ériu* 48 (1997): 41–58.

Charles-Edwards, T.M. "The Social Background of Irish *Peregrinatio*." *Celtica* 11 (1976): 43–59.

Charles-Edwards, T.M. "Review Article: The *Corpus Iuris Hibernici*." *Studia Hibernica* 20 (1980): 141–162.

Charles-Edwards, T.M. *Early Irish and Welsh Kinship*. Oxford: Clarendon Press, 1993.

Charles-Edwards, T.M. *Early Christian Ireland*. Cambridge: Cambridge University Press, 2000.

Charles-Edwards, T.M. *The Chronicle of Ireland*. 2 vols. Liverpool: Liverpool University Press, 2006.

Charles-Edwards, T.M. "Whitley Stokes and Early Irish Law." In *The Tripartite Life of Whitley Stokes (1830–1909)*, eds. Elizabeth Boyle and Paul Russell, 161–174. Dublin: Four Courts Press, 2011.

Dictionary of the Irish Language: Based Mainly on Old and Middle Irish Materials, Compact Edition, gen. ed. E.G. Quin. Dublin: Royal Irish Academy, 1983. See also *eDIL* http://www.dil.ie.

Dillon, Myles. "The Relationship of Mother and Son, of Father and Daughter, and the Law of Inheritance with regard to Women." In *Studies in Early Irish Law*, ed. R. Thurneysen et al., 129–179. Dublin: Royal Irish Academy, 1936.

Eska, Charlene M. "Varieties of Early Irish Legal Literature and the *Cáin Lánamna* Fragments." *Viator* 40 (2009): 1–16.

Eska, Charlene M. "Women and Slavery in the Early Irish Laws." *Studia Celtica Fennica* 8 (2011): 29–39.

Eska, Charlene M. "*Recholl Breth*: Why It Is a 'Shroud of Judgments'." In *Ollam: Studies in Gaelic and Related Traditions in Honor of Tomás Ó Cathasaigh*, ed. Matthieu Boyd, 173–184. Madison, NJ: Fairleigh Dickinson University Press, 2016.

Eska, Charlene M. "A Medieval Irish Legal Commentary on Wakes and Funerals from *Anfuigell* 'Wrong Judgment'." *North American Journal of Celtic Studies* 1 (2017): 27–44.

Eska, Joseph F. "Where Have All the Object Pronouns Gone? The growth of object agreement in earlier Celtic." *Zeitschrift für celtische Philologie* 57 (2009–2010): 25–47.

Etchingham, Colman. *Church Organisation in Ireland AD 650 to 1000*. Maynooth: Laigin Publications, 1999.

Finnane, Rowena. *Late Medieval Irish Law Manuscripts: A Reappraisal of Methodology and Context*. Sydney Series in Celtic Studies 13. Sydney: The University of Sydney, 2013.

Flower, Robin. "*Quidam Scotigena .i. Discipulus Boëthii* or Boëthius and the Four Conditions of the Tale." *Ériu* 8 (1916): 150–154.

Ford, Patrick K. *The Celtic Poets: Songs and Tales from Early Ireland and Wales*. Belmont, MA: Ford & Bailie, 1999.

Fry, Susan Leigh. *Burial in Medieval Ireland, 900–1500*. Dublin: Four Courts Press, 1999.

Griffith, Aaron. "Old Irish Pronouns: Agreement affixes vs. clitic arguments." In *Formal Approaches to Celtic Linguistics*, ed. Andrew Carnie, 65–93. Cambridge: Cambridge Scholars Publishing, 2011.

Gwynn, E.J. "Miscellanea." *Ériu* 9 (1923): 27–30.

Harman, Jade. "Causation in Medieval Irish Law." In *Language and Power in the Celtic World*. Sydney Series in Celtic Studies 10. Eds. Anders Ahlqvist and Pamela O'Neill, 97–122. Sydney: University of Sydney, 2011.

Heijda, Kim. "War-goddesses, Furies and Scald Crows: The Use of the Word *badb* in Early Irish Literature." Final Thesis, University of Utrecht, 2007. https://dspace.library.uu.nl/handle/1874/21638. Accessed June 1, 2018.

Kelly, Fergus. *A Guide to Early Irish Law*. Early Irish Law Series 3. Dublin: Dublin Institute for Advanced Studies, 1988.

Kelly, Fergus. *Early Irish Farming*. Early Irish Law Series 4. Dublin: Dublin Institute for Advanced Studies, 2000.

Kelly, Fergus. "Drifting on the Ocean: Are Old Irish *Cnoe Gnáe* 'Beautiful Nuts' to be Identified as Sea Beans?" In *Bile ós Chrannaibh: A Festschrift for William Gillies*, eds. Wilson McLeod et al., 211–218. Ceann Drochaid, Perthshire: Clann Tuirc, 2010.

Kelly, Fergus. "The Recovery of Stolen Property: Notes on legal procedure in Gaelic Ireland, Scotland, and the Isle of Man." In *Tome: Studies in medieval Celtic history and law in honour of Thomas Charles-Edwards*, eds. Fiona Edmonds and Paul Russell, 165–171. Woodbridge: The Boydell Press, 2011.

Kelly, Fergus. *Marriage Disputes: A Fragmentary Old Irish Law-Text*. Early Irish Law Series 6. Dublin: School of Celtic Studies, Dublin Institute for Advanced Studies, 2014.

Kelly, Matthew, trans. *Cambrensis Eversus*. 3 vols. Dublin: The Celtic Society, 1848–1854. [Trans. of John Lynch below.]

Ker, Neil. "From 'Above Top Line' to 'Below Top Line': A Change in Scribal Practice." *Celtica* 5 (1960): 13–16.

Lambert, Pierre-Yves. "The Expression of 'sense, meaning, signification' in the Old Irish Glosses, and particularly in the Milan and Saint-Gall Glosses." In *Grammatica, Gra-*

madach and Gramadeg: Vernacular Grammar and Grammarians in Medieval Ireland and Wales, eds. Deborah Hayden and Paul Russell, 85–100. Amsterdam: John Benjamins Publishing Company, 2016.

Latvio, Riita. "*Neimed*—Exploring Social Distinctions and Sacredness in Early Irish Legal Sources." In *Approaches to Religion and Mythology in Celtic Studies*, eds. Katja Ritari and Alexandra Bergholm, 220–242. Newcastle, UK: Cambridge Scholars Publishing, 2008.

Lexique étymologique de l'irlandais ancien, eds. J. Vendryes, E. Bachellery, and P.-Y. Lambert. Paris: Centre National de la Recherche Scientifique, 1959–.

Lynch, John. *Cambrensis Eversus*. Saint Malo, 1662. [Trans. by Matthew Kelly above.]

Mac Cana, Proinsias. "Ir. *Buaball*, W. *Bual* 'Drinking Horn'." *Ériu* 44 (1993): 81–93.

MacNeill, Eoin. "Ancient Irish Law: The Law of Status or Franchise." *Proceedings of the Royal Irish Academy* 36 C (1923): 265–316.

Mac Niocaill, Gearóid. "Jetsam, Treasure Trove, and the Lord's Share in Medieval Ireland." *The Irish Jurist* 6 (1971): 103–110.

McCone, Kim R. "Werewolves, Cyclopes, *Díberga*, and *Fíanna*: Juvenile delinquency in early Ireland." *Cambridge Medieval Celtic Studies* 12 (1986): 1–22.

McCone, Kim R. "Dubthach Maccu Lugair and a Matter of Life and Death in the Pseudohistorical Prolgue to the *Senchas Már*." *Peritia* 5 (1986): 1–35.

McCone, Kim R. "Hund, Wolf und Krieger bei den Indogermanen." In *Studien zum indogermanischen Wortschatz*, ed. Wolfgang Meid, 101–154. Innsbruck: Institut für Sprachwissenschaft der Universität, 1987.

McCone, Kim R. *The Early Irish Verb*, 2nd ed. Maynooth: An Sagart, 1997.

McLaughlin, Roisin. *Early Irish Satire*. Dublin: School of Celtic Studies, Dublin Institute for Advanced Studies, 2008.

McLeod, Neil. *Early Irish Contract Law*. Sydney Series in Celtic Studies 1. Sydney: University of Sydney, 1992.

McLeod, Neil. "Property and Honour-Price in the Brehon Law Glosses and Commentaries." *The Irish Jurist* 31 (1996): 280–295.

McLeod, Neil. *Bloodshed and Compensation in Ancient Ireland*. Perth: Murdoch University, 1999.

McLeod, Neil. "The Blood-Feud in Medieval Ireland." In *Between Intrusions: Britain and Ireland between the Romans and the Normans*. Sydney Series in Celtic Studies 7. Ed. Pamela O'Neill, 114–133. Sydney: University of Sydney, 2004.

McLeod, Neil. "Review Article: A True Companion to the *Corpus Iuris Hibernici*." *Peritia* 19 (2005): 136–163.

McLeod, Neil. "The Lord of Slaughter." In *The Land beneath the Sea: Essays in honour of Anders Ahlqvist's contribution to Celtic Studies in Australia*. Sydney Series in Celtic Studies 14. Ed. Pamela O'Neill, 101–114. Sydney: University of Sydney, 2013.

McLeod, Neil. "*Ón* and *airliciud*: Loans in medieval Irish law." In *Celts and their Cultures at Home and Abroad: A Festschrift for Malcolm Broun*. Sydney Series in Celtic Studies 15. Eds. Anders Ahlqvist and Pamela O'Neill, 169–196. Sydney: University of Sydney, 2013.

McLeod, Neil. "External Influences on Medieval Irish Law: AD 600–1600," *Australian Celtic Journal* 11 (2013): 31–54.

Mulchrone, Kathleen. "The Rights and Duties of Women with regard to the Education of their Children." In *Studies in Early Irish Law*, ed. R. Thurneysen et al., 187–205. Dublin: Royal Irish Academy, 1936.

Ó Coileáin, Seán, "Mag Fuithirbe Revisited." *Éigse* 23 (1989): 16–26.

Ó Corráin, Donnchadh. *Clavis Litterarum Hibernensium: Medieval Irish Books & Texts (c. 400–c. 1600)*, 3 vols. Turnhout: Brepols, 2017.

Ó Cuív, Brian. *Catalogue of Irish Language Manuscripts in the Bodleian Library at Oxford and Oxford College Libraries*. Dublin: Dublin Institute for Advanced Studies, 2001.

O'Curry, Eugene. *On the Manners and Customs of the Ancient Irish: A Series of Lectures*, 3 vols. London: Williams and Norgate, 1873.

O'Grady, Standish Hayes. *Catalogue of Irish Manuscripts in the British Museum*, vol. 1. London: The British Museum, 1926.

Oliver, Lisi. "Forced and Unforced Rape in Early Irish Law." *Proceedings of the Harvard Celtic Colloquium* 13 (1993): 93–105.

O'Neill, Pamela. "Old Irish *Muirchrech* 'Sea-Boundary'." *Ériu* 67 (2017): 1–9.

Ó Súilleabháin, Seán. *Irish Wake Amusements*. Dublin: The Mercer Press, 1967.

O'Sullivan, William. "The Book of Domhnall Ó Duibhdábhoireann, Provenance and Codicology." *Celtica* 23 (1999): 276–299.

O'Sullivan, William. "The Manuscript Collection of Dubhaltach Mac Fhirbhisigh." In *Seanchas: Studies in Early and Medieval Irish Archaeology, History and Literature in Honour of Francis J. Byrne*, ed. Alfred P. Smyth, 439–447. Dublin: Four Courts Press, 2000.

Patterson, Nerys. "Honour and Shame in Medieval Welsh Society: A study of the role of burlesque in the Welsh laws." *Studia Celtica* 16/17 (1981): 73–103.

Plummer, Charles. "Notes on Some Passages in the Brehon Laws II." *Ériu* 9 (1923): 31–42.

Power, Nancy. "Classes of Women Described in the *Senchas Már*." In *Studies in Early Irish Law*, ed. R. Thurneysen et al., 81–108. Dublin: Royal Irish Academy, 1936.

Qiu, Fangzhe. "*In senchas bith-nua:* The Traditionalisation of Early Irish Law." Medieval Law Conference, Dublin Institute for Advanced Studies, June 28, 2014. Available at https://www.youtube.com/watch?v=gIJutcPSjU8.

Russell, Paul. "The Sounds of a Silence: The Growth of Cormac's Glossary." *Cambridge Medieval Celtic Studies* 15 (1988): 1–30.

Russell, Paul. "Laws, Glossaries and Legal Glossaries." *Zeitschrift für celtische Philologie* 51 (1998): 85–115.

Russell, Paul. "*Quasi*: Bridging the etymological gap in early Irish glossaries." In *A Com-*

panion in Linguistics: A Festschrift for Anders Ahlqvist on the occasion of his sixtieth birthday, eds. Bernadette Smelik, Rijcklof Hofman, Camiel Hamans, and David Cram, 49–62. Nijmegen: Stichtig Uitgeverij de Keltische Draak, 2005.

Russell, Paul. "*Y Naw Affaith*: Aiding and Abetting in Welsh Law." In *Tair Colofn Cyfraith: The Three Columns of Law in Medieval Wales*. The Welsh Legal History Society v (2005). Eds. T.M. Charles-Edwards and Paul Russell, 146–170. Bangor: The Welsh Legal History Society, 2007.

Russell, Paul. "Poets, Power and Possessions in Medieval Ireland: Some Stories from *Sanas Cormaic*." In *Law, Literature and Society*. CSANA *Yearbook* 7. Ed. Joseph F. Eska, 9–45. Dublin: Four Courts Press, 2008.

Russell, Paul. "The Languages and Registers of Laws in Medieval Ireland and Wales." In *Law and Language in the Middle Ages*. Medieval Law and Its Practice 25. Eds. Jenny Benham, Matthew McHaffie, and Helen Vogt, 83–103. Leiden: Brill, 2018.

Simms, Katharine. "The Brehons of Later Medieval Ireland." In *Brehons, Serjeants and Attorneys: Studies in the History of the Irish Legal Profession*, eds. Daire Hogan and W.N. Osborough, 51–76. Blackrock, Co. Dublin: Irish Academic Press, 1990.

Simms, Katharine. "The Contents of Later Commentaries on the Brehon Law Tracts." *Ériu* 49 (1998): 23–40.

Stacey, Robin Chapman. "Law and Order in the *Very* Old West: England and Ireland in the Early Middles Ages." In *Crossed Paths: Methodological approaches to the Celtic aspect of the European Middles Ages*. Eds. Benjamin T. Hudson and Vickie Zieglar, 39–60. Lanham, MD: University Press of America, 1991.

Stacey, Robin Chapman. *The Road to Judgment: From custom to court in medieval Ireland and Wales*. Philadelphia: University of Pennsylvania Press, 1994.

Stacey, Robin Chapman. "Ancient Irish Law Revisited: Rereading the Laws of Status and Franchise." In *Understanding Celtic Religion: Revisiting the Pagan Past*, eds. Katja Ritari and Alexandra Bergholm, 99–119. Cardiff: University of Wales Press, 2015.

Taylor-Griffiths, Alice R. "*Gúbretha Caratniad*: Agreement and disagreement in the classroom." *North American Journal of Celtic Studies* 2 (2018): 105–132.

Thurneysen, Rudolf. "Aus dem irischen Recht I." *Zeitschrift für celtische Philologie* 14 (1923): 335–394.

Thurneysen, Rudolf. "Aus dem irischen Recht IV." *Zeitschrift für celtische Philologie* 16 (1927): 167–230.

Thurneysen, Rudolf. *Die Bürgschaft im irischen Recht*, Abhandlungen der Preussischen Akademie der Wissenschaften. Phil.-hist. Klasse; Nr. 2. Berlin: Verlag der Akademie der Wissenschaften, 1928.

Thurneysen, Rudolf. "Aus dem irischen Recht V." *Zeitschrift für celtische Philologie* 18 (1930): 353–408.

Thurneysen, Rudolf. "Allerlei Nachträge," *Zeitschrift für celtische Philologie* 19 (1933): 125–133.

Thurneysen, Rudolf. *A Grammar of Old Irish*, rev. ed. and trans. D.A. Binchy and Osborn Bergin. Dublin: Dublin Institute for Advanced Studies, 1946.

Tymoczko, Maria. "The Semantic Fields of Early Irish Terms for Black Birds and Their Implications for Species Taxonomy." In *Celtic Language, Celtic Culture: A Festschrift for Eric P. Hamp*, eds., A.T.E. Matonis and Daniel F. Melia, 151–171. Van Nuys, CA: Ford and Bailie, 1990.

Williams, J.E. Caerwyn, and Patrick K. Ford. *The Irish Literary Tradition*. Belmont, MA: Ford & Bailie, 1992.

Wooding, Jonathan M. *Communication and Commerce along the Western Sealanes AD 400–800*. British Archaeological Reports International Series 654. Oxford: Tempvs Reparatvm, 1996.

Index

Indexed items are linked to pages numbers and section numbers. Section numbers are given in bold.